This expansive collection of essays joins a growing number of efforts questioning PhD education in the theological disciplines: Is the degree too expensive and take too much time? Does it impose an intellectual pattern that is insensitive to other patterns of intellectual effort? How does it advance the work and witness of communities of faith? The essays in *Challenging Tradition* thoughtfully pursue these and other issues about advanced theological education in the Majority World. They offer both critique of Western advanced theological education and an interesting array of proposals that could enhance the intellectual, educational, and cultural value of advanced theological education in the Majority World. While the editors state that the intended audience is leaders of emerging programs of advanced theological studies in the Majority World, these essays have considerable value for theological educators in the West as well.

Daniel O. Aleshire, PhD
Former Executive Director,
The Association of Theological Schools in the United States and Canada
The Commission on Accrediting

Challenging Tradition: Innovation in Advanced Theological Education is a rich collection of the work of twenty-three global theological scholars, who share about their own life and experience serving in theological education in the Majority World for many years. This handbook blends educational theory, diverse contexts and multicultural aspects that require a mindful consideration of how we approach teaching and learning in the context where we are called to lead and teach. Dr Shaw's and Dr Dharamraj's commitment to provide theological education leaders and faculty with resources that will contribute to equipping transformational servant leaders and church ministers with creativity and innovation in each context is reflected in the topics included in this handbook. As I looked at each chapter, I started to picture in my mind how theological education would look like as readers embark on a journey toward the transformation of global theological education. Theological educators and church leaders committed to develop disciples of Jesus Christ, who are able to serve effectively in theological education institutions and churches in their own contexts, will benefit with this valuable resource.

Orbelina Eguizabal, PhD
Professor of Christian Higher Education,
Talbot School of Theology, Biola University, La Mirada, CA, USA
Former professor and academic dean at SETECA, Guatemala

This book challenges the "one-size-fits-all" approach in higher education which favors the western model of linear-empiricist study. While not discounting the strengths of this classic approach, the book points out its limitations considering the different patterns of learning and communication in Majority World contexts. It likewise offers rich theoretical reflection on the purpose of advanced study with emphasis on the development of theological leadership. But what stands out in this book are the examples of innovative approaches from different settings that have been put forth in it! Most certainly, this book will spur the much-needed changes in advanced theological studies!

Theresa Roco-Lua, EdD
General Secretary, Asia Theological Association

There has been a seismic shift in the global church, from the Global North to the Global South. The church is growing and thriving in Asia, Africa, Latin America, and other parts of the Majority World. This offers opportunities for the revitalization and renewal of the church worldwide, including fresh innovations in theological education. In *Challenging Tradition*, we are offered an invaluable insight into alternative and innovative approaches to theological education and advanced theological studies. I found the insights of this book both challenging and thrilling, and believe that this book will help renew and transform theological education worldwide.

Graham Hill, PhD
Provost, Morling College, Sydney, Australia
Author of *GlobalChurch*

Most of theological education in the world is in crisis. The problem is not the resources or the curriculum or teachers. The real problem is the lack of vision to our time. The world has changed, the church has changed, and the ministry has changed, but theological education remains the same. This book that Perry Shaw and Havilah Dharamraj have edited has the intention to change this situation with a creative and challenging approach. All who have a real concern about advanced theological education for the present and the future must read this book, not just to be aware of new ideas but to be part of this revolution.

Norberto Saracco, PhD
Founder, Facultad Internacional de Educación Teológica (FIET)

As the epicenter of global Christianity is shifting to the Global South, it is time to hear the theological and educational issues facing the changing world from the perspectives of those in the Majority World. The contributors to *Challenging Tradition* are seasoned and mature theological leaders, most of them serving in Asia, Africa and Latin America. With their experience and timely contribution to alternative innovative approaches to graduate and post-graduate programs, the global church surely will be enriched with proper changes! This is a must read for all theological educators and church leaders.

Joseph Shao, PhD
President, Biblical Seminary of the Philippines, Valenzuela City, Philippines

Challenging Tradition issues a welcome and timely call for theological institutions and educators in the Majority World to move beyond the linear-empiricist model of theological research that dominates the Western academy, adopting and adapting alternative models of research that are equally rigorous but are more suitable for non-Western ways of thinking and communicating. We who live in the Majority World and seek to do theology in service to the mission and people of God know that change is needed, urgently. *Challenging Tradition* provides practical options without sacrificing a commitment to rigour.

Kevin Smith, PhD
Principal, South African Theological Seminary, Bryanston, South Africa

A most helpful collection of writings for Asian seminaries considering alternative approaches to the traditional way of carrying out their graduate programs. The editors are to be congratulated for the choice of contributors who have given solid arguments and examples from personal experiences on the possibilities of innovation in theological education. The text has encouraged and challenged me to explore approaches that are consistent with a Trinitarian conception of learning and knowing and which form the whole person. I will recommend that my colleagues study the text for help to better equip theological leaders.

Sunny Tan, ThD
Director of Theology Programs, Asia Graduate School of Theology (Alliance)
Academic Dean, Malaysia Baptist Theological Seminary, Penang, Malaysia

ICETE Series

Challenging Tradition

Global Hub for Evangelical Theological Education

GLOBAL LIBRARY

Challenging Tradition

Innovation in Advanced Theological Education

Edited by

Perry Shaw and Havilah Dharamraj

© 2018 Perry Shaw and Havilah Dharamraj

Published 2018 by Langham Global Library
An imprint of Langham Publishing
www.langhampublishing.org

Langham Publishing and its imprints are a ministry of Langham Partnership

Langham Partnership
PO Box 296, Carlisle, Cumbria CA3 9WZ, UK
www.langham.org

ISBNs:
978-1-78368-413-7 Print
978-1-78368-426-7 ePub
978-1-78368-428-1 PDF

Perry Shaw and Havilah Dharamraj hereby assert their moral right to be identified as the Author of the General Editor's part in the Work in accordance with sections 77 and 78 of the Copyright, Designs and Patents Act 1988.

The Contributors hereby assert their moral right to be identified as the Author of their Contribution in the Work, in accordance with the Copyright, Designs and Patents Act 1988.

All rights reserved. No part of this publication may be reproduced, stored in a retrieval system or transmitted, in any form or by any means, electronic, mechanical, photocopying, recording or otherwise, without the prior written permission of the publisher or the Copyright Licensing Agency.

Scripture quotations marked (TNIV) is taken from the HOLY BIBLE, TODAY'S NEW INTERNATIONAL VERSION®. TNIV®. Copyright © 2001, 2005 by International Bible Society. Used by permission of Zondervan. All rights reserved worldwide.

Scripture quotations marked (NIV) are taken from the Holy Bible, New International Version®, NIV®. Copyright © 1973, 1978, 1984, 2011 by Biblica, Inc.™ Used by permission of Zondervan.

British Library Cataloguing-in-Publication Data
A catalogue record for this book is available from the British Library

ISBN: 978-1-78368-413-7

Cover & Book Design: projectluz.com

Langham Partnership actively supports theological dialogue and an author's right to publish but does not necessarily endorse the views and opinions set forth here or in works referenced within this publication, nor can we guarantee technical and grammatical correctness. Langham Partnership does not accept any responsibility or liability to persons or property as a consequence of the reading, use or interpretation of its published content.

Contents

Foreword..xiii

Introduction..1
    Perry Shaw and Havilah Dharamraj

Section I:
Principles for Innovation in Advanced Theological Studies....9

1 My Journey into Theological Education 13
    Ashish Chrispal

2 A Context Conducive to Innovation: How Changes in Doctoral Education Create New Opportunities for Developing Theological Leaders..........................21
    Evan R. Hunter

3 Innovation and Criteria: Ensuring Standards While Promoting Innovative Approaches.......................43
    Perry Shaw

4 "What You Get Is What You See"? Addressing the Hidden Curriculum of Doctoral Studies......................61
    Allan Harkness

5 Culture, Gender, and Diversity in Advanced Theological Studies......................................89
    Perry Shaw

6 The Imperative of Cultural Integration in Advanced Theological Studies: Perspectives from the Majority World....109
    Lal Senanayake

7 Scholarship in Our Own Words: Intercultural Rhetoric in Academic Writing and Reporting 127
    Stephanie L. Black

8 Nurturing Emancipatory Local Knowledges 145
    César Lopes

9 A Theology for Advanced Theological Studies 167
   Ian W. Payne

Section II:
   Innovative Possibilities for the Dissertation 185

10 Pathways of Integration for Theological Knowledge:
   Integrative Knowing/Learning for Thesis Construction
   in Advanced Theological Studies 189
   Paul Allan Clark

11 Problem-Based Learning in Advanced Theological Studies 209
   John Jusu

12 Action Research for Theological Impact: Reflections from
   an Arab Context 233
   Caleb Hutcherson with Bassem Melki

13 Studying Together:
   Joint and Collaborative Research 253
   Rafael Zaracho

14 Chicken Theology:
   Local Learning Approaches from West Africa 269
   Jay Moon

15 Ethnohermeneutics and Advanced Theological Studies:
   Towards Culturally Appropriate Methodologies for
   Doctoral Programs 287
   Larry Caldwell

16 Boldly Go! Tracking Trends in Comparative Literature 309
   Havilah Dharamraj

Section III:
   Innovative Forms of Advanced Theological Studies 325

17 Exploring the Possibilities of Portfolio as an Alternative
   to the Traditional Dissertation 329
   Joanna Feliciano-Soberano

18 Digital Scholarship 351
   Marvin Oxenham

19 Doing Theology from the "Land of Samba": Integrating Personal Experience in the Task of Advanced Theological Research 375
    Samuel Ewell

20 Telling Tales: Stories That Embox Theology 393
    Havilah Dharamraj

21 Proverbs as Theology 411
    Dwi Maria Handayani

22 Poetry as Theology: A Creative Path 425
    Xiaoli Yang

23 Verse by Verse: The Use of Poetry in Advanced Theological Education 447
    Havilah Dharamraj, Xiaoli Yang, Grace al-Zoughbi Arteen, and Karen Shaw

Epilogue 461

About the Contributors 465

Author Index 473

Subject Index 481

Foreword

It was in 2003 that I attended my first ICETE triennial conference at High Wycombe, England, as the relatively new (since 2001) International Ministries Director for Langham Partnership. At that time all those from the Majority World who received Langham Scholars grants for doctoral level study came to the West, mostly to the UK and USA. However, the "success" of the program, begun by John Stott in 1970, meant that there were already several seminaries in Africa, Asia and Latin America where more than one faculty member had their PhD. They were beginning to ask, and rightly so, "Why cannot we offer doctoral programs that train our own people here in our own context?"

On Langham Partnership's behalf I was conducting a survey of the field, with a questionnaire to some one hundred graduated and faculty-level Langham Scholars, to see whether and when, and on what conditions, Langham might be willing to offer grants to scholars doing doctoral study outside the West. The matter was fully discussed at board level within Langham in 2004, with the decision taken to begin cautious investment in such programs. (As a matter of record, that decision and the process described below led to the situation where now close to 60 percent of all doctoral scholars supported by Langham are studying in Majority World programs, or in split-site arrangements between Western and Majority World institutions.)

So I remember suggesting to that 2003 ICETE conference that what would really help would be some kind of agreed template of what constituted recognizable "doctorateness" – in a generic way, regardless of the cultural context. How would we know, in other words, or by what criteria could we tell, if a doctorate offered in an African, Asian or Latin American institution was of comparable rigour and value to one in a Western institution? And agreement on such a generic template would have to include, of course, colleagues from all over the Majority World – not something merely dictated by the West itself.

Well, it took some time! These things always do. I raised the question again at the ICETE triennials in Chiang Mai, Thailand, in 2006, and Sopron, Hungary, in 2009. It was taken up with vigour by ICETE and several participating agencies such as Langham Scholars, Overseas Council, and ScholarLeaders International. A consultation was convened at the Arab Baptist Theological Seminary, Beirut, in 2010, with representatives from fourteen Majority World institutions who were considering, or had already launched, doctoral programs. They committed themselves enthusiastically to forging the highest possible common standards, and the historic "Beirut Benchmarks" were born. This was followed by other related documents proposing guidelines for institutional best practice at doctoral level.

While this "Beirut Process" was undoubtedly a milestone in establishing and assessing the maturity and credibility of theological doctorates in key Majority World institutions – a moment of mutual accountability in the world of global evangelical theological education – its documents remained (as they were intended) at a very generic level. We were trying to establish indicators of what ought to be true of a doctorate anywhere, without prescribing what precise form it might take in any given cultural context – except that cultural and contextual relevance were essential.

The contributors and editors of this book take the whole process way beyond that first step and explore precisely that next question. What indeed *could* a doctorate look like in cultures outside the West? This fine book is one of the most stimulating and exciting I have read on the topic of theological education. It is challenging and disturbing, in exposing the inadequacy (as well as acknowledging some of the age-long proven strengths) of the classic form of doctoral-level studies in the Western academy, and its export to the rest of the world.

But it is far from being a merely negative critique. Chapter after chapter comes up with interesting and carefully thought-through suggestions and experiments in alternative possibilities – possibilities that aim to sustain the necessary quality and standards of what "doctorateness" should look like in any cultural context (the vision of the Beirut Benchmarks), while acknowledging that the forms, methods and outcomes that display such quality cannot and should not be determined or dictated exclusively by predominantly white western male patterns of thought and "Enlightenment" assumptions.

With its creative discussion questions and extensive bibliographical documentation for every chapter, this book should be an absolute must-read for any seminary faculty contemplating (or already engaged in) doctoral-level training. It is gratifying that the book includes at least five Langham Scholars (including one of the editors). Certainly those of us, such as Langham Partnership and ScholarLeaders, who invest heavily in doctoral-level theological education, must listen very carefully to its message.

My only worry, or perhaps it should be a hope, is that if doctoral-level work is to move in this direction, we will have to ask similar questions and do some radical thinking about the nature of theological education further upstream at bachelors and masters levels, if we are to have a flow of doctoral candidates (and their supervisors) prepared to be as innovative as this book encourages.

Christopher J. H. Wright
International Ministries Director, Langham Partnership
February 2018

Introduction

Perry Shaw and Havilah Dharamraj

The wise man sits on the hole in his carpet. (Urdu proverb)

We live in exciting times. Over the past century we have seen the church shift from being a predominantly Western institution (albeit with significant ancient churches in the Middle East) to a genuinely global community, with its centre of gravity moving increasingly south and east. In 1900 there were about 350 million Christians in Europe and fewer than 10 million on the entire continent of Africa. Today there are nearly 600 million Christians in Africa, constituting nearly one-quarter of the global Christian community. There are now over 20 million Christians in South Korea alone, and Christians in China are several times that number. Similar movements can be seen elsewhere in the world.[1]

If the church is to impact the surrounding society for the kingdom of God, in every location there is a need for theological leadership. Such leadership will not take place through the imposition of a Western approach to "scholarship," but through the development of quality reflection within communication paradigms that resonate with the local context. This book proposes possible innovative steps for the development of theological leaders who can speak to their local contexts in meaningful forms and structures. The need for innovation in advanced theological studies is particularly pressing.

This discussion is not unique to the theological academy. There is a growing acknowledgement that all is not well in global higher education. Rising costs and changing social climates have led to the questioning of classic models.[2]

---

1. Todd M. Johnson et al., "Christianity 2017: Five Hundred Years of Protestant Christianity," *International Bulletin of Mission Research* 41, no.1 (2017): 41–52. See also The World Christian Database, at http://www.worldchristiandatabase.org/wcd.

2. See, for example, The Modern Language Association of America, "Report of the MLA Task Force on Doctoral Study in Modern Language and Literature," May 2014, accessed 1 December 2016, https://apps.mla.org/pdf/taskforcedocstudy2014.pdf.

Increasing recognition has been given to questions of cultural hegemony:[3] the contemporary shape of university studies is the product of a particular region of the world (Europe) in a particular period of history (the linear empiricist heyday of the seventeenth and eighteenth centuries) for a particular group of people (white males), and this model is no longer seen as universally normative. Perhaps until now we've been carefully sitting on the hole in our carpet, but now the hole is getting bigger. The wise man knows when he should get up and begin mending the carpet. Already in the secular academy experiments in innovative approaches to advanced study are taking place.[4] Our team's work in this collection is consistent with the global discussions in other fields of study.

The innovative suggestions in this book face many obstacles. One of the greatest challenges to innovation is the inertia that comes with what has been described as the "Pike syndrome"[5] in which people come to assume they have complete knowledge of a situation because of past experiences, and these experiences become "normative." The end result is a trained incapacity that comes from rigid commitment to what was true in the past and a refusal to consider alternatives and different perspectives. We trust that the combination we offer here of quality theoretical reflection with very tangible suggestions might help to overcome this inertia.

While both Perry and Havilah have succeeded in the system of advanced theological study, we have both for some time sensed that there is something not right about the rigidity of the current processes we use. In 2011 Perry wrote

---

3. See in particular A. Suresh Canagarajah, *A Geopolitics of Academic Writing* (Pittsburgh: University of Pittsburgh, 2002).

4. See, for example, "Report of the MLA Task Force"; Cassidy R. Sugimoto, "Toward a Twenty-First Century Dissertation," accessed 1 December 2016, http://cgsnet.org/ckfinder/userfiles/files/1_1%20Sugimoto.pdf; Fernanda Zamudio-Suaréz, "An Activist Defends His Dissertation in Rap," *The Chronicle of Higher Education*, 27 February 2017.

5. The term comes from a series of experiments in which an individual pike was placed in a large fish tank. Several smaller fish were then introduced into the tank, but separated from the pike in a large glass jar, closing them off completely from the pike. In an attempt to get at this ready food source the pike hit the glass over and over until, frustrated and "conditioned," it settled at the bottom of the tank right next to the minnows. After a while the jar was lifted and the minnows were released to swim all around the pike and throughout the large tank. And yet the pike remained motionless. Indeed, the pike never tried again and eventually died of starvation, despite having a source of food and survival immediately available. Mike Greene, "Pike Syndrome," *Integrity Works Coaching*, accessed 22 July 2015, www.integrityworkscoaching.com/blog/200-pike-syndrome.html.

an article in which he suggested that the rationalist-empiricist shape that is generally seen as normative in advanced studies has overtones of culture and gender imperialism.[6] While Perry intentionally wrote in a provocative style that no doubt overstated the case, Riad Kassis liked the article in that it resonated with a lot of his own concerns.

In a conversation at the ICETE 2015 Triennial Consultation (Antalya, Turkey), Riad suggested that Perry put together a book that elaborated on the ideas he introduced in his article. The discussion is particularly germane in light of the changes occurring in Majority World doctoral programs in theological education. Perry was uncomfortable taking on such a project alone, particularly as a white Western male with limited experience in the field. He first needed a partner who could complement his own training and experience.

Perry knew Havilah personally and also saw the richness of the presentation she had done at the 2012 ICETE Consultation (Nairobi, Kenya),[7] and so we talked over the idea in Turkey. We immediately realized that an integrated anthology would better demonstrate that our concerns are widespread, and would also bring a richness of insight for innovation.

Havilah suggested that we field-test the concept in a workshop at South Asia Institute of Advanced Christian Studies (SAIACS), which we did in February 2016. The response of the SAIACS faculty was enthusiastic. We spent the next few months approaching people within the ICETE network who we felt would be sympathetic, and through recommendations from them and others we built our team. The current collection is the end result.

We have a number of goals for this collection:

- To shift our understanding of the purpose of advanced study from the development of scholars to the development of theological leadership.[8] This shift will entail a serious engagement not only

---

6. Perry Shaw, "'New Treasures with the Old': Addressing Culture and Gender Imperialism in Higher Level Theological Education," chapter 2 in *Tending the Seedbeds: Educational Perspectives on Theological Education in Asia*, ed. Allan Harkness (Quezon City: Asia Theological Association, 2010), 47–74.

7. Havilah Dharamraj, "We Reap What We Sow: Engaging Curriculum and Context in Theological Education" (presentation delivered at the ICETE Triennial Consultation, Nairobi, Kenya, October 2012).

8. This is central to Evan Hunter's chapter in this collection, "A Context Conducive to Innovation."

- with local contextual issues, but also with local patterns of rhetoric and communication.
- To realize that while the traditional approach certainly has value, it is limited and limiting, and that there are significant other approaches for generating valuable knowledge.
- To pursue stewardship in the development of theological leaders. There is no question that one learns a tremendous amount through the process of advanced study – both in content and in methodology – but are there approaches that might form theological leaders without the current level of personal, ministry, and financial cost?
- To demonstrate that creative methodology is the way of the future, and to affirm that creative approaches are already being embraced in many Western universities.
- To provide specific models that have already been tried, and to suggest others that might enhance learning for theological leadership.

For ease of reading we have divided the collection, somewhat artificially, into three sections:

The first section looks at broader philosophical, theological, and social-contextual issues which shape our understandings of advanced theological studies. The chapters in this section investigate the purpose of advanced theological education, particularly as perceived by leaders in the Majority World church.

The second section imagines some innovative possibilities for the dissertation. The assumption here is that our basic form would be retained for showing competency at the master's and doctoral levels, while reimaging the substance.

The third section imagines innovative forms other than the dissertation for showing master's or doctoral competency. Most of these are a search for local forms of expression that better serve the purpose of developing contextually competent theological leadership for the church.

We recognize that the thrust of this book and many of the suggestions offered may raise concerns in some. Is this yet another effort to "dumb down" advanced theological studies? Are we opening a "Pandora's box," the end of which will be chaos? Certainly we acknowledge from the outset that there are many strengths to the classic Western model of linear-empiricist study:

discipline, attention to detail, the desire for objectivity. However, increasingly there is recognition that there are foundational weaknesses in the classic approach: fragmentation and the consequent loss of holistic understanding, the focus on knowledge more than wisdom, the cultural dissonance in non-Western contexts. This collection seeks to investigate innovative possibilities that better resonate with the need for theological leaders.

Perry and Havilah have each brought different backgrounds and gifts to the task. Perry was raised in Australia and his first degree was in mathematics, and so has fit comfortably within the system as it is. However, nearly three decades of living in the Arab world and his consultancy work throughout the Majority World has helped him to realize the extent to which a very particular set of cultural values has surreptitiously been exported around the globe through Western-style theological education. Havilah, being an Indian and female, is comfortable in story and image, and views ideas holistically. She has learned to work within the system as it is, but recognizes the need for affirming other patterns of thinking and expression.

We present this collection as a step on the journey towards strengthening global theological leadership. However, we wish to acknowledge a major shortcoming of this collection, a weakness that in some ways supports a questionable Western hegemony over the global theological academy: the issue of language. We have felt the severe incongruity between our advocacy for contextual significance in both content and methodology, and our requirement that our writers present in English.[9] How much better would have been the match between our purpose and our presentation if Lal, César, John, Rafael, Joanna, Dwi, and Xiaoli (and perhaps others in our team) had been empowered to write in their heart languages. We are particularly grateful to each of these for their graciousness and effort in presenting in English.

---

9. This is an issue highlighted by Tim Tennent in his article, "New Paradigm for Twenty-First Century Mission: Missiological Reflections in Honor of George K. Chavanikamannil," in *Remapping Mission Discourse: A Festschrift in Honor of the Rev. George Kuruvila Chavanikamannil*, ed. Simon Samuel and P. V. Joseph (Delhi: ISPCK, 2008), 185–203. See also Namsoon Kang's discussion of the subalternization of language in "Envisioning Postcolonial Theological Education: Dilemmas and Possibilities," in *Handbook of Theological Education in World Christianity: Theological Perspectives – Regional Surveys – Ecumenical Trends*, ed. D. Werner et al. (Eugene: Wipf and Stock, 2010), 36–37.

It is important at the outset that we make clear our primary target audience: leaders of emerging programs of advanced theological studies in the Majority World. While schools in the Minority World may well find the material of interest, our concern as we look to the future is to empower the rapidly growing church in Africa, Asia, and elsewhere to develop meaningful forms and structures to the training of theological leaders. As we seek both content and methodology that resonates with the local context, there is great potential for our schools to prepare men and women who can help the churches speak meaningfully to their societies and nations, and hence bring impact in the name of Christ.

Bibliography

Canagarajah, A. Suresh. *A Geopolitics of Academic Writing*. Pittsburgh: University of Pittsburgh, 2002.

Dharamraj, Havilah. "We Reap What We Sow: Engaging Curriculum and Context in Theological Education." Presentation delivered at the ICETE Triennial Consultation, Nairobi, Kenya, October 2012.

Greene, Mike. "Pike Syndrome." *Integrity Works Coaching*. Accessed 22 July 2015. www.integrityworkscoaching.com/blog/200-pike-syndrome.html.

Johnson, Todd M., Gina A. Zurlo, Albert W. Hickman, and Peter F. Crossing. "Christianity 2017: Five Hundred Years of Protestant Christianity." *International Bulletin of Mission Research* 41, no. 1 (2017): 41–52.

Kang, Namsoon. "Envisioning Postcolonial Theological Education: Dilemmas and Possibilities." In *Handbook of Theological Education in World Christianity: Theological Perspectives – Regional Surveys – Ecumenical Trends*, edited by D. Werner, D. Esterline, N. Kang, and J. Raja, 30–41. Eugene: Wipf and Stock, 2010.

The Modern Language Association of America. "Report of the MLA Task Force on Doctoral Study in Modern Language and Literature." May 2014. Accessed 1 December 2016. https://apps.mla.org/pdf/taskforcedocstudy2014.pdf.

Shaw, Perry. "'New Treasures with the Old': Addressing Culture and Gender Imperialism in Higher Level Theological Education." Chapter 2 in *Tending the Seedbeds: Educational Perspectives on Theological Education in Asia*, edited by Allan Harkness, 47–74. Quezon City: Asia Theological Association, 2010.

Sugimoto, Cassidy R. "Toward a Twenty-First Century Dissertation." Accessed 1 December 2016. http://cgsnet.org/ckfinder/userfiles/files/1_1%20Sugimoto.pdf.

Tennent, Tim. "New Paradigm for Twenty-First Century Mission: Missiological Reflections in Honor of George K. Chavanikamannil." In *Remapping Mission Discourse: A Festschrift in Honor of the Rev. George Kuruvila Chavanikamannil*, edited by Simon Samuel and P. V. Joseph, 185–203. Delhi: ISPCK, 2008.

The World Christian Database. http://www.worldchristiandatabase.org/wcd.

Zamudio-Suaréz, Fernanda. "An Activist Defends His Dissertation in Rap." *The Chronicle of Higher Education*, 27 February 2017.

Section I

Principles for Innovation in Advanced Theological Studies

> When a poor man suddenly prospers, he will insist on an umbrella held over his head even in the middle of the night. (South Indian proverb)

In days gone by, when a king went for a walk on a summer's day, his attendant would go along, holding a richly decorated umbrella over his head. In this section, we consider why we should innovate in advanced theological studies. What exactly are we trying to do, and how best might we accomplish it? If we don't carefully think through the mantra "Fitness of purpose – Fitness for Purpose," we might well end up shading ourselves at midnight.

We open with a personal narrative from Ashish Chrispal, recently retired Asia Regional Director for Overseas Council. Ashish was one of the very first Langham scholars and has been involved in promoting advanced theological studies for forty years. His story provides something of a historical background to this collection, and speaks for thousands of theological students who have found their theological education alienating and ineffective in preparing them for the context to which God had called them for ministry.

Some years ago Andrew Kirk observed: "It is now a commonplace of much theological endeavour in the church of the global South that the verification of genuine theology is determined not so much by criteria formulated within the parameters of the academic community, as by its ability to liberate people for effective involvement in society. If it does not have this effect, it is considered an alienated and alienating force."[1] Evan Hunter's research on emerging doctoral programs in the Majority World affirms Kirk's observation, and the need to shift our focus from the development of scholars to the development of theological leadership. Evan's leadership role in ScholarLeaders has further highlighted the need for this shift. In his chapter Evan gives an overview of shifting global perspectives in higher education in general and in advanced theological education in particular. Evan's material demonstrates that innovation in advanced theological studies is now imperative.

However, are there any boundaries to what studies should be acknowledged as valid at the master's and doctoral levels? Perry investigates current global standards of quality assurance, concluding that accrediting bodies are increasingly focusing on the demonstration of competency, not the completion of a set methodology. In many countries substantial room is being given for innovation in form, and these innovations can be readily embraced in advanced theological studies.

In accepting the status quo we can easily become blind to the messages we communicate in our practices. Allan Harkness (formerly Dean of the AGST Alliance) investigates the hidden curriculum of advanced theological studies, and doctoral studies in particular, looking systematically at how the outcome, process, output, and cost of doctoral studies may serve to undermine the larger purposes of the kingdom of God.

The next four chapters of our collection look at the extent to which the current approach to advanced theological studies is structured to suit empiricist, linear-thinking white Western males. Perry examines some dominant culture

---

1. J. A. Kirk, "Re-Envisioning the Theological Curriculum as if the *Missio Dei* Mattered," *Common Ground Journal* 3, no. 1 (2005): 23–40.

and gender studies, pointing to the impoverishment that occurs through a rigid understanding of advanced studies. Lal Senanayake (Principal of Lanka Bible College and Seminary, Sri Lanka) examines the relationship between culture, communication, and research. Drawing on her many years of teaching in Africa, Stephanie Black introduces us to the world of intercultural rhetoric and its potential in academic writing. And César Lopes, speaking from his Brazilian context, calls us to the release and empowerment of local knowledges. All four chapters point to the need for greater responsiveness not only in content but also in methodology as we seek to build culturally significant theological leadership.

We trust that the four chapters on culture will raise a greater awareness of Majority World patterns of thinking and communication, and hence enable a friendlier environment in which the church is enriched through its global community. To do otherwise is to treat the rich diversity of Majority World believers as little more than "ghosts among whom we move but do not have to acknowledge as we do not see them."[2]

Is there a "theology of research"? As those who are developing Christian leaders it is valuable to consider major theological themes and their implications for the way we shape and conduct research in the theological academy. In terms of both his training and his current role as Principal of SAIACS (India), Ian Payne is ideally placed to take us on this theological journey. His chapter rightly concludes the first section of our collection.

Bibliography

Kirk, J. A. "Re-Envisioning the Theological Curriculum as if the *Missio Dei* Mattered." *Common Ground Journal* 3, no. 1 (2005): 23–40.

---

2. Mary Fisher in a personal communication with Perry Shaw, October 2016.

1

My Journey into Theological Education

Ashish Chrispal

This chapter is the story of my journey into theological education. Its purpose is to share the challenges one faces during theological studies when coming from the Majority World, but also to point out the reality of our missed missional vision and ministry goal of theological education. I am offering this to lead us to understand theology as the praise of God (*Theos Eulogeo*) rather than the study of God (*Theos Logos*). My journey seemed to begin when I entered seminary to equip myself for the ministry to which God had called me. However, after forty-two years of involvement in ministry, I have realized that my actual journey began much further back, when I was born into a pastor's family.

Childhood

I was born in Bombay to God-fearing parents. My father was a pastor and my mother a high-school teacher. We lived in a slum colony sharing an 8 feet by 10 feet room with an elderly widow, as the church could not afford rent for a separate house. The sacrificial lifestyle of my parents and the widow has gone into my being, to focus my ministry on the underprivileged and marginalized. The Word of God and prayer were central to my upbringing. My parents' transfers from one city to another also made me adaptable to life situations.

However, our second church, in the city of Surat in Gujarat, impacted me the most as we suffered at the very hands of the church. No other pastor stayed at this church for more than six months. But by God's grace my father stayed on for four years. However, this experience as a young child adversely affected me and I was determined never to become a pastor or to be in ministry. I detested being a pastor's son as I saw the struggles and difficulties my parents faced. I wanted to be a medical doctor. This led me to the next phase of my educational journey and God's calling to his ministry.

Educational Journey

We moved to the city of Ahmedabad where I did my education from middle school till graduation. My parents could not afford English medium school for me, so they put me in a Hindu school. This gave me the privilege of knowing my context of religious plurality better. It also helped me to learn Sanskrit, as for four years it was one of my main subjects. It also simultaneously exposed me to the Indian prejudicial view of Christians as outcast people who convert for material privileges.

It was during my second year of college that my hope of being a medical doctor crashed and the Lord took hold of my life. I surrendered my life to Jesus Christ as my Lord and Saviour. I completed my final two years of BSc in English medium, still hoping to go back to medical school and be a doctor, but then the Lord changed the course of my life.

Call to Ministry and Theological Education

I accepted God's call and entered seminary to do my bachelor of divinity (BD/MDiv). This call was based on the life of Abraham as depicted in Hebrews 11:8–19. He believed the unbelievable, he saw the invisible, and he inherited the unthinkable. This has ultimately become my life story. The Lord's hand was upon me and I was able to do well in my studies and ministry preparation. The biblical language studies of Greek and Hebrew came easily to me. But as a science graduate who had studied for seventeen years in the vernacular language, I found it difficult to express myself well in the English language.

I had to work harder and for longer hours to cope with the studies. I had excellent professors who were experienced pastors and missionaries.

After my BD graduation, my first year of ministry was a great challenge. I served a congregation of about 250 families. Most of the men were workers in one of the big spinning mills, while the women were teachers in the government schools or nurses in the government hospitals. I used all of my learning to minister but saw minimal results. I was also teaching at the vernacular Bible school at BTh level. This was a denominational school training evangelists and pastors for the Church of North India. After six months of ministry the Principal of the college invited me to organize an "Exposure Week" for the students to help them understand their context of ministry. It was during this week that the Lord confronted me with the reality of many of my parishioners. As we were visiting the only fully automated spinning mill I saw a single person in each room managing eight power looms. There was no personal touch, just mechanical interaction with machines. I reconsidered my ministry and learned to relate to people, to get to know their challenges and worldviews, and to help them see the transforming power of God.

It was as if I had to relearn all of my theological training to be relevant and engaged with my congregation. First, I had to understand that mere good exegesis with the use of biblical languages is not enough to prepare sermons that touch human lives. I also needed applications that dealt with the life challenges of the people. Second, I had to understand that counselling people was not about using steps in counselling techniques or mere skills, but required listening to them and their context. Third, it also meant experiencing failure and learning more of the social context within which people dealt with their life situations. I have written about my first pastoral challenge as a case study, "Who Runs My Life?"[1] This pastoral experience has stayed with me all these years. It impacted my thinking during my doctoral studies and seminary ministry, and helped me to see my doctoral studies as a preparation for being involved in the formation of students for ministry with a missional focus.

---

1. Ashish Chrispal, "Who Runs My Life?," in *Human Rights Issues in Pastoral Ministry: Indian Theological Case Studies*, ed. H. S. Wilson (Bangalore: BTESSC, 1989): 1–4.

Involvement in Theological Education

My alma mater, the Union Biblical Seminary (Yavatmal), invited me to be on the faculty in 1978. This began a new phase in our life as a family. We moved to Yavatmal with three years of pastoral ministry experience. My interest by this time was very much in biblical studies and in pastoral ministry within the context of the poor and religious pluralism. After two years of teaching I had the privilege to meet Dr John R. W. Stott in Singapore and was invited to be an EFAC scholar (today known as Langham Ministries International). I reluctantly accepted this offer at the insistence of my principal, as I was not sure whether I would survive the British model of doctoral studies, first, because the seminary decided to send me to study in the field of Systematic Theology. I saw this as my weakest area, since I always felt that Systematics were irrelevant to the realities of my context. Second, I was afraid of the level of English language required at the university and the uncertainty of knowing whether I would ever get through my thesis. I was more comfortable with the coursework, comprehensive exam, and dissertation model of doctoral studies than just a thesis. So we moved to Aberdeen with trepidation and uncertainty. It was a lonely journey.

I started my doctoral studies under Professor James Torrance and Dr Chris Wigglesworth. I was given the privilege of doing an interdisciplinary program combining Systematic Theology and Practical Theology. This was a salvaging factor; otherwise I was in the context in which theology was viewed only from the traditional categories of Lutheran, Calvinist, Barthian, and so on. My early school experience, my pastoral experience, and even my four years of teaching experience showed me that theology is a living encounter with God in and through his Word, as one engages with one's context. The Western approach to Systematic Theology, on the other hand, answers the philosophical questions of the times of theologians. I also realized that the Indian mindset is rarely analytical or logical in matters of spirituality and religious discourse. This was an uphill task, as my professor, being a strong Calvinist and a Barthian, clearly believed that there was no General Revelation. Another challenge I faced was my desire to research development theology, liberation theology, and to develop an evangelical answer to the challenges faced by the poor. But this was not possible as it would have required depth in economics and sociology.

The political changes of the time also brought in financial cuts for the universities which made it difficult to get research resources through any sort of inter-library loan scheme. We lived near the church which was supporting EFAC and hence we had very little connection with fellow doctoral students. This made my journey very lonely. In those days there were no doctoral seminars or reading of papers within the theology department as each one was looking at different theological research. But to juggle my studies with my pastoral responsibilities, the struggle of giving time to my wife and son in a foreign country, and with little help from interaction with my peer researchers in the department became difficult. I am a people person, but here we were thrown into an impersonal society context in which we had to survive. I am glad that now such seminars have become the norm.

After struggling for two years we moved back to India, to research my area further without wasting God's money by staying on in Aberdeen. It also became a struggle to support ourselves without returning to my seminary and taking up the responsibilities. I continued to complete my doctoral research while being the Academic Dean and a teacher at the Union Biblical Seminary (UBS), and pastoring a congregation about 100 km away from Pune. I always believed that my doctoral studies were by God's grace alone. This is the name of our first son, "Anugrah" ("God's grace and blessings" in Sanskrit and Hindi).

My time completing doctoral studies was ridden with difficulties. My thesis was written prior to the age of the computer, and my second advisor left the university just a year after I came back to India. The university also required British English. But the Lord took care of all these challenges. The Lord helped me to complete my studies and receive my doctorate. It was by the graciousness of my professor that Bishop Lesslie Newbigin and Dr Duncan Forrester were invited to be my external examiners. This in itself was a great blessing, to have two stalwarts who had served in India and who knew my burden and challenges. This fulfilled my need for external examiners who also knew my interdisciplinary approach to the thesis. I was glad that I had changed the course of my enquiry to focus on the nature of the church in the context of poverty and religious pluralism. My dissertation was entitled: "An Indian Perspective on the Nature of the Church in the Context of Poverty and Religious Pluralism, with Special Reference to the Works of M. M. Thomas." I served at UBS until 1994, when again the Lord guided me into an out-of-the-comfort-zone experience.

Exposure to Education

It was in 1994 that the Lord led me out to The Kodaikanal International School (K-12 school). It was difficult to accept this call, but it was an act of faith and transformation in terms of my educational and missional understanding. I served as the Dean of Students and Administrative Principal for seven years, which helped me to see the need for Christ and his love among those who are the "haves" of the world. It helped me to learn student-centred education and the emphasis on learning rather than teaching. In 2001 the Lord led me to serve with a mission organization for a year and I got involved in the ministry with grassroots workers in the remotest parts of India ministering to the poor and marginalized. I now realized that the Lord took me out of theological education to relearn the emphasis on formation. I also understood that many teachers at seminaries come back with doctorates but with no curricular, pedagogical, or administrative learning, but are thrown into the deep end as Academic Deans or Presidents, and even as teachers. This leads to the sarcastic tag that theological education is neither theological nor educational! I returned to seminary teaching in 2002 and became President of the South Asia Institute of Advanced Christian Studies (SAIACS), Bangalore, in 2004.

New Era with Renewed Vision

The year 2005 became the most difficult in our lives, as our second son went to be with the Lord after a rare illness (viral myocarditis). He had just returned to India after studying at Asbury College, Kentucky. But this reiterated my firm belief that the resurrection faith is the watershed of religions.

I was dissatisfied with the way we teach theology and the way we do theology. We require mental assent to dogmas and theories filled with irrelevant cerebral teaching. Instead of preparing agents of transformation we create stereotype professors who can speak to their constituency but have little to say to their fellow believers or their national church. Some live in two worlds, one of perceived theology and the other of pastoral ministry. This leads some to separate their faith from their theology.

Since 2007 I have served with the Overseas Council as the Regional Director for Asia, ministering in non-Chinese-speaking seminaries in fourteen countries. My ministry has helped me to be a pastor to the presidents and faculty of these partner schools. My purpose in this ministry was to become a catalyst for the transformation of theological education, which in turn would help to mentor transforming and missional leadership for the church in the days to come. My desire is that theological education would help the church to be a transforming agent to impact the society with the Lord's help. As a part of this ministry the Lord used me to participate in the development of a doctoral program at the Torch Trinity Graduate University, where every doctoral candidate is exposed to curricular and pedagogical designs, institutional leadership, and interdisciplinary learning during coursework.

My challenge to those of us who are educators is this: let us make theological education both theological and educational. We need theological leaders, not academicians. Theological education needs to form and equip students to be the disciplers for the Lord. Professor Andrew Walls, in his keynote address at Chiang Mai ICETE Triennial 2004, propounded that the centre of Christianity has moved from the West to the Majority World. Then why does theological education still look to the West for recognition and approval? Why are Majority World methodologies for research, with their more anecdotal and case-study-filled approaches, still looked down upon? Can we build frameworks that take seriously, as valid expressions of theological training, our researchers' backgrounds, their experiences of their context, and their zeal to disciple the nations? I pray that the essays in the current collection will challenge us and inspire us for a promising future for the church in the twenty-first century and beyond.

Discussion Questions

1. Take no longer than five minutes to share briefly with one or two other leaders the main contours of your own "journey into theological education." In particular, share some of the most painful moments in your experience of advanced theological studies.

2. From your own experience, what have been two or three of the most significant disconnects you have observed between your life and ministry pilgrimage and the realities of advanced theological studies?

3. Read again the final paragraph of Ashish's reflection. What do you believe are one or two of the most significant changes that need to be made in order for theological education to better function theologically and educationally, and in particular "to form and equip students to be the disciplers for the Lord"?

Bibliography

Chrispal, Ashish. "Who Runs My Life?" In *Human Rights Issues in Pastoral Ministry: Indian Theological Case Studies*, edited by H. S. Wilson, 1–4. Bangalore: BTESSC, 1989.

2

A Context Conducive to Innovation:
How Changes in Doctoral Education Create New Opportunities for Developing Theological Leaders

Evan R. Hunter

Introduction: Looking for Something Different in the Degree

The common definition of insanity is to keep doing the same thing over and over while expecting different results. That being the case, when the path you are on will not get you where you want to go, the time has come to consider alternatives. For some in theological education, that time is now. Frustration with a process can become a force for innovation, opening avenues to new ideas for accomplishing the task. Over the last decade, advocates for changes in doctoral education have pushed for new approaches to achieve better results. This context of change has implications for theological education as well as seminaries as they develop theological leaders through the PhD experience.

Earning a PhD requires great sacrifice: years of study, hours upon hours of writing, time away from family, friends, and ministry, perhaps even a relocation to a new country. However, the process of the PhD can seem disconnected from the realities of the context. When I conducted my doctoral research on newly developed doctoral programs in the Majority World,[1] I heard a common theme from leaders. These leaders, who appreciated their time of study, often felt their experience was out of sync with the intended purpose. They graduated looking for something different, more meaningful, more contextually relevant, and better connected to their career aspirations. They left with a series of questions:

- Is my degree merely academic or does it matter to the church? As one respondent stated, pursuing advanced studies means choosing between serving academia and serving the church: "When I started my PhD program I was told that the PhD research contributes scholarship, not to the church."[2]
- Does my degree serve the West or will it make a difference where I live? Until most recently, leaders from the Majority World had no choice but to travel to the West to earn a PhD. Even as new programs start, some leaders feel they may simply copy Western models, further dichotomizing the process from the context: "The Western approach is that you write for the scholarship, while . . . the African approach . . . wants to see how the community will benefit from your research."[3] For this leader, it created a tension in how to pursue his studies.
- Will this degree prepare me to teach in a relevant way? Several expressed their disappointment to discover that all the notes and classes they had taken would not translate into their home contexts. At the furthest extreme, their studies had been almost a waste of

---

1. This chapter will use the term Majority World to refer to the regions of Africa, Asia, Latin America, Eastern Europe, and the Middle East. This term has been chosen as it has preference over historic terms such as "Third World" or "Developing World," which may carry a pejorative connotation. Directional terms such as "West" and "Global South" may prove problematic, as they are not always accurate. For example, Brazil is clearly in the western hemisphere but not generally considered "the West." Australia is in the southern hemisphere, but is more often associated with the resources and power dynamics found in Europe and North America. "Majority World" is a positive term that reflects the reality of both the population in general and Christians in particular, as the majority of Christians now live in Africa, Asia, Latin America, the Middle East, and Eastern Europe.
2. Evan R. Hunter, "Stakeholder Perspectives of Contextual Engagement of PhD Programs at Select Evangelical Seminaries in the Majority World" (PhD diss., Trinity Evangelical Divinity School, 2014), 123.
3. Hunter, "Stakeholder Perspectives," 123.

time in preparation for the work to come: "When I came back, I realized that the notes I took at [my school] will not help me in my classroom because the concerns my teachers had are not necessarily the concerns my students have. If I start giving them that information, then there's going to be problems. I had to redo my notes. Actually, I don't use anything from [the school where I studied] in my teaching. I had to do everything right from scratch looking at the issues, the concerns and the problems that I see we need to address here in Africa."[4]

These statements exemplify a sentiment among many scholars within the PhD experience, for whom the output and preparation for teaching have apparently missed the mark. They believed that formal academic experience is oriented to the West and does not meet local needs. The degree has value, but these scholars long for something different, more relevant.

A Context Conducive to Creativity

Change comes slowly in academia, and doctoral programs are deeply rooted both historically and in practice in the university system. The PhD developed in the universities of Paris, Bologna, and Berlin, eventually becoming focused almost exclusively on the production of an independent dissertation.[5] The PhD holds value as the pinnacle of the academic degree, designed to prepare the recipient for a career in teaching, research, and writing. Graduates become "stewards of the discipline," demonstrating broad expertise and, through generative research, promoting innovation within their fields.[6] Doctoral education has become a large enterprise with the number of those enrolled in

---

4. Hunter, 119.
5. Madeleine Abrandt Dahlgren and Anna Bjuremeark, "The Seminar as Enacted Doctoral Pedagogy," in *Reshaping Doctoral Education: International Approaches and Pedagogies*, ed. Alison Lee and Susan Danby (New York: Routledge, 2012), 56–58.
6. See David Boud and Alison Lee, *Changing Practices of Doctoral Education* (New York: Routledge, 2009); Chris Golde and George E. Walker, *Envisioning the Future of Doctoral Education: Preparing Stewards of the Discipline*, Carnegie Essays on the Doctorate, 1st ed. (San Francisco: Jossey-Bass, 2006); George Walker and the Carnegie Foundation for the Advancement of Teaching, *The Formation of Scholars: Rethinking Doctoral Education for the Twenty-First Century*, 1st ed. (San Francisco: Jossey-Bass, 2008).

doctoral programs increasing dramatically. Since 2008, China surpassed the US as the nation producing the greatest number of graduates on an annual basis and shows little sign of slowing down as they have grown in enrollment in doctoral programs by 24 percent each year since 1978.[7]

Within theological education, the PhD prepares students as theological leaders – women and men who teach at seminaries, train the next generation of church leaders, and carry out the intellectual work of the church through their research and writing. However, the inherited structures are often "at odds" with the stated purpose of the seminary education.[8] Not only does institutional inertia perpetuate the status quo, but theology is understandably a field that shuns novelty in its commitment to historic orthodoxy.

However, the winds of change have begun to stir. Internal and external forces have asked new questions of the purpose and design of the PhD in its process, outcomes, and outputs. Research on the doctorate shows a greater demand for graduates who can think across disciplines, engage collaboratively, and address issues relevant to society. The same holds true within theological education where the desire for something different from the doctoral process harkens to Jesus's metaphor of new wine and old wineskins. This disruptive climate creates new opportunities for considering new and creative methodologies to achieve the purpose of developing theological leadership for the church.

Changes in the Landscape of Doctoral Education

As new questions arise about the kinds of graduates needed to face twenty-first-century realities, doctoral education has entered into a "state of flux."[9] Internal pressures related to overall graduation rates, completion times, and rising costs have combined with external factors related to the academic job

---

7. Geoff Malsen, "More Countries Are Asking Whether They Produce Too Many Ph.D.'s," *The Chronicle of Higher Education*, 10 April 2012.

8. Helen Bleier and Barbara Wheeler, *Report on a Study of Doctoral Programs That Prepare Faculty for Teaching at Theological Schools* (New York: Auburn Center for the Study of Theological Education, 2010), 8.

9. Claire Aitchison and Anthony Pare, "Writing as Craft and Practice in the Doctoral Curriculum," in Lee and Danby, *Reshaping Doctoral Education*, 12.

market and the need for research that addresses complex problems in society to force educators to re-evaluate doctoral program design.

The doctoral process has received attention on both sides of the Atlantic. The Bologna Declaration sets standards for higher education in Europe, harmonizing degrees so that they are transferable and comparable across borders.[10] Through standardization, they also seek to maximize graduation rates and develop the degree in ways that are "useful and efficient" to meet the needs of an increasingly globalized world.[11] In the US, the Carnegie Initiative on the Doctorate (CID) created a large-scale, multidisciplinary research initiative to evaluate and improve doctoral education. The CID focused on questions of degree purpose, vocational preparation, and assessment standards. The CID moves away from an exclusive focus on dissertation output to consideration for the "formation of scholars" with a holistic concern for graduates who can steward their disciplines.[12]

As with the student quotations above, the CID demonstrates that many PhD graduates have not been adequately prepared for postdoctoral realities.[13] The doctoral process needs to do more to address relevant societal issues. Students need better preparation for teaching and the daily realities of their vocations within and beyond the academy. Embracing the metaphor of doctoral education as a journey, these writers broaden the focus to include not only the published thesis but also the multifaceted aspects of the doctoral process.[14] Calls for reform have drawn attention to some of the emerging phenomena within higher education.

---

10. Barbara Gabrys and Alina Beltechi, "Cognitive Apprenticeship," in Lee and Danby, *Reshaping Doctoral Education*, 144–155.

11. See Maresi Nerad and Mimi Heggelund, *Toward a Global PhD? Forces and Forms in Doctoral Education Worldwide* (Seattle: Center for Innovation and Research in Graduate Education in Association with University of Washington Press, 2008).

12. See Golde and Walker, *Envisioning the Future*, 2006. Also Ronald Ehrenberg, Charlotte V. Kuh, and Cornell Higher Education Research Institute, *Doctoral Education and the Faculty of the Future* (Ithaca: Cornell University, 2009).

13. See Peggy Maki and Nancy A. Borkowski, *The Assessment of Doctoral Education: Emerging Criteria and New Models for Improving Outcomes*, 1st ed. (Sterling, VA: Stylus, 2006).

14. D. Leonard and R. Becker, "Enhancing the Doctoral Experience at the Local Level," in Boud and Lee, *Changing Practices of Doctoral Education*, 71–99.

Attention to the Rise of New Doctoral Programs in Evangelical Seminaries in the Majority World

In the midst of the turbulence around doctoral education in general, a significant shift has occurred in theological education with the rapid rise of PhD programs at reputable evangelical schools across the Majority World. In 1999, only two doctoral programs had begun among schools located in the Majority World associated with the International Council for Evangelical Theological Education (ICETE) and its affiliate regional accrediting bodies. By 2015, that number had reached twenty-three schools, hosting more than sixty different PhD programs. Those twenty-three schools have a combined enrolment in their PhD programs of more than 700 doctoral students.[15]

The number of doctoral students pursuing their PhDs at schools located in the Majority World now exceeds the total number of international students enrolled in PhD programs at schools accredited by the Association of Theological Schools. In 2015, ATS reported the number of international students in doctoral programs – including all evangelical, mainline, and Roman Catholic seminaries in the US and Canada – to be 638. The numbers represent a rapid shift in the location of enrolment of evangelical Majority World doctoral students away from the West and towards contextually based programs. Furthermore, the trend will likely continue as PhD enrolment by international students at ATS schools in North America has declined since 2003, a shift that coincides with the rise of the new programs in the Majority World.[16]

The new doctoral programs will have a significant impact on the development of the next generation of theological scholars in the Majority World. First, these programs provide greater access to PhD studies for students who would not be able to find funds or time to pursue their doctorates abroad. Students appreciate that they do not have to relocate their families to the West

---

15. Evan R. Hunter, "A Tectonic Shift: The Rapid Rise of PhD Programs at Evangelical Seminaries in the Majority World," *InSights Journal* 1, no. 2 (2016): 45.
16. Association of Theological Schools (ATS), "Head Count Enrollment by Race or Ethnic Group, Degree, and Gender: All Member Schools," *Annual Data Tables 2003–2004*, http://www.ats.edu/uploads/resources/institutional-data/annual-data-tables/2003-2004-annual-data-tables.pdf; and *Annual Data Tables 2014–2015*, http://www.ats.edu/uploads/resources/institutional-data/annual-data-tables/2014-2015-annual-data-tables.pdf, accessed 10 February 2017.

for extended periods of time to earn the degree. Furthermore, regionally based programs provide greater cost efficiency and allow many students to remain engaged in ministry during their doctoral studies. In addition, many of the programs explicitly state their intention to engage with contextual realities often overlooked in the West. For example, Nairobi Evangelical Graduate School of Theology (now Africa International University) designed its PhD program to "meet the needs of Africa and the African church."[17] China Graduate School of Theology began its doctoral program with the express purpose of encouraging "research and contextualization on the local soil."[18] Others have similar purpose statements related to preparing scholars and leaders for the church and society in Asia (Asia Graduate School of Theology – Alliance) or a PhD program focused on Christianity or Biblical Studies in the African context (Akrofi Christaller Institute for Theology, Mission, and Culture).

New programs also have the freedom to explore creative approaches better suited to the development of theological leaders for the church. Most of these programs were developed before the current literature base on doctoral education had become widely available. Yet they identified many of the same needs and have taken strides to address the gaps they see in the historical models.

Attention to Integration and Collaboration

In keeping with "useful" research, the CID advocates for more integrative and cross-disciplinary work.[19] Research that engages with real-life problems often extends beyond the boundaries of a single discipline. Manathanuga observes, "much of the cutting edge research in many fields now occurs along the gaps and cracks between disciplines."[20] Very often, such work will require

---

17. Richard Starcher and Sheldon L. Stick, "Preliminary Considerations on Theological Doctoral Program Design in an African Context," *Christian Higher Education* 2, no. 2 (2003): 94.

18. Wilson Chow, "CGST Plans Doctoral Program," *China Graduate School of Theology Bulletin*, April–June 2001.

19. Juliet Willetts et al., "Creative Tensions: Negotiating the Multiple Dimensions of a Transdisciplinary Doctorate," in Lee and Danby, *Reshaping Doctoral Education*, 128–143.

20. Catherine Manathunga, "'Team Supervision': New Positionings in Doctoral Education Pedagogies," in Lee and Danby, *Reshaping Doctoral Education*, 48.

collaborative approaches, bringing researchers and supervisors together to address larger issues.[21]

Collaboration has become the norm in certain scientific fields where relevant research is often bigger than any one doctoral candidate can undertake alone. Such an approach deviates from the historical approach of scholarship that has focused on highly individualized, independent, and original work. Referred to as "mode one" learning, traditional research usually pushes deeper into a single subject. However, collaborative, multidisciplinary work moves into "mode two" learning that focuses on integration across multiple domains.[22] Integrative work can be challenging when individuals must have facility in more than one discipline. If multiple researchers combine their expertise, they must learn to integrate their work in ways that demonstrate the capabilities of all who contribute to the project.[23] Supervisors may have to operate outside of their specialties or develop team approaches. However, operating across fields may challenge tacit assumptions as disciplines intersect and researchers integrate new ideas together. As researchers identify needs, span boundaries, and incorporate knowledge across domains, collaborative and integrative approaches will continue to draw interest in doctoral education.

Attention to Cultural Differences

Programs that begin in different settings engage cultural differences in ways often overlooked in the traditional centres of higher education. Theological education can draw from the business literature developed in the wake of globalization. With transnational companies and multinational employees, business leadership has given more attention to the differences in culture and their effect on corporate life. Building on work by Hofstede and others, the Globe Study has defined nine dimensions that serve as axes for understanding the impact of culture and context on approaches to communication and problem-solving in the business environment.[24] The categories are:

---

21. Rafael Zaracho's chapter in this volume addresses collaborative research.
22. Boud and Lee, *Changing Practices* of Doctoral Education (Kindle ed., loc. 3718).
23. Paul Clark's chapter in this volume addresses integrative learning.
24. The Globe Study conducted research across multiple business sectors in twenty-five cultural groups in sixty-two countries.

- *Power distance:* the degree to which members of a collective expect power to be distributed equally.
- *Uncertainty avoidance:* the extent to which a society, organization, or group relies on social norms, rules, and procedures to alleviate unpredictability of future events (includes tolerance of ambiguity).
- *Humane orientation:* the degree to which a collective encourages and rewards individuals for being fair, altruistic, generous, caring, and kind to others.
- *Institutional collectivism:* the degree to which organizational and societal institutional practices encourage and reward collective distribution of resources and collective action.
- *In-group collectivism:* the degree to which individuals express pride, loyalty, and cohesiveness in their organizations or families.
- *Assertiveness:* the degree to which individuals are assertive, confrontational, and aggressive in their relationships with others (includes generative and repetitive ideas).
- *Gender egalitarianism:* the degree to which a collective minimizes gender inequality.
- *Future orientation:* the extent to which individuals engage in future-oriented behaviours such as delaying gratification, planning, and investing in the future (also includes initiative vs. reactive approaches).
- *Performance orientation:* the degree to which a collective encourages and rewards group members for performance improvement and excellence.[25]

While some have critiqued the study for over-generalization,[26] the results revealed functional differences in leadership approaches across cultures. For example, the regions of sub-Saharan Africa, Latin America, and South Asia show strong values around in-group collectivism, high power distance, and

---

25. Robert House, Javidan Mansour, and Peter Dorfman, "Project GLOBE: An Introduction," *Applied Psychology: An International Review* 50, no. 4 (2001): 498–505. See also G. H. Hofstede, *Culture's Consequences: International Differences in Work-Related Values* (Thousand Oaks: Sage, 1980), revised and expanded in 2001.

26. George B. Graen, "In the Eye of the Beholder: Cross-Cultural Lessons in Leadership from Project GLOBE," *Academy of Management Perspectives* 20, no. 4 (2006): 95–101.

humane orientations. By contrast, the Anglo, Germanic, and Nordic cultures that dominate higher education value individualism, uncertainty avoidance, performance, and future orientation.[27] As descriptive values, the categories may prove helpful for theological education as it imagines creative approaches to the doctoral process.

During this same time, research in epistemology has revealed measurable differences in how people from different cultures formulate problems, make assessments, and pursue solutions.[28] Historically, this difference between "East and West" has been evident in medicine, but has proven to have deeper epistemological implications. Spearheaded by Nisbett, Peng and others, the research shows that not all cultures pursue logic in the same linear fashion as that found in the West.[29]

Western thought values formal logic that often takes strong analytical approaches, sifting data into discrete categories. By contrast, Eastern approaches tend to be more holistic and relational. Where Western logic adheres strongly to the law of non-contradiction, Eastern thought is dialectical, embracing tension and change in its analysis of data, problems, and solutions. Eastern approaches have a higher tolerance of ambiguity, while Western logic better creates succinct propositional statements.[30] Eastern approaches focus on relationships, harmony, and the larger field of focus rather than zeroing in on individual items isolated from context. This research that has contrasted Western logic with that of Asia (particularly Confucian-influenced cultures) may appeal to other non-Western cultures.

---

27. Robert House and Global Leadership and Organizational Behavior Effectiveness Research Program, *Culture, Leadership, and Organizations: The GLOBE Study of 62 Societies* (Thousand Oaks: Sage, 2004).

28. Chapters by Perry Shaw, Lal Senanayake, Allan Harkness, and Stephanie Black also address issues related to culture.

29. For more on this contrast and specific examples, see Incheol Choi and Richard E. Nisbett, "Cultural Psychology of Surprise: Holistic Theories and Recognition of Contradiction," *Journal of Personality & Social Psychology* 79, no. 6 (2001): 890–905; Richard Nisbett, *The Geography of Thought: How Asians and Westerners Think Differently . . . And Why* (New York: Free Press, 2003); Richard Nisbett et al., "Culture and Systems of Thought: Holistic Versus Analytic Cognition," *Psychological Review* 108, no. 2 (2001): 291–310; Kaiping Peng and Richard E. Nisbett, "Culture, Dialectics, and Reasoning about Contradiction," *American Psychologist* 54, no. 9 (1999): 741–754.

30. Peter Chang, "Steak, Potato, Peas and Chopsuey: Linear and Non-Linear Thinking in Theological Education," *Evangelical Review of Theology* 5, no. 2 (1981): 113–123.

Within theological education, both approaches have value. Western approaches have dominated, particularly in the development of clear, logical, systematic categorical approaches to theology. Seminaries and theological leaders may also draw from the strengths of non-Western approaches that value more holistic observation, a "big picture" field of focus, and integrated thinking that engages complexity across disciplines.[31] Attention to cultural differences encourages a more diverse approach to doctoral outputs, adding to a context that is conducive to creativity.

Implications for Theological Education

According to the CID, programs ought to evaluate each component of the doctoral process against its contribution towards the purpose of the degree. This approach focuses the degree more broadly than the dissertation so that it includes the totality of the doctoral process, including the intended, enacted, implicit (and hidden) aspects of the curriculum.[32] To adequately equip graduates, the doctorate must be more than what Lee and Danby have termed "apprenticeships in research."[33] Upon graduation, they move from the role of student to that of colleague and equal with their professors.[34] The purpose of the degree, therefore, is both to provide skills and to help socialize the student into the academic community.[35] According to the CID, schools should design the doctoral journey to fit this purpose.

For seminaries, the purpose of the research doctorate is to develop women and men who will ultimately serve as theological leaders. Theological leaders often, but not always, serve on the faculty of a school and engage in the work

---

31. Marlene Enns, "Now I Know in Part: Holistic and Analytic Reasoning and Their Contribution to Fuller Knowing in Theological Education," *Evangelical Review of Theology* 29, no. 3 (2005): 251–269.
32. Rob Gilbert, "The Doctorate As Curriculum: A Perspective on Goals and Outcomes of Doctoral Education," in Boud and Lee, *Changing Practices in Doctoral Education*, 54–68.
33. Susan Danby and Alison Lee, "Framing Doctoral Pedagogy as Design and Action," in Lee and Danby, *Reshaping Doctoral Education*, 3.
34. B. Green, "Challenging Perspectives, Changing Practices," in Boud and Lee, *Changing Practices in Doctoral Education*, 239–248.
35. See Deborah A. Colwill, *Educating the Scholar Practitioner in Organization Development*, Contemporary Trends in Organization Development and Change (Charlotte: Information Age, 2012).

of the theological school. While the seminary is often imagined in various ways, it has a consistent twofold purpose of forming leaders for the church and reflecting theologically for the church. Faculty members, therefore, must be able to teach and to help the school exercise its prophetic voice, addressing issues facing the church and society. To be "fit for purpose," as encouraged by the literature, a doctoral program should develop theological leaders with these capacities.

A Capacity to Teach[36]

Doctoral programs have consistently viewed teaching as the vocational trajectory for graduates. Yet students sometimes feel a gap between the process and their long-term objectives. The PhD is often earned in lonely corners of a library, where the scholar is far removed from contact with other people. However, shortly after graduation, those scholars are asked to enter classrooms and teach. It is as if we teach people to farm, but then ask them to cook. Both are related to the process of feeding people, but they are significantly different skills. Individual research has an important role, even helping refine what is taught in the classroom. However, often the strengths developed in research do not necessarily translate into the ability to teach. In rethinking the PhD, educators stress that good pedagogy ultimately leads to the production of knowledge and not just its transfer from professor to student. In this way, teaching also has a generative component to it and should be developed during the doctoral process. The formation of theological leaders rightly includes the development of teaching skills that will transfer to the classroom.

A Capacity to Engage with Context

The literature emphasizes that doctoral education should be "useful" and "efficient."[37] Usefulness addresses both a need to prepare people for their vocational futures as well as to generate research and dissertations that are relevant to society. Efficiency relates to streamlining completion times and

---

36. Allan Harkness's chapter in this volume addresses issues related to curriculum and teaching.
37. Nerad and Heggelund, *Toward a Global PhD?*, 9.

increasing completion rates.[38] Both the CID in North America and the Bologna Process push schools to consider how to help students both complete their doctorate and do so with research that matters within their fields.

For Majority World seminaries, new doctoral programs address both criteria. Earning a PhD in context creates more affordable opportunities that do not require the time and cross-cultural challenges of going to the West for a degree. They achieve "usefulness" through contextual relevance. To be useful to the church within a specific context, a program must do more than have geographical proximity. As Higgs explains, a program is African, not because of its geographical location but because it "directs its attention to the issues, concerns and theoretical or conceptual underpinnings of African culture."[39] Caldwell picks up a similar theme, stating that Asian programs are useful to the church in Asia because they "address Asian issues and engage Asian pedagogies."[40] Useful degrees have an inherent contextual engagement to them.

The Beirut Benchmarks, developed in conjunction with the International Council for Evangelical Theological Education (ICETE), also emphasize the importance of both "contextual relevance" and "missional impact" in doctoral research.[41] Doctoral graduates should develop abilities to engage with contextual realities in biblically informed and theologically reflective ways. Furthermore, this work should ultimately serve the broader mission of the church.

A Capacity for Prophetic Engagement

For the scholar, relevance also means embracing the second part of the calling to theological leadership found in the intellectual and prophetic work of the academy. The seminary does not operate apart from the church but is a critical part of the broader body of Christ. However, it is a unique role that Kelsey

---

38. Across all disciplines, less than 57 percent of those who begin a PhD complete the degree within ten years. See R. Sowell et al., *Ph.D. Completion and Attrition: Analysis of Baseline Program Data from the Ph.D. Completion Project* (Washington: Council of Graduate Schools, 2008).

39. Philip Higgs, "Towards an Indigenous African Educational Discourse: A Philosophical Reflection," *International Review of Education* 54, no. 3–4 (2008): 448.

40. Larry Caldwell, "How Asian Is Asian Theological Education?," in *Tending the Seedbeds: Educational Perspectives on Theological Education in Asia*, ed. Allan Harkness (Quezon City: Asia Theological Association, 2010), 32.

41. Ian Shaw and Kevin Lawson, *Handbook for Supervisors of Doctoral Students in Evangelical Theological Institutions* (Carlisle: Langham Global Library, 2015), Kindle ed., loc. 141.

describes as being simultaneously "of," "about," "with," "for," and "against" the church.[42] As such, the faculty members of the school have an obligation to engage prophetically in the issues that face the church and society. This requires development as scholars who are proficient in research and writing. Faculty members need the academic skills they have honed through schooling and a vision for applying them in service of the church. Prophetic voice is very much concerned with the "community" as well as the "academy."

A Capacity to Conduct Meaningful Research

The doctorate is not a vocational degree. While a renewed emphasis on usefulness and purpose may advocate for a broader understanding of the skills that should develop in the course of the doctoral journey, it remains a degree focused on the development of generative knowledge. Research doctorates should advance the theoretical base within a field. However, the understanding of new knowledge has expanded beyond simply delving deeper and deeper into a single subject. Increasingly, collaborative and multidisciplinary project designs have received attention. Boyer encourages the development of integrative scholarship, stating, "By integration we mean making connections across the disciplines, placing specialties in larger context, illuminating data in a revealing way, often educating non-specialists . . . what we mean is serious, disciplined work that seeks to interpret, draw together, and bring new insight to bear on original research."[43] Integration has a generative effect. Integration often has a practical genesis, but it also makes a theoretical contribution.[44]

Scholars whose thought patterns are naturally more holistic, focused on the broader field, and who draw relational connections between subject matters may be more inclined to develop integrative dissertations. These approaches can also be seen in the growth of integrated degree programs such as Peace Studies and Theology and Development at Majority World seminaries.[45] Perhaps some of these programs have developed because of the acute needs

---

42. David Kelsey, *To Understand God Truly* (Louisville: Westminster John Knox, 1992), 207.
43. Earnest Boyer, *Scholarship Reconsidered: Priorities for the Professoriate* (Princeton: Carnegie Foundation for the Advancement of Teaching, 1990), 18–19.
44. See Paul Clark in this volume.
45. Hunter, "Tectonic Shift," 49.

of the church, as well as cultural patterns that make integration more natural. Integrated programs (as well as individual dissertations) respond to practical issues, often drawing from multiple theological and social science fields. They are also fields in which students may seek new and creative expressions for their research findings.

Risks and Opportunities

However, even as more innovative approaches resonate with the purpose of the degree and cultural values found in Majority World contexts, a tension remains as new programs seek credibility in the well-established arena of doctoral education. This tension is evident in the opening quotation about writing for scholarship or the community. If a degree program or dissertation has a high degree of contextual relevance, will it still be viewed as academically rigorous and in step with the established view of a PhD? If the degree is done in a new way, will it be perceived as a viable doctorate? Innovation can be difficult for new programs, especially when factors such as a lack of history, limited faculty experience, and reduced access to resources can raise questions related to the quality of the degree. However, these two values – academic rigour (or quality of scholarship) and contextual relevance (or societal usefulness) – do not need to be at odds. Rather than endpoints on a spectrum, they are different axes on a graph. Credible programs can maximize both in the formation of scholars.

Furthermore, innovations in the doctorate respond to current gaps not met by the existing system. The CID identifies opportunities to address needs left untouched by traditional approaches. Evangelical seminaries in the Majority World have created new doctoral programs because Western training has been incomplete and at times inadequate to meet the current needs of the church. As it so often does, necessity has led to innovation.

Although by definition untried, new approaches may yield a new measure of success in the formation of today's scholars. For example, collaborative approaches[46] depart from the model of absolutely solitary work and embrace a collectivist value found in much of the non-Western world. Transdisciplinary

---

46. See Rafael Zaracho in this volume.

degrees[47] create opportunities for team supervision as research may require expertise from more than one field of study. Team supervision may also have value for the students who have increased opportunities to observe and learn from the scholarly work of multiple mentors. They both receive additional support and encouragement, but must also navigate different approaches and find their own place within the academic landscape on matters of approach and style that are often part of the socialization process of a PhD.[48] In each case, the process of the PhD more closely approximates postdoctoral realities when leaders must work together to solve complex problems that extend beyond the boundaries of their discipline.

New approaches to doctoral education have certain risks in achieving perceived credibility from the system. However, they also have significant potential to improve that same system. Greater attention to pedagogy will help develop better teachers. A concern for context will help the scholar develop a prophetic voice. A stronger PhD program will produce theological leaders better equipped to serve the church.

Conclusion

A time of change in the broader field of the doctorate creates opportunities for new approaches in how evangelical doctoral programs can better prepare theological leaders for the church. For the two dozen newly formed doctoral programs in Majority World seminaries, this moment of flux is particularly ripe for exploring new and creative methods to meet the new and changing demands of the global church in the twenty-first century. Rather than perpetuate old patterns that often yielded less than fulfilling results, new programs are often unencumbered by institutional inertia and can experiment with new solutions in response to the changing environment.

In business, the practice of "reverse innovation" challenges the conventional wisdom that the best solutions develop in historically established markets and

---

47. See Paul Clark in this volume.
48. Boud and Lee, *Changing Practices of Doctoral Education*, loc 1820.

are then exported to new areas.[49] Rather, inspired by a different set of needs and starting assumptions, innovative solutions may develop outside historical centres, creating new products that ultimately benefit all. For theological education, this may mean that schools in the Majority World take the lead as creators of new approaches to doctoral programs rather than simply existing as the implementers of Western models that are "merely derivative of 'northern' ideas, models and pedagogies."[50] Innovation in Majority World seminaries may be part of the reverse innovation that has an impact on all. This moment of disquiet may be highly conducive to innovative approaches to the practice of doctoral education.

Discussion Questions

1. What alternative pathways to master's and doctoral degrees have you seen to the traditional empiricist thesis or dissertation? What are some of the strengths and weaknesses of these approaches? While recognizing the risks involved, in what ways might opening the door to these innovative approaches enrich the global church?

2. For your own national and cultural context, give one or two key implications for your school if it shifted in understanding from the training of scholars to the training of "theological leaders." In what ways might such a shift better serve the mission of God in your region?

3. The current pattern of globalized higher education is deeply rooted in Western understandings of learning. Describe some ways in which you have seen Majority World students struggle in the Western system.

4. The fragmentation of knowledge is one of the major concerns being addressed in contemporary higher education discourse. Describe two or three ways in which your school currently promotes integration. What are some

---

49. See Vijay Govindarian and Chris Trimble, *Reverse Innovation: Create Far from Home, Win Everywhere* (Boston: Harvard University, 2012).

50. Alison Lee, "Excavating Differences: Stories of Experiences of Doctoral Education from Five Countries," in *Doctoral Education in International Context: Connecting Local, Regional and Global Perspectives*, ed. Vijay Kumar and Alison Lee (Selangor, Malaysia: Universiti Putra Malaysia, 2011), 21.

suggestions for developing greater integration, particularly in your advanced studies programs?

5. In your particular context, what are the greatest challenges to collaborative learning? Particularly in light of the church's need to strengthen cooperative approaches to ministry, describe some ways in which you could promote collaborative learning at your school.

6. What are one or two of the main barriers to innovation that stand in the way of developing and implementing new approaches to advanced theological education in your institution?

Bibliography

Aitchison, Claire, and Anthony Pare. "Writing as Craft and Practice in the Doctoral Curriculum." In Lee and Danby, *Reshaping Doctoral Education*, 12–25.

Association of Theological Schools (ATS). "Head Count Enrollment by Race or Ethnic Group, Degree, and Gender: All Member Schools," *Annual Data Tables 2003–2004*, http://www.ats.edu/uploads/resources/institutional-data/annual-data-tables/2003-2004-annual-data-tables.pdf. *Annual Data Tables 2014–2015*, http://www.ats.edu/uploads/resources/institutional-data/annual-data-tables/2014-2015-annual-data-tables.pdf. Accessed 10 February 2017.

Bleier, Helen, and Barbara Wheeler. *Report on a Study of Doctoral Programs That Prepare Faculty for Teaching at Theological Schools*. New York: Auburn Center for the Study of Theological Education, 2010.

Boud, David, and Alison Lee. *Changing Practices of Doctoral Education*. New York: Routledge, 2009.

Boyer, Earnest. *Scholarship Reconsidered: Priorities for the Professoriate*. Princeton: Carnegie Foundation for the Advancement of Teaching, 1990.

Caldwell, Larry. "How Asian Is Asian Theological Education?" In *Tending the Seedbeds: Educational Perspectives on Theological Education in Asia*, edited by Allan Harkness, 23–45. Quezon City: Asia Theological Association, 2010.

Chang, Peter. "Steak, Potato, Peas and Chopsuey: Linear and Non-Linear Thinking in Theological Education." *Evangelical Review of Theology* 5, no. 2 (1981): 113–123.

Choi, Incheol, and Richard E. Nisbett. "Cultural Psychology of Surprise: Holistic Theories and Recognition of Contradiction." *Journal of Personality & Social Psychology* 79, no. 6 (2001): 890–905.

Chow, Wilson. "CGST Plans Doctoral Program." *China Graduate School of Theology Bulletin*, April–June 2001.

Colwill, Deborah A. *Educating the Scholar Practitioner in Organization Development.* Contemporary Trends in Organization Development and Change. Charlotte: Information Age, 2012.

Dahlgren, Madeleine Abrandt, and Anna Bjuremeark. "The Seminar as Enacted Doctoral Pedagogy." In Lee and Danby, *Reshaping Doctoral Education*, 56–68.

Danby, Susan, and Alison Lee. "Framing Doctoral Pedagogy as Design and Action." In Lee and Danby, *Reshaping Doctoral Education*, 3–11.

Ehrenberg, Ronald, Charlotte V. Kuh, and Cornell Higher Education Research Institute. *Doctoral Education and the Faculty of the Future.* Ithaca: Cornell University, 2009.

Enns, Marlene. "Now I Know in Part: Holistic and Analytic Reasoning and Their Contribution to Fuller Knowing in Theological Education." *Evangelical Review of Theology* 29, no. 3 (2005): 251–269.

Gabrys, Barbara, and Alina Beltechi. "Cognitive Apprenticeship." In Lee and Danby, *Reshaping Doctoral Education*, 144–155.

Gilbert, Rob. "The Doctorate As Curriculum: A Perspective on Goals and Outcomes of Doctoral Education." In Boud and Lee, *Changing Practices of Doctoral Education*, 54–68.

Golde, Chris, and George E. Walker. *Envisioning the Future of Doctoral Education: Preparing Stewards of the Discipline.* Carnegie Essays on the Doctorate. 1st ed. San Francisco: Jossey-Bass, 2006.

Govindarian, Vijay, and Chris Trimble. *Reverse Innovation: Create Far from Home, Win Everywhere.* Boston: Harvard University, 2012.

Graen, George B. "In the Eye of the Beholder: Cross-Cultural Lessons in Leadership from Project GLOBE." *Academy of Management Perspectives* 20, no. 4 (2006): 95–101.

Green, B. "Challenging Perspectives, Changing Practices." In Boud and Lee, *Changing Practices of Doctoral Education*, 239–248.

Higgs, Philip. "Towards an Indigenous African Educational Discourse: A Philosophical Reflection." *International Review of Education* 54, no. 3–4 (2008): 445–458.

Hofstede, G. H. *Culture's Consequences: International Differences in Work-Related Values.* Thousand Oaks: Sage, 1980. Revised and expanded in 2001.

House, Robert, and Global Leadership and Organizational Behavior Effectiveness Research Program. *Culture, Leadership, and Organizations: The GLOBE Study of 62 Societies.* Thousand Oaks: Sage, 2004.

House, Robert, Javidan Mansour, and Peter Dorfman. "Project GLOBE: An Introduction." *Applied Psychology: An International Review* 50, no. 4 (2001): 498–505.

Hunter, Evan R. "Stakeholder Perspectives of Contextual Engagement of PhD Programs at Select Evangelical Seminaries in the Majority World." PhD diss., Trinity Evangelical Divinity School, 2014.

———. "A Tectonic Shift: The Rapid Rise of PhD Programs at Evangelical Seminaries in the Majority World." *InSights Journal* 1, no. 2 (2016): 41–60.

Kelsey, David. *To Understand God Truly*. Louisville: Westminster John Knox, 1992.

Lee, Alison. "Excavating Differences: Stories of Experiences of Doctoral Education from Five Countries." In *Doctoral Education in International Context: Connecting Local, Regional and Global Perspectives*, edited by Vijay Kumar and Alison Lee, 19–84. Selangor, Malaysia: Universiti Putra Malaysia, 2011.

Lee, Alison, and Susan Danby, eds. *Reshaping Doctoral Education: International Approaches and Pedagogies*. New York: Routledge, 2009.

Leonard, D., and R. Becker. "Enhancing the Doctoral Experience at the Local Level." In Boud and Lee, *Changing Practices of Doctoral Education*, 71–99.

Maki, Peggy, and Nancy A. Borkowski. *The Assessment of Doctoral Education: Emerging Criteria and New Models for Improving Outcomes*. 1st ed. Sterling, VA: Stylus, 2006.

Malsen, Geoff. "More Countries Are Asking Whether They Produce Too Many Ph.D.'s." *The Chronicle of Higher Education*. 10 April 2012.

Manathunga, Catherine. "'Team Supervision': New Positionings in Doctoral Education Pedagogies." In Lee and Danby, *Reshaping Doctoral Education*, 42–55.

Nerad, Maresi, and Mimi Heggelund. *Toward a Global PhD? Forces and Forms in Doctoral Education Worldwide*. Seattle: Center for Innovation and Research in Graduate Education in Association with University of Washington Press, 2008.

Nisbett, Richard. *The Geography of Thought: How Asians and Westerners Think Differently . . . And Why*. New York: Free Press, 2003.

Nisbett, Richard, Kaiping Peng, Incheol Choi, and Ara Norenzayan. "Culture and Systems of Thought: Holistic Versus Analytic Cognition." *Psychological Review* 108, no. 2 (2001): 291–310.

Peng, Kaiping, and Richard E. Nisbett. "Culture, Dialectics, and Reasoning about Contradiction." *American Psychologist* 54, no. 9 (1999): 741–754.

Shaw, Ian, and Kevin Lawson. *Handbook for Supervisors of Doctoral Students in Evangelical Theological Institutions*. Carlisle: Langham Global Library, 2015.

Sowell, R., T. Zhang, K. Redd, and M. King. *Ph.D. Completion and Attrition: Analysis of Baseline Program Data from the Ph.D. Completion Project.* Washington: Council of Graduate Schools, 2008.

Starcher, Richard, and Sheldon L. Stick. "Preliminary Considerations on Theological Doctoral Program Design in an African Context." *Christian Higher Education* 2, no. 2 (2003): 97–123.

Walker, George, and the Carnegie Foundation for the Advancement of Teaching. *The Formation of Scholars: Rethinking Doctoral Education for the Twenty-First Century.* 1st ed. San Francisco: Jossey-Bass, 2008.

Willetts, Juliet, Cynthia Mitchell, Abeysuriya Kumi, and Dena Fam. "Creative Tensions: Negotiating the Multiple Dimensions of a Transdisciplinary Doctorate." In Lee and Danby, *Reshaping Doctoral Education*, 128–143.

3

Innovation and Criteria:
Ensuring Standards While Promoting Innovative Approaches

Perry Shaw

As we discuss throughout this book, there is an increasing recognition that the traditional understanding of scholarship is educationally rigid and narrow. The perceived-as-normative approach to higher education reflects the preferred learning styles of only a small minority of the world's population – predominantly (but not exclusively) white Western males who approach learning through a rigid, linear, step by-step, empirical approach to reasoning.[1]

The roots of this perception are found in the so-called "Enlightenment," a term that "contains in itself a value judgment on persons and things non-Western; that is, they are not enlightened."[2] Throughout the eighteenth and nineteenth centuries the positivistic and empiricist approach of the scientific method was seen as the only "rational" approach to argument. In various guises the essence of the scientific method has been extended to other fields – even the humanities – and institutionalized as the standard of excellence, with other approaches being seen as substandard or irrational.

Being myself such a linear-thinking white Western male I have travelled "first class" throughout my academic career. The whole system of advanced

---

1. See in particular my chapter "Culture, Gender, and Diversity in Advanced Theological Studies."
2. Gary Riebe-Estrella, "Engaging Borders: Lifting Up Difference and Unmasking Division," *Theological Education* 45, no. 1 (2009): 23.

study with its emphasis on rationalism and a movement from theory to practice is geared for people with my specific kind of mindset. Consequently I have experienced relatively little trauma along the path of academia. However I have become increasingly concerned to see many highly intelligent and creative people who do not think in this particular pattern, and have consequently been forced to travel the same narrowly defined path in "economy class."[3] In the process the academy, the church, and society as a whole have been left impoverished.

The fact that the traditional emphasis on linear, step-by-step, empirical research papers has been perceived as normative is hardly surprising: the structure of global higher education is patterned after a Western university model that was in turn developed at a time when the scientific method was seen as the standard of knowledge, and in which the university was virtually an exclusive conclave for Western males. Even today over 80 percent of the "top fifty schools" listed in the influential QS World University Rankings[4] are located in the West, over 90 percent have male presidents, and over 80 percent have white presidents. The hegemony of white Western males in global higher education is overwhelming.

However, the quality of knowledge and wisdom is impoverished when so limited. Consequently an increasing number of options are emerging in Western schools in terms of learning and assessment – even to dramatically different shapes in the demonstration of competency at the master's and doctoral levels. If the Minority World[5] is recognizing the need for diversification in approach, how much more important is this for schools in the Majority World, particularly in the realm of theological education. The articles in this volume present pathways to such a diversity.

---

3. The airline imagery of first, business, and economy class for understanding global higher education is borrowed from Namsoon Kang, "Envisioning Postcolonial Theological Education: Dilemmas and Possibilities," in *Handbook of Theological Education in World Christianity: Theological Perspectives – Regional Surveys – Ecumenical Trends*, ed. D. Werner et al. (Eugene: Wipf and Stock, 2010), 36–37.
4. "QS World University Rankings," TopUniversities, accessed 27 January 2016, http://www.topuniversities.com/university-rankings/world-university-rankings.
5. The term "Minority World" is used here to refer to "the West" to emphasize the contrast with the more widely used term "Majority World."

A question often raised, however, is standards. How can we ensure that those who are seeking to demonstrate competency through non-traditional means are indeed at a comparable level to those presenting more traditional theses and dissertations? In what follows I would like to address this question through an overview of three approaches: Bloom's *Taxonomy of Educational Objectives*,[6] the European Union's Dublin Descriptors,[7] and the ICETE Beirut Benchmarks.[8] It will become clear through this synopsis that the focus throughout is not on the form of production but on the ability to demonstrate depth of learning and understanding. Consequently, even if we adopt standard Minority World understandings of learning, there is vast scope for alternative approaches to demonstrating quality of learning.

However, in describing these standards the cultural hegemony of the West in education will become strikingly clear. Numerous questions remain, and I will conclude the chapter by pointing out some of the deeper issues at stake as we discuss such matters as academic standards – in particular, the need to consider other cultural understandings of wisdom and knowledge.

Bloom's *Taxonomy and Educational Standards*

A good starting point for a conversation on educational standards is to use as a dialogue partner Bloom's *Taxonomy of Educational Objectives*. Developed in the early 1950s by a group of senior educators under the leadership of Benjamin Bloom, the taxonomy was an attempt to categorize systematically the forms and levels of cognitive learning. Bloom and his associates suggested that there are six different levels of cognitive sophistication, as follows:

---

6. B. Bloom et al., *Taxonomy of Educational Objectives, Handbook 1: Cognitive Domain* (London: Longmans, 1956).
7. European Consortium for Accreditation in Higher Education, "Dublin Descriptors," accessed 27 January 2016, http://ecahe.eu/w/index.php/Dublin_Descriptors.
8. Ian J. Shaw, Scott Cunningham, and Bernhard Ott, eds., *Best Practice Guidelines for Doctoral Programs* (Carlisle: Langham Global Library, 2015). The summary statement of the Beirut Benchmarks can also be found at ICETE, "The Beirut Benchmarks," accessed 3 October 2016, http://www.icete-edu.org/beirut/.

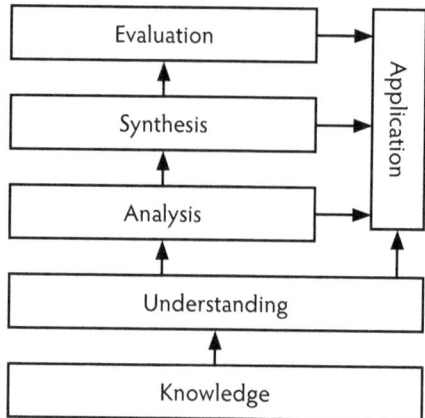

Figure 3.1 Bloom's *Taxonomy of Educational Objectives*[9]

- *Knowledge:* the ability to recall facts or information.
- *Comprehension:* the understanding of what is being communicated, and the ability to make use of the material at a simple level.
- *Application:* the ability to use abstractions in particular concrete situations.
- *Analysis:* the ability to break material down into its constituent elements or parts.
- *Synthesis:* the ability to build a structure or pattern from diverse elements, or to put parts together to form a whole, creating a more comprehensive meaning or structure.
- *Evaluation:* the ability to make judgements about the value of ideas or materials.

The simplicity of Bloom's taxonomy has led to its widespread dominance in educational literature. However, learning is far more complex than is suggested in the taxonomy, and a plethora of other models have been suggested to address the more simplistic elements in Bloom's model.[10] This said, the very simplicity

---

9. Adapted by Perry Shaw in *Tranforming Theological Education* (Carlisle, UK: Langham Global Library, 2014), 75.
10. L. Anderson and D. Krathwohl, eds., *A Taxonomy for Learning, Teaching and Assessing: A Revision of Bloom's Taxonomy of Educational Objectives* (New York: Longman, 2001); L. Fink, *Creating Significant Learning Experiences: An Integrated Approach to Designing College Courses* (San Francisco: Jossey-Bass, 2003); R. Marzano and J. Kendall, eds., *The New Taxonomy*

and understandability of Bloom's model, its widespread influence, and its ready applicability to theological education make it a good starting point for discussing standards.

While it is not completely valid, there is somewhat of a hierarchy in Bloom's taxonomy: knowledge is preliminary to comprehension; comprehension is preliminary to analysis; analysis to synthesis; and synthesis to intelligent evaluation. Moreover, the more deeply one grasps the issues related to an idea or question, the more potentially powerful the application.

To a certain extent each of these levels reflects the target of a different level of schooling:

- *Knowledge:* Elementary school. In tandem with Piaget's understanding of middle childhood as a period of concrete operational thinking,[11] the ages of 7–11 are an ideal period for providing children with a solid and broad foundation of significant knowledge. The information accumulated during this period can then be built upon as children mature. Naturally children are also encouraged to understand, and particularly as they move to the latter years of elementary school, to engage in some simple analytical work. Nonetheless the central thrust of elementary school is that children will move on to secondary school with a strong foundation of knowledge in key disciplines.
- *Comprehension:* Secondary school. As children move into adolescence, so their brains mature and become capable of more abstract thought patterns – what Piaget has termed "formal operational thinking."[12] The ability to look beyond facts to the reasons behind the facts is the goal of quality secondary education. Particularly in early adolescence there is a strong desire to see the bigger picture and to place the details within this bigger picture.

---

of Educational Objectives, 2nd ed. (Thousand Oaks: Corwin, 2006); Lee Shulman, "Making Differences: A Table of Learning," The Carnegie Foundation for the Advancement of Teaching, 2002, accessed 6 September 2013, www.carnegiefoundation.org/elibrary/making-differences-table-learning.

11. Jean Piaget and Bärbel Inhelder, *The Psychology of the Child* (New York: Basic, 1962).

12. Bärbel Inhelder and Jean Piaget, *The Growth of Logical Thinking from Childhood to Adolescence: An Essay on the Construction of Formal Operational Structures* (New York: Basic, 1958).

As students mature they should be challenged to engage in an increasing level of analytical thinking, but this is a major challenge for many, and the primary goal of secondary education remains a mastery of comprehension skills.

- *Analysis and Application:* Undergraduate study. With a strong grounding in comprehension skills from high school, the goal of undergraduate studies should be the development of robust critical-analytical skills. Through the course of a bachelor's program students should increasingly be able to see connections, and learn how to assess critically how one idea is linked to another. In senior years of undergraduate study, and particularly if there is a graduate project of some sort, students should be able to demonstrate a mastery of analytical skill, together with initial steps in synthetic thinking. In that undergraduate studies are the requirement for many professional fields, there should also be the ability to work out the analytical skills in applied practice.
- *Synthesis and Advanced Application:* Graduate study – master's degrees. A solid master's program seeks to bring a more complex dialogue of ideas, and in particular the integration of concepts from diverse fields. Graduates should be comfortable in bringing into conversation apparently contradictory ideas, seeing the strengths and weaknesses of each of these ideas, and developing well-constructed integrated models. These synthetic models become the basis for advanced practice.
- *Evaluation and Creativity:* Doctoral study. In later adaptations of Bloom's taxonomy the final level of "evaluation" has been replaced with "creativity," in the sense of the creation of new knowledge. In doctoral studies both are sought. The key to all doctoral work is original contribution, involving creative thinking – sometimes the expansion of an existing concept or approach, sometimes the creation of a new area of understanding. However, quality doctoral learning also demonstrates a high level of self-reflective and self-critical skill. In many traditional theses evaluative ability is reflected not merely in the ability to assess critically others' ideas, but also to assess the strengths and weaknesses of one's own ideas. In order

to demonstrate one's level of evaluative skill it is generally expected that doctoral candidates will include both an extended section on the limitations of their own research and a discussion of an array of possible areas for further research.

The Dublin Descriptors

Another valuable conversation partner is the Dublin Descriptors, a series of competency descriptions for each level of higher education, adopted by the European Union in 2005. This was established to encourage comparability between institutions of higher education across Europe such that students could comfortably carry their studies from country to country. The standards described in the Dublin Descriptors are typical of national and regional quality assurance standards across the globe, and close parallels can be seen with other influential documents such as those produced by the Council for Higher Education Accreditation (United States),[13] the United Kingdom Quality Assurance Agency for Higher Education,[14] and the Tertiary Education Quality and Standards Agency (Australia).[15]

The documentation for the Dublin Descriptors is quite extensive. However, a summary of the competencies given for each of the bachelor's, master's, and doctoral levels is indicative of the document as a whole:

Bachelor Level (First Cycle)

Students can:
- demonstrate knowledge and understanding in a field of study that builds upon their general secondary education, and is typically at a level that, whilst supported by advanced textbooks, includes some aspects that will be informed by knowledge of the forefront of their field of study;
- apply their knowledge and understanding in a manner that indicates a professional approach to their work or vocation, and

---

13. www.chea.org.
14. www.qaa.ac.uk.
15. www.aqf.edu.au.

have competences typically demonstrated through devising and sustaining arguments and solving problems within their field of study;
- gather and interpret relevant data (usually within their field of study) to inform judgements that include reflection on relevant social, scientific, or ethical issues;
- communicate information, ideas, problems, and solutions to both specialist and non-specialist audiences;
- have developed those learning skills that are necessary for them to continue to undertake further study with a high degree of autonomy.

The central feature of these competencies is the emphasis on the ability to develop sustained arguments and informed judgement. To a certain extent these elements run in very close parallel to Bloom's "analysis" level, although the emphasis on communication and application skills is a notable expansion on Bloom's taxonomy.

Master's Level (Second Cycle)

Students can:
- demonstrate knowledge and understanding that is founded upon and extends and/or enhances that typically associated with bachelor level, and that provides a basis or opportunity for originality in developing and/or applying ideas, often within a research context;
- apply their knowledge, understanding, and problem-solving abilities in new or unfamiliar environments within broader (or multidisciplinary) contexts related to their field of study;
- integrate knowledge and handle complexity, and formulate judgements with incomplete or limited information but which include reflecting on social and ethical responsibilities linked to the application of their knowledge and judgements;
- communicate their conclusions, and the knowledge and rationale underpinning these, to specialist and non-specialist audiences clearly and unambiguously;
- have the learning skills to allow them to continue to study in a manner that may be largely self-directed or autonomous.

The major step from bachelor to master's level is seen primarily in the third item, where key concepts are integration, complexity, sound judgements based on limited information, and social and ethical responsibility. Questions of integration and complexity resonate with the synthetic level of Bloom's taxonomy. However, the expectation even in secular education of greater ethical maturity in master's students is striking. Again, the call for quality communication skills with both specialist and non-specialist audiences is a significant challenge to those engaged in advanced theological education.

Doctoral Level (Third Cycle)

Students can:
- demonstrate a systematic understanding of a field of study and mastery of the skills and methods of research associated with that field;
- demonstrate the ability to conceive, design, implement, and adapt a substantial process of research with scholarly integrity;
- make a contribution through original research that extends the frontier of knowledge by developing a substantial body of work, some of which merits national or international refereed publication;
- engage in critical analysis, evaluation, and synthesis of new and complex ideas;
- communicate with their peers, the larger scholarly community, and with society in general about their areas of expertise;
- promote, within academic and professional contexts, technological, social, or cultural advancement in a knowledge-based society.

The more advanced elements of doctoral work are clearly evident. The expectations of a high level of independent creativity in scholarship and an original contribution to the world of learning are essential components of quality doctoral work. All three of the advanced levels of Bloom's taxonomy (analysis, synthesis, and evaluation) are specifically enumerated. Again the ability to communicate is seen as imperative, but there almost seems to be an invitation to a passion for knowledge and learning that the doctoral graduate will pass on to those with whom he or she interacts.

Throughout the Dublin Descriptors, at no point is there a specification of processes necessary to demonstrate the various levels of competency. Terms such as "thesis" or "dissertation" appear nowhere. The focus is not on means but on ends. In light of the increasing emphasis on fitness for purpose within the wider Bologna Process, there is a growing variety of means for demonstrating competency at each of these levels. Particularly noteworthy is the growing postmodern critique of the rigid linearity and supposed objectivity of the modernist understanding of learning. Consequently an increasing level of experimentation in non-linear and multi-voice conversational approaches to scholarship is emerging – even at the doctoral level. In light of the strong holistic traditions of much of the Majority World, these new forms need to be appreciated, embraced, and even extended.

The Beirut Benchmarks

As is well documented the global Christian community is now predominantly from the Majority World.[16] Recognizing the importance of local development of local thought-leaders, an increasing number of advanced master's and doctoral programs in theological education have emerged over the past few decades. In response, global leaders in evangelical theological education met in Beirut (Lebanon) in March 2010 and again in Bangalore (India) in October 2011 to discuss best practice guidelines for advanced studies in evangelical theological education. These consultations resulted in the Beirut Benchmarks, focusing on more traditional text-based research, and the Bangalore Adaptations for professional doctorates.

The Beirut Benchmarks are significant in that beyond mere academic research they emphasize the need for missional impact, the development of Christian character, and a commitment to the church. The benchmarks are introduced with three governing principles which emphasize a confessional, rational, and missional approach to advanced theological studies:

- right belief and committed trust in the living God ("the fear of the LORD is the first principle of wisdom");

---

16. See, for example, Graham Hill, *Global Church: Reshaping Our Conversations, Renewing Our Mission, Revitalizing Our Churches* (Downers Grove: IVP, 2016); and Philip Jenkins, *The Next Christendom: The Coming of Global Christianity*, 3rd ed. (Oxford: OUP, 2011).

- creative and humble use of the rationality God has granted to humans made in his own image; and
- appropriate living in the world to reflect God's calling and participate in God's mission.

These principles are detailed in a series of qualities and competencies: comprehensive understanding, critical skills, serious inquiry with integrity, creative and original contribution, contextual relevance, ability to communicate, and missional impact. For research doctorates the focus is on the breadth of systematic understanding of a field of study. For professional doctorates the emphasis is on innovative and applied reflection on practice.

In the ICETE explanatory text[17] the distinct nature of advanced *theological* studies is explained and developed. Alongside many traditional expectations, a number of more striking elements are suggested:

- The research should be something that excites evangelicals and be warmly embraced for its potential (p. 10).
- The research should be for the glory of God, and hence prayer for insight should accompany the work (p. 11). Doctoral students should be challenged to integrate their academic formation with personal spiritual disciplines and commitment to the local church community (pp. 16, 21–22).
- Advanced studies in evangelical theological education should have a missional focus, both in serving the mission of the church in the world and in a role of mission to the academy (p. 14).
- We need to take into account diversity of learning styles, and hence embrace fresh understandings of what constitutes excellence in the delivery of doctoral education. The imposition of dominant models from outside contexts should be eschewed (p. 17).
- Advanced study should be relevant to both the local educational and church context, while ensuring that theological leaders can engage meaningfully with the global academy (pp. 18–21).
- Advanced training needs to take seriously the candidates' likely future role of leadership and teaching (pp. 22–23).

---

17. Shaw, Cunningham, and Ott, *Best Practice Guidelines*.

This is an extraordinarily forward-looking document, and resonates strongly with the innovative approaches we are presenting in this book. As with secular quality assurance standards the Beirut Benchmarks and Bangalore Adaptations focus on competencies rather than process, and these particular competencies are shaped strongly by biblical-theological values.

Sadly, however, in other ICETE documentation[18] there seem to remain very traditional assumptions as to process. Subsequent discussions seem to assume a final project that is linear, rationalist, and theory-to-practice[19] in shape and completed by solitary scholars, and it is probable that the majority of master's and doctoral studies will continue to lean on these assumptions at least in the near future. However, if we take the Beirut Benchmarks seriously there is room for significant innovation and creativity in the processes we embrace in advanced theological studies.

The Doctorate Must Look Like a Doctorate

Even though Christian scholarship by its very nature needs to embrace fundamentally different values, the mere fact that we are offering master's and doctoral degrees means that the work produced needs to be recognized as of an appropriate standard and type. As Ian Shaw observes, "the final product still needs to look like a doctorate and be recognized as such in the eyes of the global academic community, as well as by local accreditors or validators, churches, and students undertaking the program."[20]

But what does this mean? Too often this claim is used among more traditional (notably Minority World) Christian scholars to justify a rigid adherence to traditional theses and dissertations. It is noteworthy that the global academy is already recognizing the inherent limitations of these modes of research and is increasingly opening the doors to new forms and approaches. The essential issue is not the form but the function: if the student

---

18. Shaw, Cunningham, and Ott, 25–26, 36–38, 41–42, 46–49; Ian J. Shaw with Kevin E. Lawson, *Handbook for Supervisors of Doctoral Students in Evangelical Theological Institutions* (Carlisle: Langham Global Library, 2015), 75–98, 113–123, 175–206, and in passing.
19. . . . if practice is evident at all.
20. Shaw, Cunningham, and Ott, *Best Practice Guidelines*, 8.

can demonstrate appropriate competencies, as described earlier in this chapter, creativity of form is embraced and in some quarters encouraged.

For example, in the United Kingdom the Quality Assurance Agency for Higher Education (QAA), in its key document "Doctoral Degree Characteristics,"[21] lists a wide variety of approaches to the doctoral award which include those shown in the table.

Award	Characteristics
Traditional PhD	Based largely on the supervised research project, examined on the basis of the thesis.
PhD by publication	Based largely on the supervised research project, but examined on the basis of a series of peer-reviewed academic papers which have been published or accepted for publication, usually accompanied by an overarching paper that presents the overall introduction and conclusions.
New route PhD	Contains significant taught elements (which are examined and must be passed), and initially developed in 2001 to provide international students with an integrated doctoral training scheme including program-related research training and personal and professional development.
Professional doctorate	Includes a significant "taught" element, and as such most have specific "learning outcomes." Based on a combination of taught modules (which are examined and must be passed), and the supervised research project, which is often smaller than the traditional PhD, is more applied, and is work-based or -focused.
Practice-based doctorate	Based on a supervised research project, usually in the performing arts, where the output involves both a written piece (which is usually much shorter than the traditional PhD thesis, and includes both reflection and context) and one or more other forms, such as a novel (for creative writing), a portfolio of work (for art and design), or one or more performance pieces (for theatre studies or music). Both forms of output are examined.

Secular British universities are embracing innovation in theological studies faster than faith-based schools. The autoethnographic approach to theology taken by Sam Ewell at the University of Birmingham, and described later in

---

21. United Kingdom Quality Assurance Agency for Higher Education (QAA), "Doctoral Degree Characteristics," September 2011, accessed 6 October 2016, http://www.qaa.ac.uk/en/Publications/Documents/Doctoral_Characteristics.pdf.

this collection,[22] signals a much-needed openness to innovation. Even more striking are the newly established MPhil and PhD programs in "Theology Through Creative Practice" at the University of Glasgow.[23] The degrees are "practice-based" and designed to enable practitioners to "address theological or religious issues through . . . creative practice in fields such as: drama, liturgy, music, sacred architecture, creative writing, homiletics, textiles, painting, ritual practice or pedagogy."

If the secular academy is embracing diversity in approach to the completion of advanced studies, how much more should the Christian academy investigate innovative approaches that better serve the missional calling of the church? An essential element must be to recognize the current disconnection between local contextual patterns of communication and the traditional emphasis in Minority World higher education on a solitary, linear-rationalist, theory-to-practice, written dissertation. The approaches and models discussed in this book are suggestive possibilities on that journey.

Questions Remain

Throughout this chapter my aim has been to advocate for innovative methodology within the current understandings of globally recognized criteria. However, there remains a discomfort rooted in several unanswered questions. I leave these questions floating with the hope that the conversation will continue to grow and develop.

- Why do we in the Christian community continue to seek to imitate and follow the secular academy rather than play a leadership role? Given that the church is now numerically dominated by Majority World believers, is there not a role to speak back to the hegemony of the West in the academy?
- Who chooses the standards? At the moment it is the West. In some cases the control of standards is direct – through the Minority World

---

22. Sam Ewell, "Doing Theology from the 'Land of Samba': Integrating Personal Experience in the Task of Advanced Theological Research."
23. "Theology Through Creative Practice," University of Glasgow, accessed 18 May 2017, http://www.gla.ac.uk/schools/critical/research/researchcentresandnetworks/literaturetheologyandtheartsatglasgow/theologythroughcreativepractice/.

leadership of influential universities, or leadership by nationals trained and shaped by Western education. In other cases the control is indirect – through global accreditation systems that are modelled after Western understandings of learning and knowledge. Might there be alternative understandings of standards that better reflect the values of other cultural contexts? Such alternative understandings are richly embedded in the ICETE Beirut Benchmarks, but the implications have yet to be worked out fully in practice.

- The analytical-hierarchical understanding of learning is rooted in Greek philosophical paradigms that are not necessarily valued in other parts of the world. This approach to learning may be important to the disciplines of the hard sciences. However, taxonomic approaches such as the work of Bloom and his associates are perhaps of lesser worth in fields that seek to appreciate and serve people. In the cultural context of the Majority World models such as Bloom's can be particularly problematic.[24]

- The definition of "critical thinking," a term repeatedly used in official documentation, is largely shaped by Minority World understandings, often in the form of the critical analysis of texts, leading to a movement of thesis-antithesis-synthesis. However, equally complex thinking can be found in seeking to see practice through theoretical eyes, comparison of case studies, or seeking harmony between apparent paradoxes. The movement from theory to practice is a preferred white Western male approach to learning. Many other contexts prefer moving from practice to theory.

- The doctorate is supposed to demonstrate a high level of synthetic-creative thinking. Why, then, can we not have creative-innovative methodology – and not simply creative-innovative content?

The Western hegemony of education is far from unique to the theological academy. One of our deepest challenges is that global higher education in all its forms and degrees is largely a legacy of the Western colonial period of the

---

24. See, for example, Maha Bali, "What I Learned from Student-Created Learning Taxonomies," *The Chronicle of Higher Education*, 19 April 2016, in which Bali documents a recent piece of research that highlights the problem of Bloom's taxonomy in the Egyptian context.

nineteenth and early twentieth centuries. If anything, secular higher education in Majority World countries is often more tied to traditional Western forms than is secular higher education in the Minority World. In the latter the critique of the modernist myth of objectivity has opened the doors to increasingly innovative approaches to advanced studies, approaches that better resonate with the natural learning patterns of Asia, Africa, and Latin America.

We do not function within a vacuum, and innovative leaders of theological education in the Majority World do not simply have to negotiate Western-dominated global accreditation patterns, but also the Western-shaped educational patterns of their own countries. And yet I often wonder if the church with its deep understanding of global sharing might play a prophetic role to the world around it by modelling culturally significant patterns of learning in its striving after godly wisdom for the global theological economy.

Summary and Conclusion

Drawing the threads together, there is a high level of international consistency in terms of what a bachelor, master's, or doctoral degree represents. In the strictly cognitive domain there is a clear movement evident from analysis to synthesis to evaluative and creative thought. Also striking is the expectation of increasing ability to communicate with clarity not only to the academy but also to the wider community. A third major contour has to do with application and mature judgement, moving from simple to more complex and nuanced discernment and utilization of knowledge.

Noteworthy throughout the majority of national and transnational documents on standards is the eloquent silence with regards to means. Rarely is there mention of a thesis or dissertation as the exclusive means by which proficiency is demonstrated, and in many national contexts a growing diversity of options for establishing competence is indeed becoming apparent. It is with this background that space is available for approaches to advanced theological study that are non-linear, innovative, and contextually aware.

Discussion Questions

1. Take time to do an audit of your faculty. To what extent does your faculty ratio lean towards white and/or male? Assess the audit results to decide whether the ratio should stay or change.

2. How many of your faculty were educated in institutions shaped by Western Enlightenment assumptions? In what ways have you seen these educational assumptions working out in your school's educational decision-making?

3. A major emphasis in quality assurance standards is the expectation that advanced study will reflect higher-order thinking, in particular, the ability to synthesize divergent ideas and engage in creative thinking and evaluative reflection. Describe some innovative ways in which your school has sought to enhance these cognitive competencies, especially by incorporating local approaches to pedagogy.

4. A growing emphasis in quality assurance standards is the ability of candidates in advanced study programs to communicate effectively, in particular the ability to communicate in simple and popular language. Describe some ways in which your school might enhance what it is already doing in developing the communication skills of students in your advanced programs.

5. How does your school nurture the uniquely spiritual dimension of advanced theological studies? Consider in particular the spiritual life of the students and the supervisors, the process of study, and the culture of the school and its programs.

Bibliography

Anderson, L., and D. Krathwohl, eds. *A Taxonomy for Learning, Teaching and Assessing: A Revision of Bloom's Taxonomy of Educational Objectives*. New York: Longman, 2001.

Bali, Maha. "What I Learned from Student-Created Learning Taxonomies." *The Chronicle of Higher Education*, 19 April 2016.

Bloom, B., M. Engelhart, E. Furst, W. Hill, and D. Krathwohl. *Taxonomy of Educational Objectives. Handbook 1: Cognitive Domain*. London: Longmans, 1956.

European Consortium for Accreditation in Higher Education. "Dublin Descriptors." Accessed 27 January 2016. http://ecahe.eu/w/index.php/Dublin_Descriptors.

Fink, L. *Creating Significant Learning Experiences: An Integrated Approach to Designing College Courses*. San Francisco: Jossey-Bass, 2003.

Hill, Graham. *Global Church: Reshaping Our Conversations, Renewing Our Mission, Revitalizing Our Churches*. Downers Grove: IVP, 2016.

ICETE. "The Beirut Benchmarks." Accessed 3 October 2016. http://www.icete-edu.org/beirut/.

Inhelder, Bärbel, and Jean Piaget. *The Growth of Logical Thinking from Childhood to Adolescence: An Essay on the Construction of Formal Operational Structures*. New York: Basic, 1958.

Jenkins, Philip. *The Next Christendom: The Coming of Global Christianity*. 3rd ed. Oxford: OUP, 2011.

Kang, Namsoon. "Envisioning Postcolonial Theological Education: Dilemmas and Possibilities." In *Handbook of Theological Education in World Christianity: Theological Perspectives – Regional Surveys – Ecumenical Trends*, edited by D. Werner, D. Esterline, N. Kang, and J. Raja, 30–41. Eugene: Wipf and Stock, 2010.

Marzano, R., and J. Kendall, eds. *The New Taxonomy of Educational Objectives*. 2nd ed. Thousand Oaks: Corwin, 2006.

Piaget, Jean, and Bärbel Inhelder. *The Psychology of the Child*. New York: Basic, 1962.

"QS World University Rankings." TopUniversities. Accessed 27 January 2016. http://www.topuniversities.com/university-rankings/world-university-rankings.

Riebe-Estrella, Gary. "Engaging Borders: Lifting Up Difference and Unmasking Division." *Theological Education* 45, no. 1 (2009): 19–26.

Shaw, Ian J., Scott Cunningham, and Bernhard Ott, eds. *Best Practice Guidelines for Doctoral Programs*. Carlisle: Langham Global Library, 2015.

Shaw, Ian J., with Kevin E. Lawson. *Handbook for Supervisors of Doctoral Students in Evangelical Theological Institutions*. Carlisle: Langham Global Library, 2015.

Shulman, Lee. "Making Differences: A Table of Learning." The Carnegie Foundation for the Advancement of Teaching, 2002. Accessed 6 September 2013. www.carnegiefoundation.org/elibrary/making-differences-table-learning.

United Kingdom Quality Assurance Agency for Higher Education (QAA). "Doctoral Degree Characteristics," September 2011. Accessed 6 October 2016. http://www.qaa.ac.uk/en/Publications/Documents/Doctoral_Characteristics.pdf.

4

"What You Get Is What You See"?
Addressing the Hidden Curriculum of Doctoral Studies

Allan Harkness

Trying to sleep on a long-haul night flight, I became aware of a stewardess trying to get my attention. "Dr Harkness, we have a medical situation, and we wonder whether you might be able to assist us." Somewhat embarrassed, I responded, "Sorry, but I'm the wrong sort of doctor." (My PhD is in Christian education.) The airline staff assumed the "Dr" title on my boarding pass made me medically qualified: but what they saw was not what they got!

In advanced theological studies – and more specifically, doctoral studies[1] – there are elements in the study process that may work against the process achieving what it is designed to accomplish. In educational terms, this refers to the presence and power of the *hidden curriculum*, well attested to in the

---

1. There are two major formats for doctoral programs: the doctorate by research dissertation/thesis and doctorate by coursework plus dissertation/thesis. There is sufficient in common between the two formats for us to consider them together in this chapter. "Thesis" and "dissertation" are often used interchangeably. Generally, in UK and British Commonwealth countries a dissertation is completed for a master's degree and a thesis for a doctorate, while in the USA the opposite tends to occur. In this chapter, "dissertation" is used to refer to the output of doctoral programs.

education literature. This chapter demonstrates that it may not be the case that (to twist the idiom) "what you get is what you see."

The Hidden Curriculum in Advanced Studies

Informed educators are well aware of the interplay between three elements in curriculum processes:

- The *explicit* (manifest, "obvious") curriculum: what is intentionally planned and articulated for learning in an educational institution. This is most commonly reflected in course syllabi and the stated objectives for a course or program.
- The *implicit* (hidden) curriculum: elements in the psycho-social and physical environment which influence the explicit curriculum. This is related to what is experienced in a learning setting – "the unwritten, unofficial, and often unintended lessons, values, and perspectives that students learn in school . . . the unspoken or implicit academic, social, and cultural messages that are communicated . . ."[2]
- The *null* curriculum: what is omitted from the explicit curriculum, intentionally or unintentionally.

The hidden curriculum is particularly powerful, as it reinforces or works against the achievement of the explicit curriculum. In advanced studies this is not a newly recognized phenomenon. For example, in 1995 a paper presented at a meeting of the Association for the Study of Higher Education highlighted the topic: "the hidden curriculum is what students perceive they must do 1) to pass individual courses of particular instructors; 2) to pass doctoral comprehensive examinations; and 3) to write a dissertation proposal and dissertation acceptable to particular professors."[3]

An example offered is where students recognized that the grade awarded to student papers by one faculty member "seemed to be determined by [their] length and number of references. He rarely made comments about any part of

---

2. Great Schools Partnership, "Hidden Curriculum," The Glossary of Education Reform, last updated 13 July 2015, accessed 15 December 2016, http://edglossary.org/hidden-curriculum.
3. Barbara Townsend, "Is There a Hidden Curriculum in Higher Education Doctoral Programs?" (paper presented at the Annual Meeting of the Association for the Study of Higher Education, 2–5 November 1995, Orlando, FL), 3.

the papers . . . and never commented on the organization or coherency of the paper. Students passed on to one another their understanding of the hidden curriculum in his classes: to get an A on any paper, just write grammatically correct, lengthy papers and use lots of references."[4]

A second example of such unintended but real learning may be seen at a deeper level too:

> The formal curriculum of all programs, including higher education doctoral programs, is politically and culturally shaped and laden . . . it can serve to reinforce the dominant culture or expose and awaken students to non-traditional political, economic, and cultural perspectives and orientations.
>
> . . . the curriculum in most higher education programs probably reflects a preponderance of works by white, male scholars even at a time when scholarship by women and people of color has contributed new insights and broadened significantly the knowledge bases in our field. An unintended outcome of this domination of the curriculum by works of white, male authors is the inference that knowledge created by and about women and people of color is not as important.[5]

Fast-forward to 2010, and we find Perry Shaw writing in similar vein: "[T]he classic approach to higher level research is linear, specific, analytic, hypothesis-driven, and individualistic-competitive . . . far more likely to suit the thinking processes of white western males than women in general, or than students from collectivist societies . . . The approach is rarely questioned."[6]

It is encouraging that while these critiques are generalizations, there are now numerous models of doctoral-level study which challenge these perceptions, as a simple search of the Internet using descriptors like "alternative models for doctoral research" will show. However, the power of the hidden

---

4. Townsend, "Is There a Hidden Curriculum," 3.
5. Townsend, 3–5.
6. Perry Shaw, "'New Treasures with the Old:' Addressing Culture and Gender Imperialism in High Level Theological Education," in *Tending the Seedbeds: Educational Perspectives on Theological Education in Asia*, ed. Allan Harkness (Quezon City: Asia Theological Association, 2010), 54–55.

curriculum is still a reality which needs to be recognized, not least in advanced theological studies.

The Focus of Evangelical Advanced Theological Studies

Official statements for some years have been explicit about the intended focus of theological education (TE) endeavours. Most recently, the Cape Town Commitment that arose from the Third Lausanne Congress on World Evangelization in 2010 espoused the intended focus of TE this way:

> The mission of the Church on earth is to serve the mission of God, and the mission of theological education is to strengthen and accompany the mission of the Church. Theological education serves *first* to train those who lead the Church as pastor-teachers, equipping them to teach the truth of God's Word with faithfulness, relevance and clarity; and *second*, to equip all God's people for the missional task of understanding and relevantly communicating God's truth in every cultural context.[7]

This vision has been applied specifically to doctoral studies in the Beirut Benchmarks,[8] which include this opening statement:

> Doctoral study within an evangelical Christian institution is founded on an understanding of knowledge that is more than academic. In the Bible, acquiring and exercising wisdom involves a combination of faith, reason and action. It requires
>
> - right belief and committed trust in the living God ("the fear of the LORD is the first principle of wisdom"),

---

7. Lausanne Movement, "Cape Town Commitment: A Declaration of Belief and a Call to Action," Lausanne Movement, accessed 12 December 2016, http://www.lausanne.org/en/documents/ctcommitment.html, II-F-4.

8. ICETE, "The Beirut Benchmarks," in *Best Practice Guidelines for Doctoral Programs*, ed. Ian Shaw (Carlisle: Langham Global Library, 2015), 1–5. This statement on excellence in doctoral programs arose from an ICETE consultation held in 2010 in Beirut, Lebanon. A second consultation held in 2011 in Bangalore, India, approved an adaptation of the benchmarks for professional doctorates. The potential of the benchmarks in practice is thoughtfully elucidated in Shaw, *Best Practice Guidelines*.

- creative and humble use of the rationality God has granted to humans made in his own image, and
- appropriate living in the world to reflect God's calling and participate in God's mission.

Doctoral study, therefore, pursued on such a foundation, will be *confessional*, *rational* and *missional*. For a Christian, doctoral study is one dimension of what it means to "love the LORD your God with all your heart and mind and soul and strength."[9]

Ideally, in any evangelical doctoral theological study program, this focus and the associated values – specifically missional and ecclesial values – will be reflected. A reality check will identify where and to what extent a hidden curriculum is influencing such programs for or against the explicit focus and values.

The Hidden Curriculum in Evangelical Advanced Theological Studies

Various stakeholders are involved in evangelical doctoral programs. The ultimate stakeholder is our sovereign creator triune God "in whom we live and move and have our being" (Acts 17:28). The main human stakeholders include:

1. The students,[10] with their vested interest in completing their program successfully and in good time.
2. Seminary faculty – supervisor(s) and committee members – who are investing effort to see their students finish well. Their reputation in academic circles is (at least partially) at stake.
3. The students' seminary, whether one in which they are already on the faculty or one they plan to join as a newly minted doctorate holder.
4. The students' families (nuclear and extended), as their primary support structure.

---

9. ICETE, "The Beirut Benchmarks." Original italics.
10. People undertaking doctoral studies are commonly referred to as candidates. In this chapter, "student" is used, better to recognize that an educational venture is in progress.

5. The wider church, as the inclusive institution of which all the other human stakeholders are usually part.

All five of these human stakeholder groups hold many assumptions, mostly unexamined, about doctoral-level education which may lead to substantial incongruity between the explicit curriculum and the potentially very powerful hidden curriculum. This may be seen in four aspects of the doctoral research process:
- The *outcome* of doctoral studies
- The *process* of doctoral studies
- The *output* of doctoral studies
- The *cost* of doctoral studies

A. The Hidden Curriculum in the *Outcome* of Doctoral Studies

In doctoral theological studies, what sort of "doctor" do we expect to see produced? We can identify a number of common assumptions relating to this question, bearing in mind that imagining the end product inevitably impacts on the process leading to its achievement.

"Doctoral Students Are Academics"

A common perspective of the stakeholders in doctoral studies is that the doctorate earned is an academic qualification giving the holder the credentials to research and to teach. A stereotyped image is of an arcane theoretician rather than an effective practitioner. Even for a professional doctorate,[11] with its stated applied focus, the "academic" label usually still sticks.

This common view of the doctorate holder as an academic (or scholar, a term that is often used synonymously) is a significant hindrance if the statement that "theological education serves *first* to train those who lead the Church as pastor-teachers" (the Cape Town Commitment statement above) is

---

11. There is a common distinction between "academic" and "professional" doctorates. The main difference lies in their orientation: the former (mostly PhD) seeks to contribute original disciplinary insights, while the latter (e.g. doctor of education, doctor of ministry) seeks to provide original implications for professional and vocational practice. There are enough similarities for us to treat them together in this chapter.

to become a reality. This emphasis is reflected in the Beirut Benchmarks: "the doctoral qualification will be awarded to students who are church members commended for faithful discipleship and recognized leadership"; and one of the seven criteria for awarding a doctoral degree is:

> *Missional impact*, having shown that they are committed, and can be expected, to use the fruit of their doctoral study, the skills it has given them and the opportunities it affords them, to promote the kingdom of God and advance the mission of the church (both local and global), through Christ-like and transformational service, to the glory of God.[12]

These statements highlight the potential for someone with a doctoral degree. What does a doctorate-bearing pastor-teacher[13] who is able to "lead the Church" and "advance the mission of the church . . . through Christ-like and transformational service" look like? Teaching and research may well be part of this – after all, "doctor" is from the Latin *docere* ("to teach") – but what pastoral qualities might mark the teaching? An implication may be that seminary faculty need to reflect that they are primarily ministers of the gospel who teach and research, rather than teacher-researchers who minister.

The "academic" assumption also impacts on determining who is suitable for doctoral studies. The fitness of Christian leaders to be able to successfully navigate their way through doctoral studies is usually gauged primarily by their prior academic performance. But this is only partly appropriate. If the

---

12. ICETE, "The Beirut Benchmarks." I have a concern about aspects of these statements in relation to the dangers of assessment based on personal commitment, an issue of educational ethics. Educational integrity is at stake when we try to merge the dispositional with the academic. A danger germinal in the assessment processes of institutions equipping people for Christian leadership/ministry is that dispositional criteria may be invoked to overrule judgements of academic deficiency during the assessment process: "The work is substandard academically, but we will pass her because she loves the Lord, and/or she needs this qualification for effective ministry/Christian leadership." A flip side of this may be, at the time of examination: "We acknowledge the academic quality of this dissertation, but we are not going to pass it because we don't think the writer has been living according to our expected behavioural norms." Warning bells ring for me here, and doctoral programs will need to demonstrate very carefully how this concern will be resolved.

13. The separate terms "pastor" and "teacher" have many connotations, some helpful and others unhelpful in the context of this chapter. I use the terms here because of the use of "pastor-teacher" in the Cape Town Commitment.

desired outcome is better-equipped pastor-teachers, then the selection process will call for greater recognition of non-formal and informal learning[14] in prior ministry and mission settings for skills acquired, achievements gained, and attitudes and values demonstrated.

"Doctoral Students Are Free to Research on Any Topic"

Are approved topics for research that have no overt missional impact acceptable in advanced theological studies? Doctoral programs likely have a good deal to answer for on this question.

Seminaries have a relationship with the church from which both stand to benefit – or to suffer from. Students have a privilege and responsibility "to consider using the intellectual creativity associated with doctoral studies to contribute to their communities' knowledge systems in these contemporary times,"[15] and this will be reflected in the chosen research topics.

There is an unlimited number of abstruse, uncontextualized topics that could be – and often are – chosen for doctoral studies. Of course "all truth is God's truth," but should these topics actually be encouraged? A blanket restrictive policy will be unhelpfully limiting, but perhaps the norm should move closer to that demonstrated by a SE Asian seminary which declined the applications of doctoral candidates who were unable to demonstrate a clear contextual, missional focus in their proposed topics.[16]

"Doctoral Students Eventually Make Effective Teachers"

A common assumption is that a person with a doctorate is able to teach effectively. With my newly acquired PhD, I soon discovered that indeed "it

---

14. *Non-formal* modes of learning are those which are intentional, but which take place in non-institutional settings; and *informal* modes are those which utilize spontaneous or coincidental opportunities through life. These are in contrast to *formal* modes, which use structured and institutionalized settings.

15. Payi Ford, "Reflections on Doctoral Candidature Experiences as an Indigenous Australian," in *Doctorates Downunder: Keys to Successful Doctoral Study in Australia and Aotearoa New Zealand*, ed. Carey Denholm and Terry Evans, 2nd ed. (Camberwell, VIC: ACER, 2012), 149.

16. The topics weren't wrong *per se*; they simply were not the sorts of topics that particular seminary wanted to encourage because of its explicit focus on building the church in SE Asia. And the students could of course opt to pursue their pet topic elsewhere.

takes 5–7 years for a person with a PhD to be able to teach effectively."[17] Year by year as cohorts of seminary students passed through my courses (mainly on educational topics, ironically) I came to appreciate unexamined assumptions I was making about the students' levels of understanding and interest in my courses, their learning competencies and preferences, and what I brought (or didn't bring) to the learning process.

"I teach as I have been taught" is a common feature of the hidden curriculum. But few seminaries challenge this by providing intentional pedagogy training opportunities to suit their ministry and missional training focus. Some of the necessary skills may be acquired by faculty along the way, but the norm should be an intentional, regular in-service faculty training program, or ensuring faculty get the equivalent from external sources.

A related point of concern is the comprehension level of language used by doctorate-holders when they come to teach. In their advanced studies they have likely become adept at understanding and interacting with scholarly thought, so have acquired language skills with a high fog index (the number of years of formal education a person needs to understand a text or speech)[18] – and unconsciously they bring that to their teaching. Initiatives for faculty training will do well to better ensure appropriately intelligible and meaningful communication with students who have not been exposed to that same level of scholarship.[19]

"The Ideal Seminary Faculty Is Full of Doctors"

It is commendable that seminaries are raising the bar in terms of the qualifications of their faculty, and many are seeking to increase the proportion of faculty members with doctorates. The implication is that the ideal faculty for effective TE is doctorate-loaded. But the issue of credentialism arises, "the concept that credentials sometimes become unnecessary and inequitable

---

17. Source unknown.
18. "Fog Index," UsingEnglish.com, accessed 1 December 2016, https://www.usingenglish.com/glossary/fog-index.html.
19. There may also be the need to sensitively but firmly debunk the perception held in some cultures and sub-cultures that the more unintelligible faculty and scholars are, the higher their intelligence must be.

barriers to gainful employment and other aspects of society."[20] Given the missional focus of TE, it is likely that "non-doctors" will make suitable faculty members: those with ministry and mission experience but without formal qualifications will often be the best credentialed to facilitate key aspects of students' ministry and missional formation – and indeed, by going through the doctoral hoops their effectiveness might actually be hindered. The perception of stakeholders – from students being assigned supervisors to accrediting agencies – *à propos* who is best equipped to provide necessary formational oversight may need to be sensitively but firmly challenged.

"Doctoral Studies Lead to Entitlement"

An aspect of the hidden curriculum of doctoral study is that attaining the "Dr" title gives the holder a sense of entitlement, with perceived rights and privileges. This is expressed in various ways, influenced and shaped by the culture of the various stakeholders. At times holding the title may be positive, such as when the title opens doors for enhanced ministry and mission contribution. But there is a clear danger for relationships with others, both in the church and beyond. If a key doctoral quality is "Christ-like and transformational service," then a number of relational attitudes and practices will likely be challenged if measured against the model of the one who "came not to be served but to serve, and to give his life a ransom for many" (Mark 10:45).

"Doctoral Studies Lead to Enhanced Christian Discipleship"

Often stakeholders assume that one who holds a "Christian" doctorate is a model of mature Christian spirituality: "The higher the degree, the greater the spirituality and holiness of the holder."[21] It is as if quantity of knowledge somehow equates to quality of life. This is open to challenge, and rightly so, as church history is littered with examples of academically well-qualified leaders who manifestly demonstrate that the fruit of the Holy Spirit (Gal 2:22–23) and other Christian qualities and virtues can't be correlated with completing

---

20. Bernard Bull, "What Are the 10 Most Critical Issues in Education Today?," *Etale* (blog), 17 September 2015, accessed 8 January 2017, http://etale.org/main/2015/09/17/what-are-the-10-most-critical-issues-in-education-today/.

21. This point is similar to the assumption that a minister, pastor, or "full-time Christian worker" is more spiritual and more holy than a "mere layperson," by virtue of the role held.

advanced theological studies. Indeed, akin to the rich entering the kingdom of God being likened to camels going through eyes of needles (Mark 10:25), so undertaking advanced studies has the potential to make dynamic discipleship harder to attain.

The extent to which the assumptions identified in the six aspects above relating to "What sort of 'doctor' do we expect to see produced?" are true has hidden curriculum impact. If they remain unexamined, they have potential to skew or sabotage the explicit purposes of advanced theological studies.

B. The Hidden Curriculum in the *Process* of Doctoral Studies

Achieving the status of "doctor" in TE circles doesn't just happen, as much as stakeholders (not least students' families) might wish otherwise. It entails an extended process: a reputable PhD usually takes a minimum of three years of full-time study or five to seven years of part-time study.

Within this time frame, the typical doctoral studies approach has worked well for many – but it has also been too tall a hurdle for numerous others. Numerous factors contribute to the drop-out rate: time management, change of priorities, loss of interest in the topic, and finance. But less commonly recognized contributing factors to doctoral success are related to students' prior educational experiences, culture, personality, and preferred learning styles. For each of these factors a hidden curriculum may be working against the achievement of the explicit curriculum.

Prior Educational Experience Matters

Doctoral students bring to their studies assumptions about what the research process entails, both its scope and its quality. Their perception of the requirements is influenced by their prior educational experiences, which dynamically interact with the elements of the research context. This interaction influences the students' view of what the research task requires and the appropriate approach to achieving it.[22]

---

22. Paul Ramsden, *Learning to Teach in Higher Education*, 2nd ed. (London/New York: RoutledgeFalmer, 2003).

Few students are likely to articulate the features of their prior learning experiences and to appreciate which of those will help or hinder their study venture. The scope of such features are described in well-known frameworks for identifying salient aspects of effective learning (e.g. multiple intelligences, learning style theory, learning levels, the impact of personality, etc.), an appreciation of the importance of metalearning ("learning how to learn"), and the concept of deep vs. surface approaches to learning.

When students fail to understand and apply how they learn most effectively and don't actively approach their studies in a deep way, they are likely, at best, to make frustratingly slow progress or, at worst, to drop out of – or be dropped from – their program. And no one wins.[23] (There is hope, when institutions offering doctoral programs ensure their students undertake a comprehensive orientation to the skills and perspectives required to move through their program successfully.)

Culture Matters

A major "elephant in the room" in advanced studies is the impact of students' culture on how they navigate through their program: a major hidden curriculum issue arises if this is not recognized. Contemporary literature on doctoral studies highlights how the cultural background of students plays a significant role in the successful completion – or non-completion – of their program. Perry Shaw's chapter on culture, gender, and diversity explores this issue in some detail, but several points are worth comment here.

Students from many cultural groups, especially in Majority World countries or as minority groups in Western nations, may experience significant cognitive dissonance while undertaking their studies within the traditional Western framework. Anne Hiha, a New Zealand Māori, has illustrated this from her experience: "I described this period as walking the edge of the sword with the Western world on one side and the Māori world on the other. I felt as though

---

23. Potential loss of face by students is at least partially addressed by doctoral programs that have several exit points – for example, an award for completed coursework but non-completed dissertation; and in some institutions an MPhil is awarded to students who are deemed not competent to move on into a full PhD.

I was being pulled both ways; and to stay on the sword I was in a tense state all the time."[24]

A major contributing element is whether the culture from which a student comes tends towards individualism or towards being communitarian.[25] The traditional dissertation approach, designed to encourage independent thinking and learning, leans heavily on the individualistic approach. But this is an ill-conceived assumption: "One of the commonest misconceptions about research is that it is an 'ivory tower' activity, far removed from reality and from social contact with others. If you say you are doing research, people will often talk to you as though you had decided to spend a number of years in solitary confinement from which, in due course, you will emerge with your new discoveries."[26]

Students from communitarian cultures naturally struggle when this perspective is reinforced, and it may take a long time (if it comes at all) for them to realize that "what is needed is collaboration, not competition"[27] – all the more so when "deeply creative projects may require many hands."[28] The message that students are alone in their doctoral journey is implied when they sense that it is solely their responsibility to find a research topic and develop a suitable research question, to plan the flow of their research, to initiate meetings with their supervisor (or committee members), and to provide the agenda for such meetings. The situation is worsened when supervisors make themselves available to students only infrequently or for very short meetings, do not read students' draft writing or take an inordinately long time to do so, and fail to discern when a student needs more interaction. These practices usually arise because supervisors supervise as they were supervised for their advanced studies.

---

24. Anne Hiha, "Being a Maori Doctoral Candidate," in Denholm and Evans, *Doctorates Downunder*, 144.
25. Perry Shaw's chapter on culture, gender, and diversity and Rafael Zaracho's chapter on joint and collaborative research develop this point.
26. Estelle Phillips and Derek Pugh, *How to Get a PhD: A Handbook for Students and Their Supervisors* (Maidenhead: Open University, 2000), 14.
27. Phillips and Pugh, *How to Get a PhD*, 16.
28. Katina Rogers, "Opportunities Created by Emerging Technologies," in Papers from the Future of the Dissertation Workshop, 28–29 January 2016, accessed 18 December 2016, http://cgsnet.org/sites/default/files/DissFwd_Print%20All%20Papers.pdf.

The individual vs. communitarian issue needs to be addressed for theological reasons also. The most conducive setting for missional-focused education is likely to be one which is intentional, collaborative, and communitarian.[29] But TE institutions have by and large lost the initiative to both the legal and the medical professions in the extensive use the latter give to the place of collaboratively-oriented enquiry- and problem-based learning strategies. Such collaborative approaches were demonstrated by Jesus and the apostolic leaders, not simply as sound educational strategies (well before "andragogy" became a catchword[30]), but because these approaches were intimately integrated with the theological beliefs they expounded. That is, their theology shaped their educational approaches.

Collaborative advanced studies have the potential for flow-on into postdoctoral ministry. "Collaborative work during the doctoral program and . . . within the dissertation, provides a strong foundation for post-doctoral success,"[31] both in ongoing research and vocational activity. Advanced TE studies lend themselves to the dynamic reflected in Sugimoto's assertion, undergirded by the theological value of collaboration in community, in the ongoing ministry and mission ventures of Christian leaders.

Personality Matters

People with particular personalities are intuitively more likely than others to navigate successfully through advanced studies, given traditional study approach expectations. For example, using the Myers Briggs Type Indicator framework, those with the INTP personality type (Introversion, Intuition, Thinking, Perceiving) tend to "prefer to spend time on their own, working through problems . . . engag[ing] their thirst for knowledge and passion for

---

29. This theme is expanded in Allan Harkness, "Assessment in Theological Education: Do Our Theological Values Matter?," *Journal of Adult Theological Education* 5, no. 2 (2008): 183–201.
30. E.g. Malcolm Knowles, *The Modern Practice of Adult Education* (New York: Association Press, 1979).
31. Cassidy Sugimoto, "Toward a Twenty-First Century Dissertation," in Papers from the Future of the Dissertation Workshop, 28–29 January 2016, accessed 18 December 2016, http://cgsnet.org/sites/default/files/DissFwd_Print%20All%20Papers.pdf.

theory"[32] – qualities typically required by doctoral students in the humanities[33] (especially those undertaking the doctorate by dissertation option). But "INTPs" represent only around 3 percent of the population,[34] so what of students with other personality types? Almost inevitably they will struggle to a greater or lesser extent with the expectations of the doctoral study process.

Learning Styles Matter

Similar concerns may be raised about the learning styles of doctoral students. There are numerous typologies for learning styles; one well-regarded model is the VARK approach developed by Neil Fleming and Colleen Mill, which identifies sensory modalities that are used for learning: Visual, Aural, Read/write and Kinaesthetic.[35]

Although academics may be multi-modal, Read/write (a preference for information presented as written words, and ability at authoring and text-editing) is the main preferred modality for them. This won't be a surprise, as Westernised systems of education have tended to be based on this modality. VARK researchers have also gathered data which points to gender trends – men having stronger Kinaesthetic and women stronger Read/write mode preferences for learning;[36] and ethnic trends – there are indications that Polynesian cultures may have a stronger Aural mode preference, while Australian Aboriginal and Torres Strait Islanders, Native Americans, and Middle East students may tend towards stronger Visual mode preference.[37]

How might the traditional processes of advanced studies impact on people with these mode preferences? Successful completion is not directly an issue of

---

32. Stephanie Small, "16 Myers Briggs Personality Types (MBTI)," GradSchools.com, accessed 19 January 2017, https://www.gradschools.com/get-informed/before-you-apply/choosing-what-study/16-myers-briggs-personality-types-mbti.
33. There is debate over whether theology (and the study of religions) rightly sits in the humanities. Given that theology is still commonly located there, I do so also in this chapter.
34. NERIS Analytics, "INTP Personality ('The Logician')," 16personalities, accessed 24 January 2017, https://www.16personalities.com/intp-personality.
35. VARK Learn, "Frequently Asked Questions," VARK, accessed 24 January 2017, http://vark-learn.com/introduction-to-vark/frequently-asked-questions/.
36. VARK Learn, "Frequently Asked Questions: Are There Differences in the VARK Preferences of Men and Women?"
37. VARK Learn, "Frequently Asked Questions: Are There Differences in the VARK Preferences of Different Cultures?"

motivation, for motivation is not the same as learning style: "Motivation is a separate and significant part of learning. However if learners are using modes that are a strong part of their preferences they are more likely to be motivated than if they have to use modes where their preference is weak. That makes common sense!"[38]

C. The Hidden Curriculum in the *Output* of Doctoral Studies

The commonly-preferred output of doctoral study in the humanities and social sciences is a dissertation: a piece of written work up to 80–100,000 words in length (rather less for a professional doctoral dissertation) that has a fairly predictable internal format. Here, the assumption of a "one size fits all" approach creates significant challenges.

Where students are pushed – implicitly if not explicitly – to undertake the traditional dissertation journey, and their prior learning experiences, cultural background, personalities, and preferred learning styles (itemized above) differ significantly from those of the stereotyped white Western male for whom the typical approach works, then there are bound to be significant challenges for them to finish well.

Fortunately in wider doctoral-level education there is growing legitimacy for a large range of alternative pathways available to be harnessed for doctorates which give greater emphasis to students' preferred learning styles and contexts. The present book showcases some of the possibilities specifically within TE, so this section will summarize only three aspects of the output of doctoral studies in which the hidden curriculum may be evident.

Originality Matters

It is commonly understood that the output of PhD research is an original contribution to knowledge. This is encapsulated in the Beirut Benchmarks:

> *Creative and original contribution*, having produced, as a result of such disciplined inquiry, a creative and original contribution

---

38. VARK Learn, "Frequently Asked Questions: Does VARK Say Anything about Motivation?"

that extends the frontiers of knowledge, or develops fresh insights in the articulation and contextual relevance of the Christian tradition, some of which merit national or international refereed publication.[39]

Statements like this raise stakeholders' expectations that the doctoral output will make peers in the discipline (and hopefully people outside the discipline) sit up and take notice of what has been achieved, a highly significant breakthrough which is likely the pinnacle of the student's academic journey. But this attitude is unhelpful, as noted Australian educator Brian Hill has warned: "Most [doctoral] students have a secret hope that they will transform the world with their dissertation. It occasionally happens in the physical sciences and maths! But the humanities are more reflective than revolutionary. The doctorate is one's union ticket . . . Time to save the world when one is in the post-doctoral phase!"[40]

What advanced studies provide is opportunity for enhanced thinking on what is probably already "out there" in one form or another, and for this to be expressed in the students' own voice. Thus "originality" is likely to have a different feel to it in different cultures. Two common approaches to learning are the master–student and the independent learner approaches.[41] It is easy to appreciate the struggles of students coming from cultures in which the educational norm, even up to tertiary level, reflects the master–student

---

39. ICETE, "The Beirut Benchmarks." This benchmark has been adapted for professional doctorates: "*Creative and original contribution*, having produced, as a result of such disciplined inquiry, a creative and original contribution that a) extends the frontiers of knowledge, b) generates new perspectives, approaches or paradigms in professional practice, and c) enhances the integration between theological reflection and Christian ministry practice, and so merits publication in national or international professional literature."

40. Brian Hill, "Supervising Research Doctorates: Insights from Personal Experience" (personal communication, undated).

41. Watkins and Biggs, cited in Margaret Kumar, "International Candidates' Transition to a 'Doctorate Downunder,'" in Denholm and Evans, *Doctorates Downunder*. Margaret Kumar (p. 155) highlights the major difference between these two "cultures of learning": "In the master–student approach, the student follows the master unquestioningly; the master is the ultimate authority on the subject. Important texts are memorised and discussion is focused on clarification and understanding. The ultimate aim is to demonstrate via tests – including examinations – that the master's knowledge has been successfully passed to the student. In contrast, the independent learning approach requires the student to question, explore and discover knowledge within a particular topic. The literature that the student reads is not memorised, but rather used as a basis

approach (e.g. the *guru-shishya* tradition in India and *shi fu-tu di* tradition in China). These students are intuitively likely to struggle to express their own views (and to wonder what plagiarism is all about!). The hidden curriculum at work in these areas is particularly powerful.

Resources – From Here, There, and Everywhere?

Estelle Phillips and Derek Pugh, in their list of what "becoming a fully professional researcher" means, include "[y]ou must be aware of what is being discovered, argued about, written and published by your academic community across the world."[42]

This can result in two polar but unhelpful expectations. When students take that point literally, they may expend incredible effort trying to ensure they have accessed everything available, and fail to progress onto their own distinctive contribution. At the other extreme, students may think that they will be able to get by with resources fairly close to hand (and often quite dated as a result), and then they wonder why their dissertation examiners knock them back on the inadequacy of their cited literature. As students seek to ensure that they have discovered the literature that is particularly significant for their research focus, the expansion and accessibility of Internet resources and electronic databases make excuses of limited resources less convincing.[43]

The matter of languages is related. For English-medium advanced studies often it is assumed that resources in English will suffice. This may be so, although

---

for them to construct their own understanding. The student engages in critical and analytical thinking and enquires about what is in the written text. Thus, any opinions are formed through reasoning. These opinions are given and argued through discussion and based on what is being read from teaching, reading and enquiry."

42. Phillips and Pugh, *How to Get a PhD*, 21.

43. "[T]he reality [is] that the familiar patterns of scholarly communication are not, in fact, etched in stone, but are instead undergoing a variety of transformations across all domains. Modes of communication are expanding to include more informal venues of exchanges, from tweets to blog posts, in addition to the traditional genres of articles, books and conference papers. Access to scholarly output has dramatically increased via the open access movement and related new entrants into the domain, such as new open access and library-based publishers, as well as individual researchers directly promoting their work across the web" (Lisa Schiff, "Creative Destruction: Open Access, Institutional Repositories and the Changing Dissertation," in Papers from the Future of the Dissertation Workshop, 28–29 January 2016, accessed 18 December 2016, http://cgsnet.org/sites/default/files/DissFwd_Print%20All%20Papers.pdf). On digital projects see Rogers, "Opportunities Created by Emerging Technologies."

students (and their supervisors) do need to be alert to significant resources in other languages. If there are, then it is proper to consider which languages students need to have sufficient working knowledge of, and sometimes expectations are unrealistically high. If advanced studies for missional impact are to be completed within a viable time frame, then language competence required for the chosen topic, and how much secondary rather than primary sources may be adequate, need to be considered carefully.

Criticality Matters

The expectation of Western-based modes of learning is that doctoral students are critical researchers: they demonstrate the ability to move beyond description to in-depth analysis and explanation of their topic. But students often fail to appreciate what critical enquiry entails, and think that it is adequate to focus on describing the knowledge already "out there." They are reluctant to critique, assuming the common usage of "critical" as commenting negatively on the insights of others. Instead, they need to learn that critical thinking entails appraising those insights, recognizing strengths and weaknesses in the content and logic, and identifying gaps. After all, it is a gap of some sort in existing knowledge that students need to identify in order to ensure originality.

What appropriate "critical analysis" means across cultural boundaries itself requires serious critical enquiry, and this is where the question of academic rigour arises, along with the level of credibility given to resources in English and from Western countries. I recollect an article on demon possession for an Asian magazine, written by an Asian seminary faculty member. The authorities cited were predominantly North American and European. Where were the informed commentators from the Majority World – the Asian, African, and S. American regions in which Christians have lived experience of demon possession and a worldview within which the phenomenon is situated? The faculty member's response was telling: "It is true that my sources are primarily Western . . . Asian theologians unfortunately have not written on the subject with the same rigour as their Western counterparts" (personal communication).

Although there is no clear consensus on a precise definition of academic rigour, it is related to the process of reviewing, critiquing, and revising ideas. Using Bloom's *Taxonomy of Educational Objectives*,[44] rigour is seen in competence in the ability to remember, understand, apply, analyse, evaluate, and create. Within these criteria, there is clearly a place for drawing on and evaluating resources which include comment on lived experience, even when generated (in various forms, written, aural, etc.) in a style not customarily perceived to fit the category of academic (or scholarly) writing. The examples presented in section three of this book demonstrate creative possibilities.

D. The Hidden Curriculum in the *Cost* of Doctoral Studies

Stakeholders in TE doctoral programs need to be aware of the implicit values expressed in the logistics surrounding the programs. Doctoral students face pressures from various directions as they seek to complete their programs within a reasonable time frame: finance, family and personal expectations and responsibilities, and work and ministry are the main forces which often derail good intentions to finish well – and all may be considered as hidden curriculum issues.

Financial Cost

Doctoral study does not come cheaply.[45] To be sure, students (especially from Majority World countries) may receive partial or full scholarships, but where does the necessary finance come from? And can the amount be justified? Answers may well be on a case-by-case basis, but an implicit value is that

---

44. Lorin Anderson and David Krathwohl, eds., *A Taxonomy for Learning, Teaching, and Assessing: A Revision of Bloom's Taxonomy of Educational Objectives* (New York: Longman, 2001).

45. For example, the (approximate) annual tuition cost of doctoral programs in accredited seminaries in Majority World countries is likely to be in the range of USD2,000 (Kenya), USD1,100–2,500 (Malaysia), and USD1,400 (Philippines). In Western countries the annual tuition bill for doctoral programs is considerably higher: e.g. in the USA, USD28,000–40,000; in the UK, up to USD26,000 for international students; and in Australia USD9,900–26,000 for international students (Mark Bennett, "How Much Does It Cost to Study a PhD in Australia?", "PhD Programs in Australia," FindAPhD, accessed 25 January 2017, https://www.findaphd.com/study-abroad/aus-nz/phd-study-in-australia.aspx#Fees-and-funding; Elke Schwarz, "How to Get PhD Funding," TopUniversities, accessed 25 January 2017, http://www.topuniversities.com/student-info/student-finance/how-get-phd-funding). And these costs exclude living costs and travel.

doctoral study is a good return on investment. However, this may need to be challenged if a missional focus is an explicit stakeholder value.

The common perception is that the best-quality doctoral programs are located in Western countries, or perhaps in a more developed country within a region, so this option is a significant attraction for many of the stakeholders in evangelical TE. Seldom is the issue of distribution of available funds the priority concern, in which the value of someone going overseas for doctoral studies is compared to undertaking studies in a local or regional institution at a fraction of the cost. There are now numerous TE institutions in the Majority World which are offering reputable doctoral programs – and surely the main factor should not be so much the reputation of the institution to which a student goes (where the quality of research generated may be more assumed than the reality) so much as the value of the focus and quality of the research for the more effective mission of the church in the student's country/region. And increasingly burgeoning Internet resources and opportunities for short-term research visits to well-equipped study centres mitigate the resource gap between local and overseas institutions.

Cost on Family Life

Doctoral study requires a good deal of time, during which students' families usually bear a heavy load. Support from family will make the program more achievable for the student, and the heavier load borne by family members may well be manageable for a defined period.

But often there is a clash of values between the explicit theological statements on the importance of family for Christians and the implicit value demonstrated by a parent being absent from the family (nuclear and extended) for an extended period of time in order to undertake a doctoral program in another country. Such separation is usually justified in terms of lack of finance and concern that if the family moves to another country for the duration of the parent's program the transition back to their home country after several years is likely to be difficult. Of course there are cultural differences relating to the dynamics of family life, but what needs to be ascertained is the extent to which what is being modelled by family separation squares with the values explicitly espoused about family life by the faith communities of the students and their families.

Cost on Personal Well-Being

Doctoral study has significant impact on the well-being of the student in all areas of life – psychological, physical, social, spiritual, and so on. A challenge facing the stakeholders – including the students themselves, often their own worst enemies – is to ensure that the explicit value of ensuring a healthy lifestyle for holistic well-being does not clash with the implied value that for the duration of the study program well-being can be subjugated to the research venture.

This incongruity is often seen in the effort by students to complete their program in as short a time as possible, and in so doing finding their hours of sleep and exercise, their recreation regime, and their diet – and yes, their personal and corporate spiritual formation too – all suffer for the sake of their studies.

A key to minimizing this incongruity will likely lie in the stakeholders appreciating that the advanced studies are not simply an add-on to the already busy life the student leads. Rather, for its duration the doctoral venture is a significant component of their life and their work, and other life and work activities – usually ministry-related – will need to be put on hold if the students are to have adequate time and energy for their program (see next section). Theologically, the concept of *kairos* (time imbued with particular opportunity) is important for well-adjusted and guilt-free doctoral students.

Cost on Ongoing Ministry and Mission

Christian leaders constitute the majority of students undertaking studies in evangelical TE doctoral programs. Certainly this is assumed in the Beirut Benchmarks: "students who are church members commended for faithful discipleship and recognized leadership."[46]

What happens to their ministry/mission roles during their doctoral ventures? It is here that further hidden curriculum issues arise, not unrelated to the family and personal well-being cost issues. For example, if the churches or organizations of the students do not see the doctoral studies of their staff members/colleagues as an integral part of their ministry/mission contribution and give adequate allowance for them, the students will likely experience a

---

46. ICETE, "The Beirut Benchmarks."

significant energy-sapping and stress-inducing disconnect between their ministry responsibilities and study programs. Burnout is not an uncommon reason for uncompleted doctoral studies.

There may be a clash of values, too, if students travel outside their country to study. It is well recognized that the growth of the church in Majority World countries is hampered by Christian leaders who go overseas to study, and then fail to return. Or they return, but with a different agenda from that arising in their home country. It is encouraging when TE institutions see as their main concern to train Christian leaders in their own context, sensing the heartbeat of their setting – but the stakeholders need to demonstrate practically the value of this through actively supporting students to study more locally, even if finance for overseas study is not an issue and the local institution doesn't yet have anywhere near the same apparent prestige as overseas institutions.

For Christian leaders in the Majority World, undertaking doctoral studies full-time and "away from home" may also have serious repercussions for the ministry of which they are part. Senior leadership positions are not usually easy to fill with a deputy for the duration of a study program. This is especially marked in small seminaries in Majority World countries: it is difficult to find someone sufficiently well qualified to cover the teaching areas of the faculty member absent for advanced studies – if such people are around, they would likely have been drawn into the faculty by now in any case – let alone have the finance available to pay a fill-in faculty member. And it is unhelpfully stressful and counterproductive to add extra course and administrative loads to already stretched faculty colleagues.

For the sake of integrity, stakeholders in TE doctoral programs need to be aware of the implicit values expressed in terms of finance, family life, personal well-being, and ministry/mission responsibilities, and seek to ensure that there is a closer correlation between the values and the associated practices they explicitly espouse. Mutual agreement on these will make it more likely that undertaking the doctoral program "seems good to them and the Holy Spirit" for the student to pursue without evoking disquiet, anxiety, and dissonance.

Conclusion

"What should we do with a hidden curriculum when we find one?"[47] reflects the question we need to bear in mind as we consider doctoral studies in evangelical TE settings. To be forewarned is to be forearmed, and this chapter has identified key areas in which a powerful hidden curriculum may be identified.

When the challenges to tradition detailed through this book are considered, it is important to bear in mind what espoused biblical/theological – and especially missional – values held by the stakeholders in advanced studies are being expressed and to weigh these up against the implicit values, in terms of the outcomes, processes, outputs, and costs.[48] And it is also worth asking, "How do (or how might) these contribute to a 'new normal'?"

Bernard Bull has asked of education in general "a fundamental pair of questions about the type of educational system that we want to support today":

> Do we want to build learning ecosystems that allow a select few with a select set of views to dominate, forcing or pressuring everyone else to follow along? Or, do we want to build an education system that leaves room for difference, acknowledging the deeply values laden nature of the education enterprise, and providing people with freedom, voice and choice about something as formative as education? These are important questions for policymakers and anyone interested in helping to shape the future of our education.[49]

Bull's questions are directly applicable to the challenge facing advanced studies in TE settings. To answer these questions well, and so to better serve the mission of God, appreciation of the dynamics of the hidden curriculum is an essential asset.

---

47. Jane Martin, "What Should We Do with a Hidden Curriculum When We Find One?," *Curriculum Enquiry* 6, no. 2 (1976): 135–151.
48. Ian Payne's chapter, "A Theology for Advanced Theological Studies," may be a worthwhile stepping-off point for further thinking on biblical/theological values.
49. Bernard Bull, "Musings on Cognitive Bias in Education Policy and Why I Deactivated My Facebook Account," *Etale* (blog), 8 November 2016, accessed 18 December 2016, http://etale.org/main/2016/11/08/musings-on-cognitive-bias-in-education-policy-and-why-i-deactivated-my-facebook-account/.

Discussion Questions

1. In your experience, where have you seen these assumptions (detailed in section A) expressed?
    - "Doctoral students are academics."
    - "Doctoral students are free to research on any topic."
    - "Doctoral students eventually make effective teachers."
    - "The ideal seminary faculty is full of doctors."
    - "Doctoral studies lead to entitlement."
    - "Doctoral studies lead to enhanced Christian discipleship."

Has the impact of these assumptions been positive or problematic, especially for a missional emphasis for theological education? Why? Do any other assumptions come to your mind to add to the list?

2. Flowing from your (and perhaps your colleagues') journey in theological education, what advice relating to perspectives in any of the four areas in section B – *prior educational experience, culture, personality* and *learning style* – would you give to a colleague planning for advanced studies, in order to enhance his or her study experience?

3. Keeping in mind section B, in what ways might the selection process for those to undertake advanced theological studies potentially impoverish the church? Weighing up your insights along with the points made in section D (the *cost* of doctoral studies), how might your school amend its selection process to reflect your answers?

4. In your advanced studies, in what ways was the *output* (see section C) less than what you had hoped for, in terms of significance and impact? Suggest changed perspectives that might lead to a more satisfying outcome.

5. Keeping in mind the focus of this chapter and with the mission statement and values of your school in hand, complete this sentence: '*For those from our school undertaking advanced theological studies, our hope is that . . .*' With which of your school's stakeholders could you have a conversation about your sentence?

Bibliography

Anderson, Lorin, and David Krathwohl, eds. *A Taxonomy for Learning, Teaching, and Assessing: A Revision of Bloom's Taxonomy of Educational Objectives.* New York: Longman, 2001.

Bennett, Mark. "How Much Does It Cost to Study a PhD in Australia?," "PhD Programs in Australia." FindAPhD. Accessed 25 January 2017. https://www.findaphd.com/study-abroad/aus-nz/phd-study-in-australia.aspx#Fees-and-funding.

Bull, Bernard. "Musings on Cognitive Bias in Education Policy and Why I Deactivated My Facebook Account." *Etale* (blog), 8 November 2016. Accessed 18 December 2016. http://etale.org/main/2016/11/08/musings-on-cognitive-bias-in-education-policy-and-why-i-deactivated-my-facebook-account/.

———. "What Are the 10 Most Critical Issues in Education Today?" *Etale* (blog), 17 September 2015. Accessed 8 January 2017. http://etale.org/main/2015/09/17/what-are-the-10-most-critical-issues-in-education-today/.

Ford, Payi. "Reflections on Doctoral Candidature Experiences as an Indigenous Australian." In *Doctorates Downunder: Keys to Successful Doctoral Study in Australia and Aotearoa New Zealand*, edited by Carey Denholm and Terry Evans, 145–152. 2nd ed. Camberwell, VIC: ACER, 2012.

Great Schools Partnership. "Hidden Curriculum." The Glossary of Education Reform. Last updated 13 July 2015. Accessed 15 December 2016. http://edglossary.org/hidden-curriculum.

Harkness, Allan. "Assessment in Theological Education: Do Our Theological Values Matter?" *Journal of Adult Theological Education* 5, no. 2 (2008): 183–201.

Hiha, Anne. "Being a Maori Doctoral Candidate." In *Doctorates Downunder: Keys to Successful Doctoral Study in Australia and Aotearoa New Zealand*, edited by Carey Denholm and Terry Evans, 138–144. 2nd ed. Camberwell, VIC: ACER, 2012.

Hill, Brian. "Supervising Research Doctorates: Insights from Personal Experience." Personal communication, undated.

ICETE. "The Beirut Benchmarks." In *Best Practice Guidelines for Doctoral Programs*, edited by Ian Shaw, 1–5. Carlisle: Langham Global Library, 2015.

Knowles, Malcolm. *The Modern Practice of Adult Education.* New York: Association Press, 1979.

Kumar, Margaret. "International Candidates' Transition to a 'Doctorate Downunder.'" In *Doctorates Downunder: Keys to Successful Doctoral Study in Australia and Aotearoa New Zealand*, edited by Carey Denholm and Terry Evans, 153–163. 2nd ed. Camberwell, VIC: ACER, 2012.

Lausanne Movement. "The Cape Town Commitment: A Declaration of Belief and a Call to Action." Lausanne Movement. Accessed 12 December 2016. http://www.lausanne.org/en/documents/ctcommitment.html.

Martin, Jane. "What Should We Do with a Hidden Curriculum When We Find One?" *Curriculum Enquiry* 6, no. 2 (1976): 135–151.

NERIS Analytics. "INTP Personality ('The Logician')." 16personalities. Accessed 24 January 2017. https://www.16personalities.com/intp-personality.

Phillips, Estelle, and Derek Pugh. *How to Get a PhD: A Handbook for Students and Their Supervisors*. Maidenhead: Open University, 2000.

Ramsden, Paul. *Learning to Teach in Higher Education*. 2nd ed. London/New York: RoutledgeFalmer, 2003.

Rogers, Katina. "Opportunities Created by Emerging Technologies." In Papers from the Future of the Dissertation Workshop, 28–29 January 2016. Accessed 18 December 2016. http://cgsnet.org/sites/default/files/DissFwd_Print%20All%20Papers.pdf.

Schiff, Lisa. "Creative Destruction: Open Access, Institutional Repositories and the Changing Dissertation." In Papers from the Future of the Dissertation Workshop, 28–29 January 2016. Accessed 18 December 2016. http://cgsnet.org/sites/default/files/DissFwd_Print%20All%20Papers.pdf.

Schwarz, Elke. "How to Get PhD Funding." TopUniversities. Accessed 25 January 2017. http://www.topuniversities.com/student-info/student-finance/how-get-phd-funding.

Shaw, Ian, ed. *Best Practice Guidelines for Doctoral Programs*. Carlisle: Langham Global Library, 2015.

Shaw, Perry. "'New Treasures with the Old': Addressing Culture and Gender Imperialism in High Level Theological Education." In *Tending the Seedbeds: Educational Perspectives on Theological Education in Asia*, edited by Allan Harkness, 47–74. Quezon City: Asia Theological Association, 2010.

Small, Stephanie. "16 Myers Briggs Personality Types (MBTI)." GradSchools.com. Accessed 19 January 2017. https://www.gradschools.com/get-informed/before-you-apply/choosing-what-study/16-myers-briggs-personality-types-mbti.

Sugimoto, Cassidy. "Toward a Twenty-First Century Dissertation." In Papers from the Future of the Dissertation Workshop, 28–29 January 2016. Accessed 18 December 2016. http://cgsnet.org/sites/default/files/DissFwd_Print%20All%20Papers.pdf.

Townsend, Barbara. "Is There a Hidden Curriculum in Higher Education Doctoral Programs?" Paper presented at the Annual Meeting of the Association for the Study of Higher Education, 2–5 November 1995, Orlando, FL.

VARK Learn. "Frequently Asked Questions." VARK. Accessed 24 January 2017. http://vark-learn.com/introduction-to-vark/frequently-asked-questions/.

5

Culture, Gender, and Diversity in Advanced Theological Studies[1]

Perry Shaw

Introduction

The central thesis of this chapter is that global higher education in general and theological education in particular has been shaped by empiricist, linear-thinking white Western males for empiricist, linear-thinking white Western males. The unquestioned assumption that the empiricist, linear-thinking white Western male way is the only true way of doing academic thinking is more a matter of ideological power than it is a desire for quality learning. There is a troubling level of culture and gender imperialism in higher level theological study – not so much in content as in the narrow understanding of scholarly methodology embedded in the empiricist, linear-analytic shape of thesis-writing that has become virtually sacrosanct in the academy.

---

[1]. Much of the material in this chapter is a development of my earlier published material as found in "'New Treasures with the Old': Addressing Culture and Gender Imperialism in Higher Level Theological Education," chapter 2 in *Tending the Seedbeds: Educational Perspectives on Theological Education in Asia*, ed. Allan Harkness (Quezon City: Asia Theological Association, 2010), 47–74; and in my *Transforming Theological Education: A Practical Handbook for Integrative Learning* (Carlisle: Langham Global Library, 2014), 236–239.

The moment I make the above assertion I know that there will be those who will dismiss this chapter. What research exists is suggestive more than comprehensive, and unfortunately has been misused to stereotype people on the basis of culture and gender. Certainly, women of the calibre of Marie Curie, Maria Goeppert-Mayer, Dorothy Hodgkin, Ada Yonath, and Maryam Mirzakhani demonstrate that making absolute statements about male–female differences is less than helpful. However, I believe that to dismiss the research, much of which demonstrates high levels of statistical significance, only serves to reinforce the existing power structures that favour empiricist, linear-thinking white Western males. Consequently, those who prefer to think and learn through networked, holistic, experience-driven, and relational-cooperative patterns are disenfranchised. Statistically, these are more likely to be those from the Majority World and women in general.

In this regard Behera[2] is scathing in her analysis:

> Do Greek and western philosophies find resonance with African and Asian philosophies and contexts, or do these continue to be imposed on the global South without consideration for a two-way exchange of information and ideas? There is an urgent need for a more holistic approach to viewing as well as constructing methodologies for theological education. This must begin with a long overdue acknowledgement from the North that colonialism has left its legacy on theological education in the South. Under the guise of enlightenment and the view to "civilise" indigenous populations, theological education has used the language of the colonisers, [and] its method of instruction has been modelled on European structures of education.

While you may disagree with some of the details, I trust that you will at least agree with the fundamental desire that undergirds this chapter, which is to affirm and advocate for greater diversity in methodology, structure, and requirements as we seek after genuine learning and understanding. Certainly,

---

2. Marina Ngursangzeli Behera, "Inequality in Theological Education Between the North and the South," in *Reflecting On and Equipping for Christian Mission*, ed. Stephen Bevans et al. (Oxford: Regnum, 2015), 125–126.

I believe that the church has become impoverished by limitations imposed on what is possible in the methodology permitted in advanced theological reflection. This book was specifically designed to investigate the possibilities and open up new vistas for the development of theological leadership across the globe.

My Own Story

I am a linear-thinking, white Western male. My undergraduate degree was in applied mathematics, and I continue to think, talk, and teach like a mathematician. This is certainly evident in the book I wrote on theological education,[3] and probably shows through this chapter. The linear and empiricist form of logic that is still perceived as normative in Western education comes naturally to me, and even when I moved from numbers to writing I experienced few struggles in my studies. Although my early writing was boring in the extreme it was logical and systematic and consequently generated high grades. For many years I assumed that a linear-empiricist approach to the world was the only intelligent way to live. If people only took time to think, surely they would be able to articulate a step-by-step logical rationale for decision-making. To do otherwise is a sign of undisciplined thinking, irrationality, and perhaps even laziness.

Two experiences fundamentally changed my perspective. The first was in the early days of the millennium, when I was asked to teach a new course in "study skills" for entering students at a theological college in Beirut. Our college informed me that an essential element of the study skills course should be to train students in writing essays – meaning (of course) writing in a linear-empiricist form of logic. Over my years of training it had been repeatedly emphasized to me that the starting point for quality writing was the establishment of a clear research question which could be addressed meaningfully in the limited space. A good example would be: "What is the connection between Christian unity and Incarnation in the first two chapters of Paul's letter to the Philippians?"

---

3. Shaw, *Transforming Theological Education*.

My more Western-educated students found little difficulty in this exercise, but I also had students from sub-Saharan Africa, some of whom seemed incapable of creating a meaningful research question. However, with gentle probing I discovered it was not inability but reticence and in one case outright opposition. When I finally broke through the intense layers of deference and politeness, one student quietly said, "But it is an insult to the Incarnation to treat this precious teaching in such a narrow way." Rather it seemed that these African students would have preferred to build up a web of ideas over a series of papers in which, in the first paper, they dealt with elements X, in the next, elements Y, and the next, elements Z (see figure 5.1).[4]

Figure 5.1: Web Network Thinking

---

4. A far more nuanced analysis of African rhetorical patterns that would better explain my experience can be found in Stephanie Black, "Scholarship in Our Own Words: Intercultural Rhetoric in Academic Writing and Reporting," in this volume. I suspect that if I had had her article at hand when I taught this study skills class, I would have been in a far better place to guide these African students.

It did not take me long to realize the richness of this approach, and that this approach possibly resonates better than does the linear-empiricist paradigm with how the Scriptures themselves deal with complex issues. But such an approach was deemed unacceptable – as it continues to be deemed unacceptable in most of the global academy.

The second and more profound experience came when I acted as doctoral field supervisor for my wife Karen. Karen is a highly intelligent and insightful woman who thinks through networks rather than in linear-empiricist structures. She was frequently on the verge of giving up on writing her dissertation. My support for her consisted mostly in translating her networked thinking into a linear and "objective" form that would satisfy the white-and-male-dominated environment of higher theological education.

Throughout her studies Karen used mind-maps to think through the networks of ideas. Within these networks were embedded rich and insightful connections. Karen's preferred writing style is narrative and interconnected, but this was not considered scholarly, and she was required to force her findings into a traditional (and far more boring) linear shape:

Introduction
Point 1
- Sub-point A
  - A.1
  - A.2
    - A.2.1
    - A.2.2
    - A.2.3
- Sub-point B
Point 2
- Sub-point A
- Sub-point B
- Sub-point C
- . . . Etc.
Conclusion

To add insult to injury, Karen's thesis revolved around the crucial nature of affectivity in communication, and yet Karen was prohibited from using any affective elements in her writing (exclamatory statements, feelings sentences, or the like) as these were perceived as unsuitable for academic writing. Karen expressed her frustration: "The thesis of my dissertation is that the affective is essential to Christian communication, and finds its source in the character of God. And yet I am required to write the wretched thing in a cold and so-called 'academic' way that clearly implies, 'The affective is unacceptable and even dangerous, and consequently must be marginalized or removed completely.'"

Throughout the process I found myself asking over and over, "Why is the system so restrictive? Why are we impoverishing the church in this way?" Even while I was working with Karen I came to realize the answer: the system has been designed by empiricist, linear-thinking white Western males for empiricist, linear-thinking white Western males, and those who don't fit the system either submit or fail. Sadly, those who succeed in the system who are not linear-thinking white Western males often end up defending the system in which they have finally succeeded.

The global church will be enriched by opening the door to greater diversity in methodology, structure, and requirements as we seek after genuine learning and understanding. There is great potential for new approaches to preparing quality theological leadership, approaches the Majority World church is now well equipped to embrace – if it has the will. The ideas suggested in this book are possible pathways along that journey.

Culture and Learning

Some years back the SVD priest Gary Riebe-Estrella observed:

> Few of us would challenge that in too many of our classrooms the learning/teaching style privileges the values of the Western Enlightenment (a term that contains in itself a value judgment on persons and things non-Western; that is, they are not enlightened) such as the prizing of the individual over the group, individual creativity and initiative over interdependence and collaboration, rational thought over emotional response, writing over orality, the

universal over the particular. In these cases as with the culture of our schools, the classroom structures and procedures that embody these values appear to the dominant group to be both normal and normative. Accommodations are seen as concessions. And rarely does this underlying value system and its historical and cultural contextuality come up for faculty discussion and critique . . . For it is the value system that produced the educational system in which most faculty have been trained and which has shaped their understanding and practice of education. That is, it is the value system that undergirds their self-understood identity. To challenge the worldview is not only to introduce change but to threaten the fundamental stability of the educational enterprise of which faculty see themselves as the center – a challenge that will sometimes be met with some technical, though rarely adaptive, change and which almost always meets with stiff resistance.[5]

Riebe-Estrella's observations point to the unconscious and yet pervasive cultural imperialism that characterizes the academy, and the seeming intransigent resistance to change. And yet in the context of a world in which the Christian centre of gravity is shifting south and east, both acknowledgement of the problem and the embrace of change are becoming imperative.

In another chapter of this volume Evan Hunter[6] asserts persuasively that the development of theological leaders should be a fundamental purpose of advanced theological studies. Certainly the church in every region is desperately in need of men and women who can be leaders in developing theological lenses for engaging with society. However, for theological leadership to be meaningful it needs to be developed and presented in conceptual patterns that resonate with the local culture.[7]

---

5. Gary Riebe-Estrella, "Engaging Borders: Lifting Up Difference and Unmasking Division," *Theological Education* 45, no. 1 (2009): 19–26.
6. Evan Hunter, "A Context Conducive to Innovation," in the present volume.
7. Robert J. Priest, "Christian Theology, Sin, and Anthropology," in *Anthropology and Theology: God, Icons, and God-Talk*, ed. Walter Adams and Frank Salomone (Lanham: University Press of America, 2000), 59–75.

Over the past few decades a growing body of research has given specific meaning to the general understandings that cultural anthropologists have intuited for decades. While the differences are not absolute, and there is wide diversity and individual variation, there are strong, statistically significant differences between the ways in which information is processed by people from different cultural backgrounds. These differences have a profound impact on the ways in which thinking, learning, and communication take place from culture to culture.

One of the most influential and extensive series of studies in this field has been that conducted by Richard Nisbett[8] with colleagues at the University of Michigan, who focused on differences in thinking and learning patterns between East Asians and European Americans. Nisbett's team suggested four areas in which Westerners and Easterners process information differently:

- *Attention and control.* In general, East Asians tend to focus on the overall field, seeing wholes and observing co-variations. Westerners tend to focus on specifics, isolating and analysing the elements as the necessary step towards generalization.

- *Relationships and similarities vs. rules and categories.* East Asian students are more likely to group words and ideas on the basis of some kind of relationship, while European American students are more likely to group words and ideas on the basis of a shared category. These different results are consistent with the communal nature of East Asian society as against the analytical–individualistic character of most Western societies.

- *Experiential knowledge vs. formal logic.* When engaging in deductive reasoning, East Asian students tend to prefer beginning with experiential knowledge based on intuitive understandings emerging from direct perception, reflecting a general understanding of truth and reality as relational and changeable. In contrast, Western students tend to rely on logic and abstract principles, reflecting a general understanding of truth and reality as consistent and logical.

---

8. Richard Nisbett, *The Geography of Thought: How Asians and Westerners Think Differently . . . And Why* (New York: Free Press, 2003); and R. Nisbet et al., "Culture and Systems of Thought: Holistic Versus Analytic Cognition," *Psychological Review* 108, no. 2 (2001): 291–310.

- *Dialectics vs. the law of non-contradiction.* East Asians and European Americans have differing levels of commitment to avoiding apparent contradiction in deductive reasoning. For example, in Western logic, rules such as the following have played a central role:
  - The law of identity: A = A. A thing is identical to itself.
  - The law of non-contradiction: A ≠ not-A. No statement can be both true and false.
  - The law of the excluded middle: any statement is either true or false.

  In contrast, East Asian logic is based on Chinese dialecticism, which embraces principles[9] such as the following:
  - The principle of change: reality is a process that is not static, but rather is dynamic and changeable. A thing need not be identical to itself at all because of the fluid nature of reality.
  - The principle of contradiction: partly because change is constant, contradiction is constant. Old and new, good and bad, exist in the same object or event, and indeed depend on one another for their existence.
  - The principle of relationship or holism: because of constant change and contradiction, nothing either in human life or in nature is isolated and independent, but instead everything is related. It follows that attempting to isolate elements of some larger whole can only be misleading.

In summary, Nisbett's team suggested that Western students tend towards information-processing that is linear, specific, analytic, theoretical, and individualistic-competitive, while East Asian students prefer to think through patterns that are circular, interconnected, holistic, experiential, and communal.

Figure 5.3 is an example of the work done by Nisbett and his team: they asked people in China, Korea, Japan, the United States, and the United Kingdom to state whether the flower at the bottom belongs with group A or group B. The East Asians overwhelmingly chose group A, while the Westerners overwhelmingly chose B. From a closer study of the groups it is evident that a

---

9. Noteworthy also is that Europeans and Americans seek "laws" while East Asians seek "principles" – in itself indicative of fundamentally different understandings of reality.

primary factor in the choice was the East Asian focus on the flower as a whole, in contrast to the Western tendency to focus on the details, in this case the stem of the flower.

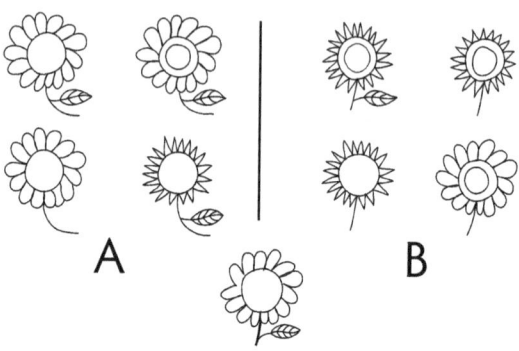

Figure 5.3: Nisbett's Flower Experiment

While the focus of Nisbett was on East Asia, similar intercultural research from elsewhere in the world suggests that the linear-analytical thinking of Greek philosophy and the "Enlightenment," which has so shaped Minority World educational systems, is globally atypical. While the specifics differ, the general pattern of information-processing throughout most of the Majority World tends towards holism and networked thinking, in contrast to the tight specificity so typical in Minority World academia.[10]

A variety of factors have been suggested for why these differences exist, but the most important factor mooted is the extent to which people grow up in independent or interdependent societies. By way of example, an international study of values priorities[11] found that the top three American values were

---

10. See, for example, C. W. Bauman and L. J. Skitka, "Ethnic Group Differences in Lay Philosophies of Behavior in the United States," *Journal of Cross-Cultural Psychology* 37, no. 4 (2006): 438–445; S. Merriam, R. S. Caffarella, and L. M. Baumgartner, *Learning in Adulthood: A Comprehensive Guide* (San Francisco: Jossey-Bass, 2007), 238–239; S. H. Schwartz, "Universals in the Content and Structure of Values: Theoretical Advances and Empirical Tests in 20 Countries," in *Advances in Experimental Social Psychology*, ed. M. Zanna (Orlando: Academic, 1992), 1–65; H. C. Triandis, "The Self and Social Behavior in Differing Cultural Contexts," *Psychological Review* 96 (1989): 506–520; J. Na, I. Choi, and S. Sul, "I Like You Because You Think in the 'Right' Way: Culture and Ideal Thinking," *Social Cognition* 31, no. 3 (2013): 390–404.
11. F. Elashmawi and Philip R. Harris, *Multicultural Management* (Houston: Gulf, 1993), 63.

freedom, independence, and self-reliance; for Japanese it was belonging, group harmony, and collectiveness; and for Arabs it was family security, family harmony, and parental guidance. From my own experience I know first-hand the tribal nature of Arab society. For example, in Arabic there are eight different ways to say "cousin," and when people meet each other for the first time, the standard opening question is, "What family are you from?" Family and community networks are of fundamental importance throughout Asia, Africa, the Middle East, and Latin America. It should not be surprising that children growing up in these highly networked relationships view reality more through interconnected wholes than through individual details.[12]

Nisbett also observed that in early language learning among children in East Asia, parents would typically begin by introducing children to verbs, while in a typical Western family children are first introduced to nouns. Nisbett posits that the relational nature of verbs as against the discrete nature of nouns would likely contribute to an Eastern preference for networked thinking as against a Western preference for discrete ideas and linear-analytic thinking.[13]

Reflecting on the implications of Nisbett's work in dialogue with her own experiences in Latin America, Marlene Enns[14] observed:

> I am learning to recognize the validity of holistic ways of reasoning and starting to realize that:
>
> - It may be just as important to discern the driving forces behind a narrative as it is to discern the rationality of the narrative.[15]

---

12. Hence the significance of Paul Clark's chapter in this collection, "Pathways of Integration for Theological Knowledge: Integrative Knowing/Learning for Thesis Construction in Advanced Theological Studies."
13. Nisbett, *Geography of Thought*, 148–152. Cf. V. Lun, R. Fischer, and C. Ward, "Exploring Cultural Differences in Critical Thinking: Is It About My Thinking Style or the Language I Speak?," *Learning and Individual Differences* 20, no. 6 (2010): 604–616.
14. Marlene Enns, "Theological Education in Light of Cultural Variations of Reasoning: Some Educational Issues," *Common Ground Journal* 3, no. 1 (Fall 2005): 76–87.
15. The significance of narrative for advanced study in the Majority World is investigated in various chapters in this collection: in particular, Stephanie Black's "Scholarship in Our Own Words: Intercultural Rhetoric in Academic Writing and Reporting," Jay Moon's "Chicken Theology: Local Learning Approaches from West Africa," Havilah Dharamraj's "Telling Tales: Stories That Embox Theology," and Dwi Maria Handayani's "Proverbs As Theology."

- Pushing back boundaries in research may happen just as much through weaving together existing topics with a different pattern and the pursuit of missing relationships as through the pursuit of new topics and of missing pieces.
- Inter-disciplinary and "broad" research may be just as necessary as intradisciplinary and "deep" research.[16]
- To point out mystery and complexity without need to come to a resolution – at least not for now – may be just as important as to explain and predict.[17]

Of course, nothing is ever simple, and the whole education system in most countries of the Majority World is a legacy of colonialism. Some years ago I led a faculty training retreat for an influential theological college in East Africa. One of the sessions revolved around culture and learning, and I began by presenting some of Nisbett's research. Nisbett's focus is on East Asian and Western university students, and I was unsure how relevant it was to the African context. And so I asked the faculty whether they related to either the East Asian or the Western patterns of thought described by Nisbett, or whether they have a totally different way of processing information. The answer was unanimously that the East Asian patterns resonated strongly with them. I continued, "The theological education at your school is largely structured and delivered on a Western pattern, and this is also the structure of the whole schooling and university system in your country. Is the educational methodology that you have experienced for years therefore contextually irrelevant?" Smiles all around the table. Finally one of the more articulate black faculty members spoke up: "It is like having schizophrenia. We live in two worlds – one is the world of life with its strong communal networks and its embrace of both/and rather than either/or. And then we enter into this box called school which has no connection to the rest of our lives but which we need to get ahead in life. Yes, we have been influenced by this box, but if we are to speak meaningfully to

---

16. Discussed in depth in Paul Clark's "Pathways of Integration for Theological Knowledge," in this collection.
17. Hence the value and significance of poetry, as seen in Xiaoli Yang's "Poetry As Theology: A Creative Path," and the final poetry anthology, in this collection.

our ministry context we have to leave that box far behind us in the villages and towns where we serve."

Gender and Learning

I recognize that the notion of cognitive difference between men and women is a sensitive issue. Many feminist writers challenge the existence of any significant distinction, concerned that a sharply dichotomous understanding will reinforce gender stereotypes to the detriment of women. Also, the extent to which the differences are due to nature or socialization is still an unresolved issue. I can sympathize with these sentiments having observed the ideological abuse of the data to further entrench the dominant power of white Western males.

However, to ignore the differences can be equally detrimental to women. My desire to delve into this "hornet's nest" is not to promote stereotyping, but rather to advocate for greater respect for diversity in thinking and learning. While there are always exceptions, and the research reflects tendencies rather than absolutes, a sensitization to statistically significant gender differences can empower serious educators to provide appropriate learning contexts for all. I long for the church to benefit from the rich diversity that exists among its best thinkers.

Among the most significant and persuasive research on gender difference has emerged from the growing field of brain research. The average male brain tends to be attuned to specificity in tasks, and prefers to compartmentalize and simplify tasks as much as possible: it is hardwired for understanding and building systems around specific content. In contrast, there is a tendency for the average woman's brain to be geared to see multiple implications and the big picture when completing tasks.[18] A clear implication would seem to be that men more than women would tend towards the study of narrow, focused research questions, while women more than men would be drawn to broad interdisciplinary study.[19]

---

18. M. Ingalhalikar, A. Smith, D. Parker et al., "Sex Differences in the Structural Connectome of the Human Brain," *Proceedings of the National Academy of Sciences of the United States of America* 111, no. 2 (January 2014): 823–828; S. Baron-Cohen, *The Essential Difference: Men, Women and the Extreme Male Brain* (New York: Basic, 2003).

19. See Paul Clark's chapter in this collection, "Pathways of Integration for Theological Knowledge."

In general, women more than men have difficulty understanding the value or meaning of theory without specific, concrete examples, and tend to do best in learning opportunities which involve hands-on, practical experiences from which the theoretical material can be deduced.[20] Stated simply, men tend to prefer to go from theory to practice, while women tend to prefer to go from practice to theory.[21]

Women also have greater interconnectivity between the verbal, reasoning, and emotional parts of the brain, and consequently tend to prefer learning in community by talking through the issues and ideas being presented.[22] In contrast, males tend to prefer processing ideas and issues without having to exercise the language parts of their brains; or, if they use speech in learning, it tends to be through debate and argument over very specific points.[23] When I first encountered this research I was immediately struck by the cold "objectivity" promoted in academic writing, and the common disdain for affective involvement in the practice of scholarship. Is this actually less due to a concern for quality learning, and more due to the difficulty many men experience in making connections between their thinking and their emotions? I wonder if it may be time for the academy to reassess the sociological factors and the epistemological claims which have led to the current virtual monopoly of a socially and emotionally distant, empiricist framework of study.

---

20. M. Philbin et al., "A Survey of Gender and Learning Styles," *Sex Roles* 32, no. 7–8 (1995): 485–494; M. F. Williamson and R. L. Watson, "Learning Styles Research: Understanding How Teaching Should Be Impacted by the Way Learners Learn; Part II: Understanding How Learners Prefer to Receive Information," *Christian Education Journal* Series 3, 3, no. 2 (2006): 343–361.

21. Hence the value of such hands-on approaches as problem-based learning and action research. See John Jusu, "Problem-Based Learning in Advanced Theological Studies," and Caleb Hutcherson with Bassem Melki, "Action Research for Theological Impact: Reflections from an Arab Context," in this collection.

22. See Rafael Zaracho, "Studying Together: Joint and Collaborative Research," in this collection.

23. L. Frings et al., "Gender-Related Differences in Lateralization of Hippocampal Activation and Cognitive Strategy," *NeuroReport* 17, no. 4 (March 2006): 417–421; M. F. Belenky and A.V. Stanton, "Inequality, Development and Connected Knowing," in *Learning As Transformation: Critical Perspectives on a Theory in Progress*, ed. J. Mezirow (San Francisco: Jossey-Bass, 2000), 71–102.

Culture and Gender Imperialism in Advanced Theological Studies

The classic approach to higher level research is linear, specific, analytic, hypothesis-driven, and individualistic-competitive: this is seen in the standard shape expected in higher research theses, almost irrespective of the discipline. The approach is deeply rooted in the West's love affair with the empiricism of the scientific method, an approach that brought great gifts to the development of knowledge in the physical sciences. The scientific method in turn emerged out of the Enlightenment's embrace of Greek analytical patterns of reasoning. Because of the great benefit experienced by Western society through this form of analytical reasoning, particularly during the Industrial Revolution, the scientific method was subsequently applied to all fields of study as the only source of sure knowledge.[24]

The linear, specific, analytic, hypothesis-driven, and individualistic-competitive approach to research is far more likely to suit the thinking processes of empiricist, linear-thinking white Western males than women in general, or than students from interdependent societies.[25] This is not surprising, given that the now internationalized model of advanced master's and doctoral education was developed in the West and in its earliest generations was a virtual "closed shop" for male students only. Up to today the most admired academic institutions in the world are in the West and are dominated by white male faculty and administration. These institutions have enormous influence on the shape of international accreditation, which in turn globally dominates the curricular decisions of higher education. The approach is rarely questioned. In part this is because most white Western males cannot understand how people could learn otherwise: repeatedly I have been asked by colleagues in the West, "Doesn't everyone learn this way?"

Sadly, I have often observed that in the process of satisfying the linear-analytical requirements of the academy, many Majority World and women scholars become increasingly Westernized and male-genderized, and so we lose the great potential gift of alternative thinking patterns they offer – in particular

---

24. T. Ziolkowski, "The Ph.D. Squid," *American Scholar* 59, no. 2 (1990): 177–195.
25. S. P. Ango, "Lessons for Effective Christian Education in Golmo: An African Traditional Approach to Teaching and Learning," *Christian Education Journal* Series 3, 4, no. 1 (2007): 17–33.

a level of holistic multidisciplinary theological reflection desperately needed by a church whose "centre of gravity" is moving increasingly east and south.

The need for holistic wisdom amongst Christian thinkers is imperative in the contemporary world. We should not completely reject Greek-based analytic cognitive reasoning; the theological world has benefited enormously from the model and can continue to do so. However, we need to be aware that it is not the only way to perceive and process information, and that it has inherent limitations. While it is probably inevitable that we will continue to have some who complete traditional empiricist dissertations, the global church must also embrace and even urge engagement in more diversity and breadth in the pursuit of advanced theological study.[26]

The proposals offered in the current collection resonate strongly with many of the issues raised in this chapter. In as much as the global church implements innovative approaches such as these, the result will be a far richer mix of diverse forms of reasoning through which we are able to assess life situations in alternative and possibly more comprehensive ways.

Conclusion: Whose Table?

If the church is to move beyond mere rhetoric about globalizing theological education serious attention needs to be paid to the current dominance of patterns of research that favour empiricist, linear-thinking white Western males. A far broader range of options needs to be made available in terms of both content and methodology. Critiques of the classic dissertation and suggestions for new paths to advanced study are becoming increasingly vocal in the secular academy.[27] Comparable discussions need to be brought to advanced theological studies. Many of the proposals investigated in this book

---

26. Stephanie Black, in her chapter in this collection, "Scholarship in Our Own Words: Intercultural Rhetoric in Academic Writing and Reporting," suggests a middle ground in which Majority World writers develop research that speaks "both to international academia and to their home communities."

27. See, for example, Modern Language Association of America, "Report of the MLA Task Force on Doctoral Study in Modern Language and Literature," Web publication, May 2014, accessed 1 December 2016, https://apps.mla.org/pdf/taskforcedocstudy2014.pdf; Institute for the Public Life of Arts and Ideas, "White Paper on the Future of the PhD in the Humanities," McGill University, December 2013, accessed 1 December 2016, http://iplai.ca/wp-content/uploads/2015/04/white_

are reflective of such a desire to enrich the knowledge and wisdom of the church through multiple doorways.

Some twenty-five years ago Paul Stevens lamented that, despite the rhetoric, in reality "the current practice of globalization tends to work against contextualization. Instead of mutual sharing and mutual learning there is usually wholesale, uncritical importing and exporting of the Western model. In other words, globalization has become the universalization of the Western model with a minimum of contextualization."[28] Evidence points to the future centre of God's work worldwide lying not in the west but in the rapidly growing church of the south and the east. The time has come for the Majority World church to recognize the strength of its holistic and relational educational traditions for the development of quality theological leaders. The main thing preventing significant creative change is the courage to challenge the white Western male dominance of the academy and to affirm the possibility of alternative methods in advanced theological education. Given the growing strength of the church in Asia, Africa, and Latin America, the issue is no longer whether methodological change will take place, but who will step out and do it.

Discussion Questions

1. Have you ever encountered people who have had the sort of difficulties described in the stories of the African students and the author's wife? What was the outcome?

2. The "East–West" research of Nisbett and his team works off a spectrum between Western Greek patterns of thinking and Eastern Confucian ways of understanding. As you read this material, where did you find yourself on the spectrum? Or do you sense that your approach to thinking and learning is quite different from both? Explain.

---

paper_on_the_future_of_the_phd_in_the_humanities_dec_2013_1.pdf; Stacey Patton, "The Dissertation Can No Longer Be Defended," *Chronicle of Higher Education*, 11 February 2013; Cassidy R. Sugimoto, "Toward a Twenty-First Century Dissertation," accessed 1 December 2016, http://cgsnet.org/ckfinder/userfiles/files/1_1%20Sugimoto.pdf.

28. R. P. Stevens, "Marketing the Faith: A Reflection on the Importing and Exporting of Western Theological Education," *Crux* 28 (2 June 1992): 6–18.

3. In what ways do the advanced programs at your school emphasize Western Greek patterns? Eastern Confucian ways? Describe one or two ways in which Nisbett's research might inform your school as to more culturally meaningful approaches to education.

4. One of the key statistical differences between the brain functioning of men and women is the level of interconnectivity between the cognitive and emotional components of the brain, with women in general better able both to understand and to articulate their feelings. To what extent is the affective domain of learning (emotions, attitudes, and motivations) affirmed in your school in terms of both the classroom culture and the nature and shape of written work?

5. Based on some of the material suggested in this chapter, name one or two specific ways in which your school might better welcome diverse learners in your classrooms.

Bibliography

Ango, S. P. "Lessons for Effective Christian Education in Golmo: An African Traditional Approach to Teaching and Learning." *Christian Education Journal* Series 3, 4, no. 1 (2007): 17–33.

Baron-Cohen, S. *The Essential Difference: Men, Women and the Extreme Male Brain*. New York: Basic, 2003.

Bauman, C. W., and L. J. Skitka. "Ethnic Group Differences in Lay Philosophies of Behavior in the United States." *Journal of Cross-Cultural Psychology* 37, no. 4 (2006): 438–445.

Behera, Marina Ngursangzeli. "Inequality in Theological Education Between the North and the South." In *Reflecting On and Equipping for Christian Mission*, edited by Stephen Bevans, Teresa Chai, J. Nelson Jennings, Knud Jørgensen, and Dietrich Werner, 116–128. Oxford: Regnum, 2015.

Belenky, M. F., and A. V. Stanton. "Inequality, Development and Connected Knowing." In *Learning As Transformation: Critical Perspectives on a Theory in Progress*, edited by J. Mezirow, 71–102. San Francisco: Jossey-Bass, 2000.

Elashmawi, F., and Philip R. Harris. *Multicultural Management*. Houston: Gulf, 1993.

Enns, Marlene. "Theological Education in Light of Cultural Variations of Reasoning: Some Educational Issues." *Common Ground Journal* 3, no. 1 (Fall 2005): 76–87.

Frings, L., K. Wagner, J. Unterrainer, J. Spreer, U. Halsband, and A. Schulze-Bonhage. "Gender-Related Differences in Lateralization of Hippocampal Activation and Cognitive Strategy." *NeuroReport* 17, no. 4 (March 2006): 417–421.

Ingalhalikar, M., A. Smith, D. Parker et al. "Sex Differences in the Structural Connectome of the Human Brain." *Proceedings of the National Academy of Sciences of the United States of America* 111, no. 2 (January 2014): 823–828.

Institute for the Public Life of Arts and Ideas. "White Paper on the Future of the PhD in the Humanities." McGill University, December 2013. Accessed 1 December 2016. http://iplai.ca/wp-content/uploads/2015/04/white_paper_on_the_future_of_the_phd_in_the_humanities_dec_2013_1.pdf.

Lun, V., R. Fischer, and C. Ward. "Exploring Cultural Differences in Critical Thinking: Is It About My Thinking Style or the Language I Speak?" *Learning and Individual Differences* 20, no. 6, (2010): 604–616.

Merriam, S., R. S. Caffarella, and L. M. Baumgartner. *Learning in Adulthood: A Comprehensive Guide.* San Francisco: Jossey-Bass, 2007.

Modern Language Association of America. "Report of the MLA Task Force on Doctoral Study in Modern Language and Literature." Web publication, May 2014. Accessed 1 December 2016. https://apps.mla.org/pdf/taskforcedocstudy2014.pdf.

Na, J., I. Choi, and S. Sul. "I Like You Because You Think in the 'Right' Way: Culture and Ideal Thinking." *Social Cognition* 31, no. 3 (2013): 390–404.

Nisbett, Richard. *The Geography of Thought: How Asians and Westerners Think Differently . . . And Why.* New York: Free Press, 2003.

Nisbett, R., I. Choi, K. Peng, and A. Norenzayan. "Culture and Systems of Thought: Holistic Versus Analytic Cognition." *Psychological Review* 108, no. 2 (2001): 291–310.

Patton, Stacey. "The Dissertation Can No Longer Be Defended." *Chronicle of Higher Education*, 11 February 2013.

Philbin, M., E. Meier, S. Huffman, and P. Boverie. "A Survey of Gender and Learning Styles." *Sex Roles* 32, no. 7–8 (1995): 485–494.

Priest, Robert J. "Christian Theology, Sin, and Anthropology." In *Anthropology and Theology: God, Icons, and God-Talk*, edited by Walter Adams and Frank Salomone, 59–75. Lanham: University Press of America, 2000.

Riebe-Estrella, Gary. "Engaging Borders: Lifting Up Difference and Unmasking Division." *Theological Education* 45, no. 1 (2009): 19–26.

Schwartz, S. H. "Universals in the Content and Structure of Values: Theoretical Advances and Empirical Tests in 20 Countries." In *Advances in Experimental Social Psychology*, edited by M. Zanna, 1–65. Orlando: Academic, 1992.

Shaw, Perry. "'New Treasures with the Old': Addressing Culture and Gender Imperialism in Higher Level Theological Education." Chapter 2 in *Tending the Seedbeds: Educational Perspectives on Theological Education in Asia*, edited by Allan Harkness, 47–74. Quezon City: Asia Theological Association, 2010.

———. *Transforming Theological Education: A Practical Handbook for Integrative Learning*. Carlisle: Langham Global Library, 2014.

Stevens, R. P. "Marketing the Faith: A Reflection on the Importing and Exporting of Western Theological Education." *Crux* 28 (2 June 1992): 6–18.

Sugimoto, Cassidy R. "Toward a Twenty-First Century Dissertation." Accessed 1 December 2016. http://cgsnet.org/ckfinder/userfiles/files/1_1%20Sugimoto.pdf.

Triandis, H. C. "The Self and Social Behavior in Differing Cultural Contexts." *Psychological Review* 96 (1989): 506–520.

Williamson, M. F., and R. L. Watson. "Learning Styles Research: Understanding How Teaching Should Be Impacted by the Way Learners Learn; Part II: Understanding How Learners Prefer to Receive Information." *Christian Education Journal* Series 3, 3, no. 2 (2006): 343–361.

Ziolkowski, T. "The Ph.D. Squid." *American Scholar* 59, no. 2 (1990): 177–195.

6

The Imperative of Cultural Integration in Advanced Theological Studies:
Perspectives from the Majority World

Lal Senanayake

Introduction

A few months ago an American professor who visited Sri Lanka as an adjunct professor to teach at Lanka Bible College and Seminary (LBCS) discussed certain assignments completed by higher-level students. He said most of the students had not engaged in independent thinking, reasoning, and assessing, but had copied from each other and from Internet resources. This was not the first such experience I have had in the academic life of our institution. Over the years I have encountered these issues repeatedly, first as the Academic Dean from 2000 and then as the President of a theological education institution from 2007.

While I sympathize with the American professor, I also know that numerous and profound cultural factors impact the way our students engage in their studies. For education to be relevant in contexts such as ours it is not enough simply to import Western patterns. Quality theological education will involve a level of cultural integration between internationally accepted standards and local patterns of learning.

The Ultimate Purpose of Advanced Theological Education (ATE)

Theological education has a significant impact on the church. Therefore, determining the imperatives in advanced theological education (ATE) is vital for the development of both pastors and their congregations. By way of background one needs to understand the ultimate purpose of theological education before understanding the necessity of cultural integration in theological education. Since the purpose determines the program and the content of the program, which in turn serves the purpose, a clear purpose for theological education is critical for the proper training of every pastor or leader. Defining the purpose of theological education is a formidable task. It involves broad and integrative thinking in relation to the needs of a particular given context.

The New Testament provides some basic but profound guidelines for understanding the ultimate purpose of theological education. One of the main themes of New Testament teaching is Christian growth and maturity. Paul advised the Colossian church that teaching must take place with all wisdom, so that we may present everyone fully *mature* in Christ (Col 1:28). Paul said to Timothy – the pastor of the Ephesian church – that the numerous gifts are given to the church, such as apostles, prophets, evangelists, pastors, and teachers, to *equip* the people for the works of service, so that the body of Christ will be *mature* and built up until they reach the unity of faith and knowledge of the Son of God, and become *mature*, attaining to the whole measure of the fullness of Christ (Eph 4:11–13).

Holistic maturation does not take place in a vacuum, but in a cultural context. Advanced theological study, therefore, must be *appropriately* integrated culturally. It must be holistic, because it involves the totality of human personality. It must be culturally integrated because, even within the same culture, people's interests vary significantly. In a context where there are diverse interests and an explosion of knowledge it is difficult to maintain a comprehensive knowledge. Like any other culture, the Majority World culture is complex and faces diverse challenges. Theological education must develop a "coherent worldview" in a given diverse context.[1]

Culture and faith (religion) are intertwined. The reality of faith and religion in a given culture also plays a significant role in human society. The ATE must provide opportunities for developing openness and skills for interfaith interaction to communicate with the wider world and to be more dialogical with people of other faiths, rather than reactive or confrontational. The Majority World still largely believes in religion and spirituality, yet there is an interfaith tension and animosity in many Majority World contexts. These socio-cultural and religious diversities must be considered when designing ATE in the Majority World.

The Nature of Cultural Reality in Higher Theological Education

Having understood the purpose of ATE, we need to look at the nature of cultural reality in the educational field, particularly in the Majority World. The socio-cultural and religious challenges – that is, relevancy of the program to the context – are seldom taken into consideration when introducing higher studies in the Majority World. Oftentimes, higher studies in the Majority World are considered a prestigious achievement and a way of acquiring credentials for securing a job or ministry position at a higher level. A Majority World student who enrols in higher education faces challenges of various kinds, as stated below.

Educational Practices: Majority World vs. Western World

First, the ATE system is largely influenced by the Western system of learning. The Western system of education involves learning skills such as critical thinking, self-directed learning, and higher-order thinking in which the learning is largely dependent on the students, not on the teacher or facilitator. However, in the Majority World, education is mostly top-down, with rote-learning as the favoured methodology. Self-directed learning, therefore, is a challenge. In spite

---

1. Gordon R. Lewis and Bruce A. Demarest, *Integrative Theology* (Grand Rapids: Zondervan, 1987), 21.

of teacher-training seminars and the introduction of new methods of teaching and learning, the old way of teaching – teacher-centred and memory-based education – continues to be the primary education methodology.

The general understanding of education in Sri Lanka is that education equals schooling and schooling equals education. The education has a formal context of the *guru–gola* (teacher–student) relationship. The *guru*, that is, the teacher, is the one who teaches and knows the subject. The responsibility of the *golayas*, the *students*, is studying – basically memorizing what the *guru* has taught. The *guru* has all the knowledge and the *golayas* must receive that knowledge from the *guru*. Pupils must have skills of memorizing and repeating the content which the *guru* gives. This practice is often done without critical reflection on the part of the students. Thus, in the traditional understanding of the *guru–gola* (teacher–student) relationship, the teacher is the authority of knowledge and the students are mere recipients of that knowledge. The basic skill required for education is the ability to memorize and reproduce more or less the same material at final examinations. Comparable patterns are found in much of the Majority World.[2] Therefore, Majority World students struggle to learn in a learner-centred, self-directed learning context. The Majority World learner in general requires a large amount of external motivation, guidance, and instructions from a teacher.

Often students do quite well in their education at the basic and secondary levels of education, which are teacher and syllabus centred. However, when reflective and research assignments are given to students for independent research, most students either copy from others, copy and paste from Internet articles, or directly copy from books without any reflection and critical engagement on the part of the student. The rote-learning culture does not identify such copying as unethical and plagiaristic.

This common pattern, even at the seminary, raises several questions. What is the nature of learning in the Majority World? Why do students struggle to engage their cognitive and metacognitive skills independently when learning? What is causing this problem? What kinds of learning skills are necessary

---

2. See, for example, Ramesh C. Mishra, "Education of Tribal Children in India," in *Educational Theories and Practices from the Majority World*, ed. Pierre R. Dasen and Abdeljalil Akkari (New Delhi: Sage, 2008), 145–167; Marlene Asselin and Ray Doiron, *Linking Literacy and Libraries in Global Communities* (New York: Routledge, 2013), 20.

for learning at higher levels of education? The concern of this chapter is to understand the role of ATE and to see what challenges are present when implementing such a program in the Majority World.

Impact of Socio-Cultural Background on Education

Educational program planning is not culturally, politically, or socially neutral. This process is replete with various socio-political and cultural values. These values implicitly or explicitly affect curriculum theory and design. Little's team, in their research on education in Sri Lanka,[3] wrote extensively on the complex interactions between politics, policy formulation, culture, and the challenges of implementing change. The learner constructs knowledge based upon his or her background knowledge, cultural frames of reference, experience, instructional influences in the culture, and so on.

The Socio-Cultural Understanding of Education

The customs and cultural practices of a society influence every individual of that particular society. If a certain individual is not educated or influenced according to the customs of that society, he or she will not be able to live harmoniously with others in that society. Therefore, Durkheim has defined education like this: "in order that there be education, there must be a generation of adults and one of youth, in interaction, and an influence exercised by the first on the second."[4] This dialectic definition sees a primary connection between two common elements – the past and the present. According to Durkheim, in order for education to take place there must be a generation of adults and another of youth. Education takes place through the influence exercised by the adults upon the youth.[5] This refers to the various ways in which society transmits knowledge across generations, including factual information and occupational skills, as well as cultural norms and values.[6] Central to the socialization process,

---

3. Angela W. Little, ed., *Primary Education Reform in Sri Lanka* (Colombo: National Education Commission, 2000). Available online at http://angelawlittle.net/wp-content/uploads/2012/07/PrimaryEdReformSriLankaFull.pdf.
4. Emile Durkheim, *Education and Sociology* (New York: Free Press, 1956), 67.
5. Durkheim, *Education and Sociology*, 67.
6. John J. Macionis, *Sociology*, 4th ed. (Englewood Cliffs: Prentice Hall, 1993), 439.

schooling serves as one cultural lifeline linking the generations.[7] Thus, there is hope for advanced theological education, because when rightly implemented it has potential for influencing the formation of a nation.

In this process of influence, the chief end of education should be to form the mental states of the individual as well as the capacity for the individual to live as a social being in harmony with collective traditions and the social and religious customs of the society. Therefore, it is essential to understand the nature of the society and the social construction of the existing reality. Since there are diverse understandings of the function of society in connection to education, this chapter seeks to examine the effect of social forces upon the implementation of advanced studies in the field of theology in Majority World contexts.

Cultural Dichotomy: High-Context vs. Low-Context Culture

Among the most significant challenges that face advanced theological education in the Majority World is the fundamental difference in communication patterns between Minority and Majority World cultures. Put simply, the Western advanced theological education system is designed in a low-context (LC) culture. This same system has then been implemented in a high-context (HC) culture. These cultural differences are illustrated below.

Edward T. Hall has elaborated on the role of "context" in meaning-making. As he pointed out, in every culture there is a "highly selective screen" between humans and the outside world. The human culture, therefore, will decide "what we pay attention to and what we ignore."[8] This "screening function" is helpful to protect the human "nervous system" from "information overload." The "context" plays an important role in the field of communication and one of the functions is handling information overload.[9] When someone relates to the outside world or outside information, the person's "selective screen" functions according to his or her preference in the "high–low-context continuum." As

---

7. Macionis, *Sociology*, 444.
8. Edward T. Hall, *Beyond Culture* (New York: Anchor, 1976), 85.
9. Hall, *Beyond Culture*, 86.

this person moves from low to the high side of the scale, awareness of the "selective process" increases. Therefore, "what one pays attention to, context, and information overload are all functionally related."[10] With reference to language and meaning translation, Hall said that the problem does not lie in the "linguistic code" but in the "context, which carries varying proportions of the meaning."[11] Therefore, the linguistic code is incomplete without the context, because the code contains only part of the meaning.

Accordingly, there are high-context (HC) cultures and low-context (LC) cultures. For example, Asian, African, and Middle Eastern cultures are generally known as high-context, and Western and European cultures are known as low-context (LC). How do we identify the distinction between the two? Hall said, "A high-context (HC) communication or message is one in which most of the information is either in the physical context or internalized in the person, while very little is in the code, explicit, transmitted part of the message. A low-context (LC) communication is just the opposite; i.e., the mass of information is vested in the explicit code."[12] Thus, high-context communication is generally indirect, with emphasis on nonverbal messages. Low-context communication, on the other hand, is direct – either spoken or written. The idea being discussed is more important than the feelings behind the statement.

Moreover, according to Hall, those from a high-context culture generally pay more attention to the physical world around them. Communication is connected to the surroundings of the environment (background), tone of voice, facial expressions, body language, colour, smell, and so on. High-context language may be very flowery and elaborate (as in South Asia and the Middle East) or succinct and understated (as in China, Japan, and Korea).[13] Even the minute details of real life communicate important information. The low-context culture, on the other hand, pays more attention to concepts, principles, facts, and ideas in communication, not so much to the physical setting – context or the tone of voice. Precise expression with verbal meaning is more

---

10. Hall, 86
11. Hall, 86.
12. Hall, 91.
13. Anne Marie Francesco and Barry Allen Gold, *International Organizational Behavior* (Upper Saddle River: Prentice Hall, 1998), 60.

important than the context of the communication. The low-context culture is more concerned about the big idea of the conversation. The conflicting nature of communication between high-context and low-context culture is further illustrated in the table.

Table 6.1 Conflict in LCC and HCC Cultures[14]

	Low-Context Communication	**High-Context Communication**
Causes of conflict	Instrumental in nature	Expressive in nature
Conflict and expectations	Individual expectations of the situation are being violated	Collective or cultural expectations of the situation are being violated
Stance and strategy	Open, confrontational, and direct	Ambiguous, non-confrontational, and indirect
Conflict management	Factual-inductive, axiomatic-deductive, or lineal-logical	Affective-intuitive, synthetic, or point-logical
Issue and person	Dichotomy between conflict and conflict parties	Integration of conflict and conflict parties
Goal	Action- and solution-oriented	"Face-" and relationship-oriented
Communication codes	Explicit	Implicit
Strategies	Open and direct	

One example of a communication barrier between LC and HC is observed in the process of research and assessment. A common tool used in the West is the Likert Scale. Likert Scale marking works in a direct communication system such as low-context. However, in a high-context culture, those surveyed will struggle to score appropriately, or they will respond according to what might be the response expected by the teacher. Therefore, such research and assessment is successful when done within a conversational context within the teacher–student relationship.

Advanced theological education, which is mostly influenced by the Western–European system, must consider the above socio-cultural communication barriers. In an educational setting in much of the Majority

---

14. Summarized from Stella Ting-Toomey, "Towards a Theory of Conflict and Culture" (paper presented at the 68th Annual Meeting of the Speech Communication Association, Louisville KY, 4–7 November 1982).

World, "one must decide how much time to invest in contexting" the other person in order to make communication effective.[15] In high-context cultures, "actions are by definition rooted in the past, slow to change, and highly stable."[16]

Religious Background

Religious background poses multiple challenges. The religious background of the students enrolling for the program is one challenge advanced theological education will face in the Majority World. The number of students coming into the Christian faith from other faiths is increasing, and many of these come into higher education without adequate biblical or theological understanding. Their church life and ministry experience may be minimal. Traditionally, advanced theological studies have been compartmentalized, with students focusing on a particular field of study – Old Testament, New Testament, theology, history, Bible, missions, and so on. Specializing in a particular discipline without overall understanding of other fields could lead to a skewed understanding of the Christian worldview. The advanced studies must be integrated and interdisciplinary.

The other challenge that advanced theological education must address within a multi-religious culture is interfaith dialogue. Often in the Majority World the relationship between Christians and people of other faiths is more antagonistic than dialogical. Most of the Majority World church leaders lack skills training and opportunities for receiving such training in a pluralistic society. Therefore, in most cases, the Christian approach to missions has been unwise and threatening.

Unprecedented Innovation of Theological Institutions

Innovation is difficult in the social learning culture of Majority World countries such as Sri Lanka. In the field of advanced theological education, however, innovation is vital. The proper development of Christian academia with required standards and socially accepted educational norms has been impeded

---

15. Hall, *Beyond Culture*, 92.
16. Hall, 93.

by the *unprecedented* development[17] of theological educational institutions. Unaccredited higher education is a common factor in social learning cultures such as ours. Therefore, much of Majority World higher education is in crisis.

Moreover, there is unprecedented awarding of doctoral degrees by certain organizations to leaders who have no recognized formal training of any kind.[18] The purpose of education, in general, is not to develop knowledge, skills, and attitudes – that is, holistic formation – but the mere accumulation of certificates or credentials for social position and prestige. This situation is the cause of several areas of concern within the Christian community.

First, while many leaders justify the validity of these free diplomas, the hard-earned accredited diplomas are equally positioned, at the same level. The holder of a hard-earned degree is undervalued and underused by the Christian community. Therefore, there is no motivation for doing hard work for disciplined advanced studies.

Second, Christian advanced studies have become a mockery within the educated community. In the Majority World context, when recruiting for work, the important requirement is credentials or certificates, not so much the formation of the individual in the areas of knowledge, skills, or attitudes that the applicant must have for a given task. Ironically, the knowledge, skills, and attitudes are measured through the certificates of the applicant.

Third, leaders are engaging in ministry without adequate training. Many of these leaders have false confidence and false security about their competency for their lives and ministries. They lack holistic formation. They are theologically, socially, emotionally, spiritually, and intellectually immature for carrying out

---

17. What is meant by the *unprecedented* development of theological institutions is that there are many training institutions mushrooming around the country mainly as a result of the culture of social learning prevailing in Sri Lanka. These institutions are not accredited, nor run by leaders with adequate formal training. The primary mode of learning in the country has been *social learning* – emulating one another. This is the social reality in the country. For example, when one person in the village or town buys a three-wheeler taxi for hiring purposes, another hundred or more will follow the same practice. The same reality can be seen in any other industry, including ministry. In most Majority World settings there has been minimal development in creative or innovative skills, and very limited creative self-direction in learning.

18. The statement does not imply that a formal setting is essential for education to take place. Nevertheless, in the Majority World culture, recognized education takes place in a formal setting – schooling. The prestige of the school where learning is taking place also matters for recognition of education in the Majority World.

their duties in the field. This in turn has created a distorted view of Christian faith among people of other faiths. Christian faith is considered to be a mere blind faith, not requiring the use of wisdom and intelligence. The general understanding, ironically, is that there is no reasoning behind Christian faith; hence Christianity has no academic value.

Work in the mission field is hampered because of the illegitimate approach to missions by untrained leaders, or rather, trained ones at unaccredited theological institutions. These men and women enter the mission field with a false sense of security and a false identity regarding their qualification for such a task. This scenario makes Christian faith a mockery among the general public, and they develop an antagonistic attitude towards Christianity. Mission and evangelistic work is largely focused on the poor and the needy because the church is incapable of dialoguing with the educated community. Therefore, the church is accused of taking advantage of people's vulnerability and poverty to convert them to Christianity. Christian preaching and teaching in many churches doesn't make sense. It is basically characterized by incoherence or irrelevance to both the biblical context and the social context. Since our culture is more oriented towards social learning, many leaders imitate the celebrity preachers and prosperity gospel preachers on television or the Internet and follow their teachings without engaging in critical reflection to understand the integrity of such teachings. Consequently, the church has no program for carrying out a meaningful dialogue with the prevailing situation of the context.

Cultural Integration in Education in the Majority World

When designing an advanced study program for the Majority World, the importance of taking a "transcultural perspective on education" cannot be overstated, because "education is a cultural process and occurs in a social context."[19] Understanding will consequently entail the intentional study and

---

19. George D. Spindler, *Education and Cultural Process: Anthropological Approaches* (Long Grove: Waveland, 1997), 272.

understanding of local cultural realities.[20] Since cultures are diverse, and each culture has its own preference and methodology of learning, it is impossible to discuss every method each culture is using or must use for the purpose of education and cultural transmission in a short paper like this. However, in this section we will discuss some basic methods that are common in the Majority World, and what methods might consequently be relevant for learning. The reader is encouraged to explore his or her own cultural context in order to understand how students study in their own context and, accordingly, which relevant methods should be implemented.

Understanding the Cultural Context

The starting point for cultural integration is to understand how "cultural transmission" is taking place within a given community.[21] Judith Lingenfelter and Sherwood Lingenfelter observed that "every training and educational situation has a cultural context of teaching and learning."[22] Steps must be taken to "clarify and value the cultural distinctives" of students.[23] Meaningful advanced theological studies will be relevant to the cultural context. Unlike many Western educational contexts, where a student is learning to "acquire knowledge" which allows him or her to "function independently" and to be a "productive member of society," in Majority World contexts such as Sri Lanka a person must "study culture in the form of poetry, art and music, social ritual, history, political theory, and ecological concerns" in order to be a full member of that society.[24]

---

20. Timothy Reagan's *Critical Questions, Critical Perspectives: Language and the Second Language Educator* (Charlotte: Information Age, 2005) and Sharan B. Merriam, Rosemary S. Caffarella, and Lisa M. Baumgartner's *Learning in Adulthood: A Comprehensive Guide*, 3rd ed. (San Francisco: Jossey-Bass, 2007) have given a rather academic and theoretical description on the topic of "Non-Western" practices and perspectives on education and learning.
21. Spindler, *Education and Cultural Process*, 272–308.
22. Judith E. Lingenfelter and Sherwood G. Lingenfelter, *Teaching Cross-Culturally: An Incarnational Model for Learning and Teaching* (Grand Rapids: Baker Academic, 2003), 17.
23. Lingenfelter and Lingenfelter, *Teaching Cross-Culturally*.
24. Merriam et al., *Learning in Adulthood*, 174.

The Centrality of Social Learning

Most Majority World cultures are characterized by social learning – that is, learning from experience, imitation, modelling others, and observation.[25] Advanced theological educational programs which are more characterized by low-context communication methods may encounter implementational challenges in high-context cultures. Therefore, theological education must connect not only to the social context, but also to social learning experiences when introducing a Western-oriented education system.

In doing so, students must not only be encouraged to study their theology for the sake of serving people of their community, but they must also learn to study with the community, the goal being that graduates work not only for the community but also with the community. This means strengthening the harmony and dialogue with the community in the design of advanced theological education.

Local Ideologies and Critical Thinking

Another factor that must be considered is that in many Majority World cultures both the church and the society are driven by dominant local ideologies. Certain prevailing ideas, inherited from prominent figures such as community leaders or pastors, have a significant influence on the younger generation of that community or denomination. These dominant ideologies play a powerful role in decision-making processes and authority structures in the society or church. In order to combat such ideologies, critical thinking must be introduced into the system of higher theological education.

As stated earlier in this chapter, the most practised method of learning at any level in Sri Lanka is a top-down model of rote-learning. While advanced students may do some level of independent research from Internet and library resources to gather additional information, higher-order thinking and critical inquiry is rarely used. Attending lectures and classes is seen as one of the primary ways of knowing and gathering information on a given subject. The levels of learning are, according to Bloom's taxonomy, predominantly the three lowest levels of remembering, understanding, and applying.

---

25. See Perry Shaw's chapter on "Culture, Gender, and Diversity in Advanced Theological Studies" in this collection.

The development of critical thinking skills helps address socio-cultural ideological forces critically in order to explore a more productive approach to life.[26] For example, many leaders believe that theological education and training is a waste of time and money, because the Holy Spirit will teach them. This idea has contributed to weakness and immaturity in the church. Carefully designing educational objectives with a proper understanding of students' cognitive and metacognitive processes will help develop higher-order thinking and critical inquiry.[27]

One cannot leave meaning to be constructed on the basis of socio-cultural values and dominant ideologies alone. Truth is above culture or society. Every human being has the right to know truth regardless of his or her cultural background. Critical thinking helps in this process by judging the "reasonableness" or "soundness" (logical validity) and "truthfulness" (accuracy) of statements (beliefs, assumptions, theories, and opinions) through careful reflection and analysis. Critical thinking does not take truth for granted, but involves accepting and believing something only after judging the reasonableness of the issue.[28] There are certain absolute principles and claims of Christianity which are worth practising universally.[29] Truth claims are universal; therefore, it is important to know and obey them, simply because being wrong has consequences in life. As Christian apologist Ravi Zacharias puts it, "The fact is, the truth matters – especially when you're on the receiving

---

26. Stephen Brookfield's work *The Power of Critical Theory for Adult Learning and Teaching* (Maidenhead: Open University, 2005) gives a broader understanding of the necessity for critical thinking in adult learning in order to develop a society that constructs meaning with relevance to a given context.

27. Paulo Freire's *Education for Critical Consciousness* (New York: Crossroad, 1974); Stephen Brookfield and John Holst's *Radicalizing Learning: Adult Education for a Just World* (San Francisco: Jossey-Bass, 2010); Barry Beyer's *Critical Thinking* (Arlington: Phi Delta Kappa, 1995); John E. McPeck's *Critical Thinking and Education* (Basingstoke: Palgrave Macmillan, 1981); and others have pointed out the importance of learning skills in the field of education. Mary C. English and Anastasia Kitsantas, in their article "Supporting Student Self-Regulated Learning in Problem- and Project-Based Learning," *Interdisciplinary Journal of Problem-Based Leaning* 7, no. 2 (2013): 128–150, identified deeply ingrained "habits" students have developed through their familiar classroom experience, in which they have been "passive recipients of knowledge," and recommended that students make a shift to rather be active learners through the development of self-regulated learning (SRL).

28. Beyer, *Critical Thinking*; McPeck, *Critical Thinking and Education*.

29. Ravi Zacharias, *Among Other Gods: The Absolute Claims of the Christian Message* (Nashville: Thomas Nelson, 2000).

end of a lie."[30] And nowhere is this more important than in the area of faith and religion.

Developing Platforms for Interfaith Dialogue

Jesus said, "you will know the truth, and the truth will set you free" (John 8:32, TNIV). Because truth matters, advanced theological education programs must consider developing solid platforms for interfaith dialogue which is non-threatening to people of other faiths. Since truth stands above culture, this truth must be carefully developed, with relevance to the existing culture, and hence non-threatening, while being uncompromising on truth. Given the pluralistic and conflicting nature of society and religions, implementation of advanced studies on Christian apologetics and interfaith dialogue is a crucial need in much of the Majority World. Asking the right questions and providing a reasonable response to the questions people may ask are essentials for maintaining a meaningful dialogue with communities of other faiths. As the apostle Peter said, "But in your hearts revere Christ as Lord. Always be prepared to give an answer to everyone who asks you to give the reason for the hope that you have. But do this with gentleness and respect" (1 Pet 3:15).

Holistic and Informal Learning

In much of the Majority World "knowledge is conceived of more broadly than that which is based on scientific method and studied in formal setting."[31] Though there is a place for formal learning in the classroom setting, reliable learning and instruction can take place in any situation that is considered to be "holistic and informal" in nature.[32] Moreover, in many Majority World cultures, people need to use their whole being – body, mind, and spirit – in order for learning to be considered valid and complete.[33]

In such contexts learning and instructional methods ought to take place in multiple ways. In a holistic learning context, there are "diverse learning styles," which require "multiple opportunities" for learning – even at higher

---

30. Zacharias, *Among Other Gods*, 55.
31. Merriam et al., *Learning in Adulthood*, 179.
32. Merriam, 181.
33. Merriam, 182.

levels. While formal learning experiences (such as lectures and formal class discussion) are appreciated and valued in much of the Majority World, formal assignments must be connected to reading and other activities such as listening, watching, experiencing, exploring, reflecting, and doing.

In addition to presenting "multiple opportunities" for learning, there also needs to be opportunity for "multiple modes of expression" whereby students are "given multiple ways to express their comprehension and mastery" of a given topic. Students' projects should be able to be presented not only in a format of formal academic writing, but also in "alternative formats" such as "oral presentations, videos, newspaper articles, photo essays, radio documentaries, community research, and web publications."[34] The availability of instructional technology enables various ways of communication through which a learner can demonstrate his or her knowledge and skills.

Another factor that needs consideration, based on the nature of learning in such Majority World contexts, is the need to provide "multiple opportunities for engagement."[35] Students must be given opportunities to be active learners. These multiple opportunities may include aspects such as allowing students to redo their work. Very few students will be able to achieve an expected learning outcome at the very first attempt at the task. The more time we give to the task, the better equipped the students will be when the situation arises somewhere else and they are asked to apply the initial learning in a new situation. Multiple opportunities will also include doing the activities in formal and non-formal settings; creative ways of expressing ideas according to the individual student's learning style; providing quick and informative feedback on their performance; and helping them to make their learning experience and presentations relevant to their ministry and meaningful to society.

Conclusion

Advanced theological education in the Majority World presents opportunities and challenges. The challenges are often rooted in the socio-cultural realities

---

34. Colorado State University, "What Is Universal Design for Learning?," http://accessproject.colostate.edu/udl/documents/what_is_udl.pdf.
35. Colorado State University, "What Is Universal Design for Learning?"

of a particular society. Identifying these challenges and carefully navigating through them will open up opportunities for effective and fruitful educational experience at higher levels of study.

Discussion Questions

1. To what extent do teachers and students in your context reflect the *guru–gola* – teacher–student – relationship described in this chapter? How might this be a particular challenge for the development of contextually significant advanced theological education?

2. Taking into account the general description of high-context versus low-context communication, briefly consider each of the following: (a) your own personal patterns of communication; (b) the general pattern of communication of your students; (c) the communication norms in the communities your graduates serve. How do you see HCC/LCC at work? Name one or two challenges that emerge from diverse communication patterns.

3. What is the nature of religious diversity in your context? How have you sought to address this diversity? Suggest at least one possible way in which your school could better address religious diversity through its programs of advanced theological studies.

4. Choose one of the areas of cultural integration suggested in the final section of the chapter. Describe one or two ways in which your school could better embrace cultural integration in this particular area.

Bibliography

Asselin, Marlene, and Ray Doiron. *Linking Literacy and Libraries in Global Communities*. New York: Routledge, 2013.
Beyer, Barry. *Critical Thinking*. Arlington: Phi Delta Kappa, 1995.
Brookfield, Stephen. *The Power of Critical Theory for Adult Learning and Teaching*. Maidenhead: Open University, 2005.
Brookfield, Stephen, and John Holst. *Radicalizing Learning: Adult Education for a Just World*. San Francisco: Jossey-Bass, 2010.

Colorado State University. "What Is Universal Design for Learning?" http://accessproject.colostate.edu/udl/documents/what_is_udl.pdf. Accessed 15 March 2017.

Durkheim, Emile. *Education and Sociology*. New York: Free Press, 1956.

English, Mary C., and Anastasia Kitsantas. "Supporting Student Self-Regulated Learning in Problem- and Project-Based Learning." *Interdisciplinary Journal of Problem Based-Learning* 7, no. 2 (2013): 128–150.

Francesco, Anne Marie, and Barry Allen Gold. *International Organizational Behavior*. Upper Saddle River: Prentice Hall, 1998.

Freire, Paulo. *Education for Critical Consciousness*. New York: Crossroad, 1974.

Hall, Edward T. *Beyond Culture*. New York: Anchor, 1976.

Lewis, Gordon R., and Bruce A. Demarest. *Integrative Theology*. Grand Rapids: Zondervan, 1987.

Lingenfelter, Judith E., and Sherwood G. Lingenfelter. *Teaching Cross-Culturally: An Incarnational Model for Learning and Teaching*. Grand Rapids: Baker Academic, 2003.

Little, Angela W., ed. *Primary Education Reform in Sri Lanka*. Colombo: National Education Commission, 2000. Available at http://angelawlittle.net/wp-content/uploads/2012/07/PrimaryEdReformSriLankaFull.pdf.

Macionis, John J. *Sociology*. 4th ed. Englewood Cliffs: Prentice Hall, 1993.

McPeck, John E. *Critical Thinking and Education*. Basingstoke: Palgrave Macmillan, 1981.

Merriam, Sharan B., Rosemary S. Caffarella, and Lisa M. Baumgartner. *Learning in Adulthood: A Comprehensive Guide*. 3rd ed. San Francisco: Jossey-Bass, 2007.

Mishra, Ramesh C. "Education of Tribal Children in India." In *Educational Theories and Practices from the Majority World*, edited by Pierre R. Dasen and Abdeljalil Akkari, 145–167. New Delhi: Sage, 2008.

Reagan, Timothy. *Critical Questions, Critical Perspectives: Language and the Second Language Educator*. Charlotte: Information Age, 2005.

Spindler, George D. *Education and Cultural Process: Anthropological Approaches*. Long Grove: Waveland, 1997.

Ting-Toomey, Stella. "Towards a Theory of Conflict and Culture." Paper presented at the 68th Annual Meeting of the Speech Communication Association, Louisville, KY, 4–7 November 1982.

Zacharias, Ravi. *Among Other Gods: The Absolute Claims of the Christian Message*. Nashville: Thomas Nelson, 2000.

7

Scholarship in Our Own Words:
Intercultural Rhetoric in Academic Writing and Reporting

Stephanie L. Black

Who Shapes the Message?

After teaching biblical studies in Africa and India for a decade and marking reams of student papers by scribbling the same corrections in the margins over and over, it finally occurred to me that what I considered mistakes in the students' writing, especially the ways they organize and present information in their papers and their forms of argumentation, are in fact specific cultural patterns that leave an imprint on their English writing. I had just finished a year-long series of Greek exegesis courses with a handful of quite able postgraduate theology students in Kenya. We completed the syllabus with a few class sessions to spare, so I used the time to work with them on how to evaluate biblical commentaries. We took paragraphs from published works and analysed authors' claims, identifying premises and inferences, and we wrote scholarly responses to conclusions we agreed or disagreed with. My students did good work in these exercises. "Aha!" I thought; "Now they've got it! I'll see these skills show up in their final papers." But no. Those very able students submitted papers with the same "problems" in the flow of information and the ways they supported their ideas that I had seen so many times over the years. It was only at that point that I realized it wasn't that they *couldn't* write the way I told them to; it was that, perhaps unconsciously, they didn't *want* to.

Curious to understand this more deeply I searched the Internet, not sure what key words or topic I was looking for. Eventually, in online conversations among ESL instructors in higher education I came across studies in *contrastive rhetoric* examining how patterns of communication from home cultures affect international students at English-speaking universities. Under the influence of Ulla Connor, this is now more often referred to as *intercultural rhetoric*.[1] From those sources I was led to Canagarajah's *The Geopolitics of Academic Writing*, something of a manifesto against Western hegemony in academic publishing.[2] As I considered all this I knew I didn't want to force my Majority World biblical studies students to become culturally Western writers of English, even though without realizing it that was what I had been trying to do. I want them to be able to write in English so that a wide audience can welcome their work. But I also want them to be free to write in words and thought patterns that clearly convey their own sense of discovery and their own significant contributions to share with the world. Since that "eureka" moment I have been exploring how to help Majority World research students become more conscious both of Western conventions of academic writing and of the ways similar communication works in their own communities, so that they can choose which practices they prefer any project to reflect.

In 2010 I began working on this quest with a cohort of PhD students from seven African countries at the Nairobi Evangelical Graduate School of Theology (NEGST), now part of Africa International University.[3] Drawing from what Kaplan calls the "five terrible questions" to be negotiated in

---

1. Ulla Connor, *Intercultural Rhetoric in the Writing Classroom* (Ann Arbor, MI: University of Michigan, 2011).
2. A. Suresh Canagarajah, *A Geopolitics of Academic Writing* (Pittsburgh: University of Pittsburgh, 2002).
3. I am deeply indebted to this cohort of PhD students for their insights and for material shared in this chapter. In a very real sense they are co-creators of this work. While about a dozen students and colleagues participated in the original classroom discussions, for reasons of convenience I draw primarily from three unpublished reflection papers (lightly edited here) submitted by the following student groups: Peninnah Kivunzi, Melles Berhane, George Mutuku; Dagalou Teme, Nathan Ndyamiyemenshi, Bernard C. Sande; Victor Lonu, Peter Kamande, George Ogalo.

intercultural rhetoric, I asked the students to consider with me how knowledge is communicated in their home contexts:

1. What may be discussed?
2. Who has the authority to speak/write?
3. What form(s) may the writing take?
4. What is evidence?
5. What arrangement of evidence is likely to appeal (be convincing) to readers?[4]

The goal was to explore potential ways to produce academic writing that is both scholarly and truly African, in spite of the fact that within Africa's primarily oral communities there are few models of culturally authentic academic writing we can turn to. (I should add that Africa is in fact too broad and diverse a region to treat as one entity. In this chapter I refer to the sum of experiences of these students from multiple nationalities and language groups as "African," but in reality this collective term obscures abundant diversity.)

One of the most enlightening things we did as a group was to have each student imagine a short episode of oral "persuasive expert rhetoric" in his or her own village or community. From a sociolinguistic perspective, what might a traditional oral language situation with similarities to academic writing look like? Most of the students chose the form of a village meeting in which a chief allows a young person who has participated in a training event elsewhere to share that information with the community. Two students chose the situation of a father speaking to his adult children. I told the students they could draft these episodes in their mother tongues and that their submissions could be oral if they preferred, but all the students felt comfortable submitting their episodes in written English.

Then we analysed the examples, looking for features reflecting Kaplan's questions. The students' written creations included engaging stories, clever proverbs, and African ways of showing appreciation for elders, along with less explicit, more involve-the-listener ways of communicating.[5] As we shared and

---

4. Robert B. Kaplan, "Foreword," in *Contrastive Rhetoric Revisited and Redefined*, ed. Clayann Gilliam Panetta (New York: Routledge, 2008), ix.

5. For further explorations in orality and transmission of knowledge, see Jay Moon, "Chicken Theology: Local Learning Approaches from West Africa," in this volume.

discussed the essays students said things like "this feels so comfortable" and "this is us." They were intrigued to start putting descriptive labels on their own styles of communication. (One said, "I didn't even know we had a style.") As one group wrote in a subsequent reflection paper, "Almost all of us realized that we were more at home in that exercise."[6]

The students were graciously open to these new ideas. In their written reflection one group commented: "With us is a guest and as one of the Kamba proverbs says: 'a guest brings the best tobacco' meaning *guests bring with them new things that are better and useful.* It is time to lay aside our tobacco and enjoy our guest's. This guest's tobacco is literacy, academic writing, and reading culture; while our old tobacco is illiteracy, oral tradition, and ignorance of knowledge preservation through writing."[7] (I was pleased that these PhD students, accomplished and articulate in standard academic English, felt free to play with indigenous forms in their final papers for this project!) At the same time, as research students they were aware that exchanging accepted conventions of academic writing for more culturally familiar modes of expression might put their future academic careers at risk. Canagarajah observes that Majority World scholars who choose to communicate in their own ways and from the standpoint of their own orientations to knowledge are unlikely to see their papers published in the international journals that influence their fields.[8] Quoting the African proverb "When two elephants fight, it is the grass that suffers," one student group advised: "In this case we, future African writers, are the grass. Our fathers and grandfathers who live in their huts and who do not think of needing to hold pens and papers, are not worried about which writing style to adopt. On the other hand, it is safe to affirm that the western world in whose system we are already immersed, is

---

6. Dagalou Teme, Nathan Ndyamiyemenshi, and Bernard C. Sande, "African Voice and Approach to Academic Writing" (unpublished paper, Nairobi Evangelical Graduate School of Theology [Africa International University], 2010), 6.

7. Peninnah Kivunzi, Melles Berhane, and George Mutuku, "A Reflection on African Voice in Academic Writing" (unpublished paper, Nairobi Evangelical Graduate School of Theology [Africa International University], 2010), 1.

8. Canagarajah, *Geopolitics*, 84.

not ready to come down to the African oral arena overnight, unless they see the indisputable worth thereof."[9]

Acknowledging that explorations in intercultural rhetoric in academic writing represent both opportunity and risk for emerging scholars in the Majority World, what follows are some of the observations we made and the students' suggestions, along with input from wider research in intercultural rhetoric.

Explorations in Intercultural Rhetoric

What May Be Discussed?

I remember my own search for a PhD topic. As an American in a British university I waded through existing research to stake out some small space, however abstract or obscure, that had not yet been mapped, so that I could demonstrate my own competence. However, in Africa and elsewhere in the Majority World, abstract knowledge is generally less valued than "situated" knowledge which benefits the local community.[10] While Western academicians may be applauded for work on theory, or for pursuing seemingly obscure areas of study or minute sub-specializations, these African students in biblical studies felt it important that their research topics be "focused on solving current problems in our respective communities."[11] As one group put it, "The Western contribution of new knowledge is anchored in the centres of research and writing. In Africa, the original contribution to the academy is not anchored in libraries, but on the community's needs and experiences."[12]

In addition, in contrast to a Western ideal of untethered academia pushing the boundaries of discovery while society struggles to keep up, students

---

9. Teme, Ndyamiyemenshi, and Sande, "African Voice," 4.
10. Samson Nashon, David Anderson, and Handel Wright, "Editorial Introduction: African Ways of Knowing, Worldviews and Pedagogy," *Journal of Contemporary Issues in Education* 2, no. 2 (2007): 1–6.
11. Victor Lonu, Peter Kamande, and George Ogalo, "Reflection Paper on Academic Writing" (unpublished paper, Nairobi Evangelical Graduate School of Theology [Africa International University], 2010), 1.
12. Kivunzi, Berhane, and Mutuku, "African Voice," 3.

suggested that "we do not lose sight of the fact that there are some culturally sensitive topics on which writing may require prior permission of a higher authority (village leader, king, etc.). Unlike the Western system in which anybody has the authority to write, the African scholar's authority is a delegated one."[13] Other students considered the value of letting potential PhD research topics be vetted and approved by leaders in their local communities. They explained, "Such an approach would address the lingering problem of doing research to simply satisfy the 'ideal' academic community, which essentially has reference to the western mind and style. Consequently, the research would benefit the African community."[14]

The choice of a research topic does not necessarily prescribe the style used to report it. However, the value of using forms that feel natural to the primary stakeholders to report to them results from the sort of community- and problem-based projects these students would like to prioritize seems self-evident. One group urged:

> The most useful journal sites should be our local council meetings, local *barazas*, among other forums, etc. The academic writing does not have to be authenticated and admitted only on the terms of western convention. It is with the problem-solving mind-set that our academic writing styles should be tilted. After going through such a demanding process to arrive at a given solution to a problem, this is a small price to pay, but a joy to see our findings being implemented.[15]

Who Has the Authority to Speak/Write?

In Western academic writing, anyone may stake a claim to be heard, without reference to the nature of the writer's relationship to his or her community. These African PhD students found that potentially troubling. They felt that as younger members of their communities it could be inappropriate to put themselves forward as sources of new knowledge. One group, echoing

---

13. Teme, Ndyamiyemenshi, and Sande, "African Voice," 3.
14. Lonu, Kamande, and Ogalo, "Academic Writing," 2–3.
15. Lonu, Kamande, and Ogalo, 6.

Canagarajah,[16] suggested that "the risk of appearing 'too pompous and overconfident' haunts us." They further explained, "We still see ourselves as the little boys and little girls of our villages. Despite our academic level, we still want to be self-effaced in our communities."[17] Others agreed that "the writer needs to portray himself not as one providing the solutions, but the one who is privileged to lead the discussion of coming up with solution(s) for the problem(s) addressed."[18] Along these lines I observed how regularly African students and colleagues took the first few moments of a presentation to express humility about the opportunity to speak, along with appreciation of those who had gone before them, to whose work they hoped to add "some small thing."

Kaplan observes that this tends to be true in traditional societies throughout the Majority World: "In U.S. composition tradition, anyone – even a lowly student – has the authority to write and to hold and express an opinion, but in more traditional cultures, the young have no such authority." Kaplan suggests this may be one reason such students tend to depend heavily on published sources in their writing rather than offering more independent insights. More problematically, these students "may be accused of failing to exercise critical thinking, but they may not see themselves as authorized to undertake such an act."[19]

The students also hesitated over the paradox of community-centred research undertaken by a single individual. They considered the possibility of multi-author doctoral projects – resulting in two or three students being awarded PhDs for joint work. One group observed, "As it is now in the academic conventions, dissertations are not only academic ventures seeking new knowledge, they are extremely individualistic, quite the opposite of African orientation."[20]

---

16. Canagarajah, *Geopolitics*, 121.
17. Teme, Ndyamiyemenshi, and Sande, "African Voice," 3.
18. Lonu, Kamande, and Ogalo, "Academic Writing," 1–2.
19. Kaplan, "Foreword," x.
20. Lonu, Kamande, and Ogalo, "Academic Writing," 7. See Zaracho, "Studying Together: Joint and Collaborative Research," in this volume, for further consideration of the potential for collaborative research in learning communities.

What Form May the Writing Take?

My initial concerns over what I considered the poor quality of African students' writing centred on their seeming inability to state a clear thesis at the beginning of a paper and then support it with explicit evidence and sustained argumentation throughout. I was also disturbed by how often they introduced a major new idea in the conclusion that had not been addressed earlier. However, as I dug deeper into concepts of intercultural rhetoric I realized that these "errors" do not necessarily reflect an inability to think clearly, critically, or consistently, but reflect discourse patterns in their home cultures that are comfortable and appealing for them, even if unfamiliar to me. I also came to understand that some of these patterns are more complex and subtle than what I myself had been taught to produce.

Kaplan is usually credited as the first to explore cultural variation in patterns of discourse, in his seminal work now often referred to, even by Kaplan himself, as the "doodles" article (1966).[21] Growing out of his work teaching reading and composition to international students at American universities, he observed differing patterns of communication in students from different cultural backgrounds. He represented these as a collection of line drawings – the "doodles": a straight line for what he considered American linear presentation, a progression of back and forth movements (like the tacking of a sailboat) for Semitic parallelism, a spiral for what he characterized as Oriental indirection, a somewhat rambling solid line for the digressions he found typical of speakers of Romance languages, and a similarly rambling dotted line for Russian speakers' "less relevant" digressions and amplifications. Kaplan's doodles have been widely criticized as overgeneralized and reductionist, expressing an inadequate view of culture and the individual, and for assuming American practices as the norm while treating other patterns prescriptively.[22] Kaplan later agreed with much of this critique while maintaining that "each language has clear preferences, so that while all forms are possible, all forms do not occur with

---

21. Robert B. Kaplan, "Cultural Thought Patterns in Intercultural Education," *Language Learning* 16, no. 1 (1966): 1–20.

22. See, for example, Clayann Gilliam Panetta, "Understanding Cultural Differences in the Rhetoric and Composition Classroom: Contrastive Rhetoric as Answer to ESL Dilemmas," in Panetta, *Contrastive Rhetoric Revisited and Redefined*, 5.

equal frequency or in parallel distributions."[23] In other words, there are different patterns of rhetoric, and different social or cultural groups may demonstrate differing preferences and tendencies in using them.

Similarly, Bliss describes discovering a range of rhetorical patterns among her diverse international students. She categorizes them as "the 'list discrete points in order to inform' languages, the 'think along with me even if I don't tell you the answer' languages, and the 'storytelling without providing the moral or logical conclusion' languages."[24] Her "list discrete points" languages are those in which speakers tend to make more explicit, linear, and deductive presentations of information. By "even if I don't tell you the answer" languages, she means those in which information tends to be presented implicitly and inductively, with much of the responsibility for making inferences resting on the hearer or reader (more on this below when we look at the arrangement of evidence). As an example of "storytelling without providing the conclusion" Bliss describes Native American Lakota speakers, who "will tell stories, often four or more, that are somehow related to the topic at hand. The speaker confirms his or her proposition through the stories, which, though they may not even mention the speaker's major claim, are intended to help the listener understand the situation and come to the same conclusion as the speaker."[25]

As I became more aware of the wealth of rhetorical diversity, I began to realize the extent to which the series of steps and moves I expected students to make in their research papers are artefacts of Western academic convention rather than essential elements of "good" writing. In the view of one group of students in the NEGST PhD cohort:

> The African style of passing information on is characterized by a catching introduction, the development of the topic in the body (sometimes with digressions) and the conclusion. The conclusion serves as the climax; and it offers a solution to the problem . . . Just the same way we know that westerners begin with the conclusion

---

23. Robert B. Kaplan, "Cultural Thought Patterns Revisited," in *Writing Across Languages: Analysis of L2 Text*, ed. Ulla Connor and Robert B. Kaplan (Reading: Addison-Wesley, 1987), 11.
24. Anne Bliss, "Rhetorical Structures for Multilingual and Multicultural Students," in Panetta, *Contrastive Rhetoric Revisited and Redefined*, 17.
25. Bliss, "Rhetorical Structures," 19.

(thesis) and then they defend it in the paper, Africans on the other hand begin with the definition of the problem and offer the solution at the end."[26]

In particular, students repeatedly told me that they found the idea of making a thesis statement at the beginning of a paper uncomfortable, even aesthetically unappealing. "The solution does not have to be implicitly proposed until the conclusion of the research."[27] A Kenyan student in another course, whom I consider a gifted writer, acknowledged that the requirement of "narrow and airtight thesis statements is inhibiting and suffocating." Bliss found comparable perspectives among her international students: "In Japanese, for example, it is typically considered rude to point out to the listener or reader what that person should believe or do. Yet, academic English often demands an overt statement about what the reader should do or believe, followed by evidence that supports the writer's claim."[28]

What Is Evidence?

Along with standard quantitative and qualitative research methods, the students affirmed the value their communities place on oral tradition and oral sources of knowledge. They also explained that metaphors, proverbs, and traditional sayings "are the ingredients that are meant to persuade the listeners to believe in the speaker's message."[29] One group said:

> Our African history has been passed on from generation to generation by a social class of people who are socially known for keeping historical records. They are called the royal praise singers. They live in royal courts. They never went to school, but they know everything about a specific kingdom, because they learnt from their fathers and grandfathers. We future African writers are the products of that African culture and cannot deny the productivity

---

26. Kivunzi, Berhane, and Mutuku, "African Voice," 3.
27. Lonu, Kamande, and Ogalo, "Academic Writing," 1.
28. Bliss, "Rhetorical Structures," 17.
29. Kivunzi, Berhane, and Mutuku, "African Voice," 4.

of that oral system. The question we are naturally tempted to ask ourselves is: Why can't we adopt this oral strategy in our writings?[30]

Students discussed ways to include oral sources as authoritative evidence in their research. One group recommended, "For oral sources attributed to individuals, their authenticity would need to be validated by tradition over the years. For any knowledge that is not validated by the community in context may not pass as authoritative even in the oral communities themselves." They also suggested, "We might need to make quotations in our native languages... A translation in English would serve the wider community, but the native language factor would reinforce not just meaning, but relevance as well."[31] For these students, oral history is a significant and potent source of knowledge about the world which is too often devalued in Western academic research.

What Arrangement of Evidence Is Likely to Appeal (Be Convincing) to Readers?

Western academic writing is inherently polemical. Authors take an assertive and argumentative stance, battling for the validity and significance of their contribution in a competitive marketplace of ideas. But as one student group said, "Whereas the Western style of writing is polemical, the African system is more of a negotiation with the audience so as to make them 'accept' our work."[32]

In this negotiation with the audience the students consistently expressed a preference not to make more explicit the connections among ideas, evidence, or illustrations in their writing. For them this represents speaking down to their audience, who can be trusted to make the connections on their own. They affirmed Canagarajah's statement that "the reader should be treated as intelligent enough to understand the evolving argument without too much guidance from the writer."[33] One group said, "African communication is mostly implicit. When a speaker is too explicit, he is perceived by the audience as trying to undermine their intelligence."[34] Another group agreed that in their

---

30. Teme, Ndyamiyemenshi, and Sande, "African Voice," 3.
31. Lonu, Kamande, and Ogalo, "Academic Writing," 4–5.
32. Teme, Ndyamiyemenshi, and Sande, "African Voice," 4.
33. Canagarajah, *Geopolitics*, 122.
34. Kivunzi, Berhane, and Mutuku, "African Voice," 4.

essays for this project, "We had our audience in mind. Sharing a mutual cognitive environment, we didn't need to explicate everything to them." They added, "While we agree that it is academically more reasonable to apply the western rules of persuasiveness, clarity, and step by step reasoning, it must also follow that we must never forget our implied audience for whom we write."[35] The third group wrote:

> There is a proverb in one of the represented languages which when translated says that "a person who is wise does not need so much detail." Since this is the preferred rhetoric practice, we agreed that for our "other" audience we could throw in logical connectors in the translation of our dissertation (of course if circumstances allow us to write it in our native languages). Care would need to be taken to reduce implicitness where the "other" readers would find difficulty, or rather to explicate where necessary.[36]

This preference is found in other areas of the world as well. For example, Zhongshe and Lan report that "Chinese writers often expect their readers to draw upon the assumingly shared knowledge to make sense of the text, instead of spelling out everything explicitly for readers. This is the Chinese way of being polite and showing respect for their readers."[37]

I have also observed that not only do African students value different forms of evidence than I might (such as oral sources in the section above), they sometimes argue from evidence to conclusions differently than I as a Westerner was trained to do. At times I have heard colleagues complain that students "aren't good at critical thinking," but this may not be a sufficient explanation. One way to look at this is to make use of the Toulmin Model of argumentation.[38] In its simplest form Toulmin's model proposes that people connect data or evidence to the claims they make by applying "warrants" they believe their audience will accept as justifying those connections. In other words, while

---

35. Teme, Ndyamiyemenshi, and Sande, "African Voice," 3.
36. Lonu, Kamande, and Ogalo, "Academic Writing," 5.
37. Lu Zhongshe and Li Lan, "Rhetorical Diversity and the Implications for Teaching Academic English," *Asian Journal of Applied Linguistics* 3, no. 1 (2016): 105.
38. S. Toulmin, R. Reike, and A. Janik, *An Introduction to Reasoning*, 2nd ed. (New York: Macmillan, 1984).

one may argue "this, *therefore* that," there is an often unspoken set of rules or beliefs that fills the space "*because* . . ." Those implicit rules and beliefs are the warrants that underlie persuasion. In academic research and reporting I was taught to value warrants grounded in syllogistic logic, elimination of other possibilities, generalizability, and so on. While my African students are able to use such warrants, and do so when required, they also appreciate warrants grounded in pragmatic factors arising from their social context. These might include elements such as the source of the data (originating, e.g., in traditional sayings), its benefit to the community, the identity or status of the person making the claim, or even the aesthetic or emotional appeal of the presentation. What these different warrants represent is not variation in the capacity for reasoning, but in the values shared by a community which shape what that community finds persuasive.

Opportunities and Risks

These reflections on Kaplan's five questions suggest that while Western academic writing tends to be individualistic, polemical, abstract, linear, explicit, and front-loaded with thesis statements, African students and the stakeholders in their research are more likely to prefer rhetorical styles that are pluralistic, self-effacing, "situated," inductive, implicit, and rich in proverbs and traditional knowledge.[39] Can such rhetorical strategies find a place in academic writing in the global environment? African research students, and the mentors and supervisors who guide them, have three possible ways forward, although these need not be mutually exclusive: they can continue to adopt Western conventions of academic writing; they can create new models of academic writing that reflect the rhetorical values of African communities; or they may forge some hybrid of styles, perhaps varying their use according to the intended audience.

Maintaining Western conventions of academic writing offers African research students more opportunity to have their work valued and authenticated

---

39. See also Shaw, "Culture, Gender, and Diversity in Advanced Theological Studies," in this volume. On Nisbett's suggestions of similar differences between Western and East Asian students see Richard Nisbett, *The Geography of Thought: How Asians and Westerners Think Differently . . . And Why* (New York: Free Press, 2003).

by international scholars, with publication in influential international journals as one metric of that validation. But it also risks loss of cultural identity, along with the unique contributions to knowledge that researchers from the Majority World offer. Students related this to "a Swahili proverb: 'muacha mila ni mtumwa,' *he who forsakes his culture entirely becomes a slave*. The African transition to academic writing should reflect an African identity lest we become slaves in thought and lifestyle."[40] Perhaps even more critically, maintaining Western conventions of academic writing limits the effective transmission of the results of Majority World research to its own community stakeholders. Students affirmed, "We are convinced that time has come to start developing African writing style to respond to the needs of the community."[41] Others agreed: "We must therefore be prouder to find our books on our African neighbours' shelves rather than on western people's shelves."[42]

But creating African forms of academic writing and reporting is also risky. First, there are few models to look to. As one of the student groups put it: "The Kamba community has a cooking saying: 'you can know whether the food you're cooking is ready by its smell.' African academic writing is food which is still in the cooking pot, and by its smell we can tell it is not ready yet. The continent is not completely empty of thinkers and writers, but the path paved by these frontrunners needs more improvement to reflect an African identity."[43]

Another concern is the extent to which international scholarship is open to alternative models of writing and reporting, leading to the potential for the work of African scholars to be sidelined. Students acknowledge that academic writing "has largely been western in its orientation. This is understandable because the West has been leading in one way or another in writing."[44] A further barrier may be internal: "The idea that 'the best things come from the West' has taken root and precedence over African culture and most of the people have adopted the western ideas of doing things. Although now there

---

40. Kivunzi, Berhane, and Mutuku, "African Voice," 1.
41. Lonu, Kamande, and Ogalo, "Academic Writing," 7.
42. Teme, Ndyamiyemenshi, and Sande, "African Voice," 3.
43. Kivunzi, Berhane, and Mutuku, "African Voice," 1.
44. Lonu, Kamande, and Ogalo, "Academic Writing," 7.

is the visible need for Africa to have an African stance, it is still regarded by some as a step backwards."[45]

For most, the answer seems to lie in some sort of creative hybridization. Students in Western-style higher education in the Majority World are already experienced in this sort of fusion. Some commented that "by the very fact of going to school, we have chosen to become intellectual and cultural hybrids: our heads glide along the Western academic universe, but our feet are entangled in the African cultural ground."[46] Canagarajah urges that rather than abandon their own traditions and rhetorical strategies, Majority World scholars "negotiate their use" among existing conventions of academic writing and reporting to "develop a creative oppositional discourse."[47] Or, as one student group more ironically proposed, "This does not mean that we have opted for separation between the Western and African styles . . . The academic aspect of writing suggests the idea of interdependence."[48] For the present, students seem willing to add their own voices to forms already laid out by Western models, suggesting that "at least for now there should be integration. As one of us said figuratively, 'Since westerners park cars in marked spaces, Africans can "park" their cows on similar spaces.'"[49]

Perhaps students like these will find or develop writing and reporting styles to use in their research that speak both to international academia and to their home communities. Or perhaps, just as speakers of multiple languages choose which language to use in a particular social or cultural setting, students and scholars will learn to shift strategies in their academic writing and reporting to meet the needs and interests of different audiences, seeking a form of "rhetorical attunement."[50] Whatever the way forward, Majority World students and scholars must continue to pursue their authentic voices in the global academic community. In this process the world will be enriched by their discoveries and their contributions to knowledge.

---

45. Kivunzi, Berhane, and Mutuku, "African Voice," 2.
46. Teme, Ndyamiyemenshi, and Sande, "African Voice," 4.
47. Canagarajah, *Geopolitics*, 294-295.
48. Lonu, Kamande, and Ogalo, "Academic Writing," 7.
49. Kivunzi, Berhane, and Mutuku, "African Voice," 3-4.
50. Rebecca Lorimer Leonard, "Multilingual Writing as Rhetorical Attunement," *College English* 76, no. 3 (2014): 227-247.

Discussion Questions

Five basic questions are raised in this chapter. For each of these questions consider the issues at stake in your own local context.

1. *What may be discussed?* What sorts of limitations on research topics exist in your own context? In some settings the limitations may be related to social concerns, while in others they may be in terms of acceptable academic fields or how narrowly focused a research topic should be.

2. *Who has the authority to speak/write?* In what ways do social and religious authority structures influence the shape and content of advanced studies in your context? Do you believe these are healthy or unhealthy? Explain.

3. *What form(s) may the writing take?* To what extent are the rhetorical patterns of surrounding cultures allowed to influence the forms in which your advanced students write?

4. *What is evidence?* How comfortable are you with oral sources of authority? Describe one or two possible strategies for thoughtfully incorporating oral sources in your school's programs of advanced theological studies.

5. *What arrangement of evidence is likely to appeal (be convincing) to readers?* To what extent is argumentation expected to be explicit in your students' presentation of their work? Describe one or two ways in which space might be given for greater acceptance of implicit communication.

Bibliography

Bliss, Anne. "Rhetorical Structures for Multilingual and Multicultural Students." In Panetta, *Contrastive Rhetoric Revisited and Redefined*, 15–30.

Canagarajah, A. Suresh. *A Geopolitics of Academic Writing*. Pittsburgh: University of Pittsburgh, 2002.

Connor, Ulla. *Intercultural Rhetoric in the Writing Classroom*. Ann Arbor: University of Michigan, 2011.

Kaplan, Robert B. "Cultural Thought Patterns in Intercultural Education." *Language Learning* 16, no. 1 (1966): 1–20.

———. "Cultural Thought Patterns Revisited." In *Writing Across Languages: Analysis of L2 Text*, edited by Ulla Connor and Robert B. Kaplan, 9–22. Reading: Addison-Wesley, 1987.

———. "Foreword." In Panetta, *Contrastive Rhetoric Revisited and Redefined*, vii–xx.

Kivunzi, Peninnah, Melles Berhane, and George Mutuku. "A Reflection on African Voice in Academic Writing." Unpublished paper, Nairobi Evangelical Graduate School of Theology (Africa International University), 2010.

Leonard, Rebecca Lorimer. "Multilingual Writing as Rhetorical Attunement." *College English* 76, no. 3 (2014): 227–247.

Lonu, Victor, Peter Kamande, and George Ogalo. "Reflection Paper on Academic Writing." Unpublished paper, Nairobi Evangelical Graduate School of Theology (Africa International University), 2010.

Nashon, Samson, David Anderson, and Handel Wright. "Editorial Introduction: African Ways of Knowing, Worldviews and Pedagogy." *Journal of Contemporary Issues in Education* 2, no. 2 (2007): 1–6.

Nisbett, Richard. *The Geography of Thought: How Asians and Westerners Think Differently . . . And Why*. New York: Free Press, 2003.

Panetta, Clayann Gilliam. "Understanding Cultural Differences in the Rhetoric and Composition Classroom: Contrastive Rhetoric as Answer to ESL Dilemmas." In Panetta, *Contrastive Rhetoric Revisited and Redefined*, 3–13.

———, ed. *Contrastive Rhetoric Revisited and Redefined*. New York: Routledge, 2008.

Teme, Dagalou, Nathan Ndyamiyemenshi, and Bernard C. Sande. "African Voice and Approach to Academic Writing." Unpublished paper, Nairobi Evangelical Graduate School of Theology (Africa International University), 2010.

Toulmin, S., R. Reike, and A. Janik. *An Introduction to Reasoning*. 2nd ed. New York: Macmillan, 1984.

Zhongshe, Lu, and Li Lan. "Rhetorical Diversity and the Implications for Teaching Academic English." *Asian Journal of Applied Linguistics* 3, no. 1 (2016): 101–113.

8

Nurturing Emancipatory Local Knowledges

César Lopes

Imagine a classroom in graduate theological studies in a Majority World setting. Well, although there are still not that many programs of this kind out there, the number is most certainly growing![1] The students in that classroom will be, with very few exceptions, originally from the region. But even if you have only national students sitting in this mental picture, there is still a fair degree of intercultural exchange going on.

It happens because the norm is that the class will have a Western-born guest teacher, or a non-Western professor graduated from a Western program.[2]

---

1. Evan Hunter, "The Purpose of the Journal: For a Time Like This," *InSights Journal for Theological Education* 1 (2015): 9.
2. At this very early point I would like to make a careful observation: establishing a sharp contrast between terms such as EuroAmerican/Western and indigenous/non-Western thought is always a delicate matter. The terms imply a gross generalization and dichotomy. Furthermore, they also tend to vilify the former, equating it with colonialism, and to associate the latter with "the primitive, the wild, the natural" (Ladislaus Semali and Joe L. Kincheloe, *What Is Indigenous Knowledge?* [New York: Falmer, 1999], 4). However, the terms still have a heuristic usefulness (Timothy G. Reagan, *Non-Western Educational Traditions: Indigenous Approaches to Educational Thought and Practice* [Mahwah: Erlbaum, 2005], 11), and the tension between predominant Western and marginalized non-Western epistemological, philosophical, and educational constructs is real (see, for example, Debbie Epstein, *Geographies of Knowledge, Geometries of Power: Future of Higher Education* [New York/London: Routledge, 2007]; Eduardo Mendieta, *Global Fragments: Globalizations, Latinamericanisms, and Critical Theory* [Albany: State University of New York, 2007]). For the lack of better expressions, and given the fact that they still communicate concrete realities, this chapter will make a careful use of these terms.

Of course you may have, exceptionally, a local teacher graduated from a local school teaching local students, but even in this case, as this volume so intentionally aims to address, classroom and assignment models are still based in a Minority World rationality. Whatever is the case, the professor in this imaginary classroom is participating in a game that has several players, layers, and dimensions, among which cultural difference is one of the most evident. This cultural dimension has been almost exhaustively addressed, especially after the last quarter of the twentieth century witnessed an explosion in the general field of cultural studies.

This explosion is a consequence of the fact that globalization and its effects have made interactions involving international players more common than ever, causing a new sensitivity to cultural issues to emerge. The field of higher education has felt the shockwaves of this explosion. Educators have grown increasingly concerned with how cultural issues have affected teaching and learning, both in their local contexts and in international exchanges. As a result, researchers have already suggested many worthy and valuable insights in order to enhance learning in Majority World and/or cross-cultural educational situations. However, a survey on the available literature on cultural issues in teaching and learning indicates that these cross-cultural educational insights tend to emphasize what I will describe below as "anthropological" and "educational" approaches – which mostly address the *shape* of the educational exchange.

In a general sense, the present volume is an attempt, by a very diverse group of authors, to deal with the prospects and limitations of innovative approaches aiming to address this reality. In my own input through this chapter, I assume that these anthropological and educational dimensions are indeed essential and should be present in such exchanges. However, my objective is to sustain that there is also a "critical" approach to this conversation, usually present in discussions of multiculturalism and postcolonialism, on cross-cultural[3] issues

---

3. There is a relative consensus in the literature around the usage of some terms to describe and discuss education in culturally diverse settings. "Multicultural" is usually employed when referring to the kind of local educational environments that mix different ethnic groups (e.g. James A. Banks and Cherry A. McGee Banks, *Multicultural Education: Issues and Perspectives* [Hoboken: Wiley, 2010]). "Intercultural" usually refers to a somewhat general concern with diversifying the school curriculum, especially in Western contexts (Gunther Dietz, *Multiculturalism, Interculturality and Diversity in Education: An Anthropological Approach*

in Majority World contexts. My suggestion is that a fundamental contribution a teacher may offer in such educational exchanges is *nurturing emancipatory local knowledges*.

Making a General Sense of the Expression "Emancipatory Local Knowledges"

Knowledges is a term that has been used especially in the context of multicultural issues. Using this uncountable noun in the plural form is actually a statement against a conception of knowledge as static, uniform, and monochromatic. Commonly accompanied by descriptors such as indigenous, situated, subjugated, or local, the term expresses the willingness "to rupture the sense of comfort and complacency in conventional approaches to knowledge production, interrogation, validation and dissemination in EuroAmerican educational settings."[4]

David Ingram describes *emancipatory knowledge* as the "genuine knowledge [that] can be realized only as a communal project in which humans have emancipated themselves from the distorted effects of social and political domination."[5] Therefore, *emancipatory local knowledges* are tentatively defined at this point as local indigenous content, methodologies, or epistemologies that trigger "insights into relations of domination that may appear to express 'natural' laws, but can potentially be changed."[6]

In the context of this chapter, I will present the three major approaches mentioned above by linking them to the three elements which are the title of

---

[Munster: Waxmann Verlag, 2009]). "Transcultural" and "cross-cultural" make reference to international teachers who cross a cultural border in order to teach abroad (Kenneth Cushner and Sharon Brennan et al., *Intercultural Student Teaching: A Bridge to Global Competence* [Lanham: Rowman & Littlefield Education, 2007]). Finally, "international education" usually refers either to *students* crossing cultural, national, and geographic borders in order to study abroad, or to universities branching overseas in order to install their *campi* in countries other than their original ones.

4. George J. Sefa Dei, "Rethinking the Role of Indigenous Knowledges in the Academy," *International Journal of Inclusive Education* 4, no. 2 (2000): 111.

5. David Ingram, *Habermas: Introduction and Analysis* (Ithaca: Cornell University, 2010), 44.

6. Raymond Allen Morrow and Carlos Alberto Torres, *Reading Freire and Habermas: Critical Pedagogy and Transformative Social Change* (New York: Teachers College, 2002), 48.

the chapter: I would suggest that the anthropological dimension deals with the *local*; the educational, with *knowledges*; and the critical, with *emancipatory*.

It is important to highlight what this chapter wants to accomplish by describing and studying these approaches. First, they are not discrete groups but overlapping tendencies that are structured enough for the establishment of some generalizations. Second, this typology does not mean to be exhaustive, but rather to offer a general description that may lead to some concrete insights for designing learning experiences in graduate theological education. Third, authors and articles quoted in one type do not necessarily exclusively remain within it, since they sometimes incorporate two or even the three approaches.

Finally, and most importantly, this chapter conveys the idea that the overall emphasis on the critical approach highlighted here does not mean a dismissal of anthropological and educational elements. On the contrary, I explore these approaches in this chapter because teachers in graduate programs in Majority World settings will greatly benefit from also taking them into consideration: *knowledges* will be actually *emancipatory* only if they are *local*. Let's explore these three dimensions.

Focusing on the *Local*: The Anthropological Approach

The first identifiable approach to evaluating the interactions going on in our imaginary classroom tends to focus on the communicational aspects of teaching. At the centre of this approach is the figure of a teacher crossing some type of cultural barrier, either locally in multi-ethnic contexts or by teaching abroad.[7] The aim is to reduce noises caused by cultural differences in order to maximize the potential of the "content" being taught and to build a set of abilities or tools that will enable a cleaner communication process in intercultural educational exchanges. A key work on this perspective, especially

---

7. It is this notion of crossing cultural barriers that distinguishes the anthropological approach described in this section from anthropology of education as a subfield. The latter is more concerned with the cultural context around the educational experience (Elsie Rockwell, "Recovering History in the Anthropology of Education," in *A Companion to the Anthropology of Education*, ed. B. A. Levinson and M. Pollock [Chichester/Malden: Wiley-Blackwell, 2011], 65–80), where the *cross*-cultural element may or may not be present. Furthermore, the educational experience of a society is much larger than the issue of schooling, and in this section the focus is on graduate education exchanges.

in the case of cross-cultural higher theological education, is Hofstede's "Cultural Differences in Teaching and Learning"[8] and his development of a four-dimensional model for explaining cultural differences.

Researchers using this approach may ask general questions such as: How can a teacher better communicate across cultural lines and "transcend cultural borders"?[9] What kind of cultural adjustments can be made in order to maximize the retention of knowledge? What kinds of "cultural global competencies" are necessary for teachers?[10]

Further research has focused on more specific issues. For instance, how do rhetorical patterns relate to language?[11] Kaplan,[12] among others, explores the idea that thought and grammar are related in a given language, and therefore an "academic sophistication" will not only sound and read differently in different languages, but will also be structured differently. Or even a seemingly simple issue, such as: How does one define what is the appropriate time a student should wait before taking his or her turn in classroom discussions?[13]

I would point out that the reaction you, as a reader, may have to the questions above is an example of the importance of the anthropological dimension of this matter. For my own Latin American culture, for instance, the last question simply does not make sense, as we tend to speak at the same time and even to have some degree of friendly or not-so-friendly competition in classroom exchanges. However, in Eastern Asian backgrounds, for example, the question bears more significance, as silence tends to be more valued in these contexts and does not necessarily mean a lack of interest or participation.

---

8. Geert Hofstede, "Cultural Differences in Teaching and Learning," *International Journal of Intercultural Relations* 10, no. 3 (1986): 301–320.
9. Olugbemiro J. Jegede and Glen S. Aikenhead, "Transcending Cultural Borders: Implications for Science Teaching," *Research in Science & Technological Education* 17, no. 1 (1999): 45–66.
10. Reyes Quezada and Cristina Alfaro, "Developing Biliteracy Teachers: Moving Toward Culture and Linguistic Global Competence in Teacher Education," in *Intercultural Student Teaching: A Bridge to Global Competence*, ed. K. Cushner and S. Brennan (Lanham: Rowman & Littlefield Education, 2007), 57–87.
11. Stephanie Black deals in greater depth with this topic in her chapter in this collection, "Scholarship in Our Own Words: Intercultural Rhetoric in Academic Writing and Reporting."
12. R. Kaplan, "Cultural Thought-Patterns in Inter-Cultural Education," in *Landmark Essays on ESL Writing*, ed. T. J. Silva and P. K. Matsuda (Mahwah: Lawrence Erlbaum Associates, 2001), 11–26.
13. Ikuko Nakane "Negotiating Silence and Speech in the Classroom," *Multilingua* 24 (2005): 77.

However, if a teacher simply remains at an anthropological level at the expense of the other dimensions, there is a dangerous implicit assumption, and that is the unconscious perception of theological knowledge as something that has already been *produced* and is somehow ready. The teacher's task would therefore be merely to "repack" it properly for the target cultural context, and the students' task would be simply to *reproduce* such knowledge. In the next sections we will discuss if this is really enough.

In summary, the anthropological approach focuses on the *local* aspects of cultural issues in a narrower sense, stresses the role of teachers in their dealings with students from a different cultural background, and has as its central concern the proper communication of the content.

Building *Knowledges*: The Educational Approach

The second approach we need to look at takes foundational educational theories and reconceptualizes them in cultural terms or vice versa. The focus here is on creating educational experiences that not only reproduce, but that actually *produce* knowledge.

Particularly meaningful for our reflection on higher theological education in Majority World contexts is Amstutz's discussion[14] of educational approaches to cultural issues. Amstutz proposes "adjustments" in order to provide meaningful learning experiences for learners coming from diverse cultural settings. Such adjustments, she sustains, are not only in *teaching* but also in *learning*, through ideas such as helping students question theories according to their own cultural experiences, promoting non-dichotomous ways of knowing, seeking alternative forms of learning, and varying strategies regarding assignments.[15]

---

14. Donna D. Amstutz, "Adult Learning: Moving Toward More Inclusive Theories and Practices," *New Directions for Adult & Continuing Education* 82 (1999): 19.
15. Some studies under this approach are basically a test on how foundational constructs such as Kolb's learning styles (David Kolb, *Experiential Learning* [Englewood Cliff: Prentice Hall, 1984]), Mezirow's transformative learning theory (Jack Mezirow, *Transformative Dimensions of Adult Learning* [San Francisco: Jossey-Bass, 1991]), or Bloom's taxonomy (Benjamin S. Bloom and David R. Krathwohl, *Taxonomy of Educational Objectives: The Classification of Educational Goals* [New York: Longmans, 1956]) play into educational settings in different cultures. Other concrete examples help illustrate the concerns of such an approach. For instance, research

Another rich example of an inquiry on the interplay between culture and education is Sharan Merriam's volume *Non-Western Perspectives on Learning and Knowing*.[16] The book includes contributors who address the manner in which some large cultural formations or worldviews approach learning. It is particularly useful to attend to Merriam's concluding remarks, which summarize the challenges of the educational dimension we are dealing with in this chapter. She points out that such non-Western educational approaches try to help learners build knowledges which (1) are more *holistic* in their approach to human beings, as opposed to the more *rationalistic* approach in the West; (2) evidence a concern for a deeper *integration* between knowledge and the real world, as opposed to the more *dualistic* view in the West; (3) are *collectivist*, concerned with the whole community, as opposed to Western *individualism*; and (4) consider people as a valuable *source* of knowledge, with a consequent narrative and oral approach to knowing, in a certain opposition to the more *descriptive and written* approach in the West.[17]

It is important to highlight that there is a deeper layer in this educational approach than is found in a purely anthropological approach. In higher theological education settings, the educational approach assumes that the simple reproduction or contextualization of theological knowledge coming from the West is not enough. However, a possible limitation of the educational approach is that it assumes that knowledge and education are value-free; in

---

into this perspective has looked at how such constructs influenced the way European and Eastern Asian students worked in groups or interacted with professors (Apfelthaler et al., "Cross-Cultural Differences in Learning and Education: Stereotypes, Myths and Realities," in *Learning and Teaching Across Cultures in Higher Education*, ed. D. Palfreyman and D. L. McBride [New York: Palgrave Macmillan, 2007], 15–35); or how a theoretical construct like transformative learning could be enhanced by the incorporation of cultural elements to it (Peggy Gabo Ntseane, "Culturally Sensitive Transformational Learning: Incorporating the Afrocentric Paradigm and African Feminism," *Adult Education Quarterly* 61, no. 4 [2011]: 307–323). Patricia Cranton's *Understanding and Promoting Transformative Learning: A Guide for Educators of Adults* (San Francisco: Jossey-Bass, 2006) starts from Merizow's transformative learning theory and filters it through the lenses of gender and culture.

16. Sharan B. Merriam and Associates, *Non-Western Perspectives on Learning and Knowing* (Malabar: Krieger, 2007).

17. Actually, many of the chapters in this volume are great attempts to deal conceptually and in practice with the points Merriam presents. See, for instance, Clark's chapter "Pathways of Integration for Theological Knowledge," Yang's chapter "Poetry As Theology," Dharamraj's chapter on the possible usage of storytelling in master's or doctoral level dissertations, among others.

other words, that they are sociologically neutral. We will address this possible limitation in the next section.

In summary, an educational approach focuses on the interface between anthropological and educational theories, stressing the role of students in building new local knowledges, in opposition to a practice which just proposes the "localization" of established knowledges.

Local Knowledges That Are *Emancipatory*: The Critical Approach

If the first two approaches described in this chapter tend to dialogue, respectively, with anthropology and educational theories, this third one tends to dialogue with sociology and political science, especially from the perspective of critical theory and, more recently, postcolonial studies.[18]

The initial impulse of the critical approach comes from a perception that traditional intercultural approaches fall short in their efforts. Gorski, warning in the title of his article that "good intentions are not enough,"[19] candidly points out that "The practice of intercultural education, when not committed first and foremost to equity and social justice . . . might, in the best case, result in heightened cross-group awareness at an individual level. But in many cases this practice is domination . . . [and] is a tool for the maintenance of marginalization."[20]

---

18. The word "critical" used to describe this third approach is an indication of the inputs this section receives from critical theory and critical pedagogy. The first is defined by Nigel Blake and Jan Masschelein ("Critical Theory and Critical Pedagogy," in *The Blackwell Guide to the Philosophy of Education*, ed. Nigel Blake et al. [Malden: Blackwell, 2003], 38), when they examine the interface between critical theory and education, "as the tradition of thought associated with the Frankfurt School of philosophy and social theory, which originated in the late 1920's," and focuses on issues such as liberation from false consciousness and ideology critique. Critical pedagogy, in its turn, "asserts that learning, like all other social interactions, is a political act with political purposes. It rests on a belief that it is in the very nature of pedagogy that it is a political, moral, and critical practice" (Jan McArthur, "Time to Look Anew: Critical Pedagogy and Disciplines within Higher Education," *Studies in Higher Education* 35, no. 3 [2010]: 301–302).
19. Sam Ewell's chapter in this present volume points in a very similar direction, as he describes his trajectory of going through "turning points" while dialoguing with both Brazilian culture and the work of Ivan Illich.
20. Paul C. Gorski, "Good Intentions Are Not Enough: A Decolonizing Intercultural Education," *Intercultural Education* 19, no. 6 (2008): 519–520.

Sonia Nieto properly describes this problem when proposing "profoundly multicultural questions." She sees a good effort being made by educators who try to include different ethnic and cultural perspectives in the curriculum. However, her evaluation continues, sometimes this kind of educational experience "is seen as little more than a way to promote self-esteem, or simply as a curriculum that substitutes one set of heroes for another."[21] On the same note, for Arroyo, waiving this deeper dimension results in an exchange that furthers the "deterritorialization, inferiorization, and subalternization" of autochthonous or local knowledges.[22]

A *critical* approach to exchanges in higher theological education in Majority World settings therefore not only asks for a variety of content in the curricular menu, for cultural sensitivity in classroom exchanges, and for a richer educational experience in terms of learning, but also seeks more fundamental themes such as fair access to education, matters of equality and inequality in terms of gender and ethnicity, social justice, achievement gaps, and especially reflection on subaltern knowledges and epistemologies. This is the approach that Sleeter and McLaren offer when they define critical education as "a particular ethico-political attitude or ideological stance that one constructs in order to confront and engage the world critically and challenge power relations."[23] The challenge is therefore taken further than the issue of "content to be taught."

Advocating this critical dimension includes the assumption that the frontiers between producing and "consuming" theology should be dissolved. Learners are theologians, and it is crucial that the "content" of their learning involves not only static theological objects that should be somehow memorized, but rather critical reflection on *whose* theology ends up enshrined as orthodoxy, and training in *how to do theology*.

It is fair to say that the critical approach is more commonly adopted by scholars writing from the perspective of groups that see themselves as

---

21. Sonia M. Nieto, "Profoundly Multicultural Questions," *Educational Leadership* 60, no. 4 (2002): 5.
22. Miguel G. Arroyo, "Os Movimentos Sociais e a construção de outros currículos," *Educar em Revista* 55 (2015): 55.
23. C. E. Sleeter and Peter McLaren, *Multicultural Education and Critical Pedagogy: The Politics of Difference* (New York: SUNY, 1995), 7.

oppressed. In fact, expressions such as oppression, liberation, ideology, hegemony, and structure are very common in this approach. This is especially due to the fact that the broad area of critical studies draws largely from Marxian tools of analysis.

At this point it is very important to localize this kind of language to the context of this book. Remember, we are trying to dialogue with non-Christian sources that may enrich our practice in higher theological education in Majority World settings. While we do so, I suspect that in the evangelical mind, even (or especially) in Majority World contexts, discussions using expressions such as ideology, social justice, and inequality are under threat of being situated in the field of radical theologies far away from evangelical orthodoxy – whatever that is!

However, an unavoidable consequence of questioning the hegemony of linear-thinking Western males over the global academy, as Perry Shaw's chapter on culture and gender in this volume points out, is to also question matters of privilege, oppression, and hegemony, pursuing educational practices that can lead to justice, liberation, and emancipation of "subjugated knowledges."[24]

Such a discussion, argue Higuera-Smith, Lalitha, and Hawk, in their excellent volume *Evangelical Postcolonial Conversations: Global Awakenings in Theology and Praxis*, is crucial for contemporary evangelicals:

> Developing a stronger theological bond between evangelical and post-colonial thought requires new, strong theologies that articulate indigenous Christianities . . . and also strive to connect theory and praxis . . . [F]or what is it to critique power if we do not create communities that intentionally interrogate the ways that we construct power and create alternative modes of social interaction – modes that concern themselves with giving voice to

---

24. For Foucault, subjugated knowledges are "a whole set of knowledges that have been disqualified as inadequate to their task or insufficiently elaborated: naïve knowledges, located low down on the hierarchy, beneath the required level of cognition or scientificity . . . It is through the reappearance of this knowledge, of these local popular knowledges, these disqualified knowledges, that criticism performs its work" (Michel Foucault, *Power/Knowledge: Selected Interviews and Other Writings, 1972–1977* [Brighton: Harvester, 1980], 81–82).

the silenced and exercising power on behalf of one another rather than over one another?[25]

Finally, it is important to remember that, despite its co-optation by certain ideologies and radical theologies, categories such as oppression, liberation, and justice are simply biblical.

A critical approach, therefore, encompasses the anthropological and educational, adding a concern that extrapolates differences in cultural background or learning styles and goes deeper into power relations by giving voice to the silenced. However, it is important to stress an idea that was briefly mentioned at other points in this chapter: a critical approach is not sufficient in itself. The categories mentioned above look and feel different in different cultural contexts. Therefore, if it lacks the cultural sensitivity espoused by the anthropological dimension, a critical approach may paradoxically further a situation of oppression and hinder people from developing a free consciousness or from being "transformed by the renewing of your mind" (Rom 12:2).

Similarly, if actions inspired by a critical approach lack an educational dimension in the terms we describe here, another paradoxical effect may take place: students may be simply invited to *un*-critically embrace ideas and formulations articulated by a professor in another context.

In summary, the three approaches described here have to be seen as complementary and mutually dependent. The attention I bring to the *critical* dimension throughout this chapter is due simply to the fact that it generally receives less attention than the other two.

Integrating a Critical Dimension into Teaching Practices

Let us now go back to that imaginary classroom from the beginning of the chapter. Remember, we assumed a situation in which a Western-born or -educated professor is in an exchange taking place in a Majority World context of higher theological education. The aim is to *nurture* emancipatory local knowledges. It is important to remember that these knowledges may only be

---

25. Kay Higuera-Smith, Jaychitra Lalitha, and Daniel Hawk, *Evangelical Postcolonial Conversations* (Downers Grove: IVP, 2014), 26–27.

built, in the case of our scenario, by the students themselves. The role of the teacher, therefore, is to try to establish conditions for the students to build local knowledges.

The anthropological and educational dimensions of that exchange are far from resolved and definitively still present challenges, but our focus here falls on the critical dimension. I would like to point out some insights on how to deal with it.

Content Integration

In the present volume, Paul Clark offers interesting insights on how to deal directly with content integration in higher theological education in response to the fragmentation of knowledge.[26] Banks and Banks' insight also helps us at this point as they expand the challenge of integration beyond the idea of knowledge, towards what in this chapter we have been referring to as *knowledges*: "Content integration deals with the extent to which teachers use examples and content from a variety of cultures and groups to illustrate key concepts, principles, generalizations, and theories in their subject area or discipline. The infusion of ethnic and cultural content into the subject area should be logical, not contrived."[27]

In practice, this wider context integration proposed by Banks and Banks would mean that a professor in an intercultural exchange must look for local sources not only in terms of "illustrations," as the quote above suggests, but also in terms of bibliographical sources and their theological formulations, biblical interpretation, missional practices, and so on. Furthermore, taking other chapters of this volume into consideration, it means to intentionally use local poetry, music, and narratives[28] in dialogue with the professor's own sources, and to stimulate the usage of these same forms for the students' production.

This sort of content integration is far from unproblematic. Even though many of the barriers in terms of access to information were shattered by the electronic advancements of the last decades, there is still a real difficulty in

---

26. Paul Clark, "Pathways of Integration for Theological Knowledge: Integrative Knowing/Learning for Thesis Construction in Advanced Theological Studies," in the present volume.
27. Banks and Banks, *Multicultural Education*, 20.
28. See in particular Havilah Dharamraj, "Telling Tales: Stories That Embox Theology," and Xiaoli Yang, "Poetry As Theology: A Creative Path," in the present volume.

terms of the availability of the "target context" literature for the professor to examine and integrate before the educational exchange happens. There is also the matter of micro-contextual theological tensions, so common in our evangelical settings: sometimes, quoting a certain local author may create more hindrances than pathways. However, it is possible to use "cultural brokers" who may guide the professor in this acquisition process, or even to propose pre-session learning tasks in which students themselves are invited to dive into their local literature.

There is another element which it is important to highlight in this matter. Michael Apple, a US scholar on critical pedagogy, candidly points to the role that professors, curriculum makers, textbooks, and bibliographies have in establishing an "official knowledge,"[29] or a sort of canon of approved texts in a certain subject area. An explicit inclusion of local sources that is "logical, not contrived" (as Banks and Banks point to in the quote above) may strengthen the subjective value attributed to local sources by local students. However, such integration must happen beyond the mere inclusion of such materials in the bibliography of a course syllabus, as the lack of usage in classroom discussions may actually provoke a reverse effect.

A final important comment: while embracing local resources it is also necessary to avoid a complacent attitude towards local formulations, as integration does not mean lack of critique. David Tracy accurately establishes a point of balance in declaring that "to hear those [local] voices is also to resist them when necessary and to insist upon the lesson that their own emphasis on conflict can teach anew: every conversation, if it is worthy of being named a conversation at all, will not shun necessary moments of conflict; every response to their readings must be critical and active, not passively receptive."[30]

Student Production and a Safe Discussion Space

When reading the literature on multicultural education it is clear that the ideal classroom envisioned by these authors is a place of minimal coercion and of free speech, with students and teachers voicing their informed opinions and

---

29. Michael W. Apple, *Official Knowledge: Democratic Education in a Conservative Age* (New York: Routledge, 2000).
30. David Tracy, *Plurality and Ambiguity* (San Francisco: Harper & Row, 1987), 107.

sharing meaningful learning experiences that enrich and enlighten each other's cultural backgrounds.

This is not a bad situation to idealize, and I believe our practice as teachers should aim towards that. However, two important observations should be made. First, as I have already pointed out in an earlier section, teachers from a different cultural background should be very careful in their efforts to guarantee student participation in the classroom. Lal Senanayake explores a similar issue when addressing high- and low-context cultures in his chapter in this collection,[31] but for the context of this chapter I highlight again the fact that in some cultures silence is now viewed with the same negative lenses as in the West.

Second, higher theological education mostly navigates within the realm of established theological schemas: the sort of "official knowledge" I referred to in the preceding section, but framed in doctrinal terms. Usually, mainstream theologies have a coordinated system – they were allowed time and space to organize themselves and "colonize" a certain context, firmly establishing their roots. To assume this *emancipatory* dimension of nurturing local knowledges means to question some of these formulations – and even if made in contextual terms, this questioning may in some contexts get too close to the questioning of faith itself.

In one of his very few personal essays, Puerto Rican theologian Orlando Costas narrated his "three conversions." A lesser-known Latin American evangelical who wrote under the holistic mission perspective for which others such as René Padilla and Samuel Escobar have global recognition, Costas[32] describes his theological pilgrimage being marked by three key turning points: first, his conversion to Christ; second, when he started to unpeel some layers of his Christian experience while studying in an American university, and went through a sort of "cultural conversion" back to his own Latin American culture; third, when he extended this reflection to his own way of thinking

---

31. Lal Senanayake, "The Imperative of Cultural Integration in Advanced Theological Studies: Perspectives from the Majority World," in the current volume.

32. Orlando Costas, "Conversion as a Complex Experience: A Hispanic Case Study," *Occasional Essays* 5, no. 1 (1980): 21–44. Orlando Costas was a very prolific writer and practitioner until his early death in 1987 at the age of forty-five.

theologically, going through a final conversion to making theology from the perspective of the powerless.

I have experienced a similar journey, and other comparable stories may also be found: a cycle involving an experience with Christ, a revision of our understanding based on the realization that other cultural experiences have shaped the theology we accept as orthodox, and finally a commitment to theologizing in a more culturally and contextually meaningful way.

Inviting students to reflect actively on the relationship between their Christian faith and their culture is not a guarantee that emancipatory local knowledges will flourish. In fact, opposite stories may also be found: when doing such reflection, people may take a step back and further reject local knowledges in favour of "orthodox" and "mainstream" forms of theology. Such voices are certainly welcome among others at the table of the kingdom. However, the kind of critical self-reflection I am advocating in this chapter is crucial for appropriating and expanding such local knowledges.

The task of the teacher in this context, therefore, is to try to establish an environment of trust and safety in which students are free to engage in new attempts at local or contextual theologizing that are by nature tentative.[33] These attempts will mostly happen in classroom discussions and in class assignments done by students. In any particular classroom, there will always be some hindrances to a free expression of tentative formulations whether done in oral or written form. Many of the hindrances are due to culture, group dynamics, or learning styles. But many are also due to coercion.

A few questions may help illuminate and uncover sources of coercion. For instance, does the teacher or the school suffer any pressure, even if involuntary, from stakeholders and/or donors to embrace a particular epistemological framework? Are there institutional pressures on students that push them towards one line of thought? What kinds of doctrinal elements may be in place that limit the students' ability to develop alternative conclusions?

---

33. In his *Transforming Mission*, David Bosch speaks about contextual theologies in similar ways, saying that a local formulation "suggests the experimental and contingent nature of all theology . . . We need an experimental theology in which an ongoing dialogue is taking place between text and context, a theology which, in the nature of the case, remains provisional and hypothetical" (David Bosch, *Transforming Mission: Paradigm Shifts in Theology of Mission* [Maryknoll: Orbis, 1991], 427).

Teachers are not unaware of these hindrances to a meaningful discussion, and there are resources to help deal with them. I find the work of Stephen Brookfield very helpful, as he actually integrates some abstract critical theory concerns in grounded classroom practice.[34] His suggestions address mostly "live" discussions, but we may adjust some ideas for high-context cultures in which student oral participation is not necessarily encouraged in the classroom. For instance, he suggests "one minute [reaction] papers" to be assigned to students after the discussion or exposition of crucial points. These may be collected by professors, revised, and addressed after a break or in the next session, without necessarily identifying the author.

Hybrid classroom models can also be strategic in facilitating active student engagement. Wherever Internet access is readily available, it is possible to set up online environments to make resources available and to promote forums of asynchronous discussion, which provide safe spaces for engagement.

However, a great space for nurturing emancipatory local knowledges is in the assignments to be done by students. Most of this volume is dedicated to exploring innovative approaches to student research and production. In the light of what has been discussed in this chapter, teachers should also ensure that assigned projects stimulate students to use their personal experience to describe and critique their theological assumptions in the light of their cultural beliefs, experiences, and practices.

In summary, the goal of a professor aiming to nurture emancipatory local knowledges should be to establish a safe classroom environment that enables students to make tentative formulations in this direction, either in classroom discussion (live or online) or in their assignments.

An Attitude of Humility and Solidarity

Far from being a pair of cliché categories, humility and solidarity are a mark of the work of Paulo Freire, an obvious example of an educator to quote under this critical perspective. When dealing with literacy programs among sugar cane workers in an impoverished region of Brazil, he strived not only to teach

---

34. There are some interesting resources available on his website (www.stephenbrookfield.com), especially under the "Resources/Workshop Materials" tab. His book *Discussion as a Way of Teaching* (San Francisco: Jossey-Bass, 2005) brings together a comprehensive list of techniques to promote a healthy environment for an open classroom discussion.

people how to read, but also to help them to be able to identify situations and dynamics of inequality and oppression. Evidently he did not necessarily have a cross-cultural educational situation in mind, but he points towards a path that may serve as a starting point for nurturing emancipatory local knowledges:

> If in fact the dream that inspires us is democratic and grounded in solidarity, it will not be by talking to others from on high as if we were inventors of the truth that we will learn to speak with them. Only the person who listens patiently and critically is able to speak *with* the other, even if at times it should be necessary to speak *to* him or her. Even when, of necessity, she/he must speak against ideas and convictions of the other person, it is still possible to speak as if the other were a subject who is being invited to listen critically and not an object submerged by an avalanche of unfeeling, abstract words.[35]

This Freirean model, permeated by humility and respect, is a good one for interactions between Western and local knowledges. An interaction in graduate studies in Majority World settings is a concrete situation in which local emancipatory knowledges may be nurtured and promoted, as long as teachers are willing to avoid talking to students "from on high" or as "inventors of the truth."

Final Remarks

The figure of a Western-born or -trained teacher crossing geographical and cultural borders in order to engage in educational exchanges in higher theological education in Majority World settings occupies the centre of this chapter. It is important once again to state that the critical approach proposed as the framework of this discussion does not rule out the anthropological and educational insights that have also been described. In fact, the opposite is more accurate: the critical perspective *cannot* be actualized without insights

---

35. Paulo Freire, *Pedagogy of Freedom: Ethics, Democracy, and Civic Courage*, Critical Perspectives Series (Lanham: Rowman & Littlefield, 1998), 110–111.

from education and anthropology, and agents involved on both sides of these educational exchanges need to be fully aware of them.

The end result may look as if a situation already charged with challenges and difficulties is now even more complicated by this critical-emancipatory dimension. Any individual who has ever been in an educational exchange which bears cultural sensitivities surely knows first-hand the complexity of the issues and details involved in such interactions, and the critical approach espoused by this paper actually adds layers to this picture.

However, if we consider that our innovative approaches to higher theological education in Majority World settings should substantially contribute to a global conversation, then nurturing emancipatory local knowledges is definitively worth the effort.

Discussion Questions

1. In what ways has your school taken seriously anthropological considerations in the content and methodologies applied in its programs of study? In particular consider the kinds of "cultural global competencies" that are expected from your faculty, and the sorts of communication norms that are encouraged or discouraged.

2. What are the key educational considerations that operate in your own local context? In particular consider Merriam's call to embrace non-Western educational approaches which are holistic, integrate knowledge and the real world, collectivist (concerned with the whole community), and include narrative and oral approaches to knowing.

3. To what extent do you feel comfortable or threatened by the material on emancipatory education? Why?

4. Consider each of the following issues: fair access to education, matters of equality and inequality in terms of gender and ethnicity, social justice, achievement gaps, and especially the reflecting on subaltern knowledges and epistemologies. Which of these are particularly significant challenges for your school? Why?

5. The chapter describes the following as possible pathways to nurturing emancipatory local knowledges: content integration; student production and a safe discussion space; and an attitude of humility and solidarity. Suggest one or two ways in which your school might better promote these potential areas of growth.

Bibliography

Adams, Tony, Stacy Holman Jones, and Carolyn Ellis. *Autoethnography: Understanding Qualitative Research*. New York: Oxford, 2015.

Amstutz, Donna D. "Adult Learning: Moving Toward More Inclusive Theories and Practices." *New Directions for Adult & Continuing Education* 82 (1999): 19–32.

Apfelthaler, Gerald, Katrin Hansen, Stephan Keuchel, Christa Mueller, Martin Neubauer, Siow Heng Ong, and Nirundon Tapachai. "Cross-Cultural Differences in Learning and Education: Stereotypes, Myths and Realities." In *Learning and Teaching Across Cultures in Higher Education*, edited by D. Palfreyman and D. L. McBride, 15–35. New York: Palgrave Macmillan, 2007.

Apple, Michael W. *Official Knowledge: Democratic Education in a Conservative Age*. New York: Routledge, 2000.

Arroyo, Miguel G. "Os Movimentos Sociais e a construção de outros currículos." *Educar em Revista* 55 (2015): 47–68.

Banks, James A., and Cherry A. McGee Banks. *Multicultural Education: Issues and Perspectives*. Hoboken: Wiley, 2010.

Blake, Nigel, and Jan Masschelein. "Critical Theory and Critical Pedagogy." In *The Blackwell Guide to the Philosophy of Education*, edited by Nigel Blake, Paul Smeyers, Richard Smith, and Paul Standish, 38–56. Malden: Blackwell, 2003.

Bloom, Benjamin S., and David R. Krathwohl. *Taxonomy of Educational Objectives: The Classification of Educational Goals*. New York: Longmans, 1956.

Bosch, David. *Transforming Mission: Paradigm Shifts in Theology of Mission*. Maryknoll: Orbis, 1991.

Brookfield, Stephen. *Discussion as a Way of Teaching*. San Francisco: Jossey-Bass, 2005.

Costas, Orlando. "Conversion as a Complex Experience: A Hispanic Case Study." *Occasional Essays* 5, no. 1 (1980): 21–44.

Cranton, Patricia. *Understanding and Promoting Transformative Learning: A Guide for Educators of Adults*. San Francisco: Jossey-Bass, 2006.

Cushner, Kenneth, and Sharon Brennan. *Intercultural Student Teaching: A Bridge to Global Competence*. Lanham: Rowman & Littlefield Education, 2007.

Dei, George J. Sefa. "Rethinking the Role of Indigenous Knowledges in the Academy." *International Journal of Inclusive Education* 4, no. 2 (2000): 111-132.

Dietz, Gunther. *Multiculturalism, Interculturality and Diversity in Education: An Anthropological Approach*. Munster: Waxmann Verlag, 2009.

Epstein, Debbie. *Geographies of Knowledge, Geometries of Power: Future of Higher Education*. New York/London: Routledge, 2007.

Foucault, Michel. *Power/Knowledge: Selected Interviews and Other Writings, 1972-1977*. Brighton: Harvester, 1980.

Freire, Paulo. *Pedagogy of Freedom: Ethics, Democracy, and Civic Courage*. Critical Perspectives Series. Lanham: Rowman & Littlefield, 1998.

Gorski, Paul C. "Good Intentions Are Not Enough: A Decolonizing Intercultural Education." *Intercultural Education* 19, no. 6 (2008): 515-525.

Higuera-Smith, Kay, Jaychitra Lalitha, and L. Daniel Hawk. *Evangelical Postcolonial Conversations*. Downers Grove: IVP, 2014.

Hofstede, Geert. "Cultural Differences in Teaching and Learning." *International Journal of Intercultural Relations* 10, no. 3 (1986): 301-320.

Hunter, Evan. "The Purpose of the Journal: For a Time Like This." *InSights Journal for Theological Education* 1 (2015): 8-16.

Ingram, David. *Habermas: Introduction and Analysis*. Ithaca: Cornell University, 2010.

Jegede, Olugbemiro J., and Glen S. Aikenhead. "Transcending Cultural Borders: Implications for Science Teaching." *Research in Science & Technological Education* 17, no. 1 (1999): 45-66.

Kaplan, R. "Cultural Thought-Patterns in Inter-Cultural Education." In *Landmark Essays on ESL Writing*, edited by T. J. Silva and P. K. Matsuda, 11-26. Mahwah: Lawrence Erlbaum Associates, 2001.

Kolb, David. *Experiential Learning*. Englewood Cliff: Prentice Hall, 1984.

McArthur, Jan. "Time to Look Anew: Critical Pedagogy and Disciplines within Higher Education." *Studies in Higher Education* 35, no. 3 (2010): 301-315.

Mendieta, Eduardo. *Global Fragments: Globalizations, Latinamericanisms, and Critical Theory*. Albany: State University of New York, 2007.

Merriam, Sharan B., and Associates. *Non-Western Perspectives on Learning and Knowing*. Malabar: Krieger, 2007.

Mezirow, Jack. *Transformative Dimensions of Adult Learning*. San Francisco: Jossey-Bass, 1991.

Morrow, Raymond Allen, and Carlos Alberto Torres. *Reading Freire and Habermas: Critical Pedagogy and Transformative Social Change.* New York: Teachers College, 2002.

Nakane, Ikuko. "Negotiating Silence and Speech in the Classroom." *Multilingua* 24 (2005): 75–100.

Nieto, Sonia M. "Profoundly Multicultural Questions." *Educational Leadership* 60, no. 4 (2002): 6–10.

Ntseane, Peggy Gabo. "Culturally Sensitive Transformational Learning: Incorporating the Afrocentric Paradigm and African Feminism." *Adult Education Quarterly* 61, no. 4 (2011): 307–323.

Quezada, Reyes, and Cristina Alfaro. "Developing Biliteracy Teachers: Moving Toward Culture and Linguistic Global Competence in Teacher Education." In *Intercultural Student Teaching: A Bridge to Global Competence*, edited by K. Cushner and S. Brennan, 57–87. Lanham: Rowman & Littlefield Education, 2007.

Reagan, Timothy G. *Non-Western Educational Traditions: Indigenous Approaches to Educational Thought and Practice.* Mahwah: Erlbaum, 2005.

Rockwell, Elsie. "Recovering History in the Anthropology of Education." In *A Companion to the Anthropology of Education*, edited by B. A. Levinson and M. Pollock, 65–80. Chichester/Malden: Wiley-Blackwell, 2011.

Semali, Ladislaus, and Joe L. Kincheloe. *What Is Indigenous Knowledge?* New York: Falmer, 1999.

Sleeter, C. E., and Peter McLaren. *Multicultural Education and Critical Pedagogy: The Politics of Difference.* New York: SUNY, 1995.

Tracy, David. *Plurality and Ambiguity.* San Francisco: Harper & Row, 1987.

9

A Theology for Advanced Theological Studies

Ian W. Payne

Keep on asking, and you will receive what you ask for. Keep on seeking, and you will find. Keep on knocking, and the door will be opened to you.[1]

Finding

When I was nine years old, I got lost in India! We were cycling home from an inter-school art exhibition in the Ketti Valley to Lushington School in Ooty. The instruction when we set out that afternoon was "Follow the railway tracks" to Ooty. But after several miles, I got separated from the rest of the group. Lost! All alone in rural India! That was until one more fellow student came by. Together we followed the rails. I was safe. When he followed his instincts and left the tracks to strike out for home another way, I kept him in my sights. And so I made it home also. Much later, I returned to the scene and realized that had I kept to the rail tracks I would have made it home via another, though longer, route. By then I was an adult working in India and my goal was no longer getting home safely; it was to explore all over India. I confidently explored similar rail tracks up to Darjeeling. In another adventure, in Nepal,

---
1. Matt 7:7.

I rode with my children on the roof of a bus. Just a week before writing this, I re-explored that journey home to Lushington, Google Mapping it from the vantage point of satellite images.

Academic explorations may have similar biographies. Sometimes we are more adventurous than at others. Slavishly following the traditional rules of an academic discipline may get us safely home, but it may not help us explore the world very deeply. There is not just one way to argue a thesis. There may be a variety of ways to explore a truth, a variety of ways to persuade people. We can't ignore the railway tracks, though they aren't the only way to explore. But explore we must. What we need is a discipline-aware humble confidence before God in exploring his world.

Receiving

Knowledge is not simply exploration – as if the knowledge gained was entirely deserved by our valiant efforts. Especially when it is interpersonal, it is ultimately grace. The known allows itself to be known. When I was at university, I was fascinated with a girl in my home town. Of course, we "knew" each other. But it took years for me to pluck up the courage to strike up a real conversation, and even longer to ask her out on a date. Then it was months to get beyond the pain of her response: "No." Still wishing her well, I set out to forget her. How surprising, then, when, nearly a year later, she opened the door, willing now to be known! The week before I wrote this chapter we celebrated thirty-eight years of married life, and revisited the spot where we first held hands! Academic fascinations can have similar mutuality. We find ourselves receiving.

Having the Door Opened

Surprises come sometimes, yes! Academic journeys can have such turning points, "Aha!" moments, when something we at last grasp begins to shed light on new and unexpected dimensions. I was tremendously excited to discover in Karl Barth patterns in epistemology I had noticed before in less theological contexts.

Let me explain. I did an MTh thesis and a PhD thesis on the same subject but from entirely different logical directions, from below and from above. Epistemology from below starts from the phenomenology of our *experiences* and can seek to bring them into coherent relation to the *revelation* of God in Christ. I discovered three important themes, and began to wonder whether they were Trinitarian. But then the question became: Was I imagining it? Was there any connection with God apart from the number three? Was I simply reading into things what I wanted to read into them? So I set out to work in the other direction: working from *revelation* to *experience*. I asked what could be learned for epistemology by looking at God's knowing and then at human knowing. Imagine how my heart glowed when I discovered those same themes in Barth! Or were they shown to me? Who knows! All I can say is that they keep on illuminating my world.[2] All I can do is share my delight and see if lights come on for others. I'll come to the three themes soon, but first a little more of my story.

After completing my doctorate, I was given the responsibility of leading my denomination's Bible college in New Zealand. Pathways College was on the verge of closing down. Fewer churches trusted it, and fewer students were signing up for its residential classroom-centred courses. After listening carefully to blunt opinions, we could see radical change was needed. Was learning best offered as knowledge conveyed to receptive minds in classrooms? Mmm – that didn't seem so sure. Or was there a place for learning in context? I thought so. Could we rebuild the trust by sharing with churches the privilege of seeing students learn while helping in ministry? The result was an internship mode of learning which was dramatically transformative. Knowledge was excitingly discovered in practice and in relationships. There was room for the learner's exploration and it was not so easy to forget the need for grace.

---

2. For instance, see my "Reproducing Leaders through Mentoring," in *Tending the Seedbeds: Educational Perspectives on Theological Education in Asia*, ed. Allan Harkness (Quezon City: Asia Theological Association, 2010), 167–191.

Keeping on Knocking

After five years at Pathways, we were called to work at the South Asia Institute of Advanced Christian Studies (SAIACS), India. I had studied at SAIACS before but nine years' experience of academic leadership in a South Asian context has been exciting. I discovered that context-based learning works just as transformatively in India. But it has also raised many more questions for me about epistemology and pedagogy. What differences does this new cultural context make? Many of our students are working on research and a thesis; does the traditional emphasis on theory and linear logic continue to be productive? Is there something too limiting about the supremacy of the traditional approach to academic theses? Does the South Asian mind find linear Western logic congenial to its own way of thinking? Do the traditional Western disciplines become compartments that isolate South Asian students from a holism that might be more natural for them?

I had already been wrestling with the question whether the experience versus revelation dilemma means one approach is better than the other. Should we always go from above to below (or vice versa)? Should we insist students argue a particular way? The same dilemma can be seen dressed in cultural clothes: Should we always argue from text to context, or alternatively, from context to text? Or, to put it another way, should we promote systematic thinking or contextual thinking? What happens to authority when we emphasize context or experience? Does Scripture become relativized? Do the voices of the context deafen us? What remains as criteria to help us navigate? If we don't, how do we speak relevantly? We could go on: Is there one truth? Or many truths? Is coherence possible? Or should we simply rejoice in the multiplicity of voices in the theological market? What can we say regarding so-called adjectival theologies (like green theology, feminist theology, dalit theology)? Does perspective trump all? What makes them Christian?

So Where Do We Find the Answers?

Just because there are many questions doesn't mean there are no answers. I believe a theology of advanced theological studies can guide teachers and their students to engage in Christian academic work with humility, confidence, and joy. A humble, confident epistemology will open the door to humble, confident academic exploration. It will do so because what I propose is ultimately an epistemology of love. It will balance *committedness* and *openness* and *involvement* (yes, my three themes!). It will be grounded in who God is and how he knows and loves.[3] Confirming light comes from some other Christian wrestlings with experience and philosophy around us.[4] Love is not simply rational and linear. Nor is it easy. It is not safe! But it is something for which we were all made. It is not the prerogative of white Western males (though I happen to be one). Love relishes examining the gem from every side. Love is not afraid of the mutuality and the mystery. Love delights in exploring the beauty, goodness, and truth of the world our good God has made. In what follows I can only begin to point the way to a theology of advanced theological studies.

Setting the Scene

For the last five hundred years, the West has been dominated by modernist thinking. René Descartes' famous words, "I think, therefore I am," have influenced us to think increasingly of ourselves as rational individuals. The way to be certain about anything is by doubting and questioning. This meant ditching the medieval willingness to trust authorities like the church. If you want truth, modernists assumed, you must maintain your distance, be objective. Faith became unpopular; reason was the way to go.

This epistemological assumption has influenced advanced studies. Teaching and learning enshrined this "objectivity." Doctoral theses were expected to be written without first person language, or any indication of the personal circumstances of the researcher. Similarly, any enthusiasm or passion for a subject was understood as evidence of bias. For the researcher, there must be no involvement.

---

3. See also Ian Payne, *Wouldn't You Love to Know? Trinitarian Epistemology and Pedagogy* (Eugene: Wipf and Stock, 2013). Hereafter *WYLTK*.
4. See also Esther Lightcap Meek, *Loving to Know: Covenant Epistemology* (Eugene: Cascade, 2011); Lesslie Newbigin, *Proper Confidence: Faith, Doubt and Certainty in Christian Discipleship* (Grand Rapids: Eerdmans, 1995); Nicholas Wolterstorff, *Reason Within the Bounds of Religion* (Grand Rapids: Eerdmans, 1976); N. T. Wright, *Christian Origins and the Question of God*, Vol. 1, *The New Testament and the People of God* (London: SPCK, 1992), in particular p. 64.

Of course, modernism's confidence in questioning was opposed or ignored by others placing their confidence in trusting. Classical approaches to learning clung to an emphasis on trusting authorities. This promoted conformity rather than individualism. The authority of traditions, church, or scriptures was not to be surrendered lightly. In theological education, liberals welcomed questioning, fundamentalists emphasized trusting. Tellingly, however, both were convinced that certainty was the goal. In Asia, Africa, and South America, knowing and learning remained largely classical. In the West, knowing and learning were predominantly focused on "objectivity."

To a large extent this attempt to be objective, this disciplined effort to pay attention to the subject, has been the reason for the fruitfulness of science. It's been hugely successful. But increasingly there were nagging doubts. As Carver Yu put it, modernity was characterized by "technological optimism and literary despair."[5] The rise of postmodernism is more evidence that all was not well. The promise of certainty has not been delivered. Doubts have remained. Supposed neutrality has been questioned. The widespread assumption that everyone thinks the same way and can be persuaded the same way has become questionable. There simply is no representative faceless universal person with a universal rationality. Everyone is different. Everyone comes from somewhere at a particular period in history. What persuades one does not persuade another.

Eventually with postmodernism this conviction has become so widespread that notions of truth itself have changed. What is true for you isn't necessarily true for me. Knowledge has become seen to be relative, personal, and perspectival. A person's perspective is unquestionable; his or her faith is once again permitted though it is no longer universally true. Along with privatization, pluralization, and relativization, however, comes fragmentation. Indeed, with widespread pessimism about knowing things as universally true, life has become "liquid."[6] I'm obliged to keep on changing. Permanence is suspect. If there is no overarching metanarrative, globalization must be

---

5. Carver Yu, quoted by Lesslie Newbigin, *Truth to Tell: The Gospel as Public Truth* (Grand Rapids: Eerdmans; Geneva: World Council of Churches, 1991), 19.
6. See Zygmunt Bauman, *Liquid Modernity* (New York: Wiley, 2000). Bauman sees "postmodernity" as an extension of modernity.

the enemy. This deep-rooted alienation and distrust has led to populism in geopolitics, to Brexit and Donald Trump.

Of course, the watching Majority World has a myriad of other competing religious and political factors. The loudest voice is fundamentalism, whether Islamic or Hindu. If the West has lost its epistemological certainty, perhaps fundamentalism from the East can provide it? Only at the cost of our personal and religious freedom, it would seem, lost to terrorists or demagogues.

So, if reason fails us, do we reassert faith? Are we best served by questioning everything or by trusting our valued authorities? Despair settles for believing nothing or everything, for nothing is certain. Fanaticism believes with certainty, but stops listening. No, the goal of certainty is a chimera.

The answer is simply this: that sort of certainty belongs only to God. Humans must settle for "walk[ing] by faith, not by sight" (2 Cor 5:7). Faith and reason go hand in hand. Listening to God, reason is faithful, and listening to others, faith is reasonable. The answer is not distrust and self-assertion. It is love. This is as true at the level of contemporary philosophy and geopolitics as it is of academic studies. Truth is worth the effort and risks of exploration, worth the mysteries and depth of mutual personhood, worth the endless richness, questions, and wonder. Truth is God's gift in grace. Truth is worth loving for.

A Theology of Knowing

The best way to know anything is to follow God's example. He loves. The best way for us to know something is to love it. If we think about people, the best way to know someone is to love him or her. Indeed, that's what explains the intimacy of friendship and marriage. It's also true of knowing God: the best way to know him is to love him. We are to love God with all our strength, mind, and heart; we must pay attention to God in Christ and by the Spirit. This is the intuition that underlies this theology for advanced theological research. But can we call it a theology?

Yes, we can. As I have argued elsewhere,[7] God's (self-revelation of God's own) knowing guides how humans should know. We ought to relate responsibly to others as God does. That is, we should imitate God's epistemic stance – his

---

7. *WYLTK*.

love. This is the best model for knowing anything. Love should be committed, open, and involved.

We find in the three themes of *committedness*, *openness*, and *involvement* an echo of the Trinitarian God. God expresses his committedness to us in revealing himself, by giving himself to us, in his Son; he shows his openness to us by remaining the Lord who claims our obedient response; and he demonstrates his involvement with us by the indwelling of his Spirit. This is how he knows us. He loves.

If the way God knows is shaped by the ideas of committedness, openness, and involvement, then our knowing *God* ought to be also. We ought to love him the way he loves us. We ought to trust and question him at the same time. Being fully committed is what we usually call faith; being fully open to him is what we usually call submission, but it can extend to daring request or daring complaint; involvement is what we usually call fellowship, the life of loyal faith. These are the dimensions of biblical covenant-keeping.

If our knowing God involves (or ought to involve) committedness, openness, and involvement, then our knowing *anything* should do also. We ought to pay careful attention to the object, not presuming we already know everything about it. This means knowledge is personal and relational. Knowledge is not the possession of individuals, who imagine themselves to be "masters of the universe," justifying domination and exploitation.[8] The goal is not alienated objectivity. Knowledge allows us to responsibly learn about and care for the world around us. Learning is joyful, thankful worship of God before whom we stand. As the nearby diagram[9] seeks to show, loving means *trusting* and *questioning* the object – in a relationship that irrevocably involves us as human beings and before God. In this relationship, we both give ourselves to and expect things of the object we wish to know. The attitude faith adopts towards the object is committedness; openness is the attitude reason adopts towards the object.

God's committedness to the world justifies a fundamental *realism*, an optimism about the reliability of our knowledge. God's openness to the world

---

8. Colin Gunton blames Immanuel Kant's view of the mind's assertive activity for such attitudes. *Enlightenment and Alienation* (Grand Rapids: Eerdmans, 1985), 25.
9. Adapted from *WYLTK*, fig. 4.16.

guarantees its <u>intelligibility</u> and encourages our exploration. It justifies in us a *critical* realism. God's eschatological goal for his creation guarantees the <u>meaningfulness</u> of the world, but also underlines the <u>provisional</u> nature of our knowledge. What humble confidence these affirmations lead to, in all fields, and especially in theological studies! There is a real world about us which we can confidently and humbly explore.

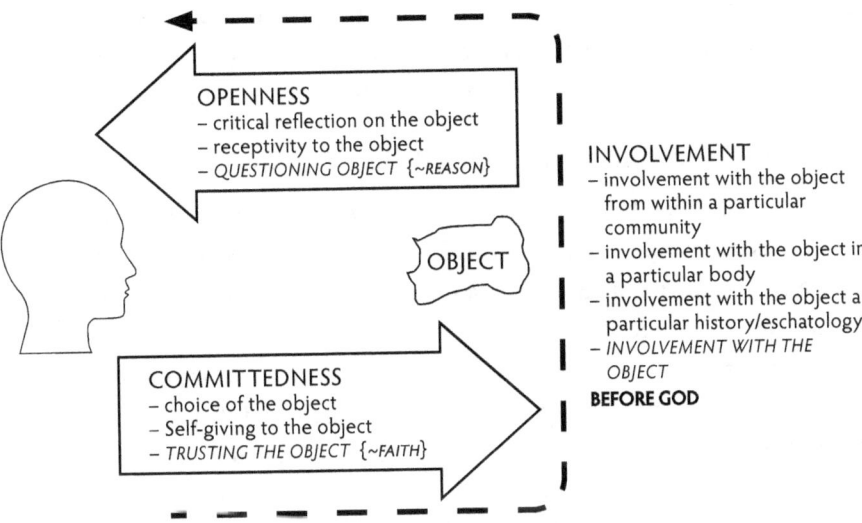

Figure 9.1 Our Optimal Epistemic Stance Towards Any Object

Applications to Advanced Theological Education

Several applications emerge from this Trinitarian relational epistemology of love. Unpacked simply from the diagram above, we will see that this epistemology suggests we must treat knowledge (and so theological education) as *relational* and as a balance of *faith* and *reason* and *missional action*. These convictions also underlie the Beirut Benchmarks. "Doctoral study," it says, "will be confessional, rational and missional. For a Christian, doctoral study is one dimension of what it means to 'love the LORD your God with all your heart and mind and soul and strength.'"[10]

---

10. ICETE, "The Beirut Benchmarks," March 2010, www.icete-edu.org/beirut/.

Knowledge as Relational

Knowledge is available only as we take up *involvement* with the object. The traditional definition of knowledge is "justified true belief."[11] This correctly identifies justification, accuracy, and rationality as three important factors in knowing. Yet it greatly oversimplifies what is going on, and all too quickly leads to problems such as individualism, intellectualism, ethnocentrism, unacknowledged bias, exclusion of passion, knowledge as possession, and knowledge as domination. With each factor, the problems are eased if they are understood in their necessary context of involvement. Simply put, knowledge is *perspectival*. Each of us knows from an inherently human perspective.

We Can't Be Satisfied with Isolated "Justification"

We are not justified by claiming neutrality. We ought not to pretend that our knowledge is entirely objective, entirely passionless, entirely unbiased towards the object. We are not justified by claiming we are unaffected by our knowledge. We are not unchanged.

We are not alone in knowing something. Rather we are embedded in a particular community, using particular language to think and communicate about the object. There is no universal rationality.[12] People from different cultures are persuaded by different approaches and reasons. This recognition is a primary motivation for this book. Diversity of rationality frees us to explore but it doesn't, however, mean we disregard tradition; rather we navigate aware of traditions and of our own tradition. To echo the introductory story of cycling home, we need to be aware of the railway tracks but recognize that exploration may leave them behind from time to time. New railway tracks may even need to be developed!

We Can't Pretend to Have Isolated (Access to) "Truth"

We ought not to imagine that we have absolute certainty. Our knowledge is inherently risky. It doesn't work to exclude risk by our definition of knowledge.

---

11. This definition goes back to Plato (*Theaetetus* 201; *Meno* 98). Edmund L. Gettier highlighted some difficulties in his "Is Justified True Belief Knowledge?," *Analysis* 23, no. 6 (June 1963): 121–123.
12. Alasdair C. MacIntyre, *Whose Justice? Which Rationality?* (London: Duckworth, 1988).

Our embeddedness and finiteness make certainty impossible. Only God possesses this. We must be satisfied with more modest claims, trusting that our faith in him can be shown to be reasonable.

Our attitude to truth is also cultural-linguistically embedded. There is no realm of abstract propositions delineating what is true; there are only particular human attempts to portray truth. And particular humans always inhabit particular cultures and languages. Moreover, knowledge cannot be summarized *only* by lists of propositions, but is often better described by narratives. We are surrounded not so much by brute facts as by "a story-laden world."[13] As noted in several chapters of this book, this observation suggests new options for the form of a dissertation.

There is some justification for postmodern suspicion about metanarratives as covert grabs for power. Of course, having no metanarrative is just as impossible as standing nowhere. So Christians need not and must not abandon the Christian metanarrative; we do, however, need to watch for any element of coercion in our efforts to persuade. The ultimate authority of Scripture is definitive of Christian evangelical identity, but it doesn't give us absolute certainty; it gives us what Lesslie Newbigin calls "proper confidence."[14]

We are involved with the object *before God*. The full truth about anything cannot exclude God. As Christians, we see God as the ultimate context for everything. The object we want to know finds its ultimate meaning in connection with God.[15] All knowing is intrinsically theological. The human knower similarly stands before God who judges his or her knowing. In other words, relational epistemology is intrinsically ethical. We ought to condemn attitudes to knowing that dominate or exploit the known in unloving ways. Similarly, advanced theological education is vitally concerned with integrity and responsibility in learning. It is vitally concerned with nurturing a spirit of worship in the learner. Not only is church and mission the natural focus

---

13. N. T. Wright, *Christian Origins and the Question of God*, Vol. 1, *The New Testament and the People of God* (London: SPCK, 1992), 42. In speaking like this, he is not adopting relativism, but avoiding naïve realism.

14. See Newbigin's book of the same title. By identifying Scripture as "our" authority, I am not suggesting that it has no authority over other religious communities. Christ is Lord over all, and Scripture is his Word; nevertheless, our grasp of what Scripture means is fallible.

15. Eph 1:10 indicates the significance of Jesus's identity for all things. Similarly, he is "the true light, which enlightens everyone," John 1:9.

of theological education, but encouraging the learner him- or herself to be embedded in church and mission is an ethical imperative.

We Can't Be Satisfied with Isolated "Belief"

The object does not sit in glorious abstract isolation in the knower's mind. Cognitive argument can't claim to be the only way to persuade others. We are more than minds: we are human beings that exist in relationship. There is more to knowledge than self-conscious cognition. Michael Polanyi, an influential scientific philosopher, highlighted how much of our knowledge is not focal and explicit but tacit.[16] In using a tool, for instance, we "indwell" it in order to focus on what we are using the tool to do. Similarly, we trust certain things in order to question what we are focused on. The tacit assumptions may need critique too, but they are an integral part of knowing. Like icebergs, not all that we believe is explicit. This means that as we adopt new assumptions there will always be new ways to critique the focus. Conclusions in advanced theological education have to be continually open to review.

Knowledge is not the act of a mind but of a human. Polanyi argued there is no knowledge without a knower. Because knowing is an act of skill, it involves the personal participation of the knower. It is "neither an arbitrary action nor a passive experience but a responsible act claiming universal validity," he said. "[I]nto every act of knowing there enters a passionate contribution of the person knowing what is being known, and . . . this coefficient is no mere imperfection but a vital component of his knowledge."[17] So learning involves passion and action. Similarly, theological education will not privilege attempts to be entirely dispassionate. It should permit passionate commitment. Reporting in first person language will not be disbarred. Since knowing is action, theological education will not privilege the "pure" sciences but may encourage the humanities. Theological education will oppose the dichotomy between theory and practice, between biblical studies and theology on the one hand and mission and practical theology on the other. Human knowledge is not better for being theoretical, or for being practical.

---

16. Michael Polanyi, *Personal Knowledge: Towards a Post-Critical Philosophy* (Chicago: University of Chicago, 1962).
17. Polanyi, *Personal Knowledge*, vii–viii.

In summary, in knowing, our justification is community-rooted and contextually framed, our grasp of truth is limited, narrative-shaped and accountable, and our beliefs are improvable and self-involving. Knowledge is justified, true belief, chastened and flourishing in an inextricably human setting.

Knowledge as a Balance between Faith and Reason

We both trust and question at the same time. We hold to both faith and reason. The balance is between committedness and openness. This balance is the way through the dilemma between modern/postmodern rationalism and fundamentalism. Uncritical faith eventually leads to incommensurable rivalries and to suicide bombers. But unfaithful reason leads to the liberal malaise of relativism, to postmodern pessimism, and to intolerant political correctness. This is the balance between realism and idealism; it is the balance proposed by critical realism. It is what is needed in geopolitics today: "From Warsaw to Washington, the political divide that matters is less and less between left and right, and more and more between open and closed."[18]

My argument is that it is also the balance taught and modelled by God in Scripture. It requires right belief and committed trust in the living God ("the fear of the LORD is the beginning of wisdom"); it requires creative and humble use of the rational faculties we have as made in God's image. It also requires of us "appropriate living in the world to reflect God's calling and participate in God's mission."[19]

Knowing Should Display Committedness

Subjective commitment is inevitable and integral to all knowing. Any attempt to have no presuppositions is doomed to failure. Rather theological education should embrace confessionalism. Prior committedness to our framework of thinking must be acknowledged, but, without such commitments, knowledge is impossible. There is no need for advanced theological education to be

---

18. "Drawbridges Up," *The Economist*, 30 July 2016. https://www.economist.com/news/briefing/21702748-new-divide-rich-countries-not-between-left-and-right-between-open-and, accessed 1 March 2017.
19. ICETE, "The Beirut Benchmarks."

embarrassed by Christian commitments; rather they are distinctive of the "children of the light" (John 12:36).

Additionally, committedness to the object you want to know is essential. It takes choice and focused time to study, time and focus that could be given elsewhere. Committedness is also trusting the object to reveal itself. We do not presume to know before we start. Especially in the humanities, study is by permission and grace. To conceive of academic knowledge as *love* is to transform the mundane; it is to imbue it with heavenly or missional purpose. Love gives dignity to what is studied; it does not demand conformity to preconceptions. It does not take knowledge as a means of exploitation or domination.

Knowing Should Display Openness

Openness is receptivity to what the object really is and then also critical reflection on it. It is *questioning* the object. Openness is essential for objectivity. For optimal learning, we need to seek to be as objective as possible; we need to diligently pay attention to the object. If God has given us adequate intellectual and sensory abilities, then to learn well we are obliged to use those abilities. If the truth exists outside ourselves,[20] then we must examine what lies beyond us. We are not simply projecting our wishes onto something if we are truly open to evidence. We may not expect it or like it, but, as Jesus said, "the truth will set you free."

Openness involves critical analysis. Advanced learning would expect independent appraisal of primary and secondary source materials, and creation of new and related concepts developed through consistent argument. Discovery of new knowledge owes much to the ability to question. But it is the balance with committedness that is valuable. To echo Polanyi again, in every act of knowing there is a focal point of attention surrounded by a vast area of tacit knowledge; that which is in question is surrounded by much that is not questioned.

In Asian contexts, with the greater emphasis on submission to the teacher, learners often find themselves diffident in developing the skill of independent

---

20. Some forms of Buddhism, Hinduism, and New Age thought deny the distinction between the "I" and the world. While this claim can be examined, it should be noted that it denies the reality of the distinction between things and God, and so it denies the value of openness.

critical thinking, but their commitment can be an asset. Contrastingly, Western students are usually more adept at critical analysis and independent thinking, but are often less willing to accept the authority of teacher and tradition, and this lack of committedness can impede their learning.

Knowledge as Missional Exploration

We need to balance faith and reason while acting. Trusting and questioning are verbs. Knowledge is more than content in our heads; it must issue in behaviour and lifestyle. It ought to be evident as wisdom, the virtuous outworking of knowledge in practice. Of course, I don't mean any action: I mean Christian action. For our actions to be meaningful they need to be congruent with mission, with God's mission. This combination of committedness and openness with action makes learning an adventure, exploration in service of the King.

Especially for advanced theological education, we expect students to undertake a significant academic journey. They should "demonstrate the ability to conceive, design and implement a substantial project of inquiry resulting in a sustained and coherent thesis."[21] We have already suggested that greater diversity in the form of a thesis will be valuable. I want to make some other points.

The thesis should implicitly or explicitly point to Christ. That is, it should be Christo-telic in *method*. To begin with, this means that it should be biblical, taking Scripture as its authority. We can't speak for Christ if we speak against his Word. In the end, Christian action takes its mandate *from* him. Moreover, in the end Christian action should witness *to* Christ. Each discipline has its own methodology, its own railway tracks, to be sure. But ultimately, what makes our Christian academic efforts Christian is the degree to which they point to Christ. To illustrate, with comparative literature as a method: Dr Havilah Dharamraj's chapter ("Boldly Go!") gives a fascinating description of the discipline, illuminating it as academic adventure into new territory. The attention properly paid to the Common Reader is distinctive of the method, and it expands the applicability of biblical studies to current issues. Let's encourage usage of this new method.

---

21. ICETE, "The Beirut Benchmarks."

How could a comparative literature thesis be Christo-telic? Anyone can simply compare Deuteronomy with *Manu Smitri*, say. What would make such a thesis evangelical and Christian? Does the writer have to explicitly move from Old Testament to New Testament to historical theology to contemporary application before the comparison is trustworthy for Christians? That would ensure a coherent analysis that doesn't omit or contradict Jesus; however, with sufficient depth, it might make the task too long. Sometimes explicitly routing the argument through reference to Jesus may not be needed. For instance, comparison of the attitude to widowhood in disparate texts is straightforward, with the obligation to care for widows being equally found in the Old Testament, in Jesus's teaching, in the New Testament, and in historical theology. Sometimes, however, reference to Jesus does significantly enrich such a comparison. For instance, comparing kingship in Old Testament narrative and Babylonian texts can hardly ignore the theme of Jesus as the true king, the King of kings, in the New Testament. Again, inter-religious textual comparison of the attitude to religious reasons for taking rest (Sabbath-keeping) should not bypass Christ's fulfilment of the Sabbath described in the New Testament. While each discipline has its area of focus, we must guard against treating disciplines as separate compartments. Christian thinking is integrated around the figure of Jesus.[22] Leaving Jesus out of a thesis argument may distort or truncate what can be Christianly said. The method of thesis argument should be explicitly (or at least implicitly) Christo-telic.

Second, the thesis should serve Christ's purposes. It should be Christo-telic in *purpose*. It should demonstrate relevance to its context, be readily communicable to Christian communities, and have potential for missional impact.[23] The academic adventure is not for its own sake. Yes, love and respect for something demands that we pay attention to it before we jump to pragmatic concerns for relevance. On the other hand, all our efforts are *ultimately* to please Christ, to promote the kingdom of God, and to advance the mission of the church.

---

22. Over recent years at SAIACS, we have identified biblical theology as one of the greatest gaps in many applicants' preparedness for MTh.
23. These are the last three concerns of the Beirut Benchmarks.

Conclusion

We can find our way home by seeking; we can get answers by asking; we can have doors opened to us if we continue to ask, seek, and knock.

We can recommend a Trinitarian theology for advanced theological education that models itself on love, seeking to balance faith and reason in missional action; a love that balances committedness and openness in a robust relationship which recognizes its human context and divine orientation. Academic study will then be part of loving God with all our heart and mind; it will be patient, disciplined, aware of the "railway tracks," without losing its character as adventure for the sake of the glory of God. Let us bring a smile to his face.

Discussion Questions

1. With one or two others discuss the dominant educational practices that take place in your school, particularly in its advanced programs of study. What do you believe is the implicit epistemology that undergirds these practices? To what extent are your practices based on a modernist emphasis on "objectivity," a classical emphasis on group "conformity," a postmodern emphasis on individual "subjectivity," or a more relational approach?

2. The central theme of this chapter is the application of an epistemology of love, seen in a balance between committedness, openness, and involvement as reflective of Trinitarian love. This involves the following three key perspectives:

   a. "Knowledge as relational." Taking seriously the explication given in this chapter – Each of us knows from an inherently human perspective; We can't be satisfied with isolated "justification"; We can't pretend to have isolated (access to) "truth"; We can't be satisfied with isolated "belief" – how do you personally seek to live out this perspective in your own teaching and/or leadership roles? To what extent is this perspective taken seriously in the approach taken to advanced studies? Give one or two suggestions for better implementation of the relational nature of knowledge in your educational context.

   b. "Knowledge as a balance between faith and reason." If you were to place on a set of "scales" faith and reason as practised in your school, and particularly in the programs of advanced study, to which side do you think the scales would lean? Why? Describe one or two practical steps you personally could take to better promote a healthy balance between faith and reason.

c. "Knowledge as missional exploration." Describe one or two key features of your school that you believe reflect the "Christo-telic" missional emphasis described in this chapter. To what extent are dissertations in your setting congruent with mission? To what extent does this understanding undergird your advanced programs of study? What do you think might be done better?

Bibliography

Bauman, Zygmunt. *Liquid Modernity*. New York: Wiley, 2000.

Gettier, Edmund L. "Is Justified True Belief Knowledge?" *Analysis* 23, no. 6 (June 1963): 121–123.

Gunton, Colin. *Enlightenment and Alienation*. Grand Rapids: Eerdmans, 1985.

ICETE. "The Beirut Benchmarks." March 2010. www.icete-edu.org/beirut/.

MacIntyre, Alasdair C. *Whose Justice? Which Rationality?* London: Duckworth, 1988.

Meek, Esther Lightcap. *Loving to Know: Covenant Epistemology*. Eugene: Cascade, 2011.

Newbigin, Lesslie. *Proper Confidence: Faith, Doubt and Certainty in Christian Discipleship*. Grand Rapids: Eerdmans, 1995.

———. *Truth to Tell: The Gospel as Public Truth*. Grand Rapids: Eerdmans, 1991.

Payne, Ian. "Reproducing Leaders through Mentoring." In *Tending the Seedbeds: Educational Perspectives on Theological Education in Asia*, edited by Allan Harkness, 167–191. Quezon City: Asia Theological Association, 2010.

———. *Wouldn't You Love to Know? Trinitarian Epistemology and Pedagogy*. Eugene: Wipf and Stock, 2013.

Polanyi, Michael. *Personal Knowledge: Towards a Post-Critical Philosophy*. Chicago: University of Chicago, 1962.

Wolterstorff, Nicholas. *Reason Within the Bounds of Religion*. Grand Rapids: Eerdmans, 1976.

Wright, N. T. *Christian Origins and the Question of God*. Vol. 1, *The New Testament and the People of God*. London: SPCK, 1992.

Section II

Innovative Possibilities for the Dissertation

If you eat salt, you will have to drink water. (South Indian proverb)

The second section of our collection investigates innovative possibilities for the dissertation. Few people are aware of the origins of the current shape of theses and dissertations. Ziolkowski points out that the PhD originated in Germany during "the heyday of positivism," and was from there exported to the United States and the rest of Europe. He concludes: "The Ph.D., as it was imported into the United States from Germany . . . was neither a teaching certificate (as James pointed out) nor a cachet of culture (as Babbitt stressed). It was essentially a badge of research competence in the sciences, introduced into this country by presidents who were German-trained scientists and monitored for the past century by graduate-school deans who have come preponderantly from fields of science or engineering."[1]

---

1. Theodore Ziolkowski, "The Ph.D. Squid," *American Scholar* 59, no. 2 (Spring 1990): 192.

The linear-empiricist shape is familiar to all who have engaged in advanced studies. In some contexts it is a required shape: Introduction (chapter 1); Literature Review (chapter 2); Research Methodology (chapter 3); Results and Discussion (chapter 4); Conclusion (chapter 5). The whole structure is designed closely on the scientific method, even in fields which call for more integrative understandings. The outcome is predictably negative – as predictable as eating salt is followed by thirst.

William Pannapacker regards the traditional dissertation as little more than "a hazing ritual passed down from another era, retained because the PhDs before us had to do it."[2] Similar sentiments were expressed to Perry when he interviewed a number of doctoral candidates and experienced supervisors of doctoral theses:

1. "Going through doctoral studies is like going through a university fraternity process, where they do all they can to humiliate you; every time you cross a hurdle they put up another barrier."
2. "I think you have to realize that it's not about learning; it's about paying your dues to the academy."
3. On the viva: "In some countries they devote their time to testing what you don't know rather than what you do know."
4. "The learning is not commensurate with the work."

Only those who have completed the process will be heard to critique the process, but by then you have invested so many years in the process that there is fear that your critique undermines the authority of your credentials.

Reflecting specifically on advanced theological studies Michael Griffiths has described the process as "theological circumcision."[3] And Walter Wink concludes that much of what we do is develop "trained incapacity to deal with the real problems of actual living persons in their daily lives."[4] Some of the best minds of the church sacrifice the best years of their lives writing

---

2. Quoted in Stacey Patton, "The Dissertation Can No Longer Be Defended," *The Chronicle of Higher Education*, 11 February 2013.
3. Michael Griffiths, "Need the Two-Thirds World Travel West for Theological Circumcision?" (unpublished paper delivered at Regent College, Vancouver, British Columbia, Canada, 1990).
4. Walter Wink, *The Bible in Human Transformation: Toward a New Paradigm in Bible Study* (Minneapolis: Fortress, 2010), 6.

something that virtually no one will read, and likely will have minimal if any impact on the world for Christ. This second section of our collection brings suggestions for innovations that may provide better paths for the development of theological leadership.

Paul Clark (Overseas Council) opens this section by pointing to the need for greater integration in thesis construction. This integration should be not merely interdisciplinary but also engaging of the whole integrated person.

John Jusu (Africa Regional Director for Overseas Council) has done extensive work on problem-based learning as a contextually significant model for the African church. John guides us through the philosophy and process of applying the model to advanced theological studies.

Action research is an approach in which the questions and answers to significant issues are generated and solved collaboratively between the researcher and the community in which the research is taking place. Caleb Hutcherson (Faculty Lead at the Arab Baptist Theological Seminary) has used this approach in projects at the master's level. In his chapter he draws in Bassem Melki (Dean of Students at ABTS) as a dialogue partner. Bassem is currently completing a PhD in Peace Studies using action research as his methodology.

The solitary nature of research has regularly been highlighted as one of the key negative features of advanced studies. Moving to more collaborative approaches is appropriate in the light of growing calls for collaboration in the secular academy, the potential resonance with the communal nature of most Majority World societies, the destructive nature of competitive and solitary leadership in the church, and ubiquitous theological imperatives. Rafael Zaracho has experimented with a variety of collaborative approaches in Paraguay, and brings insights and suggestions for advanced theological studies.

Jay Moon (Professor of Intercultural Studies, Asbury Seminary) has extensive experience engaging with oral communities in the Majority World. His chapter brings insights on how the global church might both empower theological leadership in these communities and benefit from the insights leaders in these communities bring to the church.

Through his many years of service in the Philippines, Larry Caldwell (Chief Academic Officer at Sioux Falls Seminary) came to see that our hermeneutical approaches are culturally shaped. The key idea in his chapter is to allow students to use dynamic culturally appropriate hermeneutical methods as they approach the biblical text. Larry also describes the work of graduate students who he has guided through the application of ethnohermeneutical principles to the text of Scripture, producing a final product that is both relevant and read.

Every culture has a rich corpus of literature – both classic and contemporary. And yet often in advanced theological studies the study of Scripture is divorced from this heritage. In the development of theological leadership it is imperative that the literature that shapes people's thinking is brought into dialogue with the Bible. In the final chapter of this section Havilah traces current trends in comparative literature studies, demonstrating how "literature" is more than text, and investigating the implications of comparative studies for both the content and the shape of work that we might encourage among our best thinkers.

Bibliography

Griffiths, Michael. "Need the Two-Thirds World Travel West for Theological Circumcision?" Unpublished paper delivered at Regent College, Vancouver, British Columbia, Canada, 1990.

Patton, Stacey. "The Dissertation Can No Longer Be Defended." *The Chronicle of Higher Education*, 11 February 2013.

Wink, Walter. *The Bible in Human Transformation: Toward a New Paradigm in Bible Study*. Minneapolis: Fortress, 2010.

Ziolkowski, Theodore. "The Ph.D. Squid." *American Scholar* 59, no. 2 (Spring 1990): 177–196.

10

Pathways of Integration for Theological Knowledge:
Integrative Knowing/Learning for Thesis Construction in Advanced Theological Studies

Paul Allan Clark

Integration in a Fragmented World: The Need for Integration Today

Integration of learning has become a part of my teaching. Teaching through the New Testament in the Alliance Bible Institute (SEMIBA) in São Paulo, Brazil, I found building integrative charts on the whiteboard helpful to me and my students. These charts made connections between the culture in the church and city and the text of Paul's epistle, or they drew parallels between the Gospels, making the comparison of pericopes more easily grasped. These experiences also piqued my desire to make connections between my theology and my educational practice. Integrative approaches to learning can prepare people in theological studies for interaction in more effective ways with the social, cultural, economic, philosophical, political, and even pragmatic dimensions of life in their context of ministry.

Call for Integration in Learning and Knowing in Theological Education

From within theological education there has been a call for integration between knowing, being, and doing, as seen in titles such as *Integral Ministry Training*, *A Guide to an Integrated Approach to Theological Education*, and *Beyond Fragmentation: Integrating Mission and Theological Education*.[1] The Manifesto for the Renewal of Theological Education, which grew out of the Consultations of ICETE (International Council for Evangelical Theological Education) on the issue of integration in theological education, states: "Our programs of theological education must combine spiritual and practical with academic objectives in one holistic integrated educational approach. We are at fault that we so often focus educational requirements narrowly on cognitive attainments, while we hope for student growth in other dimensions but leave it largely to chance. Our programs must be designed to attend to the growth and equipping of the whole man of God" (ICETE Manifesto, June 1983).[2]

This call comes not exclusively from the West, but also from theological educators in India and Africa.[3] Mwangi and de Klerk conclude that "we have now realised how dysfunctional and inhibiting the Western model is to positioning the African leadership to respond to the needs of the ever growing church in Africa."[4] If there is a call for integration in a fragmented world, in order to be able to prepare leaders for the church, what then are these spheres of fragmentation?

---

1. Robert Brynjolfson and Jonathan Lewis, eds., *Integral Ministry Training: Design and Evaluation* (Pasadena: William Carey Library, 2006); Paul Mohan Raj, *A Guide to an Integrated Approach to Theological Education* (Bangalore: Theological Book Trust, 2008); and Bernhard Ott, *Beyond Fragmentation: Integrating Mission and Theological Education* (Oxford: Regnum, 2001).
2. Appendix A in Robert W. Ferris, *Renewal in Theological Education: Strategies for Change* (Wheaton: Billy Graham Center, 1990), 144.
3. Tim Dearborn, "Preparing New Leaders for the Church of the Future: Transforming Theological Education through Multi-Institutional Partnerships," *Transformation: An International Journal of Holistic Mission Studies* 12, no. 4 (1995): 7–12; Jesudason Jeyaraj, *Christian Ministry: Models of Ministry and Training* (Bangalore: Theological Book Trust, 2002); and James K. Mwangi and Ben J. de Klerk, "An Integrated Competency-Based Training Model for Theological Training," *HTS Teologiese Studies/Theological Studies* 67, no. 2 (2011), accessed 26 January 2017, http://www.hts.org.za/index.php/HTS/article/viewFile/1036/1920.
4. Mwangi and de Klerk, "An Integrated Competency-Based Training Model," 5.

Spheres of Fragmentation Creeping into Theological Education

It is possible to identify at least four spheres in which theological education studies have experienced this fragmentation. First, there is a divide between theory and practice, between theology and life. Mwangi and de Klerk cite a study from Africa in which "The trainers have been accused of being 'theoretical' rather than 'practical' in training for ministry."[5]

A second sphere is the lack of integration of the "ABCs of Learning" – Affective, Behavioural, Cognitive (or Head, Heart, Hands) – with an overemphasis on cognitive learning, to the near-exclusion of the affective and behavioural aspects.[6] While in theological education there is a growing emphasis on skills acquisition and character–spiritual formation, there is a need for further integration of these areas for theological education and ministry formation.[7]

Third, the disciplinization of theological education, as it entered the world of the university, has left the marks of fragmentation common in other areas of higher education. Edgar Morin, in a philosophical call to tackle what he identifies as the "predominance of fragmented learning divided up into disciplines," states that this "often makes us unable to connect parts and wholes; it should be replaced by learning that can grasp subjects within their context, their complex, their totality."[8] The antidote to this, Morin responds, is that "we should develop the natural aptitude of the human mind to place all information within a context and an entity. We should teach methods of grasping mutual relations and reciprocal influences between parts and the whole in a complex world."[9] Morin's call for reform in education was a call for integration of learning.

The fourth sphere of fragmentation that creeps into theological education is the sacred–secular divide, between the clergy and the laity, between the vocational and the congregational. Bernhard Ott in Europe and Darren

---

5. Mwangi and de Klerk, 1.
6. Perry Shaw, *Transforming Theological Education: A Practical Handbook for Integrative Learning* (Carlisle: Langham Global Library, 2014), 76.
7. See chapter 9 in this volume, Ian Payne on "A Theology for Advanced Theological Studies."
8. Edgar Morin, *Seven Complex Lessons in Education for the Future* (Paris: UNESCO, 1999), 1.
9. Morin, *Seven Complex Lessons*, 2.

Cronshaw in Australia have both pointed to this in their writings, asking for a missional and holistic integration as the basis for renewing theological education.[10]

These tendencies of fragmentation in the world of higher education from the disciplinization, specialization, and departmentalization of advanced studies have entered theological studies, bringing a need for greater integration. The result is a lack of application of theological learning in a given context.

Integrative Approaches Are Needed in Theological Doctoral Programs

The nature of Christian theology and theological education requires us to develop an integrative approach in theological doctoral programs.

1. Integration is necessary by virtue of the nature of the thinking/knowing being that humans are. Human beings are wired to think in a holistic and integrated manner, drawing on all senses, forming responses from different sources, and working to integrate this variety of sources into a viable response. This is confirmed in recent brain science and learning studies.[11]

2. There is a need for conversation of theology with other disciplines in the process of developing theological reflection. The nature of theological reflection is not exclusively theological, but is an interaction of theology with reality and context. In order to effectively converse with the context, theology must draw on a variety of areas of knowledge and ways of knowing, to form the theological responses.[12]

3. While advanced theological studies seek to build the thinking capacity, this must be oriented towards the development of practicable theology.

---

10. Ott, *Beyond Fragmentation*; Darren Cronshaw, "Reenvisioning Theological Education and Missional Spirituality," *Journal of Adult Theological Education* 9, no. 1 (2012): 9–27.

11. G. Caine and Nummela Caine, *Education on the Edge of Possibility* (Alexandria: Association for Supervision and Curriculum Development [ASCD], 1997); D. Sousa, *How the Brain Learns*, 4th ed. (Thousand Oaks: Corwin, 2011); J. D. Zull, *The Art of Changing the Brain: Enriching the Practice of Teaching by Exploring the Biology of Learning* (Sterling, VA: Stylus, 2002).

12. See chapter 1 in this volume, where Ashish Chrispal speaks of his experience and the challenge of integrating theology and context for missional effectiveness.

As the church continues to expand into new areas of the world, theological students face the ever-increasing need for developing applicational (deeply practical) theology for these developing churches, which are ministering in cultural and contextual realities that differ from those where the Christian church originated and was strong until the shift towards the Majority World.[13]

4. The reason why many enter doctoral studies in theology is their desire to teach in theological education. While this may be allied with the goal of training and research in theology, these must develop their capacity to explain theological thinking and methodology to students. Integrative approaches could prepare them for communication with students in the teaching–learning setting of theological education.

As theological studies at the doctoral level meet the realities of the church in recent decades, intentional work must be done to prepare leaders who are capable of integrating their faith, their theological understanding, and their lives into the contexts of that church they are serving. This will require intentional work at the doctoral level towards integrational studies, and even integrational dissertations.

Applying Integrative Approaches in Theological Doctoral Programs

In order to move in this direction of applying integrative approaches in doctoral programs in theological studies, we must keep in view the aim of these advanced studies. While there is the contribution of knowledge and theory to the realm of theological studies, doctoral studies are also a preparation of scholars for three principal areas – for theological development (contributing knowledge to the disciplines of theology, biblical studies, and ministry), for ministerial vocation (contributing to the development of pastoral, missional, and ancillary ministries), and for theological education (preparing teachers

---

13. In this volume, Lal Senanayake addresses cultural questions arising from the context, in "The Imperative of Cultural Integration in Advanced Theological Studies: Perspectives from the Majority World." Also in this volume, César Lopes speaks of the need to apply an anthropological and critical approach, as we approach the cultural context with a heart of humility to learn, and bring freedom to the expression of local understandings of theology.

for a role in the formation of leaders-servants for ministries). In line with the urging of the Cape Town Commitment, we must keep the advanced studies under the guidance of the role of theological education in supporting the church in its fulfilment of the *missio Dei* in the world.[14]

An additional motivation is derived from the opportunity for conversations across disciplines. This has become more and more common in the areas of practical theology and missiology, as these bring into the theological conversation areas such as sociology, political science, anthropology, economics, and psychology. Drawing on this motivation, Ray Anderson goes even further, saying that this need for integration should lead us to define the degrees in a theological seminary "in terms of ministry or vocational outcomes, drawing on a faculty rich in interdisciplinary fields related to the total mission of God in the world through his people."[15]

The changes in our world, and in the way people think, should motivate us to look for integrative approaches that will aid in the formation of leaders for various contexts in our postmodern world. Robert Kegan challenges readers of his two volumes to think beyond the scientific epistemologies of the Enlightenment. He posits five levels of consciousness relating to thinking and knowing: Instinctual (Atomistic view of an infant); Personal (Durable category view of a child); Traditionalism (Cross-categorical view of a teen and young adult); Modernism (Systemic view of adults); and Postmodernism (Complexity view of some adults).[16] As we advance into a time that is characterized as "postmodern," the concerns expressed by Kegan for approaches to teaching-learning and curriculum that will address the complexity of the times will affect even the field of theological studies.

One of the results of moving into the "postmodern" mode of thinking, as Kegan suggests, is the necessary capacity to hold differing points of view in tension, as the mind processes through the divergences. We live in a world

---

14. Lausanne Committee for World Evangelization, "Cape Town Commitment," 2011, accessed 20 December 2016, https://www.lausanne.org/.

15. Ray Anderson, *The Shape of Practical Theology: Empowering Ministry with Theological Praxis* (Downers Grove: IVP, 2001), 326.

16. Robert Kegan, *The Evolving Self: Problem and Process in Human Development* (Cambridge, MA: Harvard University, 1982); *In Over Our Heads: The Mental Demands of Modern Life* (Cambridge, MA: Harvard University, 1994).

characterized by polarization of views and loss of middle ground, and we need theologians and theological educators who are able to bridge these divides to make theology meaningful in our time and in our contexts.

Potential Contributions from Integrative Theological Studies

Practical theology may take on new expressions, as this conversation moves out into the realms of economics, sociology, history, politics, psychology, and even the life and physical sciences.

With a growing need for theology to enter the marketplace and public sector, an integrative approach to theological studies can bring the voice of theology into conversation for forming practical responses to social, economic, and political needs. This can generate new possibilities for ministry in our world in which Christian theology is often marginalized from the public *praça*.[17] In all parts of the world there is a need for marketplace and public theologies, which will not develop without this kind of approach.

Our world is characterized not only by a marginalization of theology, but by outright opposition to Christian theology. This opposition may come from secularizing forces in the west, or from fundamentalists of majority religious groups in the east and south. But the time has come for Christian theologians to be able to converse with the theologies of their context about issues other than just the confrontation of world religions. It is time for Christian theology to contribute to the well-being of the nations with theological understanding of government, of poverty, of opposition, of persecution, of justice, and of so many other topics of great concern to the humanity we must serve as members of Jesus Christ's church. As theological knowledge expands its integration with other spheres of knowledge, it will be able to speak more clearly in our varied contexts around the world.[18]

---

17. The public square.
18. In this volume, Evan Hunter addresses the importance of integration and collaboration in advanced theological studies.

Foundations for Integrative Knowing and Learning in Theological Studies

Three foundational points are indicated for an integrative approach to knowing and learning as a basis for use in advanced theological studies. First, integration in knowing and learning can demonstrate the interconnectedness of knowledge and truth. This is the recognition that "all truth is God's truth, but not all truth is Scriptural or Theological truth; some truth is in the scientific and humanities realms, but falls outside of Scriptural or Theological understanding at this time."[19] Kevin Smith uses the illustration below to graphically show what he means. When we understand truth in this way, we see that studies that seek integration will lead to a potential expansion of theological understanding in the realms of science and the humanities, as this integrational conversation opens up these areas that were previously outside of theological and scriptural discussion. In my case, it was educational studies, but it could be connecting neuroscience with theology, or aesthetics with worship.

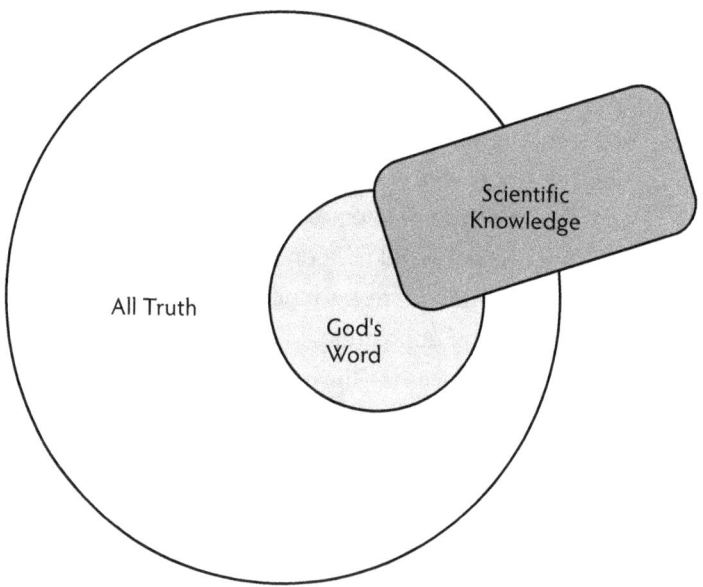

Figure 10.1 Integrative Knowing and Learning in Theological Studies

---

19. Kevin G. Smith, *Integrated Theology: Discerning God's Will for Our World* (Johannesburg: South African Theological Seminary, 2013), 117. Figure 10.1 used by permission.

Second, an integrative approach to knowing and learning will bring together a variety of voices on a particular subject. Osmer's model of Practical Theology points to learning through listening to four kinds of voices.[20] These voices arise from four tasks in theological reflection: (1) the descriptive-empirical task: "What is going on here?"; (2) the interpretive task: "Why is it going on?"; (3) the normative task: "What ought to be going on?"; and (4) the strategic task: "How might we respond?"[21] The first task gives rise to data from empirical and descriptive research into the context and phenomenon; thus it is a voice of "priestly listening," taking into consideration a thorough understanding of the situation. The second task gives rise to wisdom through "sagely reading" of the natural and spiritual world by way of the natural, social, and human sciences, giving insight into the contextual reality. The third task enables us to hear the voice of "prophetic discernment" incorporating both theology and the great traditions of biblical interpretation into the exploration of relationships and implications in the context. This voice also brings an ethical reflection to bear by applying guidelines for moral action. The final voice grows into a servant-leadership response in the form of a plan of action, which becomes "models of practice and rules of art."[22] To sum up, empirical research leads to consulting theories from the arts and sciences, engaging in theological interpretation and ethical reflection, which in turn leads to models of good practice, which are put into effect through action as servant-leaders. This model demonstrates the integration of varied perspectives for a thoroughgoing practical theology.

Third, this use of integration for learning and knowing will develop the habit of inclusion and holism, and combat the tendency in our time of exclusion and reductionism. A 2014 National Research Council report on "Convergence" suggested that advanced studies should foster rich and deep interdisciplinary learning that gives opportunities to develop some of the following proficiencies: (1) Developing the intellectual capacity to deal with complex problems; (2) Building confidence and willingness to approach

---

20. Kevin G. Smith, "Impact Studies and Curriculum Review," (unpublished paper presented at Institute for Excellence, Johannesburg, South Africa, 4 August 2016, Indianapolis: Overseas Council).
21. Richard R. Osmer, *Practical Theology: An Introduction* (Kindle ed.; Downers Grove: IVP, 2008), as discussed in Smith, *Integrated Theology*, 96–102.
22. Osmer, *Practical Theology*, loc. 2072.

problems from multiple perspectives; (3) Strengthening abilities to make decisions in the face of uncertainty (reflective judgement); and (4) Helping understand strengths and limitations of different disciplinary perspectives.[23]

Examples of an Integrative Mode of Knowing/Learning

One example of an integrative approach is the dissertation presented by Reginaldo P. Braga to Columbia University's Teachers College.[24] In this Brazilian study, he brought together a variety of disciplines ranging from the educational thought of Freire, to reformed theology, to the psychology of Frankl and Kernberg, for an integrative pedagogy for religious education for the Congregationalist tradition in north-eastern Brazil. He used the metaphor of the dance to describe how these areas need to interact, getting close and interacting with the movements of each part. This picture of the dance is summarized in various integrative charts in his conclusion.[25]

A second example is my own dissertation which brings together the areas of theological anthropology, adult education theory, and teaching practice.[26] To understand the practice of professors at seminaries in São Paulo, Brazil, it was necessary to bring these diverse areas into conversation for a theoretical and integrative framework. From theological anthropology, we understand the human being as relational and reflective, seeking to understand the reality that surrounds it, and also as a being in development. While theology gives us some of the understanding of how the human being is a learning being, educational

---

23. National Research Council, *Convergence: Facilitating Transdisciplinary Integration of Life Sciences, Physical Sciences, Engineering and Beyond*, Committee on Key Challenge Areas for Convergence and Health, Board on Life Sciences, 2014.
24. Reginaldo Paranhos Braga, Jr., *Towards a Pedagogy of Grace: In Search of Transcendence and Integration in Paulo Freire* (dissertation presented at Teachers College, Columbia University, New York, 2003).
25. In section three of this volume, examples of innovative approaches to doctoral theses show the use of wisdom literature, poetry, and various forms of story. This requires the integration of differing perspectives to show learning. Samuel Ewell brings out his own voice in his chapter "Doing Theology from the 'Land of Samba,'" bringing together the contrasts of form and function, and the influence of Brazilian culture and music, especially Samba.
26. Paul Allan Clark, "Para Uma Teologia Prática do Ensino Teológico" ("Towards a Practical Theology of Theological Teaching"; PhD diss., Programa Doutoral Latino-Americano, Facultad Internacional de Educación Teologica, Buenos Aires, Argentina, 2017).

and psychological studies inform us by giving us additional perspective on the relationality, reflectivity, and development of the human being. An integration of these perspectives yields foundational material for a practical theology of teaching practice for theological education.

Challenges of Integrative and Interdisciplinary Studies

The first challenge of integrative studies is to enter the world of interdisciplinary studies. This entrance brings the student and scholar into a conversation between radically different disciplines, which requires the recognition of different kinds of thinking, different sets of presuppositions, and the need to learn the language and thought patterns of that discipline as well as of one's primary discipline. On entering each additional domain of knowledge, learning to think in the patterns of each additional discipline is the challenge. The more varied the disciplines, the longer the stretch for the individual. In the conversation it is possible for each discipline to learn from the other. There may arise points of theory, understanding, and practice that may be integrated from one discipline to another, but rarely surface a new understanding of the whole.

An integrative approach would permit a deeper process of mutual influence between the disciplines. It might be possible not only to integrate limited points across the disciplinary lines, but also move towards a new conception of the whole. This new conception would go beyond bringing key thought schools together in an intermingling of ideas and practices; in the conversation a mutual transformation would bring change, and the potential for forming new patterns of thought and entering new areas of knowledge.

The potential for both sides profiting from this conversation is pointed out by Thomas G. Long, in his explanation of the place of theologians on the university campus: "When practical theologians engage in conversation with other disciplines, all parties gain. Clearly practical theologians draw wisdom from sociology, linguistics, ethnography, psychology, and other fields of knowledge, but those disciplines are also potential beneficiaries of these conversations."[27]

---

27. Thomas G. Long, "Practical Theology on the Quad: Doctoral Study in Practical Theology in the University Context," in *For Life Abundant: Practical Theology, Theological Education, and Christian Ministry*, ed. Dorothy C. Bass and Craig Dykstra (Grand Rapids: Eerdmans, 2008), 253.

A second challenge that an integrative approach to advanced theological studies presents is the skill set necessary for both sides of the teaching-learning encounter. The supervisor will need to operate on the level of Kegan's "postmodern" mindset. This will be necessary to see the complexity of systems, and the interaction of factors and variables. Since no simple solutions will arise, it will require a capacity to create relationships in areas of apparent divergence. This will require patience for the supervisor and perseverance for the student, along with flexibility for both. It may also require the capacity of the supervisor to gather a team of consultants from various specialized areas. The supervisor will see the whole, and the consultants will contribute their expertise to ensure that nothing is overlooked or misrepresented in the process of integration.

The student will need to develop the ability to hold apparent divergences in tension, while working on understanding the dynamics of the differing disciplines, and not be satisfied with harmonizing solutions to the dissonance. This student will hold two or more ideas in tension for a time in order to see the connections and relationships, instead of seeing them as mutually exclusive. In theology, this may mean to hold the love of God and the justice of God in tension, and as a result gain a deeper understanding of God and his working out of our salvation. In consideration of other disciplines, the tension between an atheist educator such as Freire and a theological perspective of human development may not seem to yield connections, but Freire's view of man as unfinished yields a point of entrance and conversation. This process requires a time of holding the ideas in tension, to allow them to truly converse with one another.[28]

A third challenge arises from the necessity of a team approach to develop new knowledge. Though speaking of the reality in the sciences, Dr Alan Leshner compared the historic reality of research with the current situation. In times past, the scientist often conducted research in a solitary enterprise. But with the changing of the times, science has become much more a team activity. This team effort holds out the hope of discoveries: "Many of the most interesting and important scientific questions require multidisciplinary approaches to

---

28. In this volume, Caleb Hutcherson and Bassem Melki, "Action Research for Theological Impact: Reflections from an Arab Context," address the use of action-reflection research within a multidisciplinary approach.

tackle them, and virtually no single individual has all the needed expertise. Therefore, it is essential that modern scientists be able to work productively in teams, and that they have some experience doing that before they go off into the field themselves. Graduate schools need to find some way to integrate those experiences into the curriculum."[29]

Suggested Pathways for Reflection in Integrative Thesis Construction

An integrative approach to doctoral studies and dissertation processing begins from a holistic perspective as opposed to a linear model, taking in various dimensions of the research picture, or various approaches to that point of research. So there may not be a "standard" beginning point in a certain kind of literature review, but a broad taking of perspectives and a variety of entry points for reflection, research, and revelation. The goal is not a single view, but an integration of various perspectives in a new understanding of theology, and its intersection with the larger spheres of knowledge.

The process will be dialectical, or even conversational, as different perspectives come into contact with one another. This is not an orderly pathway of investigation, but a taking in of differing angles and investigating relationships. The process is a search for connection between the differing spheres of knowledge. Graphics and tables may be useful for tracking the different connections that appear along the conversational journey.

In time, two processes will give rise to points of integration. First is what I would call "congealing," as the connections firm up through iteration, though never becoming fully concretized. This leaves room for a certain toleration of flexibility, uncertainty, and tentativeness in the conclusions, at least at the initial stages. The second process can be identified as convergence, in which points

---

29. Alan I. Leshner, "Rethinking the Dissertation in Science" (Alan I. Leshner, Chief Executive Officer Emeritus, American Association for the Advancement of Science), unpublished paper presented at the Council of Graduate Studies' Conference on the Future of the PhD Dissertation, Washington, DC, 28–29 January 2016; accessed 15 January 2017, http://cgsnet.org/sites/default/files/DissFwd_Print%20All%20Papers.pdf.

of intersection, alignment, and coherence begin to surface, giving foundation to integration of the differing spheres of knowledge.[30]

While many programs of advanced theological studies aim at individual effort, integrative approaches may open up possibilities of community learning. At the differing stages of the process, the student-researcher will find it necessary to process these points of potential integration with others, even with specialists in different fields of study. This may be through sharing stories, or living the truth discovered in community. In many cultures in the world, truth and knowledge are not an individual commodity, but a community treasure – which brings the implication that even the processing of that knowledge to give rise to truth needs to be a community process. For integrative approaches this may be even more important, so that the community can validate the processing of those connections.[31] At the same time, by its more conservative nature the community may inhibit some extreme applications of truth. Yet, even in the West, many recognize the importance of the social element. In the words of Claire Cain Miller: "For all the jobs that machines can now do – whether performing surgery, driving cars or serving food – they still lack one distinctly human trait. They have no social skills. Yet skills like cooperation, empathy and flexibility have become increasingly vital in modern-day work."[32] Integration is a particularly human activity.

The word "messy" may be the best one to describe this processing. It is not linear, not orderly, not mechanical. Rather it is circular, even spiral. It can even seem to be a wandering exercise as one journeys through different realms of knowledge, seeking points of integration. But as we develop the skills of dealing with "messy" problems that are not single-factor issues with simple (or simplistic) responses, we will discover that the processing towards potential solutions is messy just like the problems faced.

---

30. In this volume, Marvin Oxenham treats "Digital Scholarship," pointing out the necessity of making connections – and in the digital world, this is not only between ideas, but among people.
31. In this volume, Stephanie Black draws on her experiences in theological education in Africa to show that community is a vital part of learning in many cultures, not only in developing a "community of learning" but also in the community aspect of knowledge and learning.
32. Claire Cain Miller, "Why What You Learned in Preschool is Crucial at Work," "'The Upshot' Editorial," *New York Times*, 28 October 2015, accessed 20 December 2016, https://www.nytimes.com/2015/10/18/upshot/how-the-modern-workplace-has-become-more-like-preschool.html?_r=0.

This processing will be more textual than numerical. This reality will call for approaches that are more hermeneutical than statistical.[33] In a very real sense, this approach is more human, for it seeks to communicate by way of connections in much the same way that the brain makes its connections over its synapses – not in a linear fashion, but over a network of vast connectivity.

Though not wanting to make this a gender issue, I would point out that an integrative way of learning is more characteristic of female thought patterns. However, as I have encountered more men involved in the discussions of integrative learning, I believe that it is not an exclusive domain.

Conclusion

To overcome the fragmenting of knowing and learning in theological education in our twenty-first-century world, and to provide the foundation for deepening theological understanding and interaction with the expansion of knowledge in our twenty-first-century world, we must pursue the integration of theology with other realms of knowledge, and that can be encouraged through a more integrative approach to advanced theological studies, and the capstone project.

To overcome the divide between theory and practice, between diverse disciplines, and between the sacred and the secular, the integration of theological studies in a model more like that of a school of medicine may be helpful. Hibbert and Hibbert point out four elements of the medical school model that may be advantageous for integration: (1) incorporating practical ministry experience into every semester; (2) developing learning communities with graduates; (3) faculty intentionally serving as holistic role models; and (4) adopting a problem-based approach to learning.[34] In order to take advantage of these four elements, the faculty guiding this process must develop their own levels of integration. This kind of integrative doctoral studies will stretch both

---

33. For a deeper look at a hermeneutical approach, in this volume, Larry Caldwell emphasizes the role of culturally appropriate hermeneutics in the approach to the biblical text. This is an important case study on applying alternative approaches in order to integrate other fields of learning with theological studies.

34. Richard Hibbert and Evelyn Hibbert, "Addressing the Need for Better Integration in Theological Education," in *Learning and Teaching Theology: Some Ways Ahead*, ed. Les Ball and James R. Harrison (Eugene: Wipf and Stock, 2012), 113–115.

supervisor and scholar, will test systems and complexities, and will generate new categories and new perceptions of living the old truths in our times.

An integrative approach to advanced studies can nurture skills that will be useful in the process of teaching, research, and practice. The interdisciplinary conversation that is necessary will bring appreciation for and learning of different epistemological approaches, beyond the theological approach. It will introduce the student to knowledge bases, but more importantly to the ways of processing in the new disciplinary areas. An integrative approach will encourage thinking at higher levels of cognition of analysis, synthesis, and critical evaluation. This can open up to creative thinking as the possibility of new understanding flourishes. This will also lead to a capacity to carry on conversations with scholars in other disciplines, because of the deepened knowledge, appreciation, and thought processes. These conversations will go beyond the books to real personal conversation, and in these is an opportunity for collaborative integration and creation of knowledge.

An integrative approach will require stretching our normal thinking about doctoral studies in theology, so that our theology interacts with our practice, with the world of knowledge, and brings theology and the rest of knowledge into conversation. This way, theology can make a deeper contribution to our world, through leaders who are able to think theologically about the rest of knowledge.

Discussion Questions

1. Four major areas are suggested in which we need to encourage integration: (1) integration between theory and practice, between theology and life; (2) integration of the "ABCs of Learning" – Affective, Behavioural, Cognitive; (3) integration between the various disciplines of theological education; and (4) integration of the sacred and the secular.

Consider each of these areas in turn and describe one or two ways in which you see fragmentation or integration in your own school and its programs of studies.

2. In your own experience of advanced theological studies, what were some of the ways in which you brought dialogue between theological understandings

and the realms of science and the humanities? What did you sense was missing in your own advanced theological work?

3. Describe one or two of the most innovative approaches to integration that you have observed in other schools that you think your school might benefit from. You may like to consider some of the examples given in this chapter.

4. Looking to the future, to what extent in your faculty development plans are you preparing your emerging faculty to engage with interdisciplinary study and innovative integration? Describe at least one specific step that your school could take to better meet the need for developing faculty who are comfortable in integrative and interdisciplinary studies.

5. Hibbert and Hibbert point out four elements of the medical school model that may be advantageous for integration in theological studies: (1) incorporating practical ministry experience into every semester; (2) developing learning communities with graduates; (3) faculty intentionally serving as holistic role models; and (4) adopting a problem-based approach to learning. In what ways are these elements already in place at your school? Describe one or two ways in which your school could incorporate or further strengthen these four elements.

Bibliography

Anderson, Ray. *The Shape of Practical Theology: Empowering Ministry with Theological Praxis*. Downers Grove: IVP, 2001.

Braga, Reginaldo Paranhos, Jr. "Towards a Pedagogy of Grace: In Search of Transcendence and Integration in Paulo Freire." Dissertation, Teachers College, Columbia University, New York, 2003.

Brynjolfson, Robert, and Jonathan Lewis, eds. *Integral Ministry Training: Design and Evaluation*. Pasadena: William Carey Library, 2006.

Caine, G., and Nummela Caine. *Education on the Edge of Possibility*. Alexandria: Association for Supervision and Curriculum Development (ASCD), 1997.

Clark, Paul Allan. "Para Uma Teologia Prática do Ensino Teológico" ("Towards a Practical Theology of Theological Teaching"). PhD diss., Programa Doutoral Latino-Americano, Facultad Internacional de Educación Teologica, Buenos Aires, Argentina, 2017.

Cronshaw, Darren. "Reenvisioning Theological Education and Missional Spirituality." *Journal of Adult Theological Education* 9, no. 1 (2012): 9–27.

Dearborn, Tim. "Preparing New Leaders for the Church of the Future: Transforming Theological Education through Multi-Institutional Partnerships." *Transformation: An International Journal of Holistic Mission Studies* 12, no. 4 (1995): 7–12.

Ferris, Robert W. *Renewal in Theological Education: Strategies for Change*. Wheaton: Billy Graham Center, 1990.

Hibbert, Richard, and Evelyn Hibbert. "Addressing the Need for Better Integration in Theological Education." In *Learning and Teaching Theology: Some Ways Ahead*, edited by Les Ball and James R. Harrison, 107–118. Eugene: Wipf and Stock, 2012.

Jeyaraj, Jesudason. *Christian Ministry: Models of Ministry and Training*. Bangalore: Theological Book Trust, 2002.

Kegan, Robert. *The Evolving Self: Problem and Process in Human Development*. Cambridge, MA: Harvard University, 1982.

———. *In Over Our Heads: The Mental Demands of Modern Life*. Cambridge, MA: Harvard University, 1994.

Lausanne Committee for World Evangelization. "Cape Town Commitment." 2011. Accessed 20 December 2016. https://www.lausanne.org/.

Leshner, Alan I. "Rethinking the Dissertation in Science." Unpublished paper presented at the Council of Graduate Studies' Conference on the Future of the PhD Dissertation, Washington, DC, 28–29 January 2016. Accessed 15 January 2017. http://cgsnet.org/sites/default/files/DissFwd_Print%20All%20Papers.pdf.

Long, Thomas G. "Practical Theology on the Quad: Doctoral Study in Practical Theology in the University Context." In *For Life Abundant: Practical Theology, Theological Education, and Christian Ministry*, edited by Dorothy C. Bass and Craig Dykstra, 243–260. Grand Rapids: Eerdmans, 2008.

Miller, Claire Cain. "Why What You Learned in Preschool Is Crucial at Work." "'The Upshot' Editorial." *New York Times*, 28 October 2015. Accessed 20 December 2016. https://www.nytimes.com/2015/10/18/upshot/how-the-modern-workplace-has-become-more-like-preschool.html?_r=0.

Morin, Edgar. *Seven Complex Lessons in Education for the Future*. Paris: UNESCO, 1999.

Mwangi, James K., and Ben J. de Klerk. "An Integrated Competency-Based Training Model for Theological Training." *HTS Teologiese Studies/Theological Studies* 67, no. 2 (2011). Accessed 26 January 2017. http://www.hts.org.za/index.php/HTS/article/viewFile/1036/1920.

National Research Council. "Convergence: Facilitating Transdisciplinary Integration of Life Sciences, Physical Sciences, Engineering and Beyond." Committee on Key Challenge Areas for Convergence and Health. Board on Life Sciences, 2014.

Osmer, Richard R. *Practical Theology: An Introduction*. Downers Grove: IVP, 2008.

Ott, Bernhard. *Beyond Fragmentation: Integrating Mission and Theological Education*. Oxford: Regnum, 2001.

Raj, Paul Mohan. *A Guide to an Integrated Approach to Theological Education*. Bangalore: Theological Book Trust, 2008.

Shaw, Perry. *Transforming Theological Education: A Practical Handbook for Integrative Learning*. Carlisle: Langham Global Library, 2014.

Smith, Kevin G. "Impact Studies and Curriculum Review." Unpublished paper presented at Institute for Excellence, Johannesburg, South Africa, 4 August 2016. Indianapolis, IN: Overseas Council.

———. *Integrated Theology: Discerning God's Will for Our World*. Johannesburg: South African Theological Seminary, 2013.

Sousa, D. *How the Brain Learns*. 4th ed. Thousand Oaks: Corwin, 2011.

Zull, J. D. *The Art of Changing the Brain: Enriching the Practice of Teaching by Exploring the Biology of Learning*. Sterling, VA: Stylus, 2002.

11

Problem-Based Learning in Advanced Theological Studies

John Jusu

All life is problem solving. (Karl Popper)[1]

Life is always a problem; one is either in one, or getting out of one or getting into one. (African saying)

As both the opening sayings suggest, life is a school of great learning opportunities. People in general spend their lives solving problems and through the solutions they find to their problems they learn to survive. Unfortunately, our present educational methods are oblivious to this characteristic of life and continue to use methods that violate the natural way humans learn.

In typical African settings, solutions to communal problems often require collaboration among community members. This approach to problem-solving partly explains why there were no specialized institutions of learning in African traditional education. The concept of the East African "*baraza*" and

---

1. Karl Popper, *Alles Leben ist Problemlösen: Über Erkenntnis, Geschichte und Politik* (Munich: Piper Taschenbuch, 1994).

the West African "*palaver* hut"[2] suggest the communal nature to the solution of problems. The cumulative experiences of people as they solve problems become a reservoir of strategies to solve other mundane problems.

What was for the Africans a natural way of learning first emerged in Western education in the 1950s as an organized school-based learning model now referred to as Problem-Based Learning (PBL). Though its initial use was in the medical sciences, PBL is now a method of choice in many disciplines. While it seems to be a new development in educating people,[3] it has been the African way of learning for centuries.

This chapter will attempt a definition of PBL, investigate its theoretical base and assumptions, state its characteristics, identify the key players and issues in the learning mode, and examine ways to assess PBL. The chapter will close with suggestions for implementing PBL in advanced theological studies.

Definition

PBL is an approach to learning that uses real-life problems in a context that allows for the acquisition and integration of knowledge. Barrows and Tamblyn[4] define PBL as "the learning that results from the process of working towards the understanding of a resolution of a problem. The problem is encountered first in the learning process." According to this definition, learning is embedded in a response to a problem – a complex and ill-defined situation that needs a resolution. Allen, Doch, and Groh[5] conceptualized an "ill-defined problem" as one that needs more information to understand it, continues to mutate as new information about it is discovered, generates conflicting perspectives, and is complex. Nevertheless, the need for a resolution to such a problem is motivating to those who engage with it. Thus, PBL presents an opportunity

---

2. The Baraza and Palava Hut are meeting places where elders often gather, not necessarily to adjudicate grievances but to discuss matters of mutual concern in a bid to find a solution.
3. D. Boud and G. Feletti, *The Challenge of Problem-Based Learning*, 2nd ed. (London: Kogan Page, 1997).
4. H. S. Barrows and R. Tamblyn, *Problem-Based Learning: An Approach to Medical Education* (New York: Springer, 1980).
5. D. E. Allen, B. J. Doch, and S. E. Groh, "The Process of Problem-Based Learning in Teaching Introductory Science Courses," in *Bringing Problem-Based Learning to Higher Education: Theory and Practice*, ed. L. Wilkerson and W. H. Gijselaers (San Francisco: Jossey-Bass, 1996), 43–52.

to students to learn life-long lessons through the process of investigating and solving real contextual problems.

PBL is neither learner-centred nor teacher-centred. Its focus is on learning that generates knowledge through the process of solving real-life problems. Unlike other forms of learning models, its focus is on the process of learning rather than on the product of learning.

Foundations of Problem-Based Learning

When God said in Gen 1:26 (NIV) "Let us make mankind in our own image," he meant "let us make people who will look like us." The phrase "look like us" has received different theological interpretations, including one that indicates that people have some attributes they share with God. These sharable attributes include the abilities to co-create, think independently, demonstrate metacognition, and live and function within communities.

Whether consciously or not, these "look like us" attributes are strongly assumed in the learning theory that has become known as constructivism[6] – the fundamental roots of PBL. Generally, constructivism refers to the theory that humans create knowledge either individually or within social communities from their experiences.[7] Like Kilpatrick[8] and Dewey,[9] constructivism takes the experience of learners seriously.

A great advocate of constructivism was the Brazilian educator Paulo Freire.[10] His concepts of conscientization, praxis, dialogue, and experience[11] provide the basis for PBL. His critical pedagogy includes intra-group dialogue and other meaning-making strategies in conversations that matter. These pedagogies are relevant in discovering problems, understanding their nature, and discussing and negotiating the most appropriate solutions from several

---

6. See Marvin Oxenham's chapter in this book.
7. D. C. Phillips, "The Good, the Bad, and the Ugly: The Many Faces of Constructivism," *Educational Researcher* 24, no. 7 (1995): 5–12.
8. W. H. Kilpatrick, "Dangers and Difficulties of the Project Method and How to Overcome Them: Introductory Statement: Definition of Terms," *Teachers College Record* 22 (1921): 282–288.
9. J. Dewey, *Experience and Education* (New York: Macmillan, 1938).
10. See Sam Ewell's chapter in this book.
11. Paulo Freire, *Education for Critical Consciousness* (New York: Continuum, 1987).

possible options. The principles help students to learn the complexity of problems, and understand the multidisciplinary or multi-voice perspectives a problem can generate.[12]

Phillips[13] gives two broad categorizations of constructivism: psychological and social constructivism. Jean Piaget,[14] a psychological constructivist, maintains that meaning-making happens at the individual level. Thus education is for individual cognitive development. Social constructivist Lev Vygotsky[15] posits that meaning is socially constructed. Individuals do not make meaning in isolation from the cultural, political, social, and economic contexts in which they exist. Phillips suggests that these two perspectives have created a dichotomy between the individual and the context in meaning-making. To avoid this dichotomy, a third perspective has emerged. This hybrid approach posits that knowledge is both personally constructed and socially mediated.[16] While the student receives and processes complex realities at the individual cognitive level, that process depends on and is mediated by the context in which the student lives. The evidence of this approach in PBL is when students individually research and process information and then gather as a group to process, share, and validate what they have learnt individually. This shade of constructivism resonates with the African style of meaning-making summed up by the adage "I am because we are."

Project-based learning and experiential learning are other forms of learning approaches embedded in constructivism. Like PBL, these learning approaches are driven by a process of enquiry.[17] Common among these learning

---

12. Woei Hung, David H. Jonassen, and Rude Liu, "Problem-Based Learning," in *Handbook of Research on Educational Communications and Technology*, ed. J. Michael Spector et al., 3rd ed. (Abingdon: Taylor & Francis, 2008), 485–506.
13. D. C. Phillips, "How, Why, What, When and Where: Perspectives on Constructivism in Psychology and Education," *Issues in Education* 3, no. 2 (1997): 151–194.
14. J. Piaget, *Origin of Intelligence in the Child* (London: Routledge and Kegan Paul, 1936).
15. L. S. Vygotsky, *Mind in Society: The Development of Higher Psychological Processes* (Cambridge, MA: Harvard University, 1978).
16. K. Tobin and D Tippins, "Constructivism as a Referent for Teaching and Learning," in *The Practice of Constructivism in Science Education*, ed. K. Tobin (Mahwah: Lawrence Erlbaum Associates, 1993), 3–21.
17. P. Kahn and K. O'Rourke, "Understanding Enquiry-Based Learning," in *Handbook of Enquiry-Based Learning: Irish Case Studies and International Perspectives*, ed. T. Barrett, I. Mac Labhrainn, and H. Fallon (Galway: AISHE and CELT, NUI Galway, 2005), 1–12.

approaches is the quest to bring solutions to complex problems. What makes the approaches different is the structure of the problem and where it is encountered in the learning cycle. In project-based learning and experiential learning, the problem provides the platform for students to demonstrate that they have acquired the knowledge and skills required to solve daily life issues. In contrast, PBL does not assume that students have the repertoire of knowledge and skills required to solve the problem. In PBL, the students encounter the problem first, and through the process of addressing the problem they acquire the required knowledge and skills. Referring to the uniqueness of PBL, Savin-Baden says, "students are not expected to acquire a predetermined series of 'right answers.' Instead they are expected to engage with the complex situation presented to them and decide what information they need to learn and what skills they need to gain in order to manage the situation effectively."[18] Thus, quite unlike project-based learning and experiential learning, the goal of PBL is not merely to solve a problem using predetermined ways, but to acquire knowledge and skills during the problem-solving process and the ability to transfer those skills and knowledge in solving new problems.

Characteristics of PBL

In this section, we will look at the characteristics of PBL using a case study of how some African youths solved a complex problem.

Case Study 1: Open-Discovery Method in PBL

As boys growing up in a farming community in Africa, one of our responsibilities was to keep rodents from ravaging the rice plants. Allowing rodents to destroy the farm would attract severe punishment. One morning, we discovered that a rodent or several rodents had breached the barrier and had started destroying the crops. We had a serious problem: How could we keep the rodents away from the farm?

Faced with this problem, we started providing solutions from our limited experiences on how to keep the rodents away, but none of what we knew at

---

18. M. Savin-Baden, *Problem-Based Learning in Higher Education: Untold Stories* (Buckingham, PA: Open University, 2000), 55.

that time was sufficient to solve the problem. Suggestions like sleeping on the farm or scaring the animals away were not tenable, as they might attract other unfavourable consequences. Finally, we decided to track and kill the rodents. To do this, we needed to know the habits of the rodents, and we needed a tracker to help us trace the animals. After finding them, we needed to devise a means of catching them – alive or dead.

A plan was created. We started to track them. In the process of following their trail, we discovered other animals in the surroundings. We came across succulent fruit trees, which made us very cautious because where those fruits were, one would normally find a boa constrictor – a large snake capable of swallowing any one of us whole. We learned about the terrain of the land. We also learned a lot about rodents – how they move, who leads the pack, and so on. We even learned that they can swim. Eventually, we were able to trap and kill three large rodents. But the question remained: How did they breach the fence? Finding how they had breached the fence and preventing them from doing so was another area we needed to explore. And through several hypotheses, trials, and failures, we realized that the rodents did not actually breach the fence, but swam through a nearby stream into the farm. The fence did not cover the stream. So we went to work to build a fence in the stream.

What we learned in the process of keeping the rodents away from the farm was more than any lesson we could have received from any other person. It was by solving the problem that we learned a lot about keeping pests away from the farm and also about the habits of rodents – all by ourselves. As I reflect on that activity, I remember a particularly interesting part that I need to mention. As we rested from the hard work of building the fence in the water, we recounted the experiences we had had. We shared in laughter how we had missed the trail by following the footprints of a dog, and how one of us could not swim and had had to be carried on the back of another boy, who eventually slipped, causing both to fall in the water. We reflected on many things and concluded that, next time, we could do certain things better.

This case represents the use of an open-discovery method in PBL in which the learners were free to set their own goals and design activities in reaching those goals. However, due to learning regulations and expectations, students need to be guided in setting goals in PBL. The other PBL model that fits this is the guided-discovery method.

If we imagine that the goal of keeping the animals from the farm was a required learning outcome in a formal school situation, the following characteristics of PBL might be deduced:

1. *A focus on the problem:* Learning for the children was focused on the problem. The children confronted with the rodent problem had to examine the issues thoroughly. Students in PBL begin learning by understanding and addressing authentic but ill-structured problems. They proffer solutions to problems after careful analysis of different possibilities of addressing the issues. They have the freedom to explore various options and not necessarily implement ready-made solutions.
2. *Collaborative learning:* The children had a common goal – to eliminate pests from the farm. Teamwork was required. In PBL, students work together to solve problems of mutual concern as they learn from each other. PBL is self-directed in the way that learners individually and collaboratively take responsibility for learning.
3. *The role of previous experience:* The children embedded the solution within things they already knew. The problem was embedded in their daily experiences, hence the solution was also embedded in that context. By bringing previous knowledge to the solution of the problem, students in PBL are in effect highlighting the further knowledge they need to have to solve the problem. What one already knows about a problem becomes an effective tool in evaluating the extent of knowledge required to solve the problem. Further, knowledge creation that is embedded in the context of solving a problem will help the learners develop flexible knowledge that is transferable to other novel situations.
4. *Unique learning responses:* The children faced with the rodent problem had a real-life issue at hand. The goal of stopping the rodents from coming to the farm created the intrinsic motivation for learning. Solving a real-life problem in PBL becomes a motivation for learning. Since the students manage the process of learning, the learning exercise becomes self-directing, one in which they cultivate reflective, critical, and creative thinking skills.

The characteristics of PBL described above correspond to elements in Freire's critical pedagogy that provide the philosophical basis of PBL. Critical consciousness is built when the learner becomes aware of the problem, focuses on it, and understands it. After understanding the problem there should be a unique learning response. Praxis involves a conscious and intentional response to a problem situation. It includes self-determination, creativity, and rationality within a concrete reality. Through praxis, the students engage in an action-reflection-action mode as they interact with the issues. Building critical consciousness and responding to a problematic situation involves collaboration with others.

The Process in PBL

Using our case study we can present the design of a PBL class as follows:

1. The students are confronted with a real-life problem that needs a resolution. The problem itself is authentic, and embedded in a real-life context that the student deals with on a daily basis.
2. Through brainstorming, the students try to understand the problem with all its ramifications. This will require the students to bring their previous knowledge to bear on the problem.
3. When the problem is understood, the students study the problem (independently or collectively). They consult books in the library, Web resources, informed persons (at some stages this might include their teachers), and peers.
4. With the information and facts obtained during the study period, the students share their findings as they forge a collective response to the problem.
5. A strategy is developed and implemented.
6. The students review the process to identify critical learning points and mistakes to avoid, and to celebrate new knowledge acquired.

The Players in PBL

The idea that PBL is student- or learner-centred may seem to denigrate the role of the teacher in the learning process. However, PBL is more about learning as an activity than about the individuals involved in it. Consequently, both teacher and students have a critical role to play in the process of learning.

The Teacher

Formal educative processes rise and fall with the teacher. Accreditation and government regulations require the teacher to play a significant role in higher education. While the role of the teacher continues to metamorphose in light of extant research findings, response to these changes is not always automatic and teachers are often not very successful in making the epistemological and axiological shifts research evidence requires. Marincovich asserts, "It is easy to overlook the many ways in which PBL goes against the grain of faculty and postsecondary educational life. While faculty are devoted to their discipline, eager to dispense knowledge, and content oriented, PBL asks them to be student centred, guiding rather than directive and power-oriented."[19] PBL requires a paradigm shift in instructional strategy – from a teaching paradigm to a learning paradigm – a process which, according to Margetson, could be threatening to the traditional teacher who still wants to control the learning environment and prefers passive students.[20]

Being part of the learning community, teachers participate in the PBL process not as knowledge sources or custodians of knowledge, but rather as facilitators and unobtrusive guides to the process. Quite unlike in the rodent scenario, where there was no teacher or accreditation guidelines to follow, teachers may use the guided-discovery method to provide learning outcomes that enhance knowledge construction in more structured ways to accommodate accreditation and other statutory requirements.

As facilitators who model the process of PBL, teachers guide the group processes in developing and maintaining interpersonal dynamics in the

---

19. M. Marincovich, "Problems and Promises in Problem-Based Learning," in *Problem-Based Learning: Educational Innovation Across Disciplines*, ed. O. S. Tan, P. Little, S. Y. Hee, and J. Conway (Singapore: Temasek Centre for Problem-Based Learning, 2000), 1.
20. D. Margetson, "Why Is Problem-Based Learning a Challenge?," in Boud and Feletti, *The Challenge of Problem-Based Learning*, 36–44.

learning process. To do this successfully, the PBL teacher must be able to scaffold student learning, bridging the gaps between what the students know and what they need to know to solve the problems at hand. When the teacher scaffolds, he or she provides a platform that students use with incremental steps to climb higher in the learning tasks. The teacher does this not by "telling" them what should be done, but by embodying the metacognitive skills required in PBL.[21] The teacher's interaction with the students should bring the students to the point where the students are aware not only of their own learning abilities and capabilities, but also of what they know and ought to know to solve a problem. The teacher should also guide students to know how to transfer newly acquired learning to other novel situations. The teacher is an active listener in the conversations around the problems, interjecting with questions that seek clarity, and guiding the students to remain on course and not stray away from the real issues.

Students who are new to PBL should be given more attention by the teacher. However, as they mature in the process and start to display metacognitive skills the teacher becomes more inconspicuous. As Hmelo-Silver advises, "Facilitators progressively fade their scaffolding as students become more experienced with PBL until finally the learners adopt many of the facilitators' roles. The facilitator is responsible both for moving the students through the various stages of PBL and for monitoring the group process. This monitoring assures that all students are involved and encourages them both to externalize their own thinking and to comment on each other's thinking."[22]

The scaffold is removed when the students are able to evaluate critically the information from the research data they collect and to question and probe their own thinking ability. The PBL approach is very helpful in building life-long learners and developing critical thinkers.

---

21. C. E. Hmelo-Silver, "Collaborative Ways of Knowing: Issues in Facilitation" (unpublished paper, Rutgers, The State University of New Jersey, 2003).
22. C. E. Hmelo-Silver, "Collaborative Ways of Knowing: Issues in Facilitation," in *Proceedings of CSCL*, ed. G. Stahl (Mahwah: Erlbaum, 2002), 199–208.

The successful teacher in PBL builds what Schmidt and Moust call "cognitive consonance"[23] with the students. The teacher communicates to the students in words and expressions they can understand, using concepts students use so that there is no communication barrier. Students should be able to understand the teacher with complete clarity.

The PBL teacher also has the responsibility of ensuring that student learning happens in a safe and non-threatening environment. As students work in peer groups, the teacher helps to build group synergy that ensures proper group dynamics, and appropriate intra-group communication. The teacher ensures that students are well integrated into the group and that the group stays focused on the issues.[24]

The PBL teacher should be aware that students also struggle to make the shift from what is traditionally expected of them and what PBL expects. The teacher has a role to play in this transition. The teacher in PBL should make the roles and responsibilities of the students very clear. The teacher should explain the learning expectations to the students and how they should live up to those expectations. Thus, in PBL, the role of the teacher is still critical as a "backstage" actor – supporting and guiding the activities of the students who are the real "on-stage" players in the learning process.

The Students

One of my graduate students was frustrated by my using an autonomous approach to learning. One afternoon, she voiced her frustration: "Please, sir, we have paid our fees for you to teach us. Why are you not teaching us? You are just giving us projects, problems to solve, and many readings; you just need to teach us." I said, "But you are learning, aren't you?" "No, sir; you first need to teach, then we will learn."

This short episode in a graduate class shows common student perceptions about the learning process. For many students, learning happens when a teacher provides all the information the student needs, and the student then

---

23. H. Schmidt and J. Moust, "Factors Affecting Small Group Tutorial Learning: A Review of Research," in *Problem-Based Learning: A Research Perspective on Learning Interactions*, ed. D. Evenson and C. Hmelo (London: Lawrence Erlbaum Associates, 2000), 19–52.

24. P. Mayo et al., "Student Perceptions of Tutor Effectiveness in a Problem-Based Surgery Clerkship," *Teaching and Learning in Medicine* 5, no. 4 (1993): 227–233.

memorizes the facts for the exams. When the student passes the course with a good grade (so the students believe), learning has occurred.[25]

Like their teachers, students need a paradigm shift from the teaching model to a learning model. Students need to see themselves as initiators of their own learning, as knowledge creators through problem-solving and not only as knowledge consumers. They should come to the learning forum as active participants in learning rather than passive empty silos to be filled with knowledge from the expert. PBL espouses a learning model in which the students take control of their own learning. The goal is that the student becomes an independent learner whose motivation for learning is embedded in the desire to solve real-life problems.

PBL develops in students the spirit of collaboration. While the societal rhetoric is about "teamwork," in reality traditional methods espouse competitive individual learning. PBL promotes a team spirit in students; it exposes their inadequacies and gives them the motivation to bridge those inadequacies through collaborative efforts. Thus students who properly tune into PBL cultivate critical life skills required for survival in the job market. They come out with the abilities to continue constructing an extensive and flexible knowledge base. They develop effective problem-solving skills and demonstrate self-directed and life-long learning skills. They become good team players and effective collaborators who are intrinsically motivated to work and learn. They also leave the school with the ability to integrate knowledge from multidisciplinary sources to solve problems as they link theory and practice in real time and space. Undoubtedly, these are the types of graduates that society cherishes.

The Problem

Critical to the success of PBL is the statement of the problem. It is the design of the question that elicits the learning in PBL. Generally, the problems presented in a PBL class are not clearly defined or structured.

---

25. J. K. Jusu, "Patterns of Epistemological Frameworks among Master of Divinity Students at the Nairobi Evangelical Graduate School of Theology" (PhD diss., Trinity International University, 2008).

Traditional pedagogical methods are familiar with "well-structured problems." These are problems that usually have a right answer and they often test understanding of previously taught and hopefully learned knowledge. In the traditional mode, there is often a general consensus about what will constitute a correct answer or procedure, with only slight variations among experts in the field.[26] While well-defined problems are often appropriate in the natural sciences and mathematics, they may be less relevant in fields such as theological education.

Unlike well-structured problems, the "messy problems" used in PBL don't yield a particular right answer. The facts available to the students dealing with a messy problem are often vague, ambiguous, inconclusive, and sometimes conflicting.[27] When dealing with a messy problem it is not quite certain which concepts, processes, rules, and principles are needed to solve the problem.[28] A good problem in PBL:

1. *Relates to the life and context of the student.* A problem that is situated in the context of the learner is more likely to elicit passion and motivation for the student to be engaged with the learning. An additional motivational force in PBL is when the student has access to the resources required to solve the problem.

2. *Requires a multidisciplinary approach.* Everyday life problems do not come in isolated silos. They are complex and integrated, hence finding solutions to them may take the student across disciplines. For example, a student confronted with a problem of witchcraft may require several content areas, including politics, economics, legal issues, theology, sociology, and anthropology. The student acquires all this knowledge, not for the sake of the information, but to help solve the problem.

---

26. M. A. Luszcz, "Theoretical Models of Everyday Problem Solving in Adulthood," in *Everyday Problem Solving: Theory and Application*, ed. J. D. Sinnott (New York: Praeger, 1984), 24–37.
27. P. K. Wood, "Inquiring Systems and Problem Structure: Implications for Cognitive Development," *Human Development* 26 (1993): 249–265.
28. R. J. Spiro et al., "Cognitive Flexibility Theory: Advanced Knowledge Acquisition in Ill-Structured Domains," *Cognitive Science* 12 (1988): 257–285.

3. *Requires multiple intelligences.* The multidisciplinary approach to PBL may require several different abilities and skills. Howard Gardner,[29] explaining the multiple intelligences theory, posits that humans have several ways of acquiring and using knowledge. When students work in collaboration, they bring to the table their unique intelligences required to solve the problem.
4. *Promotes active research.* A well-crafted problem has the capacity to engage both students and teachers in a research process. In resolving the problem, the students develop important critical research skills, such as delineating a problem, building hypotheses to explain the problem, and selecting a research design to solve the problem.

Depending on the type of learning required, problems can be presented to students in many ways – from reading popular materials to complex research documents. The teacher can also create scenarios, cartoons, poems, or just use physical elements to present a problem. What is important is that the problem attracts and sustains the attention of the student. Schmidt and Moust declared that the level of attention, interest, and time a student wants to invest in learning to solve a problem depends on the quality of the question or task.[30] The design and framing of the question may also determine whether a deductive, inductive, retroductive, or a spiral combination of these approaches is appropriate for a solution or explanation.

Assessing Problem-Based Learning

Most authors in the field, including Savin-Baden and Major,[31] and Schwartz, Mennin, and Webb,[32] have claimed that inadequate attention has been given to assessment in PBL. Faculty members are encouraged to use PBL but have no idea how to assess the learning; consequently they continue to apply traditional

---

29. Howard Gardner, *Intelligence Reframed: Multiple Intelligences for the 21st Century* (New York: Basic, 1999).
30. Schmidt and Moust, "Factors Affecting."
31. M. Savin-Baden and C. H. Major, *Foundations of Problem-Based Learning* (Buckingham, PA: SRHE/Open University, 2004).
32. P. Schwartz, S. Mennin, and G. Webb, *Problem-Based Learning: Case Studies, Experience and Practice* (London: Kogan Page, 2001).

methods of assessment to PBL. This creates a pedagogical misalignment between the mode of learning and the mode of assessment.

Assessment in PBL, like other learning approaches, starts with the outcomes. Aligning the learning outcomes with instructional strategies and assessment procedures is necessary for effective and coherent learning. Since PBL is focused more on the processes of solving a problem, the assessment strategy should adopt a more holistic and divergent approach. Reynolds writes, "assessment needs to fit the philosophy of active learning rather than passive reproductive learning ... It may be preferable, and more rigorous, for assessments to follow the PBL philosophy and to require the individual to analyze a problem, search for and then apply relevant information."[33]

A well-formed learning outcome in PBL will empower the assessor to answer the critical questions of what to assess, when to assess, where to assess, how to assess, who will be assessed, what type of feedback students receive, and how they receive it. Above all, it will also help address the critical question of "Why assessment?" Depending on the types of learning outcomes one needs to attain, a choice can be made among many assessment techniques in PBL. Some of these techniques are presentations (group and individual), student self-assessment, reflective journaling, reports, or a combination of these.

Using Problem-Based Learning in Graduate Theological Studies

Case Study 2: Guided-Discovery Model

I was asked to co-facilitate a quarter-long module on Divisive Ethnicity in a master of divinity class. The class required students to:

1. Identify the causes of perennial ethnic cleansing that has characterized the nation since its independence.
2. Design theologically sound intervention strategies (proactively or retroactively) to address the issues of divisive ethnicity.

---

33. F. Reynolds, "Studying Psychology at Degree Level: Would Problem-Based Learning Enhance Students' Experiences?," *Studies in Higher Education* 22, no. 3 (1997): 272.

3. Defend their intervention as a best-practice model for the church in conflict situations.

Approach

Graduate-level students, irrespective of the discipline of study, are expected to demonstrate certain research competences which most lecturers at this level take for granted. Each graduate-level student is expected to:

1. Discern and generate research concerns from relevant social concerns in the areas of study – that is, moving deeper down into asking the "why" questions in the discipline.
2. Discover new information relevant to specific research concerns, not losing sight of previous social and lived experiences.
3. Assess the sources and quality of new information while being aware of the fallibility of his or her own opinions.
4. Integrate information into conceptual and theoretical frameworks.
5. Create and test hypotheses to address research concerns.
6. Communicate the results of research findings in the language of the field.

It is not advisable to relegate these competencies to only a specific research class. A well-designed PBL in any discipline will naturally nurture these integrative graduate-research skills in students. Thus, in this class, developing these competences was as important as helping each student meet the explicit course content requirements. Teachers who use PBL naturally blend these competences into courses they teach and as they naturally prepare their students for graduate-level dissertation work.

Procedure

1. Like all PBL users, my first concern was to develop a question or a problem whose solution would have empowered the students to exhibit graduate-level competences in research and attain the specific course outcomes. In this case, I had to work backwards from the course outcomes to the problem.

2. There were fifteen students in the class. I pre-assigned the students to groups of five, making three groups.
3. On the first day of class, we watched three video clips of eight minutes each. Each clip showed an era of violence just after elections held at different times within a fifteen-year period, ending with the then-just-concluded election violence in which hundreds of people were killed, others were displaced, and property worth millions of dollars was destroyed.
4. I explained to the class the learning approach that had been adopted and our expectations of them. I clarified the role of the facilitators in their learning activities.

Assessment

A multifaceted approach was used to assess student learning.

1. Each group presented their work to a panel of ten. The class (not including the group presenting) constituted the panel. The group presenting had to convince the panel that their approach was the most appropriate.
2. Each student presented the portion of the paper he or she worked on (for grading).
3. Each student provided a critical reflection on his or her experiences within the group dynamics the student was engaged in.
4. Each student prepared an integrated research paper (from all the presentations and panel interactions) on "Theological Approaches to Conflict Management."

The Problem

The issues that were critical in this course were very fresh in the minds of the students. Their country had just gone through a terrible civil conflict and everyone – theologians, pastors, and others – was seeking answers and solutions to the problem of divisive and negative ethnicity. A source of regret and baffling to the entire nation was the participation of Christians in these senseless killings and the mayhem. It was a widespread social concern. The purpose of the class was to take the problem beyond a social concern to a research concern so that students could be involved in some sort of theological theorizing about ethnic conflicts. Thus the question of concern was: Why would Christians perpetuate gross human-rights violations against each other over election results?

Debriefing

After the task was completed, the students came to a debriefing session. A summary statement was delivered by one student on behalf of the others:

> At first it was difficult for us to work with each other. In our group, we all come from different ethnicities that were literally at war with each other just a few weeks ago. The task made us sit together and approach the issues from God's perspective. We were able to understand each other. I think our model is the best because it incorporated the views of at least five tribes. We have decided to stay together to prepare a manual that we can use to teach our people about peaceful co-existence as God's desire for us.

When asked about the process, the student had this to say:

> We needed to have a clear definition of the problem and be able to state it. We discussed it identifying its ramifications. Then each of us took a segment of it for further individual investigation. After a week, we came back together to put our pieces together, design a method to collect the data, to analyze it and report our findings.
>
> Our search for information took us to the colonial archives where we discovered that the Churches were divided along ethnic lines as a result of a colonial policy. We discovered how colonial administration instituted a latent hatred of one tribe towards the other by the way social amenities were provided and the ways in which land and work were distributed. As we went to the field to collect information, we saw firsthand what the violence did to other communities. We studied ethnicity and violence from a sociological, economic, and theological perspective and [saw] that politics is just the vehicle many ethnic groups are using to preserve themselves from annihilation by other ethnic groups.

We were delighted to listen to the various solutions our colleagues provided. We never thought of bringing reconciliation to our people in the way that group 3 did. Our group has a lot to learn from them. We see their perspective about the "why" of ethnic violence [as] a little bit misleading, but it gives us something to think about.

I am from the east of the country and it was very difficult for me to follow my colleague here to his home in the west to talk to people about violence. I thought I would be killed, but my safety was assured. I have never been to those ends of the country. Interacting with his people dispelled my fear. I then noticed that my assumptions about this tribal group were all false assumptions.

So what have we learnt?

- Learning together as we have just experienced will help us build relationships that will transcend the classroom. This is very healthy for national integration.
- Wrong assumptions fuel ethnic violence. Perhaps we need to introduce civic education in our curriculum.
- Ethnic integration has not happened since independence. Churches should "de-tribalize" to permeate all regions of the country.
- Perhaps we need to revise the election laws to ensure that each political party has a certain percentage of votes from all regions before they could form a government.

Using Problem-Based Learning: Conclusion

Institutions may opt to use PBL in all their educative processes, or it may be that only a few faculty members will want to use this approach to learning. Whatever the situation, the following guidelines may help to ensure a successful use of the process:

1. Create appropriate means for training faculty members to understand the theoretical framework and practical use of PBL in a classroom situation. The institution should not take it for granted that the skills

required can be acquired easily. Avenues such as faculty orientation, staff development activities, training, mentoring, coaching, and refresher courses in best practices should be pursued.
2. Training should be provided in the use of best practices in advising, coaching, and supervising student projects and learning. PBL is a daunting task that will require faculty to know how to manage the challenges that may arise as a result of students working together. The ability to handle intra-group conflicts and the management of projects should be developed by the faculty members.
3. The institution should have robust policies on the use of PBL as a learning mode. These policies should touch on issues of faculty and student workload, assessment procedures and policies, and workspace for students that may hinge on class size.
4. Faculty should be able to model metacognitive competences.
5. Resources that are needed for the students to solve the problems must be available and accessible to students at all times.

Discussion Questions

1. Describe a significant complex situation that you are currently facing (or which you have faced in the near past) calling for multifaceted reflection before action can (could) be taken. What are some of the key areas of knowledge and skill that would need to be brought to bear on this situation in order that a wise Christian decision could be made?

2. In what ways have you seen PBL being used (if at all) in your college or community? Are there particular cultural elements that need to be brought into the process? Explain.

3. John mentions several key ways in which PBL enhances learning: a focus on problems; collaborative learning; the role of previous experience; unique learning responses. Why might these elements be particularly significant in theological education?

4. John lists key players in PBL as the teacher, the students, and the problem. As you look at how these players function at your own school, what do you see as

some of the challenges you might confront in seeking to use PBL as a learning methodology? Describe some specific action-steps you might recommend for addressing one or more of these challenges.

5. Using the guidelines and examples given in this chapter, work with one or two others in sketching out a doctoral-level project for your local context that might be shaped and developed using PBL as the primary paradigm. Keep in mind the key stages of process for PBL projects, and the particular centrality of a well-structured problem.

Bibliography

Allen, D. E., B. J. Doch, and S. E. Groh. "The Process of Problem-Based Learning in Teaching Introductory Science Courses." In *Bringing Problem-Based Learning to Higher Education: Theory and Practice*, edited by L. Wilkerson and W. H. Gijselaers, 43–52. San Francisco: Jossey-Bass, 1996.

Barrows, H. S., and R. Tamblyn. *Problem-Based Learning: An Approach to Medical Education*. New York: Springer, 1980.

Boud, D., and G. Feletti. *The Challenge of Problem-Based Learning*. 2nd ed. London: Kogan Page, 1997.

Dewey, J. *Experience and Education*. New York: Macmillan, 1938.

Freire, P. *Education for Critical Consciousness*. New York: Continuum, 1987.

Gardner, Howard. *Intelligence Reframed: Multiple Intelligences for the 21st Century*. New York: Basic, 1999.

Hmelo-Silver, C. E. "Collaborative Ways of Knowing: Issues in Facilitation." In *Proceedings of CSCL*, edited by G. Stahl, 199–208. Mahwah: Erlbaum, 2002.

———. "Collaborative Ways of Knowing: Issues in Facilitation." Unpublished paper, Rutgers, The State University of New Jersey, 2003. http://citeseerx.ist.psu.edu/viewdoc/download?doi=10.1.1.513.6684&rep=rep1&type=pdf.

Hung, Woei, David H. Jonassen, and Rude Liu. "Problem-Based Learning." In *Handbook of Research on Educational Communications and Technology*, edited by J. Michael Spector, M. David Merrill, Jeroen van Merriënboer, and Marcy P. Driscoll, 485–506. Abingdon: Taylor & Francis, 2008.

Jusu, John K. "Patterns of Epistemological Frameworks among Master of Divinity Students at the Nairobi Evangelical Graduate School of Theology." PhD diss., Trinity International University, 2008.

Kahn, P., and K. O'Rourke. "Understanding Enquiry-Based Learning." In *Handbook of Enquiry and Problem-Based Learning: Irish Case Studies and International Perspectives*, edited by T. Barrett, I. Mac Labhrainn, and H. Fallon, 1–12. Galway: AISHE and CELT, NUI Galway, 2005.

Kilpatrick, W. H. "Dangers and Difficulties of the Project Method and How to Overcome Them: Introductory Statement: Definition of Terms." *Teachers College Record* 22 (1921): 282–288.

Luszcz, M. A. "Theoretical Models of Everyday Problem Solving in Adulthood." In *Everyday Problem Solving: Theory and Application*, edited by J. D. Sinnott, 24–37. New York: Praeger, 1984.

Margetson, D. "Why Is Problem-Based Learning a Challenge?" In Boud and Feletti, *The Challenge of Problem-Based Learning*, 36–44.

Marincovich, M. "Problems and Promises in Problem-Based Learning." In *Problem-Based Learning: Educational Innovation Across Disciplines*, edited by O. S. Tan, P. Little, S. Y. Hee, and J. Conway, 1–9. Singapore: Temasek Centre for Problem-Based Learning, 2000.

Mayo, P., M. B. Donnelly, P. P. Nash, and R. W. Schwartz. "Student Perceptions of Tutor Effectiveness in a Problem-Based Surgery Clerkship." *Teaching and Learning in Medicine* 5, no. 4 (1993): 227–233.

Phillips, D. C. "The Good, the Bad, and the Ugly: The Many Faces of Constructivism." *Educational Researcher* 24, no. 7 (1995): 5–12.

———. "How, Why, What, When and Where: Perspectives on Constructivism in Psychology and Education." *Issues in Education* 3, no. 2 (1997): 151–194.

Piaget, J. *Origin of Intelligence in the Child*. London: Routledge and Kegan Paul, 1936.

Popper, Karl. *Alles Leben ist Problemlösen: Über Erkenntnis, Geschichte und Politik*. Munich: Piper Taschenbuch, 1994.

Reynolds, F. "Studying Psychology at Degree Level: Would Problem-Based Learning Enhance Students' Experiences?" *Studies in Higher Education* 22, no. 3 (1997): 263–275.

Savin-Baden, M. *Problem-Based Learning in Higher Education: Untold Stories*. Buckingham, PA: Open University, 2000.

Savin-Baden, M., and C. H. Major. *Foundations of Problem-Based Learning*. Buckingham, PA: SRHE/Open University, 2004.

Schmidt, H., and J. Moust. "Factors Affecting Small Group Tutorial Learning: A Review of Research." In *Problem-Based Learning: A Research Perspective on Learning Interactions*, edited by D. Evenson and C. Hmelo, 19–52. London: Lawrence Erlbaum Associates, 2000.

Schwartz, P., S. Mennin, and G. Webb. *Problem-Based Learning: Case Studies, Experience and Practice*. London: Kogan Page, 2001.

Spiro, R. J., R. L. Coulson, P. J. Feltovich, and D. K. Anderson. "Cognitive Flexibility Theory: Advanced Knowledge Acquisition in Ill-Structured Domains." *Cognitive Science* 12 (1988): 257–285.

Tobin, K., and D. Tippins. "Constructivism as a Referent for Teaching and Learning." In *The Practice of Constructivism in Science Education*, edited by K. Tobin, 3–22. Mahwah, NJ: Lawrence Erlbaum Associates, 1993.

Vygotsky, L. S. *Mind In Society: The Development of Higher Psychological Processes*. Cambridge, MA: Harvard University, 1978.

Wood, P. K. "Inquiring Systems and Problem Structure: Implications for Cognitive Development." *Human Development* 26 (1993): 249–265.

12

Action Research for Theological Impact:
Reflections from an Arab Context[1]

Caleb Hutcherson with Bassem Melki

Introduction

As he completes his final year of theological studies, Saʿid looks forward to ministry after graduation in a local church in the region of his home village. In the course of study, he conducted a significant research project on peacemaking strategies, analysing various approaches used by leading international experts on peacemaking. Out of that project, he developed an ambitious plan for starting a grassroots peacemaking training program when he returns home. He had hoped that by implementing this well-researched plan, the training would be a catalyst for significant progress within his minority community in the context of the majority, non-Christian society. Yet after returning home, he finds the realities of church ministry much more complex and time-consuming than he imagined in his study. The community seems resistant to the strategies he developed. The problems he identified are not felt by the community. He senses the community does not care about peacemaking at all. And he feels

---

1. This chapter adapts and expands my article Caleb Hutcherson, "Toward Theological Integration Using Action Research: Reflections from an Arab Context," *InSights Journal for Global Theological Education* 1, no. 2 (2016): 31–39.

at a loss for how to begin reworking his study when all his time is focused on simply doing ministry. The dissonance between the theory developed in the seminary classroom and the reality of work on the ground leaves him feeling confused and distanced from his community.

For theologian-pastors and faith-based social workers trying to effect change in society, "real-world" problems require integrative multidisciplinary approaches. Quite often, the complexity of even knowing where to start looms large. In the process of researching and planning a social action, the very situation that was observed initially has changed, along with the researcher himself or herself, so that the original observations no longer apply. In reality, research for social change is too complex to be studied solely (or even primarily) using a linear experimental methodology. Moreover, theological research resulting in a "completed" project with no actual action having occurred seems to miss something essential to the very nature of Christian theology. Perhaps more detrimentally, most "traditional" research approaches fundamentally privilege the theory of the *researcher* over the praxis of the *researched* in order to develop "better" action.

In this chapter, I explore how an action research approach might be used in advanced-level theological studies in a Majority World context. I trace the experiences of action research by students and a faculty member at the Arab Baptist Theological Seminary (ABTS) in Beirut, Lebanon. Throughout, I bring these experiences into conversation with a growing body of work advocating for and using action research approaches in theological studies.[2] This conversation will walk through a description of action research, look at some key reasons for using action research in theological studies, and finally look sidelong at recommendations for implementing action research. We have found action research methodology very well suited to the kinds of theological reflection and community reconciliation work we hope will characterize our alumni as they serve their societies through the church. While this chapter is not meant

---

2. Two initial entries developing theological action research are John Swinton and Harriet Mowat, *Practical Theology and Qualitative Research* (London: SCM, 2006); and Helen Cameron, Deborah Bhatti, and Catherine Duce, *Talking about God in Practice: Theological Action Research and Practical Theology* (London: SCM, 2010). Elaine Graham provides an incisive review of both in her article "Is Practical Theology a Form of 'Action Research'?," *International Journal of Practical Theology* 17, no. 1 (2013): 148–178.

as an argument against the use of traditional research methodologies, I hope that it might advance valuation of more diverse methodologies in advanced theological research.

What Is Action Research?

Broadly speaking, action research is a spiral-like reflective process consisting of a "family of research methodologies that pursue dual outcomes of action and research."[3] As a research approach, it is "uniquely suited to researching and supporting change. It integrates social research with exploratory action to promote development."[4] While various methodologies and methods can be included within the family of action research, nearly all emphasize the participatory nature of researching for social change.[5] It is research "with people, not on people"[6] that facilitates the sort of theological leadership for which Hunter's chapter in this volume calls. Action research values both the knowledge of a "professional" researcher and the "practical knowledge of local stakeholders."[7] It gets its hands dirty, identifying as data-driven research, as opposed to theory-driven.[8] Action or praxis, rather than theory, is the starting point.

---

3. Bob Dick, "Postgraduate Programs Using Action Research," *The Learning Organization* 9, no. 3/4 (2002): 159, http://www.aral.com.au/resources/ppar.html.
4. Bridget Somekh, "Action Research," in *The SAGE Encyclopedia of Qualitative Research Methods*, ed. Lisa M. Given and Bridget Somekh (Los Angeles: SAGE, 2008), 4.
5. Bob Dick, "Reflections on the SAGE Encyclopedia of Action Research and What It Says about Action Research and Its Methodologies," *Action Research* 13, no. 4 (2015): 432, doi:10.1177/1476750315573593. Theological action research shares this feature, as in Cameron, Bhatti, and Duce, *Talking about God in Practice*, Kindle loc. 757. Related methodologies and approaches in this book include problem-based learning (PBL) by John Jusu and collaborative learning by Rafael Zaracho.
6. Myles Horton and Paulo Freire, *We Make the Road by Walking* (Philadelphia: Temple University, 1990), 148.
7. Davydd J. Greenwood and Morten Levin, *Introduction to Action Research: Social Research for Social Change* (Thousand Oaks: SAGE, 2007), 53.
8. Dick, "Postgraduate Programs Using Action Research." Of course, this is not to say that action research is theory-less research. But the *driver* is data emerging from action, rather than theories and hypotheses needing application.

There is growing interest among contemporary practical theologians in the use of action research approaches in theology.[9] Rather than starting out by describing the theory of action research, in what follows I will let a master's-level theology student's project[10] demonstrate an approach to it in practice. Accompanying this description, I will highlight relevant discussion concerning the theory of action research.

Miriam came to faith in Christ in an Arabic-speaking Lebanese church through a neighbourhood outreach program. In recent years, she had begun to lead a small group made up of newly displaced Syrian refugees who had landed in the town of her church. These outsiders to this traditional Christian community differed from the community economically, culturally, and religiously. The Arab evangelical church community in which she served was already a minority within the traditional Christian community, but now the Christians, both traditional and evangelical, were faced with a Muslim majority in their town for the first time that any of them could remember. Through aid and development ministries of the church and some small-group Bible studies they offered, a number of the refugees had also become followers of Jesus. While the church was cautiously glad about this, many people seemed to be uncomfortable with any kind of integration between the two groups of believers. The differences seemed overwhelming to most, and real reconciliation undesired by a loud contingent. Miriam decided that she wanted to work on researching how to reconcile these two groups.

Rather than starting from a theoretical study of reconciliation in Scripture or traditional theological texts, her research began with observation and informal interviews, acknowledging her own bias towards seeing the two brought together. Through the interview process, she sought out key participants in

---

9. Beyond the specific work I mentioned in the introduction by practical theologians on theological action research, other related work includes Elizabeth Conde-Frazier, "Participatory Action Research: Practical Theology for Social Justice," *Religious Education* 101, no. 3 (2006): 321–329; Paul R. Dokecki, J. R. Newbrough, and Robert T. O'Gorman, "Toward a Community-Oriented Action Research Framework for Spirituality: Community Psychological and Theological Perspectives," *Journal of Community Psychology* 29, no. 5 (1 September 2001): 497–518; Cameron Harder, "Using Participatory Action Research in Seminary Internships," *Theological Education* 42, no. 2 (2007): 127–139.

10. Because of security issues in our region and the very personal content of many of the projects students undertook, I will offer here an amalgamation that represents issues my students engaged with for this project.

the church, asking them what they wanted to find out about their practices of being a community. As this was going on, she was also studying ecclesiology in a series of classes in an integrated module that introduced students to the theme of the church as a restored and restoring community. This theme was explored in classes taught by a team of faculty that considered biblical-theological, historical-theological, socio-cultural, and personal-ministerial lenses on the overall theme. Through these multidisciplinary lenses, Miriam analysed the situation and began to develop an action plan to try out in a short time frame. The plan emerged out of a theme that kept coming up in her interviews: get people talking to each other by holding a focus group meeting between key participants from both groups.

In line with the participatory nature of action research, Miriam's approach involved both the participants and the researcher in a collaborative process. While the participants work to solve a problem, the researcher works with them to see what can be learned from their practice.[11] Action research emerged as an approach particularly suited to research problems where the researcher is both an observer and a stakeholder in the project. It is rooted in social action intended to develop or repair intergroup relationships.[12] While numerous approaches exist within action research,[13] they share a common emphasis on the formative role of not only the researcher but also the participants, who in traditional approaches are often merely "objects" of research. In nearly all action research approaches, the *researcher* participates together with the *researched* to set the research question.[14]

Through the focus group meetings, Miriam recognized the emergence of some very interesting themes. The focus groups, with her prodding questions, began to surface various perspectives within both groups, each with unique questions and concerns about reconciliation. How will integrating with "them"

---

11. Cameron, Bhatti, and Duce, *Talking about God in Practice*, Kindle loc. 719.
12. Kurt Lewin, "Action Research and Minority Problems," *Social Issues* 2, no. 4 (1946): 35.
13. Dick, "Reflections on the SAGE Encyclopedia of Action Research." Cameron, Bhatti, and Duce (*Talking about God in Practice*, Kindle loc. 760) trace three primary streams from which action research developed: Northern Industrial Action Research (Lewin), Southern Participatory Action Research (Freire, liberation theologians, etc.), and professional practice research (Argyris/Schön and others).
14. Harder, "Using Participatory Action Research," 136. Also in Dick, "Reflections on the SAGE Encyclopedia of Action Research."

change us? Does reconciliation require integration? Would integration be sustainable when the refugee community return "home" and the new cultural-religious identity they have taken on is not accepted by the dominant majority? Good questions were being generated, but not the ones she had in mind when she started. And perhaps more importantly, they were emerging from the praxis of the objects of the research. They had begun to shape and be shaped by the research process.

Action research approaches recognize that by simply observing and researching a person or a group of people, the specific situation initially being observed will change.[15] The researcher both conceptualizes and participates in the process of constructing transformative social actions. Rather than developing a control by which to compare the issue under research, action research understands that the research is embedded in the community, and will, in the course of research, make a positive contribution to the community.[16]

After the initial round of action, Miriam wrote an evaluation of the focus group, reflecting on both the content generated by the participants and their interactions with each other. Out of this evaluation, she began to realize several new issues for further study, moving the analysis into areas like ecclesiology, missiology, and identity formation. This was not where her study on reconciliation had begun, but it fit within the framework of an action research approach. Even the situation being observed had changed as the participants from the initial focus group connected and continued the discussion outside of her official meetings. New potential actions began to emerge in the light of all of these changes.

By design, action research brings multidisciplinary perspectives to bear on a specific practice or social issue. Rather than ending with a set of propositions for what "ought to be," the action research project develops as a spiral of observation and analysis, critical reflection, planning and taking action, and

---

15. The close relationship with soft systems methodology is clear here. Soft systems methodology is particularly helpful in settings where the researcher seeks "to find ways of understanding and coping with perplexing difficulties in taking action to 'improve' the situations which day-to-day life continuously creates and continually changes." Peter Checkland and Jim Scholes, *Soft Systems Methodology in Action* (New York: Wiley, 1999), A4.

16. Colin Todhunter, "Undertaking Action Research: Negotiating the Road Ahead," *Social Research Update* 34 (2001), http://citeseerx.ist.psu.edu/viewdoc/summary?doi=10.1.1.304.3849.

evaluation leading to new observations as the cycle repeats.[17] Each action-reflection cycle is "bridged" by engaging in planned action, evaluating it, and then returning to the observation stage with new unanswered questions. Most approaches develop these questions through the direct input of the participants of the study. Thus, action research empowers participant individuals and communities as *co-researchers*, rather than their remaining merely objects and recipients of research.[18] In the Middle East and North Africa region where many of our graduates serve, this dynamic of community engagement and empowerment is greatly needed.

Why Use Action Research in Theological Studies?

Bassem Melki, Dean of Students at ABTS and my friend and colleague, describes himself as a "practical guy," the kind who prefers to jump into the middle of a situation to work at making it better by trying things and seeing what works.[19] As he began his own doctoral studies, he perceived a gap between the espoused theology of reconciliation of Lebanese pastors and the practised theology within Lebanese evangelical churches. Bassem is currently developing a research proposal for the Asia Graduate School of Theology in which he uses an action research approach to study pastoral practices that have the potential for transforming the Lebanese evangelical community's responses to conflict.[20] Sitting on the sidelines to theorize about the situation for three to five years while working on a PhD did not appeal to Bassem. If he was not going to be able to be a part of transformative change *during* the PhD research process, he felt it would be a waste of his time and effort.[21]

This dynamic of placing *action or practice as the primary emphasis* of action research features in early action research theory such as Lewin's 1946 work. He

---

17. Cameron, Bhatti, and Duce argue helpfully for recognizing every step of this cycle as theological, using their "four voices of theology" as a theological hermeneutic. Cameron, Bhatti, and Duce, *Talking about God in Practice*, Kindle loc. 952.
18. Cameron, Bhatti, and Duce, *Talking about God in Practice*, Kindle loc. 952.
19. Bassem Melki (ABTS faculty and Dean of Students), personal interview with Caleb Hutcherson, Mansouriyeh, Lebanon, 17 February 2017.
20. Melki, interview.
21. Melki.

argued that "research that produces nothing but books will not suffice."[22] Dick identifies this driving focus on action as a characteristic feature of the action research family of approaches.[23] The dynamic of holding action at the centre of research and knowledge is not new. It corresponds closely to the ethical value of doing, rather than merely knowing, in both Paul's (1 Cor 13:1–2) and James's (Jas 1:22 – 2:26) accounts of true Christian faith. Mere knowledge is not sufficient. In our Arab context, this action-oriented framework corresponds to the traditional Islamic emphasis on orthopraxy. The eleventh-century Muslim philosopher al-Ghazali exemplifies action's centrality to faith, stating: "My child, knowledge without action is insanity, but action without knowledge is not action. Know that all knowledge cannot save you from sin and will not make you obedient, and will not free you from the fire of hell, unless you really act according to your knowledge."[24]

Locating action and change as central to theological research, rather than its hoped-for outcome, seems to suggest that action research approaches may be at least as appropriate to theological studies as more traditional approaches that relegate action to recommendations for application in a concluding chapter. In saying this, I do not claim that faithfulness in theological studies requires social science approaches. However, the embodied, practised nature of Christian faith suggests that theological studies remain unfinished if they do not include some form of transformed action.

In Bassem's research proposal, he recognized the need for responsiveness and flexibility in the approach to researching the practice of peacemaking amongst Lebanese evangelical pastors. A traditional research approach would have forced him to artificially freeze the research to describe a specific incident at a point in time, rather than dealing responsively within the complex and changing situation of developing peace-building initiatives among these pastors and communities.[25] The input and participation of the pastors, and

---

22. Lewin, "Action Research and Minority Problems," 35.
23. Dick, "Reflections on the SAGE Encyclopedia of Action Research," 437.
24. al-Ghazali, *Ayyuha al-Walad* [*Letter to a Disciple*], trans. G. H. Scherer (Beirut: Catholic Press, 1951), quoted in Mehdi Nakosteen, *History of Islamic Origins of Western Education A.D. 800–1350, With an Introduction to Medieval Muslim Education* (Boulder: University of Colorado, 1964), 91–92.
25. Melki, interview, 17 February 2017.

the flexibility of the research methodology, are understood as essential to the research process.

This characteristic of Bassem's project highlights another important reason for using action research in theological studies: *participation and empowerment*.[26] One important value in the 1990 ICETE Manifesto is that any form of theological education should be modelled from and exist for the needs of its specific context.[27] It is because action research values and seeks out participation from the "objects" of the research, it is research "with people, not on people."[28] By developing research questions based on the input of those being studied, action research supports contextualization through participation. Cameron points out that many of the foundational influences contributing to action research started from political and theological concern for "disrupting existing power relations."[29] While there remains a danger that action research may replicate these corrupted power relationships, with careful and intentional research design it can serve as a tool that values the kingdom ethics of giving preference to the marginalized.[30] Thus theological action research can serve to develop the kind of contextualization that is most needed for theological education to have real significance in a given context.

Bassem is heavily involved in the practice of pastoral ministry both inside the seminary and in church and denomination. While he values practice and doing, he observes how time and Arab cultural dynamics tend to inhibit the practice of explicit reflection in this context.[31] Dominant educational

---

26. Dick, "Reflections on the SAGE Encyclopedia of Action Research," 434ff.
27. International Council for Evangelical Theological Education (ICETE), "ICETE Manifesto on the Renewal of Evangelical Theological Education," 1990, http://icete-edu.org/manifesto/.
28. Horton and Freire, *We Make the Road by Walking*, 148, as quoted in Dick, "Reflections on the SAGE Encyclopedia of Action Research," 434.
29. Cameron, Bhatti, and Duce, *Talking about God in Practice*, Kindle loc. 817.
30. A focus that, while closely associated with liberation theology, reflects a growing body of evangelical scholarship that recognizes a canon-wide moral ethic in Scripture. See, for example, Glen H. Stassen and David Gushee, *Kingdom Ethics: Following Jesus in Contemporary Context* (Downers Grove: IVP, 2003).
31. Melki, interview, 17 February 2017.

influences in Arab contexts tend to shun critical reflection.[32] Bassem values action research because of the way he perceives that, beyond his dissertation research, the approach might provide a process of critical reflection on action that is needed in Lebanese politics and public theology.[33]

The development of skills and disposition for *critical reflection* is another reason for using action research in theological studies. Swinton and Mowat argue that action research promotes "movement from practice (action) to theory, to *critical reflection* on practice, to revised forms of practice developed in light of this spiralling process."[34] Dick identifies two senses of "critical" amongst action researchers, one pointing to "penetrating and analytical thinking" and the other concerning sensitivity to power dynamics.[35] Both senses are supported by the cyclical movement between action and reflection that promotes deeper enquiry and learning from tacit knowledge embedded in practice.[36] Professional education holds reflective practice as a core competency for practitioners. Action research appears to promote this competency by promoting critical reflection on practices, and by making explicit the tacit knowledge of practitioners.[37] Swinton and Mowat's critical conversation model of theological reflection in action research corresponds to the fundamental dynamic of reflective practice[38] where theory and practice are brought into discourse, developing together.

As Bassem and I discussed his reasons for using action research, these three themes emerged. They are consistent with broad themes that Dick synthesizes from action researchers across other disciplines.[39] *Emphasis on*

---

32. Perry Shaw, "Madrasa and Church: A Comparative Study of Muslim and Christian Approaches to Religious Education," *Theological Review* 22, no. 2 (2001): 235; George Sabra, "The Challenges of Theological Education in the Middle East," *International Review of Mission* 89, no. 352 (2000): 71.
33. Melki, interview, 17 February 2017.
34. Swinton and Mowat, *Practical Theology and Qualitative Research*, Kindle loc. 4680.
35. Dick, "Reflections on the SAGE Encyclopedia of Action Research," 438.
36. Dick, 438.
37. Somekh, "Action Research," 6.
38. E.g. Donald A. Schön, *The Reflective Practitioner: How Professionals Think in Action*, 1st ed. (New York: Basic, 1983); Jennifer A. Moon, *Reflection in Learning and Professional Development: Theory and Practice*, 1st ed. (London: Kogan Page, 1999).
39. Dick, "Reflections on the SAGE Encyclopedia of Action Research," 438.

action, participation and empowerment, and *critical reflection* were seen to be significant values implicit to action research methodology that align with values within theological studies. While the value of critical reflection may be a point of conflict in Arab cultural contexts, recognition and development of culturally appropriate forms of critical reflection oriented around action may be a way forward.

Implementing Action Research: Openings and Challenges

At this point I pivot the exploration of action research to consider some recommendations for including and implementing action research in a graduate program of theological studies. I base my recommendations on our own experimentation with it in our particular setting in Lebanon. Rather than offering these as generalized principles, I suggest them as possible points of theorizing for other settings. I develop these recommendations in conversation with Bob Dick's general action research guides and the recent work by Helen Cameron and colleagues on theological action research.

Openings for Implementing Action Research

At ABTS, our implementation of action research came about through one faculty member's awareness of it and suggestion for using it as a learning task in an integrated learning module. The development of that learning task, the teaching to familiarize students with it, and the growing familiarity with it among the faculty on the module contributed to broader awareness of it among the broader faculty. Having one faculty member committed to researching it and using it as a learning task led to student use and interest, which pushed us to further research and use in other courses. Several faculty members participated in writing articles or research proposals that used or discussed the use of action research. The overall commitment to theological integration and reflective practice by our faculty was foundational to this entire process.

As might be evident from the first two sections of this chapter, an action research approach might be particularly suited for people who tend towards activism and practical action, yet who want to do so reflectively. In fact, action research is underpinned by a pragmatic epistemology.[40] Ministry practitioners, bivocational pastors, parachurch workers, and theologian pastors may find this approach more suited to researching realities of ministry they face than more traditional research approaches. Curiosity about practice and interest in understanding it theologically can kick-start an action research project.[41] For action research in theology, however, action cannot be for action's sake, "but always action in the service of revelation and mediation of the gospel."[42] In our attempts at using the process at ABTS, students and faculty with a desire to deal with the "what works?" questions seemed to fit most naturally within an action research framework. The overall approach opens up ways of bringing rigorous theological reflection into discovering pragmatic "this does!" answers to those questions.

Because action research remains a lesser-known approach to theological studies, contextually aware guides for conducting theological action research are needed. Broadly speaking, there are several skill sets that contribute to successful completion of an action research study of an appropriate standard. Swinton and Mowat argue for the essential place of qualitative research methods in order for individuals and communities to be faithful to God and his mission in the world.[43] This requires familiarity with and practice using qualitative research methods and social science approaches that may be unfamiliar for theologians trained in humanities-based approaches. Good people skills and the ability to tolerate ambiguity in the research process are important.[44] Because of the way action research values responsiveness rather than rigidity, the capacity to think laterally and responsively to new developments as the research progresses contributes significantly to successful completion.

Gaining familiarity with a variety of reporting formats for action research is necessary for successful implementation. Dick suggests orienting the final

---

40. Helen Cameron and Catherine Duce, *Researching Practice in Ministry and Mission: A Companion* (London: SCM, 2013), Kindle loc. 853.
41. Cameron, Bhatti, and Duce, *Talking about God in Practice*, Kindle loc. 1418.
42. Swinton and Mowat, *Practical Theology and Qualitative Research*, Kindle loc. 4719.
43. Swinton and Mowat, Kindle loc. 4711.
44. Bob Dick, "You Want to Do an Action Research Thesis? How to Conduct and Report Action Research," *Chapel Hill, QLD: Interchange (Mimeo)*, 1993, http://www.aral.com.au/resources/arthesis.html#a_art_whatisar.

report around the contribution to knowledge that results from the study.[45] Because the methodology lies outside of traditional experimental research or humanities' argumentation formats, careful explanation is often needed for why an action research approach was used. The introductory chapter should give the background for the situation needing research, justifying the reasons for the study. A brief literature overview may be needed in the early sections or chapters, but the primary focus should be an argument for the need for responsiveness in the situation or practice being studied. A methodology chapter then outlines the process of action research and the methods being used. Here the rigorousness of the methods will need to be demonstrated; the nature of the knowledge claims being made will need to be outlined.

The main body chapters can be organized around major findings the cyclical action–reflection research process made. Each of these chapters might draw from data derived during the research process, bringing it into critical conversation with relevant bodies of literature. There will be a need to engage with various bodies of literature across the chapters of the thesis.[46] The multiple visits to related literature and the progressive, developing nature of those trips highlights the interdisciplinary nature of action research in practical theology. Finally, and most importantly, the entire reporting of action research ought to read as a narrative development rather than an empirical account of research. The contribution to knowledge occurs as a journey of transformative learning involving both the researcher and the participants. Thus, people and their story are central to the action research report.

Challenges to Implementing Action Research

Despite the overall success of our experience using action research at ABTS, I have several concerns that emerge from both our use of it and my ongoing review of the literature. These may present challenges for using action research approaches in theological education in general, and in the Majority World in particular.

It is a common perception (misperception) that the purpose of research is to extract "best practice" from actions in specific contexts. These disembodied

---

45. Dick, "You Want to Do an Action Research Thesis?"
46. Dick, "You Want to Do an Action Research Thesis?"

"best practice" principles can then be exported and applied in other contexts.[47] This perception assumes that practices can be separated from the circumstances in which they are developed.[48] Thinking about action research in this way misunderstands the kind of knowledge that action research develops. Action research does not seek to build generalizations, but rather a very specific, contextualized understanding of the practice being researched. This context-specific knowledge, critically understood, allows for theorizing. In other words, it can be "offered to other contexts as a part of their exploration of their experience."[49] But knowledge claims made based on action research are not meant to generalize or indicate normativity. The ephemeral nature of these knowledge claims may be perceived as a weakness for those working in more positivist/essentialist epistemological settings.

Another challenge for action research in theological studies emerges in the setting of academic theology, theology done in university theology departments. Because of the typical location of departments of theology in humanities faculties, there may be negative perceptions of action research as being too practically focused. Cameron, Bhatti, and Duce note that this may lead to difficulty with classifications for research assessment.[50] With recent interest in action research in practical theology and the opening of theological research centres using action research,[51] increased recognition exists. But as action research is not yet a mainstream research paradigm in theological studies, there remains a broad lack of understanding of action research among supervisors and examiners. This chapter and the book containing it aim to contribute to efforts towards increasing understanding of theological action research.

---

47. Cameron, Bhatti, and Duce, *Talking about God in Practice*, Kindle loc. 691.
48. Cameron, Bhatti, and Duce, Kindle loc. 691.
49. Cameron, Bhatti, and Duce, Kindle loc. 816.
50. Cameron, Bhatti, and Duce, Kindle loc. 700.
51. The Heythrop Institute for Religion and Society at University of London has developed and used theological action research in a number of large-scale projects exploring theology and social change, including the project documented by Cameron et al. (*Talking about God in Practice*). See "The Heythrop Institute for Religion & Society," Heythrop College: Philosophy & Theology – University of London, accessed 8 February 2017, http://www.heythrop.ac.uk/organisation/research/heythrop-institute-religion-society.

The *process* of action research also presents some unique challenges. During the beginning stages of traditional research approaches, researchers typically develop and clarify research terms and questions through literature surveys. This is counterproductive in an action research approach. Rather, the research process begins with establishing the action research methodology intended to be used. The actual research process develops in "rounds" of reflective or experiential learning. The lack of clarity about the "research construct" even during data collection/analysis may be unsettling to a researcher or supervisor not used to action research approaches. The multiple rounds of research will lead to ongoing return trips to the literature to "disprove" preliminary interpretive findings during the data collection periods. Additionally, the reporting process will likely be more difficult than in a traditional approach because it documents several rounds of research, rather than one. The nature of an action research study resembles a large program of traditional research with multiple research cycles developing. This indicates something of the increased cost and time that an action research project incurs in comparison with more traditional, linear approaches. Moreover, the final research report will likely require either significant brevity on the part of the author or institutional accommodation to longer maximum word limits.[52]

Critiquing pure social science models of action research, Swinton and Mowat point out that "the focus of action tends to be on generating solutions to particular problems."[53] Problem-solving is the fundamental *telos* of action research. While practical theology does share this ethos of being grounded in the particular structure of a situation, its fundamental purpose is not merely pragmatic. It has the goal of interacting with these situations, asking "What must be done?"[54] It finds its *telos* in enabling the people of God "to remain faithful to God and to participate fully in God's continuing mission to the world."[55] This mission is ultimately about God's glory, not fixing problems. Keeping this difference in mind and prominently before theology students being introduced to action research is important. Particularly in the contexts where

---

52. Dick, "You Want to Do an Action Research Thesis?"
53. Swinton and Mowat, *Practical Theology and Qualitative Research*, Kindle loc. 4687.
54. Graham, "Is Practical Theology a Form of 'Action Research'?," 168.
55. Swinton and Mowat, *Practical Theology and Qualitative Research*, Kindle loc. 4711.

my students serve, it is quite common to feel hopeless about ever seeing things change. The promise of a "new" methodology can lead to disappointment when change is slow or non-existent. With the *telos* of *theological* action research in mind, we remember that the final assessment criteria look for faithfulness to God's mission in the world.

Conclusion

In this chapter I traced experiences with action research in theological studies in an Arab theological education setting. These experiences highlighted key themes that I brought into conversation with the literatures of action research, broadly, and theological action research in practical theology, specifically. This conversation focused on describing action research in theological studies and reasons for using it. Our experiences with using it suggest ways forward for implementing it more widely in theological studies. However, they also call attention to possible challenges that may impede its use in traditional settings. While these challenges are not insurmountable, they are important issues to consider when beginning theological action research.

In social and contextual settings like the Middle East and North Africa, we have found action research to be a powerful tool for promoting theological integration in life and ministry that seems to lead to needed social change. This is the kind of tool that can help a Middle Eastern woman conceptualize how to make a difference in her community and to reflect on that process theologically. The approach helps her plan out and experiment with actions that promote change in her community, and empowers the participation of the community in the process. Rather than objectifying the community and seeking out what is wrong, theological action research offers a way to seek out what is strong in the community and use this for transformative change in faithful participation with the mission of God in the world.

Discussion Questions

1. Briefly discuss one or two major issues that confront society in your own local context but on which the church currently seems to have little or no

impact. What are some of the theological, political, and psychological factors that can make change difficult in these areas?

2. Describe where a candidate applying the principles of action research might begin approaching these issues. Make a list of the various stakeholders who might be consulted as a starting point for the research. What are one or two key culturally sensitive approaches that would need to be in place to ensure that the stakeholders are respected and empowered in the process?

3. Who among your faculty might be well placed to supervise action research projects? In what context within your current program structures might action research projects fit in? How might the rest of the faculty support the process? How might you advocate for such an approach within your school's accreditation structures?

4. In recognition of the call for the development of theological leadership for the church's praxis, action research is a particularly strategic methodology for schools to work on jointly. Working with two or three other members of your faculty, sketch out a possible action research project that your school as a whole might implement in service of the missional call of the church in your region.

Bibliography

al-Ghazali. *Ayyuha 'L-Walad [Letter to a Disciple]*. Translated by G. H. Scherer. Beirut: Catholic Press, 1951.
Cameron, Helen, Deborah Bhatti, and Catherine Duce. *Talking about God in Practice: Theological Action Research and Practical Theology*. London: SCM, 2010.
Cameron, Helen, and Catherine Duce. *Researching Practice in Ministry and Mission: A Companion*. London: SCM, 2013.
Checkland, Peter, and Jim Scholes. *Soft Systems Methodology in Action*. New York: Wiley, 1999.
Conde-Frazier, Elizabeth. "Participatory Action Research: Practical Theology for Social Justice." *Religious Education* 101, no. 3 (2006): 321–329.
Dick, Bob. "Postgraduate Programs Using Action Research." *The Learning Organization* 9, no. 3/4 (2002): 159–170. http://www.aral.com.au/resources/ppar.html.

———. "Reflections on the SAGE Encyclopedia of Action Research and What It Says about Action Research and Its Methodologies." *Action Research* 13, no. 4 (2015): 431–444. doi:10.1177/1476750315573593.

———. "You Want to Do an Action Research Thesis? How to Conduct and Report Action Research." *Chapel Hill, QLD: Interchange (Mimeo)*, 1993. http://www.aral.com.au/resources/arthesis.html#a_art_whatisar.

Dokecki, Paul R., J. R. Newbrough, and Robert T. O'Gorman. "Toward a Community-Oriented Action Research Framework for Spirituality: Community Psychological and Theological Perspectives." *Journal of Community Psychology* 29, no. 5 (1 September 2001): 497–518.

Graham, Elaine. "Is Practical Theology a Form of 'Action Research'?" *International Journal of Practical Theology* 17, no. 1 (2013): 148–178.

Greenwood, Davydd J., and Morten Levin. *Introduction to Action Research: Social Research for Social Change*. Thousand Oaks: SAGE, 2007.

Harder, Cameron. "Using Participatory Action Research in Seminary Internships." *Theological Education* 42, no. 2 (2007): 127–139.

"The Heythrop Institute for Religion & Society." Heythrop College: Philosophy & Theology – University of London. Accessed 8 February 2017. http://www.heythrop.ac.uk/organisation/research/heythrop-institute-religion-society.

Horton, Myles, and Paulo Freire. *We Make the Road by Walking*. Philadelphia: Temple University, 1990.

Hutcherson, Caleb. "Toward Theological Integration Using Action Research: Reflections from an Arab Context." *InSights Journal for Global Theological Education* 1, no. 2 (2016): 31–39.

International Council for Evangelical Theological Education (ICETE). "ICETE Manifesto on the Renewal of Evangelical Theological Education." 1990. http://icete-edu.org/manifesto/.

Lewin, Kurt. "Action Research and Minority Problems." *Social Issues* 2, no. 4 (1946): 34–46.

Moon, Jennifer A. *Reflection in Learning and Professional Development: Theory and Practice*. 1st ed. London: Kogan Page, 1999.

Nakosteen, Mehdi. *History of Islamic Origins of Western Education A.D. 800–1350, With an Introduction to Medieval Muslim Education*. Boulder: University of Colorado, 1964.

Sabra, George. "The Challenges of Theological Education in the Middle East." *International Review of Mission* 89, no. 352 (2000): 70–75.

Schön, Donald A. *The Reflective Practitioner: How Professionals Think in Action.* 1st ed. New York: Basic, 1983.

Shaw, Perry. "Madrasa and Church: A Comparative Study of Muslim and Christian Approaches to Religious Education." *Theological Review* 22, no. 2 (2001): 216–244.

Somekh, Bridget. "Action Research." In *The SAGE Encyclopedia of Qualitative Research Methods*, edited by Lisa M. Given and Bridget Somekh, 4–6. Los Angeles: SAGE, 2008.

Stassen, Glen H., and David Gushee. *Kingdom Ethics: Following Jesus in Contemporary Context.* Downers Grove: IVP, 2003.

Swinton, John, and Harriet Mowat. *Practical Theology and Qualitative Research.* London: SCM, 2006.

Todhunter, Colin. "Undertaking Action Research: Negotiating the Road Ahead." *Social Research Update* 34 (2001). http://citeseerx.ist.psu.edu/viewdoc/summary?doi=10.1.1.304.3849.

13

Studying Together:
Joint and Collaborative Research

Rafael Zaracho

History is not written from the past, but from the present and the future that we hope or we fear. (Justo González)[1]

Introduction

What I would like to offer in this chapter is based not so much on what we have experienced and come to know, but on what we would hope to experience and provide for our learning community. I will emphasize the need to see our theological structures and models as "faithful intentions"[2] and as servant structures.[3] Seeing them through these lenses will help the learning community to engage in the process of evaluation and adjustment of our current theological programs. In addition, as we (the learning community) locate and see our theological models and structures as being part of the

---

1. Justo L. González, *Breve Historia de la Preparación Ministerial* (Barcelona: Editorial Clie, 2012), 10.
2. For the notion of faithful intentions, see Rafael Zaracho, "Formación Teológica Desde la Perspectiva Bíblica y Anabautista," in *Registro de un Peregrinaje: Instituto Bíblico Asunción, 50 Años Formando Obreros con la Palabra de Dios*, ed. Víctor Wall, Martha Florentín, and Flavio Florentín (Asunción: Instituto Bíblico Asunción, 2014), 189–199.
3. For the notion of servant structures, see Donald B. Kraybill, *The Upside Down Kingdom* (Scottdale: Herald, 1978), 171–177, 256–272.

ministry of God, we will be more determined to promote and create spaces for diverse and multiple models of teaching, learning, and final work. With these principles in mind, I will present three short examples that can be used as alternatives alongside the traditional path of the thesis. My observations and proposals are partial and above all they are an invitation to expand, exemplify, and deepen what is suggested here in the context of communities of faith that seek to listen, experience, live, and be constantly renewed by God and his Word (Rom 12:1–2).

Learning Together: An Invitation

Reflecting on my own experience of having gone through four processes of writing theses (two in my own country and two abroad),[4] I can summarize them as eminently very solitary experiences. I remember the many hours of reading and reflection as necessary steps and the price to be paid to get the degrees. I have to confess that I enjoyed those times because I am oriented to a more "reflective" style of learning. At the same time, I have come to realize that at many moments during those months and years I felt lonely, because in general there were few people and spaces to share the findings, questions, and new concerns that came out of the readings and reflections. In addition, I am sure that I would have benefited greatly if there had been more opportunities to share with groups of fellow researchers in more formal and systematic settings as part of the research process.

At the most basic level, my own experience of teaching courses on research methodology and guiding students through the process towards the realization of their final work confirms the need to create and promote formal and intentional spaces where students can share and express their concerns and findings at each step of the research. However, more than this, the reality in many theological institutions, at least in Latin America, is that there are no other options or alternatives for the final work. As the "traditional" path of the thesis is the only option, there is a need to create and promote the alternatives and options for the final work that I will propose later in this chapter. Our

---

4. My first two degrees are from Paraguay (Licentiate in Theology and Psychology), my master's in theology from the USA, and my PhD in theology from the United Kingdom.

alternatives and options, however, need to be seen as an essential part of the culture and emphases of our institutions.

Accents of the Spirit

Let me start by suggesting that to learn together we need to promote and grow in awareness of our own (and others') denominational and theological-institutional particularities and emphases. We should recognize, certainly in the context of Latin America, interinstitutional and interdenominational efforts through theological consultations with the aim of bringing together institutions in order to reflect together and learn from each other.[5] However, in many theological institutions a common reality is a lack of recognition or interest in what other institutions are doing, creating a general sense of fragmentation and duplication of efforts.[6]

There is an increasing need, at least in Latin America, to be led by the Spirit to form alternative communities in which we come together to celebrate our similarities and differences, and to work together for the extension of God's kingdom. Theological education has an important place and a key role in this process of recognizing, affirming, and celebrating our historical-theological similarities and differences. I would like to invite you to see the historical and theological emphases of our communities of faith and our institutions as "accents" of the Spirit.[7] The image of "accents" suggests the central place of our believing communities in and through which we name, prioritize, celebrate, and conserve dimensions of our relationships with our God, our brothers and sisters, and our contexts. Seeing our own (and others') historical and theological communal emphases as "accents" of the Spirit can help us to honour how the different communities and theological institutions across time and

---

5. See, for instance, René Padilla, ed., *Nuevas Alternativas de Educación Teológica* (Buenos Aires: Nueva Creación, 1986); Samuel Escobar, "Fundamento y Finalidad de la Educación Teológica en América Latina" (presented at "El diálogo del milenio," São Paulo, Brazil, 1995); Ross Kinsler, ed., *Viabilidad de la Formación Ministerial en el Mundo de Hoy* (San José: Seminario Bíblico Latinoamericano, 1994).

6. Matthias Preiswerk, *Contrato Intercultural: Crisis y Refundación de la Educación Teológica* (La Paz: CLAI, 2011), 101–108. The entire section (35–108) is very helpful in understanding and getting the sense of the "map" of theological education in Latin America.

7. As part of my doctoral dissertation I developed the notion of "accents" of the Spirit. Rafael Zaracho, "The Role of Preferences in the Context of Believing and Discerning Communities: A Maturanian Reading" (PhD diss., University of St Andrews, 2014).

cultures have been seeking to be faithful to God's kingdom. It invites us, in addition, to test and judge our own and others' theological emphases in light of our reading of the Scriptures in our contexts (local, regional, national) as we seek to become learning communities guided by the Spirit.

Faithful Intentions in Vernacular Particularity

Seeing our own (and others') historical and theological emphases as accents of the Spirit calls us to become discerning communities in which we investigate honestly the course and consequences of our beliefs and practices. It invites us to value and judge the diversity of our own (and others') believing communities and seminaries by their life-giving quality and by their promotion of a reconciled creation. The implication for our theological education is that we must promote and work towards a "vernacular"[8] face for our theological institutions and structures. That is, we need to recognize, acknowledge, and honour the "embarrassment of particularity"[9] in the distinctive theological and cultural emphases of our denominations and seminaries.

In the process of promoting and growing in awareness about our own and others' identities, we become aware, as members of our learning communities, about the extent to which we fall short in our task of believing, discerning, celebrating, and mediating God's presence in and through our experiences and in the world. At this point, it becomes crucial to see the historical-theological differences of our institutions as "accents" of the Spirit because it will allow us to recognize how the Spirit has been working and still works in and through our own and others' learning communities of faith. Then we can share with others the gifts of the Spirit that have been present in and through our own learning communities, and we will be open to learn from other learning communities that seek to become listening and obedient communities to the guiding of the Spirit. In this process in the context of our theological institutions, we can value and judge our own and others' *faithful intentions* in how to mediate, name, and celebrate God's work and presence in our midst and in the world.

---

8. Kosuke Koyama, "Theological Education: Its Unities and Diversities," *Theological Education* 1 (1993): 101–102.

9. John D. Roth, *Teaching That Transforms: Why Anabaptist-Mennonite Education Matters* (Scottdale: Herald, 2011), 67.

Kingdom, Church, and Structures in Service of God's Shalom

As we grow in awareness of our own and others' faithful intentions incarnated in and through the cultural and theological emphases of our seminaries, it is important to frame and locate our faithful intentions within the concept of *ministry*. The notion of ministry is fundamental and the primary nature of our theological institutions.[10] Our institutions, as any of our ministries as the people of God, find their roots and shape their intentionality on the basis of God's ministry. God's ministry is expressed in his seeking to reconcile the entire world to himself.[11] Consequently, the *theological* and *educational* dimensions of our institutions emerge from and find their paradigm in God's shalom project.[12] The "faithful intentions" of our theological and cultural emphases need to be revisited from time to time to evaluate if they continue to be attuned to the kingdom's principles and the particular needs of the context.

Kraybill's distinctions are appropriate here in relation to kingdom, church, and structure.[13] First, the *kingdom of God* has been initiated, according to the Gospels, with and through the life, ministry, death, and resurrection of Jesus. This kingdom works in and through the Holy Spirit in our lives and relationships. Second, the *church* is the assembly of those who have accepted and welcomed God's rule in their lives and relationships. As the church, we are the members of a visible community who live by the kingdom's principles. Finally, the *structures* are the "social vehicles" such as institutions and programs to meet our own and others' needs. The structures of the church (denominations, liturgy, mission agencies, etc.) should reflect the kingdom's principles, but it is important to remember that they are "neither the kingdom nor the church itself."[14] Kraybill suggests, "we must periodically overhaul these organized structures, these

---

10. For the notion of theology as the ministry of the church, see Karl Barth, "The Place of Theology," in *Theological Foundations for Ministry*, ed. Ray Anderson (Edinburgh: T&T Clark, 1979), 22–58.

11. For a precise and short treatment of the idea that "all ministry is God's ministry," see Ray Anderson, "A Theology for Ministry," in *Theological Foundations for Ministry*, ed. Ray Anderson (Edinburgh: T&T Clark, 1979), 6–21.

12. This shalom project finds its full expression in the incarnation. For the theological notion of the incarnation as a paradigm for theological education see, Roth, *Teaching That Transforms*, 65–92.

13. Kraybill, *Upside Down Kingdom*, 171–178.

14. Kraybill, 173.

human creations, to assure they remain servant structures."[15] Accordingly, it is crucial to remember and locate our role and work as educators and the role of our theological institutions within the framework of God's kingdom work.

Kraybill's distinction of these concepts is a helpful reminder and motivation to see our educational models and alternatives as "structures." As such, they are helpful as long as they facilitate our role as members of the church. In other words, seminary training is just one part of the bigger picture of the educational role of the church.[16] Kraybill suggests that we should have "institutional sabbaticals – periodic times when we review programs and projects."[17] As the church, we must evaluate according to the kingdom's values whether the current models and "culture" of our educational structures are promoting service to others and edification of the community of faith in our particular contexts.

The Challenge of Change

We may all agree that we need to revise and adjust our theological models and alternatives from time to time. However, as soon as we want to suggest and introduce changes we will find and perceive some initial resistance or even opposition. The implication for us as members of a learning community is that we need to be very aware that any suggestion of change needs to take into account the many actors and relationships involved in the decision. For instance, the denomination–seminary relationship needs to be in constant dialogue and revision because of tensions that may emerge, such as regarding the place and role of the church and seminary, "professional" clergy vs. the priesthood of all believers, and so on.[18] Another tension point is the relation of the theological institution to the state, where there is increasing pressure from the government to formalize and regulate the educational system. In addition, we might add the

---

15. Kraybill, 173.
16. Matthias Preiswerk, "For a Quality Theological Education: Manifesto," accessed 16 January 2017, http://www.oikoumene.org/en/folder/documents-pdf/WOCATI_2008_-_Manifesto_from_Latin_America_-_english_version.pdf.
17. Kraybill, *Upside Down Kingdom*, 176.
18. Alfred Neufeld, "Dificultades, Necesidades, Limitaciones y Desafíos en América Latina que que Enfrentan la Formación Teológica a Principios del Milenio Venidero" (presented at "El diálogo del milenio," São Paulo, Brazil, 1995).

economic relations of dependency and collaboration of an institution related to a congregation or denomination, international agencies, and so on.[19] These and other elements are in play and need to be on the table of conversation when we want to propose and introduce changes in our institutions.[20]

In the process of seeking to be faithful to God in our particular contexts, we must necessarily propose and introduce adjustments to our communal walking as we seek to hear and be obedient to the guiding of the Holy Spirit in our everyday life. These "adjustments" speak of our "faithful intentions" in the process of naming and categorizing our relationships with God, each other, and the rest of creation. The notion of "faithful intentions" communicates the idea of a discerning community of believers who seek to see, hear, taste, and live out their lives in profound relationship with God and with each other. In addition, it links with the idea of the provisory or "playful"[21] nature of our intents. Accordingly, if we see our theological institutions as servant structures or as expressions of our faithful intentions, we may be more inclined to get involved in the process of evaluation and work towards the necessary adjustments. In what follows I will present three examples or models that can be seen as alternatives or options alongside the traditional path of thesis.

Creating Spaces as Learning Communities

The fact that we are sharing common spaces such as classrooms, buildings, chapel time, and ministerial trips does not necessarily mean that we are studying and learning as an *intentional* community of learners. I am assuming that all of our theological institutions have their intentional dimension expressed by a vision and mission statement. However, this is not enough. A

---

19. Preiswerk, *Contrato Intercultural*, 77–79.
20. For those interested in engaging in the process of evaluating our educational models, two wonderful examples of case studies are, first, by Shaw in Lebanon and, second, by Preiswerk in Bolivia. Shaw and Preiswerk offer practical and helpful steps to take into account in the process of transforming our current educational models. See Perry Shaw, *Transforming Theological Education: A Practical Handbook for Integrative Learning* (Carlisle: Langham Global Library, 2014), 1–13; and Preiswerk, *Contrato Intercultural*, 177–224. For a historical overview of theological models and alternatives, see Bernhard Ott, *Understanding and Developing Theological Education* (Carlisle: Langham Global Library, 2016); and González, *Breve Historia*.
21. On the notion of theology as "games," see Rubem Alves, *La Teología Como Juego* (Buenos Aires: La Aurora, 1982).

genuine intentional community of learners is where the vision and mission are understood, embraced, and applied by the different actors such as faculty, students, board, staff, and so on.[22] In addition, the vision and mission are expressed and incarnated in and through the presence or absence in the institutions of objects (icons, photos of the founders, theologians, former principals, etc.), the disposition of the classroom, the architecture, and so on.[23] In short, the members of an intentional community of learners are aware of the dynamic of their interdependent existence as a group in the light of the nature and purpose of their calling in ministry.

The three examples or alternatives that follow are meaningful only if they are seen as an integral and core part of a larger theological agenda and responding to the vision and mission of the institution, discussed in the context of a discerning and intentional community of learners.[24] If we believe and emphasize the importance of "learning and studying together," this aspect should be reflected not only as an option for final work such as a thesis, but also as an approach to teaching and learning that can be experienced and lived in and through our many "academic" activities.[25] Consequently, as learning communities we should seek to create and promote multiple *spaces* to cultivate the process of learning together.

---

22. Shaw, *Transforming Theological Education*, 15–16.
23. Preiswerk, *Contrato Intercultural*, 51–63.
24. In my own experience of teaching, I have allowed and invited the students to explore different styles and find their styles of learning. I have allowed as final work for an Old Testament theology class, for instance, an original painting that conveyed main themes or doctrines of the OT. Another student for the same class wrote a poem dealing with the images of God in the OT. At the same time, I have invited my students to be intentional in the process of seeking and working with different students during the time of preparation. The notion of a community of learners invites us to give full voice to and to create as many spaces as possible for those who are part of these communities to be active parts of their process of learning. Very helpful on this theme is Roth, *Teaching That Transforms*, 93–156.
25. "Why do we (need to) learn what we are learning?" is a central question for all the actors of our community of learners. Trying to answer this question will give us the chance to evaluate and judge our current programs and options. Helpful on this theme is bell hooks, *Teaching to Transgress: Education as the Practice of Freedom* (New York: Routledge, 1994); Jason Ferenczi, *Serving Communities: Governance and the Potential of Theological Schools* (Carlisle: Langham Global Library, 2015), 149–159; Lee Wanak, "Developing an Operational Philosophy of Theological Education," in *Leadership in Theological Education: Foundations for Academic Leadership*, eds. Fritz Deininger and Orbelina Eguizabal (Carlisle: Langham Global Library, 2017), 33–64; Rupen Das, *Connecting Curriculum with Context* (Carlisle: Langham Global Library, 2015), 1–21.

Collaborative Research

The first option comes from my experience in our "Research Center Marturía"[26] at Instituto Bíblico Asunción where two of our graduates led a collaborative research.[27] My role as director of Marturía was to coordinate and guide the whole process of the research. The research was conducted among pastors in two towns in Paraguay using open-ended interview questions. The questions dealt with the perceptions of the pastors in relation to the needs and problems of the community, as well as the churches' responses. The research revealed that pastors are very aware of the needs and problems that are facing their particular towns and are willing to do something about the problems and needs perceived. The recommendation was that evangelical churches should regularly analyse the problems and needs of their communities to participate intentionally in the mission of God.

The two researchers worked side by side during each step of the project. The only time when they worked separately was for the interviews with the pastors. They worked together to overview the theological and historical background. They came to agreement in defining the elements and aspects that they would explore in the communities. They worked collaboratively in designing the questions and variables to take into account during the interviews. When the questionnaires were ready, each went to the chosen town and held the interviews with the pastors. After the interviews, they met again to organize their results and discuss their joint findings.

The research lasted for one academic year that included orientation meetings, background research, identification of main problems, compilation of data, and so on. The final document is about seventy pages long. Below is a rough and tentative calendar that we used:

- March: orientation
- April: preliminary research to identify topic, relevance, implications, etc.

---

26. Marturía promotes and supports research on themes related to church, leadership, ministerial, and theological issues. Each year Marturía offers three research grants for its graduates.

27. Full description of the research can be found at http://www.teologia-iba.edu.py/shurance-molas-necesidades-y-problemas-de-la-comunidad.

- May–June–July: define theme, propose steps, design of instrument, etc.
- August: interviews
- September–October: analyse and compare the data
- November: first draft
- December: Final document, socialize results

The nature of the research throughout was collaborative and comparative. It was collaborative because the emphasis was in creating and promoting an academic, spiritual, and friendly environment of support and learning from each other. It was comparative because the researchers were challenged to find similarities and differences between these communities. In this process, there was a special emphasis on creative and innovative thinking as the two students were invited to think through and find elements of unity and diversity in their data and results. This exercise was a great opportunity to build awareness of the similarities and differences in the perspectives of each of the researchers and to learn to "negotiate" at each step of the research.

I think that, with some adjustments, this model of collaborative research and comparative emphasis might be a suitable model for final works of bachelor, master's, or doctoral degrees.

Senior Seminar

The second alternative is the "senior seminar" that is one of the options for final work in the master's programs at Fresno Pacific Biblical Seminary.[28] The senior seminar is different from the thesis because of the communal and collaborative nature of the course, and these aspects are present at each step of the course. The main project is to write and present one senior paper in which the goal is to create "the opportunity to integrate key themes of learning around a topic of interest."[29] Many of my classmates were part of the senior seminar course and expressed great joy and enthusiasm about the communal, encouraging, and supportive environment and nature of the experience.

---

28. The other option is the traditional thesis, which I did because of the recommendation of my supervisor in view of my interest in pursuing doctoral studies.
29. The quotes and citations in this section are from the current syllabus provided by Valerie Rempel, Dean of the Seminary. Lynn Jost, "Senior Seminar course," Fresno Pacific Seminary, 2017.

I think the senior seminar offers a valid alternative to the thesis. The course lasts for one semester (15 weeks), requiring face-to-face meetings and "attendance at other presentations, reading seminar papers written by fellow students, and critiquing papers written by fellow students."[30] This course is designed to create and promote an interactive learning environment. The students participate in class through presentation of the materials at the different stages of the senior paper. At the same time, they engage in critique of both the oral and written materials of their fellow students. The first class sessions focus on scheduling and preparing the senior paper. The other sessions create the space for presentations of the different parts and elements of the senior paper. The evaluations are based on written assignments, attendance, and oral presentation. Below are some of the steps and elements used in this course:

In preparation for this course and during the first weeks, students are asked to:

1. *Read five of the senior papers from previous years and write a short paragraph for each paper.* This is an opportunity to gather ideas for how the students might construct their own senior seminar papers. The students are asked to include some critical interaction with each paper based on engaging questions such as: What was the thesis statement? How did the student support it? How was the biblical passage integrated into the paper? How was the paper organized and formatted?
2. *Select paper method, topic, and context, and write a thesis sentence.* Students are asked to choose one of the five options as the method they will use for the paper (dealing with the starting point: problem/issue, biblical passage, theological theme, cultural text, etc.). They are asked to come to the first class session prepared to state what option they have selected and to read to the rest of the seminar participants their written answers, bringing three extra copies of the document for the peer feedback activity in class.

---

30. Jost, "Senior Seminar Course."

During the rest of the course, students are involved and invited to engage with the following:

1. *Reading student papers/responses.* Students are to read other students' senior papers prior to each presentation. In preparation for the class discussion, they also write two or three comments. The comments may be something they learned from the paper, a response to the paper, something they will do or think differently, a question they would like to ask about the paper, or a question the paper leads them to ask. After reviewing the comments, the instructor will give them to the author of the paper.
2. *Peer reader.* Consultation will be formally available to each student from two peer readers assigned to each paper. The peer reader receives a draft copy of the assigned paper at least three weeks before the presentation. Students are required to complete an evaluation of this experience of both giving feedback to classmates and receiving feedback from peer readers.
3. *Senior seminar.* The main body text of the paper should be 25–30 pages long, double-spaced. The paper is integrative in nature, bringing together theological, biblical, contextual, and practical issues in three major sections: (1) introduction and analysis of the issue; (2) biblical and theological discussion; and (3) integration and application. The context element should be present in each section.[31] In addition to the main body text of the essay, a completed final paper will include a Table of Contents, an Abstract, and a Bibliography.

Based on conversation with those who went through this experience and taught this course, it is important to mention the collaborative environment present among the students at and through each step of the course. In addition, it creates a sense of belonging and partnership that is rare to find among those who are engaged in the traditional path of the thesis.

---

31. For a similar option, see Shaw, *Transforming Theological Education*, 98–100.

Supervised Ministerial Practice

The third option is one year of supervised ministerial practice that can be used as final work. This is an idea I proposed at the Instituto Bíblico Asunción for the program of bachelor of theology where a thesis is required to obtain the degree.[32] The general idea is that after four years in the theological program, those interested can have the opportunity to choose this one year of supervised ministerial practice. One of the goals is to provide formal supervision to those who are taking their first steps in the different areas of ministerial work (e.g. church planting, evangelism, pastoral roles, etc.). It aims also to create and promote spaces where other students on the same path can join together and reflect on their challenges, successes, and concerns.[33] The students are encouraged to keep a ministerial journal during the time of supervision which will be used during the different stages of supervision to see progress, concerns, and challenges.

I imagine that this year of supervised ministerial practice would include, in general, a monthly joint meeting with the supervisor and the students to provide the opportunity to share successes, raise concerns, and pray together. Individual face-to-face meetings with the supervisor every other month would create the space to deepen the relationship and trust. During the year, the plan is to have two retreats with all the members of the program for a time of fellowship, personal and ministerial sharing, and so on. As one of the elements of this year, the students would be required to prepare a report based on their affective, behavioural, and cognitive learning. Shaw offers some helpful insights and notes of caution related to these types of "non-classroom" activities in which it is possible to find combined the elements of "field education," "mentoring," "small groups," and "theological reflection on life experience."[34]

---

32. The idea was well received, but it is necessary to work with the university and government requirements to implement this option as an alternative.
33. This year in which I'm writing, for instance, four of our students who have completed the four-year academic program (bachelor) are starting their first ministerial experiences, but they need to first finish the thesis to get their degrees. A common scenario is that engaging in full-time ministerial work allows little space to finish their final work to get their degrees. Sadly, we have many cases of students who do not finish or who postpone their graduation for many years, and the common complaint is lack of time. For these students to have the opportunity to combine final work and ministerial experience will be of great benefit.
34. Shaw, *Transforming Theological Education*, 109–115.

Conclusion

In this chapter I have emphasized the need to see our theological structures and models as "faithful intentions" and as servant structures. I have proposed that seeing our theological programs and models through these lenses will help the learning community to engage in the process of evaluation, adjustment of our current theological programs, and finding alternatives for the final piece of work. The implication for us as members of a learning community is that our proposals need to be seen to be integral and attuned to the vision and mission of the institution. As learning communities, whether we decide to introduce alternatives or options for the final work for bachelor's, master's, or doctoral degrees, our first task is to discern that our institutional vision and mission are attuned to and nurtured by the notion of God's ministry. Consequently, we will be intentional in creating spaces for varied and multiple models of teaching, learning, and final work. If we believe and emphasize the importance of "learning and studying together," we will seek to ensure that, as learning communities, this aspect is reflected, experienced, and lived in and through our many "academic" activities, becoming an essential part of our institutional culture. It is my hope and prayer that, as members of learning communities, we may engage together in the continual process of discerning how best to create and promote *spaces* where we can learn together.

Discussion Questions

1. To what extent does your own experience of advanced theological studies resonate with Rafael's description of loneliness and isolation? In what ways might this solitary approach be seen as problematic theologically and practically?

2. In your own context, what are some interinstitutional and interdenominational efforts you have observed which honour "accents" of the Spirit? And to what extent has the "vernacular" face of your theological institution been understood and acknowledged? Describe one or two practical ways in which you personally and your school as a whole might develop faithful intentions in these areas.

3. What are one or two key learning spaces through which your school currently encourages collaboration? How might collaboration be further enhanced, particularly in your programs of advanced theological studies?

4. Consider in turn each of the case study examples included in this chapter: collaborative research; senior seminar; and supervised ministerial practice. Which of these examples might your school adapt and use to better promote collaborative learning?

Bibliography

Alves, Rubem. *La Teología Como Juego*. Buenos Aires: La Aurora, 1982.
Anderson, Ray. "A Theology for Ministry." In *Theological Foundations for Ministry*, edited by Ray Anderson, 6–21. Edinburgh: T&T Clark, 1979.
Barth, Karl. "The Place of Theology." In *Theological Foundations for Ministry*, edited by Ray Anderson, 22–58. Edinburgh: T&T Clark, 1979.
Das, Rupen. *Connecting Curriculum with Context*. Carlisle: Langham Global Library, 2015.
Deininger, Fritz, and Orbelina Eguizabal, eds. *Foundations for Academic Leadership*. Nürnberg: VTR, 2013.
Escobar, Samuel. "Fundamento y Finalidad de la Educación Teológica en América Latina." Presented at "El diálogo del milenio," São Paulo, Brazil, 1995.
Ferenczi, Jason. *Serving Communities: Governance and the Potential of Theological Schools*. Carlisle: Langham Global Library, 2015.
González, Justo L. *Breve Historia de la Preparación Ministerial*. Barcelona: Editorial.
hooks, bell. *Teaching to Transgress: Education as the Practice of Freedom*. New York: Routledge, 1994.
Jost, Lynn. "Senior Seminar Course." Fresno Pacific Seminary, 2017.
Kinsler, Ross, ed. *Viabilidad de la Formación Ministerial en el Mundo de Hoy*. San José: Seminario Bíblico Latinoamericano, 1994.
Koyama, Kosuke. "Theological Education: Its Unities and Diversities." *Theological Education* 1 (1993): 87–106.
Kraybill, Donald B. *The Upside Down Kingdom*. Scottdale: Herald, 1978.
Neufeld, Alfred. "Dificultades, Necesidades, Limitaciones y Desafíos en América Latina que que Enfrentan la Formación Teológica a Principios del Milenio Venidero." Presented at "El diálogo del milenio," São Paulo, Brazil, 1995.
Ott, Bernhard. *Understanding and Developing Theological Education*. Carlisle: Langham Global Library, 2016.
Padilla, René, ed. *Nuevas Alternativas de Educación Teológica*. Buenos Aires: Nueva Creación, 1986.

Preiswerk, Matthias. *Contrato Intercultural: Crisis y Refundación de la Educación Teológica.* La Paz: CLAI, 2011.

———. "For a Quality Theological Education: Manifesto." Accessed 16 January 2017. http://www.oikoumene.org/en/folder/documents-pdf/WOCATI_2008_-_Manifesto_from_Latin_America_-_english_version.pdf.

Roth, John D. *Teaching That Transforms: Why Anabaptist-Mennonite Education Matters.* Scottdale: Herald, 2011.

Shaw, Perry. *Transforming Theological Education: A Practical Handbook for Integrative Learning.* Carlisle: Langham Global Library, 2014.

Wanak, Lee. "Developing an Operational Philosophy of Theological Education." In *Leadership in Theological Education: Foundations for Academic Leadership*, volume 1. Edited by Fritz Deininger and Orbelina Eguizabal, 33–64. Carlisle: Langham Global Library, 2017.

Zaracho, Rafael. "Formación Teológica Desde la Perspectiva Bíblica y Anabautista." In *Registro de un Peregrinaje: Instituto Bíblico Asunción, 50 Años Formando Obreros con la Palabra de Dios,* edited by Víctor Wall, Martha Florentín, and Flavio Florentín, 189–199. Asunción: Instituto Bíblico Asunción, 2014.

———. "The Role of Preferences in the Context of Believing and Discerning Communities: A Maturanian Reading." PhD diss., University of St Andrews, 2014.

14

Chicken Theology:
Local Learning Approaches from West Africa

Jay Moon

After living in Ghana, West Africa, for several years, it gradually dawned on me that Ghanaians thought and expressed themselves in very different patterns from those I was used to. Not a day would go by without someone using a proverb, story, symbol, or even a song to portray something. This was very different from the linear, propositional, abstract approach to learning that I soaked up in my own education. Eventually, I wondered, "How are the local people evaluating my own teaching?" Even more troubling was the question, "How are the local people evaluating what my students learned, as these former students are now ministering among them?"

In this chapter I will:

1. Provide an example of a local learning process in Ghana, West Africa;
2. Demonstrate a local taxonomy for learning to compare with Bloom's taxonomy; and
3. Recommend approaches for higher education based on oral learning approaches.

To start, we need to visit the Builsa culture in the Upper East Region of Ghana, as the local pastors gather to discuss theology.

Under the Baobab Tree: Observing a Local Learning Process[1]

There was no lack of laughter or excitement around the circle as they sat in the shade of the great baobab tree. Someone asked the question, "What really helps you to stay firm in your Christian faith, even amidst trials?" The group quieted down as Kofi, a church leader, took his place in the centre of the circle. A hush settled as the group prepared to hear the proverb that best defined his faith. He leaned slightly forwards as he uttered,

> "Nurubiik a labri ka kpiak kawpta po."
> (A human being hides in the feathers of a chicken.)

It was a dramatic pause with a very puzzling ending. Joe, the Western missionary present at the time, thought, "Really? Is that it? What do chicken feathers have to do with Christianity and discipleship?"

Kofi explained, "In the life of the Builsa people, chickens are used to hide shame from problems. If someone has money troubles, they can sell some of the chickens at market and then use the money to solve the problem. If someone has sickness, infertility, drought, or famine, the traditional Builsa culture allows sacrifice of chickens to the ancestors or earth shrines. Growing up, I knew that we were always protected from shame as long as we had chickens, because we could always hide inside their feathers.

"They also help us initiate friendships," Kofi continued. "If I want to start a friendship with someone, then I offer them a chicken for us to share a meal together, or I give him a chicken to take home.

"Now that I am a *Kristobiik* [Christian], I feel that *Yezu* [Jesus] is the chicken that I hide under. When problems come, I can run to *Yezu* in prayer and ask him to cover my shame and protect me. He will bear the full impact of the problem that has come upon me, and I can safely rest in his feathers."

Another Builsa Christian, Immanuel, chimed in: "When we rest in the feathers of *Yezu*, then we no longer need to have charms, juju, or any other black

---

1. The author was an SIM missionary doing church planting, theological education, and water development among the Builsa people in Ghana, West Africa, from 1992 to 2001. Some of the stories and quotes in this chapter are adapted from the book W. Jay Moon, *African Proverbs Reveal Christianity in Culture: A Narrative Portrayal of Builsa Proverbs Contextualizing Christianity in Culture*, American Society of Missiology Monograph Series 5 (Eugene: Pickwick, 2009).

medicine to protect us. The feathers of *Yezu* will cover us – our relationship with him assures us that he will cover us with his wings. *Naawen Wani* [the Bible] says that *Naawen* [God] will 'cover you with his feathers, and under his wings you will find refuge; his faithfulness will be your shield and rampart' (Ps 91:4)."

Immanuel continued, "This proverb has touched me deeply and it helps me to understand the heart of *Yezu*. When I hear this proverb and read Matthew 23:37, I can feel *Yezu's* heart and desire for us Builsa. *Yezu* says, 'How often I have longed to gather your children together, as a hen gathers her chicks under her wings.' That is *Yezu's* desire for us – to protect us, cover our shame, and receive the brunt of our difficulties. That is a closer friend than I have ever known!"

Another Builsa Christian chimed in: "Do you remember how Ruth was a widow? Like our widows here, she had little hope for the future. When she placed herself under *Naawen's* feathers, *Naawen* brought about a wonderful blessing. Listen to the praise she received from Boaz in Ruth 2:12: 'May you be richly rewarded by the Lord, the God of Israel, *under whose wings you have come to take refuge.*'"

This lively conversation around "chicken theology" was about to take on another layer of meaning as they recounted the following story:

> A man rested his hoe over his shoulder as he walked towards his bush farm to prepare the ground for planting. When he returned home that night, his heart sank from afar as he saw only the scorched remains of his house. He forgot his weary arms and legs as he sprinted to his home, heart pounding.
>
> The earth, his hut, and his animals were covered in black embers. Everything had been destroyed by fire.
>
> Angered over his loss, he kicked the black scorched body of a lifeless chicken that lay amidst the earth. He screamed and raised his fists in the air to try to stop the all-consuming panic. As he sat in the deathly stillness, he heard a faint sound.
>
> He stopped.
>
> Bending over, he picked up the dead chicken to find live chicks under her limp wings. It was only then that he realized how the

mother hen saw the approaching fire and gathered the chicks under her wings. As she sat on top of the chicks, the fire burned the mother hen while the chicks remained safe!

"That is what it means for Christians to hide under the feathers of Jesus. He takes the fire as we remain protected and safe," he concluded.

This chicken theology was so vivid and concrete that it was easy to remember – in fact, impossible to forget. Joe the missionary would thankfully recall it to help him through a tense time.

Months later, sitting in his house as harvest time approached, Joe heard a sound from far away: "Waaaaa-hoo." The sound gradually increased in volume, as people from neighbouring houses used this call to drive away a *sakpak* (witch) who was said to wander among the tall millet in the fields.

"WAAAAA-HOO," came the shout from Joe's neighbours as they provided the traditional response to push the *sakpak* away from the house. Joe was reminded of the proverb "A human being hides in the feathers of a chicken," and his faith rose as he began to sing the song he learned in church:

> *Wa [Yezu] chawgsi mu, Wa chawgsi mu, Wa chawgis mu.*
> *Wa chawgsi mu, Wa sum jam chawgsi.*
> *Wa chawgsi mu, Satana yaa de mu,*
> *Wa chawgsi mu, Wa sum jam chawgsi.*
>
> He [Jesus] wraps me tightly, he wraps me tightly, he wraps me tightly.
> He wraps me tightly, he really does wrap me tightly.
> He wraps me tightly, even though Satan wants to destroy me,
> He wraps me tightly, he really does wrap me tightly.

As he continued to sing, his faith strengthened and the fear subsided. Instead of shouting, "WAAAAA-HOO," hiding under the feathers of Jesus provided a powerful response to this serious spiritual issue. The proverb, story, and song combined to teach him how to remain strong in his Christian faith in the face of fear.

Then it dawned on him. He had learned a powerful discipleship process, but it was very different from the Western process he had grown up with. The various oral genres can be usefully applied to foster deep learning and transformation for primary oral learners. The "chicken theology" described above revealed to him that theological education among oral learners has a different starting point and follows a different process from that used among print learners. Yet it is very effective in making disciples.

Indigenous Taxonomy for Learning

The above true story provides a window into a local learning approach. While all of the Builsa would agree that they had a substantial learning experience, the path to get there was very different from the path chosen by most Western institutions. Instead of using linear logic, general propositions, or abstract theories, this learning experience was conveyed through various oral genres. In this instance, the genres included proverb, story, and song to communicate in a way that was highly communal, holistic, image-rich, memorable, experiential, and sensory-laden. Often, the discussion of oral literature is devalued in higher education in favour of more lecture-based teaching. The question, though, remains: "Did the local people learn and become transformed by this teaching approach?"

To evaluate cognitive learning levels, Bloom's taxonomy is often cited. As shown in figure 14.1, this taxonomy starts with the lowest level of learning at the bottom and moves upward for higher levels.

- *Knowledge:* The foundation for higher-order thinking is to retain bits of information.
- *Comprehension:* Understanding of the information is demonstrated in written papers.
- *Application:* Then the learner puts this information into practice for a "practicum."
- *Analysis:* Advanced learners break down problems into discrete parts to critique them.
- *Synthesis:* Then they join various parts together to form a unique whole.
- *Evaluation:* The ultimate level of thinking is to judge the validity of ideas.

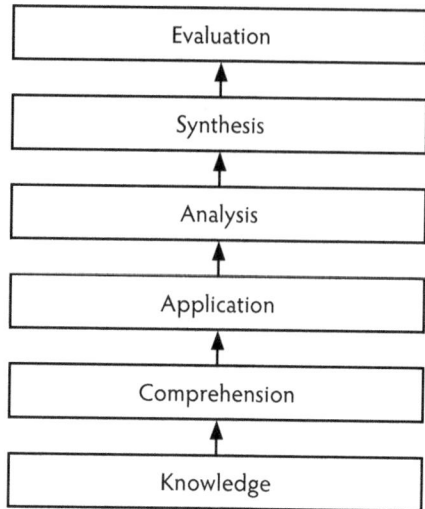

Figure 14.1: Bloom's Taxonomy for Learning[2]

Bloom's taxonomy assumes that learners start at the bottom of the ladder and gradually work their way up, a step at a time. Is it possible, though, to reach higher levels of learning via alternative paths? The Builsa learners in the case study above clearly synthesized various genres from their treasure chest of oral literature in order to interact with various sections of Scripture in the Old and New Testaments. This resulted in a unique, innovative, and memorable articulation of faith that was transformative in the local culture. *But they did not follow Bloom's taxonomy to get there!*

Instead of using Bloom's taxonomy, what local taxonomy would the Builsa use to evaluate their level of learning? Based on my ethnographic research among the Builsa people, I observed that the art of speaking (*biik*) can be classified into three levels.[3] The levels are graduated to show the degree of directness intended for the general audience, as shown in figure 14.2.

---

2. B. Bloom, M. Engelhart, E. Furst, W. Hill and D. Krathwohl, *Taxonomy of Educational Objectives. Handbook I: Cognitive Domain* (London: Longmans, 1956).
3. Moon, *African Proverbs*.

Chicken Theology

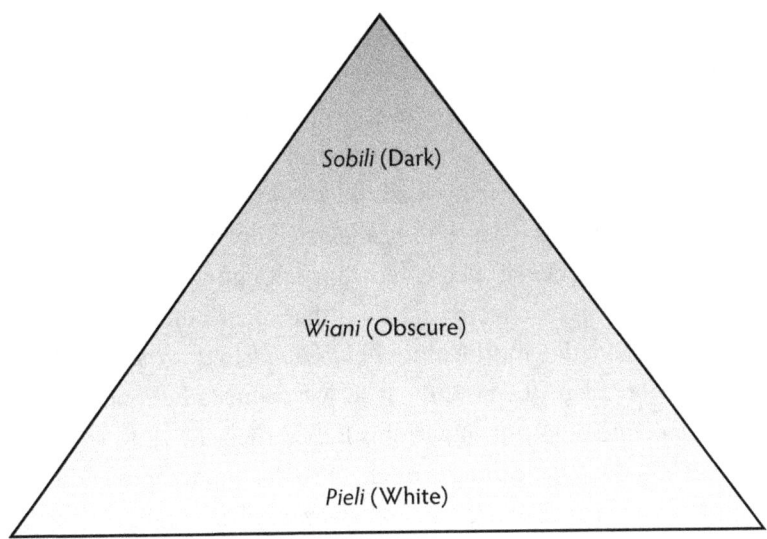

Figure 14.2: Builsa Taxonomy for Learning

The table translates and summarizes the Buli terms listed in figure 14.2.

Buli Term	Term for Clarity	Degree of Directness
Biik-pieli	White	Direct, straight to the point
Biik-wiani	Obscure	Somewhat indirect
Biik-sobili	Dark	Indirect, listen for the point

Biik-pieli is used to speak very clearly and simply. It is direct and straight to the point. A child or someone speaking to a child uses this type of speech. If you speak to adults in this manner, though, they will feel either that your message is not very important or that you are not respecting their reasoning ability. They may feel patronized as you are speaking "down" to them.

Biik-wiani is used to speak in a way that obscures the meaning so that some of the listeners will not understand the meaning (even though they may understand every individual word spoken). This can be used when adults do not want children to understand what is being discussed. Humorously, it can also be used to insult people without their realizing it (until later!). Understanding and using this type of reasoning indicates that you understand the Builsa people and their culture. This elevates the speaker from being a child who uses *biik-pieli* to a skilled adult who uses *biik-wiani* in the appropriate context. In explaining the usage of *biik-wiani*, one Builsa explained that Jesus spoke this way. Jesus spoke in obscure speech so that his enemies could not trap him; yet those who were truly interested could come back and learn more.

Biik-sobili is used by the truly wise and learned. Usually, using this speech indicates that you are an elder who has learned ancient wisdom or that you have been in the presence of such elders long enough to understand this type of learning. Often, archaic words are used that most Builsa do not normally use. A Builsa explained to me the usage of *biik-sobili* in this way: "If a boy wants to learn *biik-sobili*, you [the boy] must sit with your father and ask him [the meaning]. If a child does not sit with his father, then the child will not know *biik-sobili*. If you ask the meaning though, the elder will want to know why you are asking the meaning. They fear that you may use the meaning to hurt them."[4]

Looking back at the articulation of "chicken theology," the Builsa leaders did not waste time at the *Biik-pieli* level of learning; rather, they entered the *Biik-wiani* level right away. They used a local proverb that indirectly talked about the protection they find in Jesus. If children heard the proverb, they would understand the words but they would not understand the meaning. The process of learning through indirect reasoning elevated the discussion to a level worthy of higher indigenous education, in their minds. While they did not utilize the path advocated by Bloom's taxonomy, the well-worn local path helped the learners arrive at the synthesis level of learning.[5]

---

4. Moon, *African Proverbs*, 12–13.

5. Comparing local taxonomies to Bloom's taxonomy is a ripe area for research (beyond the scope of this chapter). For example, while the Builsa "white" level has some parallels to Bloom's "knowledge" level, the Builsa "black" level results in elaborate conclusions without the dissection into pieces for analysis and then synthesis that Bloom describes. In her chapter, "Telling Tales," Havilah Dharamraj noted that many cultures uncritically respect the wisdom of the elders; therefore, these cultures do not have a direct parallel to Bloom's "evaluation" level. This further highlights that there is a very different process for learning in oral cultures to receive, process, remember, and pass on information. Part of this difference may be attributed to the key role of memory in oral cultures when compared with print-learning contexts.

Recommendations for Higher Education

Clearly, local taxonomies for learning can differ from Bloom's taxonomy in very significant ways. It is important to realize, however, that these local patterns for learning accomplish what they set out to do – create higher levels of learning for adults. Based on the above discussion, the following recommendations are offered for theological education in the Majority World:

1. Early in their theological education journey, students should be asked to learn some of their mother-tongue culture's oral literature. This would include proverbs, stories, and songs. It could also include other genres, such as symbols, rituals, dance, and drama. These may be important sources for local discipleship, even though the path to get there may not be familiar to Western sensibilities.[6] Joseph Healey observed, "Our examples of African stories and oral literature are like diamonds that need theologians and others to cut and polish more incisively to display their richness and beauty."[7] When cultural studies are then combined with biblical studies, critical contextualization[8] can promote theological formation that is both biblically sound and culturally relevant.

2. Help students to acknowledge and appreciate that there are various taxonomies for learning that are effective. While Bloom's taxonomy is one valid approach for certain contexts, this does not mean that other indigenous approaches are less effective. This is particularly important when engaging with learners from oral cultures. Examples such as the Builsa taxonomy above should encourage students to consider the local learning approaches in their own cultures. Understanding and then working with these local learning approaches can result in future pastors/teachers who are able to minister effectively in their mother-tongue cultures. Unfortunately, the dismissal of local learning patterns can result in theology school graduates who are able to write papers well but are not able to communicate well within their mother-tongue

---

6. In my recent book, *Intercultural Discipleship: Learning from Global Approaches to Spiritual Formation*, Encountering Mission Series, ed. Scott Moreau (Grand Rapids: Baker Academic, 2017), I demonstrate how these various genres have been used for discipleship both in the worldwide church and in history.

7. Joseph Healey and Donald Sybertz, *Towards an African Narrative Theology* (Nairobi: Paulines; Maryknoll: Orbis, 2000), 377.

8. Paul G. Hiebert, "Critical Contextualization," *International Bulletin of Missionary Research* 11, no. 3 (1987): 104–111.

cultures since they have now learned and adopted a foreign reasoning process. The sad result is that these graduates are now only "at home" in academia.

3. While the classic dissertation following a Western model of logic has been regarded as the apex of learning, the appreciation of various learning taxonomies should result in creative approaches to demonstrating higher learning. For example, the growing popularity of narrative writing has been slowly making its way into dissertation writing.[9] My own dissertation[10] relied upon composite characters to develop a coherent narrative in order to portray the development of contextual theology. Instead of simply providing a linear 1–2–3-step approach to contextual theology, the narrative helps readers to find themselves as one of the characters such that this portrays the development of contextual theology in a creative and engaging manner. In addition, Aminta Arrington's dissertation "Hymns of the Everlasting Hills: The Written Word in an Oral Culture in Southwest China" (Biola University, 2014) includes several chapters in narrative prose.

4. Instead of merely assuming that Western academic approaches to theological education are preferable, the unique learning processes in local cultures should be explored and utilized as much as possible. To design learning experiences that are appropriate for oral learners, the acronym CHIMES[11] summarizes suggestions for professors to consider, as follows:

- *<u>C</u>ommunal:* Assume that students learn best as they interact with others.[12] How can you encourage the group to learn from each other (e.g. small groups, group discussions, panels, visits, rituals, etc.)?
- *<u>H</u>olistic:* Assume that they learn best when projects/topics are related to concerns in their own context. How can you connect what they

---

9. For more details see the chapters on narrative (Havilah Dharamraj), proverbs (Dwi Maria Handayani), and poetry (Xiaoli Yang) in this collection.
10. Moon, *African Proverbs*.
11. W. Jay Moon, "Re-Wiring the Brain: Theological Education Among Oral Learners," in *Reflecting on and Equipping for Christian Mission*, ed. Stephen Bevans et al., Regnum Edinburgh Centenary Series 27 (Eugene: Wipf and Stock, 2015), 166–180.
12. The significance of relational and collaborate learning is developed in more depth in Rafael Zaracho's chapter in this collection.

are learning to other areas of life so that you are adding onto and critiquing what they already know?[13]

- *Images:* Assume that words put together into outlines are not the most effective way to organize thoughts. Instead of using an outline to map out a dissertation, for example, encourage students to arrange their thoughts via a mind map. For learning experiences, consider what images, symbols, and object lessons could be used so that words are not the only communicator of meaning. In fact, assume that words are not the most effective communicators of meaning for deep values and emotions.
- *Mnemonics:* What genres can you use to "hook" the audience and then form memory "triggers" for later recall? In addition to proverbs, stories, and songs, consider symbols, rituals, dance, drama, and art. To encourage greater memory potential, consider the use of storyboards and interiorizing Scripture as described by Boomershine.[14]
- *Experiential:* Assume that linear, propositional truths learned at a distance from real life will not result in transformative learning by themselves.[15] How can learners experience something and then later reflect on it? Consider the use of exercises, activities, field trips, rituals, and festivals that engage the learner through participation.
- *Sensory:* Assume that learners prefer to engage multiple senses for learning (cf. 1 John 1:1). Consider the use of audio books over traditional print books alone. A new application called the Digi-Book is now available on i-Books[16] in order to engage the twenty-first-century learner with the process of Graze, Dive, and Connect.[17]

---

13. See Paul Clark's chapter in this collection.
14. Thomas E. Boomershine, *Story Journey: An Invitation to the Gospel as Storytelling* (Nashville: Abingdon, 1988).
15. The preference of many Majority World peoples for practically oriented learning is addressed in more depth in Perry Shaw's chapter, "Culture, Gender, and Diversity," in this collection.
16. For more information on Digi-Books see, https://digibooks.io/about/.
17. W. Jay Moon, "Theological Education for the 21st Century: The Oral Learning Renaissance," in *Orality and Theological Training in the 21st Century*, ed. W. Jay Moon (Nicholasville: DOPS, LLC, 2017), 2–19.

Turner[18] describes how symbols are uniquely suited to connect the senses with an ideology to foster deep learning.

5. The CHIMES acronym also provides helpful suggestions for students with an oral learning preference who feel frustrated by the print preference assessment rubrics. For example, the classic doctoral dissertation can be quite stifling for oral learners who prefer other means of expressing their learning. Students should consider the following:

- *C̲ommunal:* Give oral presentations that elicit feedback, and have someone record the question/answers discussed for later review. This feedback is "gold dust" since it often stimulates reflection and promotes new discoveries. Conferences or schools can provide opportunities for student presentations. For example, I observed student presentations at the Akrofi Christaller Institute in Ghana that included feedback and questions from the audience (including Dr Kwame Bediako and the gardener). When the presentation was published as an article, the discussions following the presentation were also included.
- *H̲olistic:* Draw upon topics that relate to your own culture, using concepts from your own mother tongue. Only back-translate into a lingua franca after the conceptualization process has been completed. This will likely draw in other oral genres discussed above.
- *I̲mages:* Instead of using outlines to organize thoughts (in linear patterns), try using a mind map that relies upon a central image and branches extending from this central theme (in a pictorial pattern[19]). I have observed students finally get "unstuck" with their dissertation process by switching from an outline format to a mind map that promotes more free thinking and association with images.
- *M̲nemonics:* Since memory is central to the oral learning process, draw upon memory hooks, such as proverbs, stories, and drama, to

---

18. Victor Turner, *The Ritual Process: Structure and Anti-Structure* (New York: Aldine de Gruyter, 1995).
19. This approach was developed by Tony Buzan to simulate the way the brain is naturally structured in non-linear forms. For examples, see http://www.mindmapping.com/.

move from what you know to what you do not know. The "memory palace" can effectively store and retrieve key concepts for later recall.[20]

- *Experiential:* A narrative writing style can be used for dissertations by developing composite characters. For example, give a name to one person (e.g. Kofi) who is representative of the experiences of many people in your study. Everything that happens to Kofi actually occurred in your research – it just did not happen to one person. Then the dissertation can be written in a more narrative form, with Kofi as a central character.[21]
- *Sensory:* As much as possible, engage the senses in the research and writing process. In addition to using audio books and Digi-Books to gather information, try to create rituals for reflection and writing; for example, some use special background music, light a candle, or burn sage as symbols to create liminality inside a ritual space. This stimulates the students to "want to do" what they "should do," especially when they are frustrated or overwhelmed by the dissertation process.

6. An oral learning renaissance is getting a breath of fresh air due to the widespread adoption of technology. When people receive the majority of their information via digital media vs. print media, they start to exhibit the characteristics of oral learners as opposed to print learners. This new learning

---

20. Basically, this memory technique uses a familiar location to store, associate, and retrieve information in your mind. For more details, see "Develop Perfect Memory with the Memory Palace Technique," Litemind, https://litemind.com/memory-palace/.

21. In addition to the dissertations previously described, there is precedence for the narrative genre being used in scholarly anthropological writing. Muriel Dimen-Schein (*The Anthropological Imagination* [New York: McGraw-Hill, 1977]), as well as James P. Spradley and George E. McDonough (*Anthropology Through Literature: Cross-Cultural Perspectives* [Boston: Little, Brown, 1973]), encouraged the analysis of narrative in order to stimulate anthropological reflection. Victor Turner and Edith Turner (*Image and Pilgrimage in Christian Culture* [New York: Columbia University, 1994]) also presented pages of narrative with periodic commentary for reflection and analysis. This added to the authenticity of the writing. Clifford Geertz's "thick description" in writings such as "Deep Play: Notes on the Balinese Cockfight" contains narrative that is very engaging as well as insightful (*The Interpretation of Cultures* [New York: Basic, 1973]). He recreates the context and the action that took place so that the readers participate in the original context as much as possible. This creates an authentic presentation for the reader, while still combined with analysis and reflection. These authors have shown that a narrative presentation can be combined with reflection and analysis in a way that is scholarly as well as engaging.

preference is called "digit-oral" learning.[22] As digital technology continues to grow, educators can get ahead of the curve by developing learning approaches for digit-oral learners using the approaches recommended above, aided by digital resources.[23]

Conclusion

Peter was concluding his graduate theological studies. He regularly met with other African pastors to discuss their local proverbs and then reflect on their meaning amidst their theological studies. One day, he shared the proverb, "When a man is in love, he doesn't count how long and steep the road is to his fiancée's house."

He recalled how he walked a long and dangerous path to visit the home of his fiancée and did not even consider staying at home – his love compelled him to go. As he shared this, smiles appeared on many faces as the other pastors began to picture their own journeys to visit their fiancées. Since most of these pastors were from exogamous people groups, they had had to walk a long way to visit their fiancées.

Peter explained, "We often display love through actions instead of words. We 'show' love instead of just 'speak' words of love. The tangible expression is more meaningful than words that can easily be spoken but not sincerely felt."

Immanuel chimed in: "When a friend is sick, we go and visit them to show them that we care. When there is a funeral, we go to visit and greet the family to express our sympathies. In the same way, to show a young girl that we love her, we will walk the long distance to her house and visit her and her family. That is what I mean by we 'show' love instead of 'speak' love."

As the group analysed the proverb and its cultural meaning, they reflected on the love of God expressed in an African manner. Just as they often showed love through actions and not through words alone, God also showed love

---

22. Jonah Sachs, *Winning the Story Wars: Why Those Who Tell (and Live) the Best Stories Will Rule the Future* (Boston: Harvard Business Review, 2012).
23. For more information on the digit-oral learning preference, see W. Jay Moon, "I Love to Learn But I Don't Like to Read: The Rise of Secondary Oral Learning," *Orality Journal* 2, no. 2 (2013): 55–65. See also Marvin Oxenham's chapter in this collection.

through his actions. "But God demonstrates his own love for us in this: While we were still sinners, Christ died for us" (Rom 5:8, NIV).

The group returned to the imagery of the initial proverb, "When a man is in love, he doesn't count how long and steep the road is to his fiancée's house." Another student noted, "God is in love with his fiancée too. His fiancée is the church. Because of this intense love for his bride-to-be, he did not count how long or steep the road was from heaven to earth. He knew the suffering of the cross and the rejection by his own people that awaited him on that road. Yet he did not consider the option of staying home since his love compelled him. God did not just speak his love for us. He showed us his love by coming to earth in the form of Jesus to visit the home of his fiancée, the church."

Peter was so excited about this theological understanding that he exclaimed, "I can't wait to return to Kenya soon for an evangelistic ministry! I will use this proverb to express Christianity in a way that is African and Christian."

When he returned to his home, he did not forget the discussion of proverbs and Scripture. He wrote back to share how six hundred people had come to Christ over the summer. He explained, "I used many proverbs at home, and the people became very excited when I told them the proverbs. The young people were taught in the past to leave the old things behind, but the messages were very foreign. Now, they see me as a wise man and I speak wisdom in a way they can understand."

Based on a local evaluation of learning, Peter's theological education was a success! He learned theological truth from the Bible well. Yet this truth was gained by engaging his local oral literature with Scripture. This contextual learning approach followed a local taxonomy for learning and it helped him to relate well to his mother-tongue culture. In the end, the church recognized that his theological education helped him to "speak wisdom in a way they can understand."

That sounds like a good metric of success for any theological school.

Discussion Questions

1. In what ways does oral communication shape the way people learn in your own local context? Briefly share a story you remember that in some way helped you in your personal pilgrimage of faith or in the growth of someone you know.

2. The chapter presents a Builsa taxonomy for learning which emphasizes levels of directness in communication as possible phases in learning maturity. To what extent might this reflect learning patterns in your context? What other alternative frameworks for learning do you believe are relevant for the students in your school?

3. Consider carefully each of the elements in the CHIMES framework: Communal; Holistic; Images; Mnemonics; Experiential; Sensory.
- To what extent does each element play a significant role in learning in the local communities where your graduates serve?
- How might each of these elements be brought into the educational methodologies used in your programs of study?
- Suggest at least one practical way in which these elements might be explored and empowered in your advanced theological programs of study on the path to approaches and projects that better resonate with church and society.

Bibliography

Boomershine, Thomas E. *Story Journey: An Invitation to the Gospel as Storytelling.* Nashville: Abingdon, 1988.

Dimen-Schein, Muriel. *The Anthropological Imagination.* New York: McGraw-Hill, 1977.

Geertz, Clifford. *The Interpretation of Cultures.* New York: Basic, 1973.

Healey, Joseph, and Donald Sybertz. *Towards an African Narrative Theology.* Nairobi: Paulines; Maryknoll: Orbis, 2000.

Hiebert, Paul G. "Critical Contextualization." *International Bulletin of Missionary Research* 11, no. 3 (1987): 104–111.

Moon, W. Jay. *African Proverbs Reveal Christianity in Culture: A Narrative Portrayal of Builsa Proverbs Contextualizing Christianity in Culture.* American Society of Missiology Monograph Series 5. Eugene: Pickwick, 2009.

———. "I Love to Learn but I Don't Like to Read: The Rise of Secondary Oral Learning." *Orality Journal* 2, no. 2 (2013): 55–65.

———. *Intercultural Discipleship: Learning from Global Approaches to Spiritual Formation.* Encountering Mission Series, edited by Scott Moreau. Grand Rapids: Baker Academic, 2017.

———. "Re-Wiring the Brain: Theological Education Among Oral Learners." In *Reflecting on and Equipping for Christian Mission*, edited by Stephen Bevans, Teresa Chai, J. Nelson Jennings, Knud Jørgensen, and Dietrich Werner, 166–180. Regnum Edinburgh Centenary Series 27. Eugene: Wipf and Stock, 2015.

———. "Theological Education for the 21st Century: The Oral Learning Renaissance." In *Orality and Theological Training in the 21st Century*, edited by W. Jay Moon, 2–19. Nicholasville: DOPS, LLC, 2017.

Sachs, Jonah. *Winning the Story Wars: Why Those Who Tell (and Live) the Best Stories Will Rule the Future*. Boston: Harvard Business Review, 2012.

Spradley, James P., and George E. McDonough. *Anthropology Through Literature: Cross-Cultural Perspectives*. Boston: Little, Brown, 1973.

Turner, Victor. *The Ritual Process: Structure and Anti-Structure*. New York: Aldine de Gruyter, 1995.

Turner, Victor, and Edith Turner. *Image and Pilgrimage in Christian Culture*. New York: Columbia University, 1994.

15

Ethnohermeneutics and Advanced Theological Studies:
Towards Culturally Appropriate Methodologies for Doctoral Programs

Larry Caldwell

Introduction: Why Ethnohermeneutics?

"If Jesus or Paul were in my hermeneutics class, they would have failed!"

This sentence uttered by my seminary professor startled me. I was a first-year seminary student sitting in my first course on Bible interpretation. For the past several weeks we had been examining many of the grammatical-historical techniques considered necessary for good Bible interpretation. With a bit of trepidation I raised my hand to ask the esteemed professor a question. "Sir," I said, "this is all good material that we're learning here. But I'm wondering why Jesus and Paul didn't use these grammatical-historical techniques when they interpreted the Old Testament. They just seemed to pull verses totally out of context and use them for their own purposes. What do you think of their methodology?"

And thus my professor's reply that began this chapter. Of course, he said this half-jokingly, and everyone in the class laughed. But his answer got me to thinking: "If the Son of God would have failed your hermeneutics class, whose fault would it be?" I laughed along with the others, but today I laugh no longer.

The reply of my professor put me on a quest that has lasted almost forty years now: What are the best ways to interpret the Bible, especially ways that are culturally appropriate? I found that both Jesus and Paul weren't just pulling verses out of context; rather they were using a culturally appropriate first-century hermeneutical technique known as *midrash*.[1] *Midrash* "actualizes" the text; in other words it makes the Old Testament text come alive for, in this case, their New Testament audiences. Both Jesus and Paul were experts in this hermeneutical technique, as well as in other hermeneutical techniques that were a part of their first-century hermeneutical milieu.

And this is precisely what ethnohermeneutics is all about: looking for and using hermeneutical methods that are already a part of the culture, rather than importing predominantly Western methods like the ones that I was learning in that seminary classroom. Here's my definition of ethnohermeneutics:[2]

> Bible interpretation done in cross-cultural, multi-cultural and multi-generational contexts that, whenever possible, uses culturally appropriate dynamic hermeneutical methods already in place in the culture; the primary goal being to interpret the Bible, as well as to communicate the truths of the Bible, in ways that will be best understood from within the worldview of the receptor culture.

In a nutshell, ethnohermeneutics empowers individuals to use their own dynamic culturally appropriate hermeneutical methods as they approach the

---

1. For a more in-depth analysis of the apostle Paul's hermeneutical methods, particularly *midrash*, see Larry W. Caldwell, "Reconsidering Our Biblical Roots: Bible Interpretation, the Apostle Paul and Mission Today," Parts 1 and 2, *International Journal of Frontier Missiology* 29, nos. 2–3 (2012): 91–100 and 113–121.

2. For more information on the discipline of ethnohermeneutics see, for example, Larry W. Caldwell, "Towards the New Discipline of Ethnohermeneutics: Questioning the Relevancy of Western Hermeneutical Methods in the Asian Context," *Journal of Asian Mission* 1, no. 1 (1999): 21–43; and "Towards an Ethnohermeneutical Model for a Lowland Filipino Context," *Journal of Asian Mission* 7, no. 2 (2005): 169–193.

Bible. At the same time, ethnohermeneutics places a high priority on making the results of this approach understandable to the local people.

So what does the discipline of ethnohermeneutics have to do with questions about new ways of doing advanced theological studies? Precisely the fact that my professor's attitude – in regards to the supposedly substandard hermeneutical techniques of Jesus and Paul – is the same attitude that many seminary and graduate school professors have today in regards to the best methodologies to follow in order to obtain an advanced theological degree. Though the subject matter is different, the logic is the same. It goes something like this:

> If a Majority World student is in my doctoral program they will fail if they do not follow accepted Minority World methods that ultimately produce a written dissertation.[3]

In other words, it is basically a case of "doing it my way" (i.e. a typical doctoral dissertation arrived at through scrupulously following standard Minority World methods), "or not doing it at all" (i.e. your Majority World culturally appropriate ways of researching and expressing doctoral-level expertise are not allowable).[4] As with ethnohermeneutics so, too, with culturally appropriate ways to demonstrate advanced theological expertise. We today who are involved in the training of doctoral candidates in advanced theological studies need to look at alternatives to the way we do doctoral education.[5] This will include looking at both culturally appropriate methodologies and culturally appropriate demonstrations of doctoral-level expertise, "actualized"

---

3. I am following the nomenclature used by Perry Shaw elsewhere in this book. The term "Minority World" is used instead of "the West" or the "Western world," while the term "Majority World" is used instead of "the non-West" or the "non-Western world." It is time that scholars, especially Western scholars, recognized the realities of our twenty-first-century world.

4. Here in this chapter I am speaking especially for Majority World students enrolled in our Minority World seminaries and graduate schools. However, what I write here advocating for more flexibility in the research and dissertation models applies equally to all Minority and Majority graduate students studying in both Minority and Majority World seminaries and graduate schools worldwide.

5. This is increasingly important as more and more Majority World theological schools begin offering their own doctoral programs; see, for example, Evan Hunter, "A Tectonic Shift: The Rapid Rise of PhD Programs at Evangelical Theological Schools in the Majority World," *InSights Journal for Global Theological Education* 1, no. 2 (2016): 41–60.

methodologies and demonstrations that will make such academic work come alive for both church-based and secular audiences.

To that end the remainder of this chapter will explore the possibilities of using Majority World culturally appropriate demonstrations of advanced theological studies and doctoral-level expertise through the grid of ethnohermeneutics.[6] Part 1 will frame the discussion through asking the question, "Why Culturally Appropriate Methodologies?" Part 2 will continue the discussion by drawing upon ethnohermeneutics for possible culturally appropriate strategies, culminating in a "Culturally Appropriate Strategies for Doctoral Programs" scale. Part 3 will look at four examples that illustrate how culturally appropriate strategies might be carried out in advanced theological studies. Finally, the chapter will conclude with five recommendations towards culturally appropriate methodologies in advanced theological studies.

Part 1: Why Culturally Appropriate Methodologies?

The short answer to "Why culturally appropriate methodologies?" is easy: because using culturally appropriate hermeneutical methodologies, coupled with receptor-oriented demonstrations of doctoral-level expertise, will help ensure that the final doctoral product is both relevant and read (or listened to, or watched, or participated in, and so on).

The long answer is more difficult. We look for culturally appropriate advanced degree methodologies because if we do not do so we will continue the long line of colonialist thinking that has plagued graduate-level education for at least the last century: the hegemony of mainly white male scholars and what they deemed to be proper advanced theological education. Most of us have probably never thought about the possibility that our understandings of advanced theological studies are rooted in issues of racism and colonization. However, this reality must be squarely faced before any talk of culturally appropriate methodologies can move forward.

Elsewhere I have written at length about colonization in relationship to Asian theological education, especially in regards to curriculum relevance

---

6. The discussion in this chapter will primarily be in regards to doctoral programs, but the analysis applies to master's level programs as well.

and to the dismissing of local ways of teaching and learning.[7] In brief, recent ethnographic research has come to label the influence of colonization under the category of "authoritative knowledge." This categorization shows how the colonizers came to other cultures with what they considered to be authoritative knowledge: knowledge that was seen by the colonizers as superior to any knowledge found at the local level. In the case of advanced theological education this came to mean a "correct" or "standard" way to both do research and demonstrate an expertise in that knowledge. Eventually, those who were colonized, including graduates of Western-oriented seminaries and graduate programs, eventually took on as authoritative a certain way of thinking or knowing that was foreign to their particular culture.

Anthropologist Brigitte Jordan expands upon this colonization process:

> . . . frequently one kind of knowledge gains ascendance and legitimacy. A consequence of the legitimation of one kind of knowing as authoritative is the devaluation, often the dismissal, of all other kinds of knowing . . . The constitution of authoritative knowledge is an ongoing social process that both builds and reflects power relationships within a community of practice. It does this in such a way that all participants come to see the current social order as a natural order, that is, the way things (obviously) are.[8]

Jordan's words concerning the dismissal "of all other kinds of knowing" are particularly relevant to doctoral-level education. The norms of Minority World authoritative knowledge have not allowed us, either as Majority or Minority World scholars, to value the other kinds of knowing that we have mostly categorically dismissed. Minority World scholars, as the colonizers, have not even thought of this possibility; Majority World scholars, as the colonized, have oftentimes forgotten the relevancy of their own culture's learning and knowing

---

7. See Larry W. Caldwell, "How Asian Is Asian Theological Education?," in *Tending the Seedbeds: Educational Perspectives on Theological Education in Asia*, ed. Allan Harkness (Quezon City: Asia Theological Association, 2010), 23–45.

8. Brigitte Jordan, "Authoritative Knowledge and Its Construction," in *Childbirth and Authoritative Knowledge*, ed. Robbie E. Davis-Floyd and Carolyn F. Sargent (Berkeley: University of California, 1997), 56.

styles. Indigenous anthropologist Linda Tuhiwai Smith calls this "establishing the positional superiority of western knowledge."[9]

As a result, both Minority and Majority World scholars must re-examine the validity of other ways of knowing and see how these other ways might be better incorporated into doctoral-level programs. This will give all of us more of an awareness of the transcultural perspective of education. As educational anthropologist George D. Spindler notes: "a transcultural perspective on education is essential, for education is a cultural process and occurs in a social context. Without attention to cultural difference and the way education serves those differences, we have no way of achieving perspective on our own culture and the way our educational system serves it or of building a comprehensive picture of education as affected by culture."[10] What it all really comes down to is recognizing that our traditional ways of doing advanced theological studies have originated from positions of power, power of the minority over the majority. In this regard I'm reminded of the African proverb: "Until the lion learns how to write, every story will glorify the hunter."

While in the past we have been largely ignorant of this power differential, today we have no excuse. As Spindler says, "a transcultural perspective of education is essential." Thus, as we address the issue of culturally appropriate strategies, we do well to keep these past colonization and power issues in mind.

So, if we are going to equip both Minority and Majority World students to use more culturally appropriate advanced degree methodologies, what might this look like? To that we turn next.

Part 2: Culturally Appropriate Strategies for Doctoral Programs

Elsewhere I have argued – in relationship to the overall ethnohermeneutical Bible interpretation process – for the need to exegete at length *both* the biblical text as well as the cultural context in which that text is to be interpreted and

---

9. Linda Tuhiwai Smith, *Decolonizing Methodologies: Research and Indigenous Peoples*, 2nd ed. (London/New York: Zed Books, 2012), 62.
10. George D. Spindler, *Education and Cultural Process: Anthropological Approaches*, 3rd ed. (Long Grove: Waveland, 1997), 272.

applied.[11] In that article I devised a gradation scale of minimal, mid-level, and maximal strategies specific to both the context of the biblical text and the interpreter's particular cultural context.[12] In like manner, I would like to propose a similar gradation scale of culturally appropriate strategies especially for doctoral-level research. The purpose of the "Culturally Appropriate Strategies for Doctoral Programs" scale is twofold. First, as an evaluative template, the scale can be used to assist schools in assessing where they are at present in terms of culturally appropriate strategies. Second, the scale can be used to challenge schools to work step-by-step towards maximal levels.

This scale is designed primarily for Majority World doctoral students but it has implications for the doctoral programs of Minority World students as well. The scale is suggested here merely as a starting point in the discussion of culturally appropriate doctoral-level strategies; some Minority and Majority schools have already made some progress in these strategies. Furthermore, the scale assumes that both Majority and Minority World doctoral students will be thoroughly trained in appropriate, culturally neutral, Minority World academic methods that are part and parcel of the established norms and procedures of the particular academic discipline.[13] The scale is shown in figure 15.1.

---

11. See Larry W. Caldwell, "Interpreting the Bible *With* the Poor," in *Social Engagement: The Challenge of the Social in Missiological Education*, APM Association of Professors of Mission (Wilmore: First Fruits, 2013), 165–190. For a practical application of these ethnohermeneutical principles, see Larry W. Caldwell, *Doing Bible Interpretation! Making the Bible Come Alive for Yourself and Your People* (Sioux Falls: Lazy Oaks, 2016).

12. Caldwell, "Interpreting the Bible *With* the Poor," 177–183.

13. By this I mean training in basic research methods, how to compile, analyse, and interpret data, how to demonstrate a unique contribution to the discipline, and so on.

> **Minimal culturally appropriate doctoral strategies:**
> 1. Accepting the legitimacy of the student's specific culture.
> 2. Recognizing that the student is an expert of his/her own specific culture.
> 3. Forming doctoral committees made up of both majority and minority world advisers.
>
> **Mid-level culturally appropriate doctoral strategies:**
> 4. Demonstrating language fluency (speaking, reading, and writing) by the student in his/her area of doctoral research.
> 5. Discovering by the student how his/her doctoral research relates to issues/problems/questions relevant to his/her specific culture.
> 6. Presenting familiarity with the culture-specific oral and written literature in the student's doctoral research.
>
> **Maximal culturally appropriate doctoral strategies:**
> 7. Completing the final project using the student's native language.
> 8. Relating a significant portion of the final project to issues/problems/questions found in the student's specific culture.
> 9. Exhibiting in the final project the student's ability to dialogue with his/her specific culture's oral and written material.

Figure 15.1: Culturally Appropriate Strategies for Doctoral Programs

Let us examine the scale in more detail.

First, Regarding the "Minimal" Culturally Appropriate Doctoral Strategies

1. Accepting the Legitimacy of the Student's Specific Culture

This strategy may seem obvious but it is foundational to any culturally appropriate strategy. *Both* the faculty and the student, whether from the Majority or Minority World, must recognize the validity of the student's culture and that it merits significant research efforts at the doctoral level. This validity will include the totality of the student's culture, including the culture's learning styles and how they demonstrate expertise and competency.

2. Recognizing That the Student Is an Expert of His/Her Own Specific Culture

Once again, this strategy may seem obvious at first glance, but what it really implies is that expertise is not in the hands of faculty only but it is also in the hands of the doctoral student. The role of the faculty is to assist the student in using his or her cultural expertise to the betterment of his or her overall doctoral research. In this regard the faculty member is more of a curator of the specific discipline than the all-knowing expert. Recognizing the student as a fellow expert also applies to minority faculty and students who, though they are from the same cultural group, most likely will still have significant generational (age) gap differences that are essentially cultural differences. Incorporating this strategy will help both faculty and student move beyond issues of authoritative knowledge and power.

3. Forming Doctoral Committees Made Up of Both Majority and Minority World Advisers

This strategy will not always be possible since it depends on the faculty make-up of the particular institution. However, it is a goal to be worked towards, undoubtedly reflecting the need for most faculties to recruit more diverse members.[14]

Second, Regarding the "Mid-Level" Culturally Appropriate Doctoral Strategies

4. Demonstrating Language Fluency (Speaking, Reading, and Writing) by the Student in His/Her Area of Doctoral Research

This strategy relates to the student's ability to adequately handle the language(s) necessary for the successful completion of doctoral research. For example, for Bible-related doctoral study this will typically mean a familiarity with Greek and/or Hebrew; it will not necessarily mean handling tangential languages

---

14. Some Majority World institutions, like the South Asia Institute of Advanced Christian Studies (SAIACS) in India, are already doing this. When they have a dissertation that is specific to a particular culture they get the SAIACS supervisor (if not of the same cultural group) to coordinate with a consultant from that culture. This consultant is usually an academic or a practitioner. The wide alumni network of SAIACS makes this relatively easy.

(e.g. Latin, German, and French) that may relate more to the power needs of Minority World academics than to achieving academic prowess in the particular discipline. In fact, it may be more appropriate for Majority World scholars to have an ability in a cognate language from their own geographical/cultural area; for example, Swahili for African context students, Mandarin for Asian context students, and so on.

5. Discovering by the Student How His/Her Doctoral Research Relates to Issues/Problems/Questions Relevant to His/Her Specific Culture

Here the doctoral student begins to wrestle with the question of research relevancy. Scholarship in the Majority World in the past has been relevant to very few. And it did not need to be; it was just an understood part of primarily white male minority privilege. As Professor Paul Yachnin points out: "Most faculty members have made their way in the profession along the well-established lines of the conference presentation and journal and book publication. The audience or readership they seek to engage is comprised of faculty members, postdocs, and senior graduate students. They have learned to write in ways that are familiar within their disciplines but often inaccessible to people outside their disciplines."[15] Today, with the pressing needs of the Majority World, this Minority World privilege of restricted relevancy is no longer warranted. Majority world doctoral research must be geared to issues facing the Majority World, and Majority World doctoral students must be encouraged to pursue such relevant research.[16]

6. Presenting Familiarity with the Culture-Specific Oral Traditions and Written Literature in the Student's Doctoral Research

This strategy goes without saying. All cultures have vast oral traditions, with many also having significant written literature. However, in the past

---

15. Paul Yachnin, "Instruments of Knowledge: Toward the Reform of the Ph.D. Dissertation," Council of Graduate Schools, accessed 20 January 2017, http://cgsnet.org/sites/default/files/DissFwd_Print%20All%20Papers.pdf.
16. Some Minority World groups, like Langham Partnership International, do encourage doctoral students that it sponsors to develop dissertations that are relevant to their cultural context. May their tribe increase.

these resources were neglected in favour of minority language preferences for English, German, French, or Dutch, with most of the doctoral research restricted to these privileged languages. Such neglect has no place in culturally appropriate doctoral programs. Here doctoral students must be empowered to use resources that are particular to their culture. Specifically, familiarity with oral sources germane to their area of expertise – and recognizing that they are as academically valid as the minority academic emphasis upon written texts – is especially necessary here.[17]

Third, Regarding "Maximal" Culturally Appropriate Doctoral Strategies

7. Completing the Final Project Using the Student's Native Language

If the "minimal" and "mid-level" strategies outlined above are followed, then this first maximal strategy is a natural outgrowth of all that has come before. Certainly this will take some creativity on the part of the doctoral faculty. There will be challenges related to fluency issues for minority faculty, and the like. However, there are ways around this, including comprehensive overviews of the dissertation research and summative results in the minority language of the faculty. What also needs to be addressed here is whether or not the minority view of scholarship – in reference to stylistic matters concerning footnotes, bibliography, and so on – is appropriate for Majority World scholarship. In my way of thinking, the stylistic tyranny of the Minority World should have little place in Majority World scholarship; it is a holdover from colonial thinking and has much to do with issues of power and control. While there is legitimate concern for guarding intellectual property, and giving proper credit to whom it is due, nevertheless Majority World doctoral students oftentimes spend an inordinate amount of their time with the *Chicago Manual of Style*, or some such Minority World instrument of academic torture.

---

17. While the academic discipline of orality studies does recognize the value of oral sources, this has not really taken root yet in advanced theological studies.

8. Relating a Significant Portion of the Final Project to Issues/Problems/Questions Found in the Student's Specific Culture

This strategy is perhaps most vital of all. It builds upon strategy 5: doctoral research that is culturally relevant. Now, at the end stages of the doctoral program, the doctoral student should make every effort to show how his or her long years of research and study relate directly to issues/problems/questions found in his or her own culture. The research results should not just be read by a handful of minority scholars and then put on a dusty library shelf, never to be disturbed again. Rather, the results should, as much as possible, be made relevant and applicable to the specific culture of the doctoral student. In this way scholarship is no longer just a part of the world of a privileged few but rather is made accessible to a much broader audience.

9. Exhibiting in the Final Project the Student's Ability to Dialogue with His/Her Specific Culture's Oral and Written Material

Again, if the above "minimal" and "mid-level" strategies are followed, this strategy will naturally happen as well. Creativity, like that mentioned above in strategy 7 with the uses of native language, will likewise need to occur here.

The above "Culturally Appropriate Strategies for Doctoral Programs" scale is but the "skeleton" for some of the foundational elements as we move towards a framework of culturally appropriate advanced theological studies. There is a growing literature of what the "flesh" of such studies might look like, including many of the chapters found in this book.[18]

So what is my own involvement with culturally appropriate advanced theological studies? It is now time to look at some examples of how this has worked out in my own experience.

---

18. See also the "Dissertation Model Discussions Papers" from the Council of Graduate Schools (USA) "Future of the Dissertation" Workshop held in January 2016, http://cgsnet.org/future-dissertation-workshop. Though geared to the Minority World of the North American context, there are many helpful suggestions of possible ways forward for both Minority and Majority World scholarship. Cf. the #alt-academy website that also examines the future of the dissertation, accessed 28 February 2017, http://mediacommons.futureofthebook.org/alt-ac/cluster/beyond-dissertation-1.

Part 3: Culturally Appropriate Advanced Theological Studies: Four Examples

What follows are four examples of culturally appropriate advanced theological studies that I have been directly or indirectly involved in over the years. They come from both Minority and Majority World contexts: the Philippines, Tonga, Cameroon, and North America. As these four examples are discussed here they will also be compared with the above "Culturally Appropriate Strategies for Doctoral Programs" scale to illustrate how various strategies of the scale might be implemented.

1. From the Philippines

I was director of the doctor of missiology (DMiss) program of the Asia Graduate School of Theology–Philippines (AGST–P) for many years. Though the AGST–P required a dissertation, we strived to make the final products of the DMiss doctoral students as relevant and useful to their ministry settings as possible. In so doing we easily incorporated the above "minimal" strategies while at the same time using some of the "mid-level" and "maximal" strategies as far as possible. To this end we had several dissertations that resulted either in direct publication in book form or simultaneously in the form of a doctoral project and a book. Let me here give one example of the latter.[19]

Jojo Manzano, a Filipino missions leader, did extensive research on developing appropriate training models for Filipinos involved in cross-cultural ministry while also examining existing cross-cultural training models available in the Philippines. His final dissertation project was a written summary of his research in typical dissertation format combined with a locally published eight-lesson church-based training course for Christian Filipinos who would soon be leaving the Philippines as overseas foreign workers. This training course in book form is entitled *Worker to Witness: Becoming an OFW Tentmaker*.[20]

---

19. Other examples of my former students' dissertations to books, especially using strategies 5 and 7, include the following: Antonia Leonora van der Meer, *Missionários Feridos: Como Cuidar dos que Servem* (Viçosa: Ultimato, 2009); Patrick Lai, *Tentmaking: The Life and Work of Business as Missions* (Colorado Springs: Authentic, 2005); and Anne C. Harper, *Understanding the Iglesia Ni Cristo: What They Really Believe and How They Can Be Reached* (Baguio City: APTS, 2014).

20. Jojo Manzano and Joy C. Solina, eds., *Worker to Witness: Becoming an OFW Tentmaker* (Makati: Church Strengthening Ministry, 2007).

The book takes the readers, together with their local church, step-by-step through the preparation process of planning, application, departure, and actual employment as overseas foreign workers (OFWs). It provides a basic practical understanding of the essential elements needed for Christian OFWs to become viable witnesses and tentmakers for Christ in a cross-cultural context.

In relationship to the "Culturally Appropriate Strategies for Doctoral Programs" scale, Manzano's doctoral program certainly incorporated strategies 1 and 2, though strategy 3 used Minority World committee members (though they all lived in the Philippines). Strategies 4 and 7 were not issues since English is a national language of the Philippines, while strategies 6 and 9 were not applicable. It was in strategies 5 and 8 that the final book project especially demonstrated that the doctoral research related to issues/problems/questions found in Manzano's specific culture, namely the high number of Christian OFWs and the need for them to receive some kind of cross-cultural training prior to their deployments overseas. Manzano's example is a good model for those doctoral programs that wish to maintain more rigid minority academic qualifications while at the same time continue to be relevant to the student's primary ministry context.

2. From Tonga and Oceania

Tongan Old Testament scholar Nāsili Vaka'uta has recently completed a pioneering work in the field of ethnohermeneutics. It is entitled *Reading Ezra 9–10 Tu'a-Wise: Rethinking Biblical Interpretation in Oceania*.[21] In what was originally his doctoral dissertation from the University of Auckland, New Zealand, Vaka'uta gives high praise to his doctoral advisors who, in his words, "allowed this work to be different."[22] And indeed it is. Drawing

---

21. See Nāsili Vaka'uta, *Reading Ezra 9-10 Tu'a-Wise: Rethinking Biblical Interpretation in Oceania*, International Voices in Biblical Studies 3 (Atlanta: Society of Biblical Literature, 2011). Cf. his "Tālanga: Theorizing a Tongan Mode of Interpretation," *Alternative* 5, no. 1 (2009): 127–139. For an entire listing of Vaka'uta's publications, many incorporating ethnohermeneutical principles, see http://www.trinitycollege.ac.nz/images/Publications.pdf, accessed 28 February 2017. See also the collection of ethnohermeneutically related works found in Jione Havea, David J. Neville, and Elaine M. Wainwright, eds., *Bible, Borders, Belonging(s): Engaging Readings from Oceania*, Semeia Studies 75 (Atlanta: Society of Biblical Literature, 2014), including Vaka'uta's chapter: "Border Crossing/Body Whoring: Rereading Rahab of Jericho with Native Women," 143–155.

22. Vaka'uta, *Reading Ezra 9–10 Tu'a-Wise*, xi.

upon the work of myself, Justin Ukpong, and R. S. Sugirtharajah,[23] Vaka'uta uses ethnohermeneutical principles, which he calls "contextual biblical interpretation," in order to use his own Tongan culture as a valid jumping-off place for an indigenous hermeneutical methodology. His brilliant result is a landmark study on how to do Majority World ethnohermeneutics in a format conducive to Minority World academic sensibilities.

Vaka'uta summarizes his approach as follows:

> Reading *tu'a-wise* (Tongan *lau faka-tu'a*) is an attempt to interpret the Bible based on Tongan cultural resources and social arrangement, through the "eye-/I-s" of a Tongan commoner (*tu'a*). *Lau faka-tu'a* emphasizes contextualizing the task of biblical interpretation rather than contextualizing the Bible per se. Contextualizing interpretation uses contextual or specifically indigenous categories of analysis, while contextualizing the Bible applies the insights from one's reading to one's situation. *Lau faka-tu'a* offers "an-other," uniquely Oceanic, way of reading[,] . . . engages critically with existing literature on contextual biblical interpretation and existing interpretations of the chosen text, Ezra 9–10, and aims at making biblical interpretation practice-based, nonelitist, noncontinental, transparent, and accountable.[24]

His overarching purpose "is to develop, on the one hand, an 'alternative' approach to biblical interpretation from a Tongan standpoint and to depart, on the other hand, from theories and methods that dominate biblical scholarship."[25]

In relationship to the "Culturally Appropriate Strategies for Doctoral Programs" scale, clearly strategies 1, 2, and 4 were followed, and especially strategies 5, 6, 8, and 9. Strategy 7 was not followed, but nevertheless the work uses many Tongan words and phrases throughout, complete with a lengthy glossary of Tongan terms. Vak'uta's work merits serious study by all Minority World scholars who are doing advanced theological studies with Majority World students.

---

23. Vaka'uta, 3, n. 8.
24. Vaka'uta, back cover.
25. Vaka'uta, 2.

3. From Cameroon

I recently returned from Cameroon where I facilitated a course on the general topic of contextualization with a doctor of ministry (DMin) cohort made up of mostly Cameroonian students. I use the word "facilitated" purposefully since they were definitely the experts of their own culture and I treated them as such. I brought with me some general characteristics of what good contextualization is and looks like. But that was the extent of my contribution. From then on, through a collaborative process over several days, they came up with a consensus concerning what the relevant theological issues were for Cameroon and Cameroonians, those that needed to be contextualized, and what that contextualizing might look like. Though we talked about the need to contextualize Minority World theological topics – such as God, the Bible, Jesus, sin, salvation, the church, the Holy Spirit and the last things – we all quickly came to see that the Cameroonian worldview demands much more. It demands a contextualization that deals with their own specific Cameroonian Majority World theological needs concerning topics such as death and resurrection; witchcraft and occultism/spiritism; child initiation and secret societies; and family issues dealing with marriage, singleness, polygamy, inheritance and succession, to name but a few. Furthermore, they would address these issues through the framework of ethnohermeneutics, a discipline they had just recently been exposed to. This is an ongoing process. They are trying to move beyond the Minority World "authoritative knowledge" that their Cameroonian seminaries instilled in them and attempt to rediscover their own Cameroonian hermeneutics. They are hoping that their final project will be a collaborative effort demonstrating their expertise through developing a practical theology concerning many of the issues listed above for the Cameroonian people. This end product will hopefully then be published by their Cameroonian denominational press and distributed throughout their Cameroonian constituency.

In relationship to the "Culturally Appropriate Strategies for Doctoral Programs" scale, we at Sioux Falls Seminary are committed to implementing as many of the strategies as possible with this particular DMin cohort. We see this as an opportunity "to do doctoral education right." Time will tell how well we were able to do this, but I am hopeful.

4. From North America

One of my recent MA in Bible and Theology pre-PhD students – Jordan Minnich Kjesbo – did his thesis on the theology of former Beatle John Lennon as contrasted with the theology of Jesus.[26] By using Lennon's famous song *Imagine*, Kjesbo sought to compare and contrast Lennon and Jesus through the grid of ethnohermeneutics. Kjesbo's motivation was an attempt to reconcile the gospel of Jesus with the postmodern world's deconstruction worldview and its effect on Christians today, especially Christian millennials. By deconstructing the idea of "the gospel," Kjesbo compares it with *Imagine*: "*Imagine* . . . has themes that have superficial resonance, such as promoting peace and rejecting materialism, and dissonance, like imagining a world without religion, with contemporary Christian teachings. Additionally it deals with themes such as soteriology through its challenge to imagine no heaven and hell . . . *Imagine* is fundamentally a song about transformation . . ."[27]

Kjesbo's purpose is to seek "to find points of resonance between critiques of the gospel . . . in an attempt to more clearly understand what the gospel is not and is" and, additionally, "finding the points of resonance and dissonance between *Imagine* . . . and the Gospels."[28] With that backdrop he then proceeds to compare and contrast the messages of Lennon and Jesus through exegeting the words of *Imagine* – especially the phrases "imagine there's no heaven," "imagine there's no countries," "imagine no possessions," and "you may say I'm a dreamer" – and comparing and contrasting them with the words of Jesus.

In relationship to the "Culturally Appropriate Strategies for Doctoral Programs" scale, Kjesbo's work significantly demonstrates strategies 5, 6, 8, and 9. This is especially seen in his use of an oral source that still greatly impacts cultures worldwide (Lennon's song, "Imagine") and deconstructing Jesus and the gospel in light of that oral source. Kjesbo's thesis shows how advanced

---

26. See Jordan Minnich Kjesbo, "The Gospel of John . . . Lennon" (master's thesis, Sioux Falls Seminary, 2016). Kjesbo has recently applied his same ethnohermeneutical principles to *Imagine*, this time using Paul's speech in Athens in Acts 17; see his "John Lennon and the Unknown God" (paper, Evangelical Missiological Society North Central Meetings, 18 March 2017).

27. Kjesbo, "Gospel of John . . . Lennon," 22–23.

28. Kjesbo, 24.

theological studies can dig deeply into the biblical text while at the same time resonate with the realities of modern culture.[29]

Conclusion: Towards Culturally Appropriate Methodologies

I, as a Minority World scholar, must honestly ask myself (as must we all): How am I doing in terms of developing culturally appropriate methodologies for my doctoral students? As with most of us – Minority and Majority World alike – I believe that I, and we, are on the way. Though the journey will be long, and filled with lots of twists and turns, I believe that this is the direction that most of us want to go. However, we still have some way to go. What follows are five recommendations that will hopefully help continue to move us in the right direction.

1. *Name past colonialism and the controlling role of Minority World power.* We need to acknowledge the fact that our current system of advanced theological education is rooted in a colonial past in which the Minority World was both powerful and fully in control. As a result, this minority was able to make the "rules" for what constitutes today's understandings of what advanced theological education should look like. Acknowledging this will help us to better understand why we need to move beyond where we currently are.
2. *Recognize Majority World realities and resulting changes that must occur.* As the Eagles sang in the lead song on their 1976 album *Hotel California*, "there's a new kid in town." The "new kid" in advanced theological studies is the Majority World and the innumerable Majority World scholars who have arisen over the past several decades. This number will only increase in future. Consequently, these Majority World scholars must move beyond accepting Minority World "authoritative knowledge." Instead they need to shape advanced

---

29. It should be noted that Kjesbo's primary thesis reader, a Minority World theologian, wrestled for a while with some of the ethnohermeneutical manoeuvrings Kjesbo was doing with both the biblical text and the *Imagine* text. Happily he came around in the end.

theological studies in their own image, in ways that make sense for their Majority World.

3. *Rethink academic vocabulary.* We need to rethink what we mean by using words and phrases like "academic," "scholarly research," "original contribution," "significant academic achievement," and the like. Vocabulary must be redefined so that it meets the needs of Majority World scholarship and not just that of the Minority World. These revised definitions will greatly assist in this task.

4. *Rethink the purpose of the final project/dissertation.* All advanced theological scholars need to show both originality and significant academic achievement, but there are other ways to do this besides the written dissertation. Everyone – Majority and Minority World scholars and graduate programs – must come up with viable and relevant alternatives that are both original and significant. There already is a growing acceptance of such alternatives in scholarship outside the realm of advanced theological studies.[30]

5. *Rethink relevancy.* Advanced theological studies can no longer afford to be irrelevant. While this is true for the Minority World, it is especially pertinent for the Majority World. The old Minority World model of a dissertation read by three people and then placed on a shelf hidden somewhere in the depths of a library is untenable today. There is just too much time, money, and energy invested in advanced theological studies to allow this to continue to happen. Again everyone – Majority and Minority World scholars and graduate programs alike – must make every effort to ensure that the work of their scholars is accessible and relevant for the church – and world – at large.

This chapter has covered much ground. Using the discipline of ethnohermeneutics as a grid for looking more closely at developing culturally appropriate methodologies in advanced theological studies, we have seen that the discipline has much to offer in terms of both where we have been and where we need to go. Certainly there is much for us to ponder as we seek to make

---

30. For example, see the "Dissertation Model Discussions Papers" referred to above in footnote 18.

advanced theological studies in our seminaries and graduate institutions as effective as they might be.

Discussion Questions

1. What feelings were aroused as you read the opening section of this chapter? Fear, anger, repulsion, amusement, hope . . . ? Why do you think these emotions emerged?

2. To what extent do you agree with Larry's suggestion that the grammatical-historical approach to hermeneutics is culture-bound? What concerns would you have in embracing ethnohermenutical approaches to biblical interpretation? What are some of the strengths and benefits that you see potentially for your own context?

3. What are some ways in which there is dissonance between the grammatical-historical methodology and standard interpretive approaches common in your situation? Describe one or two tacit hermeneutical patterns that you believe shape the worldview of people in your own local context, and which might be used to better communicate the biblical message. Explain.

4. Imagine what it might look like if you were to empower the use of local hermeneutical strategies for a master's or doctoral project. Briefly describe what you think might be key features of such a project in terms of both the content and the methodology. Which of the elements described in the section on "culturally appropriate doctoral strategies" do you think could/should be embraced and developed?

5. Consider in turn each of the four case study examples of ethnohermeneutical approaches to Scripture. Which of these do you think would best resonate with students in your own local context? Why?

Bibliography

Caldwell, Larry W. *Doing Bible Interpretation! Making the Bible Come Alive for Yourself and Your People*. Sioux Falls: Lazy Oaks, 2016.

———. "How Asian Is Asian Theological Education?" In *Tending the Seedbeds: Educational Perspectives on Theological Education in Asia*, edited by Allan Harkness, 23–45. Quezon City: Asia Theological Association, 2010.

———. "Interpreting the Bible *With* the Poor." In *Social Engagement: The Challenge of the Social in Missiological Education*, APM Association of Professors of Mission, 165–190. Wilmore: First Fruits, 2013.

———. "Reconsidering Our Biblical Roots: Bible Interpretation, the Apostle Paul and Mission Today." Parts 1 and 2. *International Journal of Frontier Missiology* 29, nos. 2-3 (2012): 91–100 and 113–121.

———. "Towards an Ethnohermeneutical Model for a Lowland Filipino Context." *Journal of Asian Mission* 7, no. 2 (2005): 169–193.

———. "Towards the New Discipline of Ethnohermeneutics: Questioning the Relevancy of Western Hermeneutical Methods in the Asian Context." *Journal of Asian Mission* 1, no. 1 (1999): 21–43.

Council of Graduate Schools (USA). "Dissertation Model Discussions Papers." From the "Future of the Dissertation" Workshop held in January 2016. Accessed 28 February 2017. http://cgsnet.org/future-dissertation-workshop.

Harper, Anne C. *Understanding the Iglesia Ni Cristo: What They Really Believe and How They Can Be Reached*. Baguio City: APTS, 2014.

Havea, Jione, David J. Neville, and Elaine M. Wainwright, eds. *Bible, Borders, Belonging(s): Engaging Readings from Oceania*. Semeia Studies 75. Atlanta: Society of Biblical Literature, 2014.

Hunter, Evan. "A Tectonic Shift: The Rapid Rise of PhD Programs at Evangelical Theological Schools in the Majority World." *InSights Journal for Global Theological Education* 1, no. 2 (2016): 41–60.

Jordan, Brigitte. "Authoritative Knowledge and Its Construction." In *Childbirth and Authoritative Knowledge*, edited by Robbie E. Davis-Floyd and Carolyn F. Sargent, 55–79. Berkeley: University of California, 1997.

Kjesbo, Jordan Minnich. "The Gospel of John . . . Lennon." Master's thesis, Sioux Falls Seminary, 2016.

———. "John Lennon and the Unknown God." Paper, Evangelical Missiological Society North Central Meetings, 18 March 2017.

Lai, Patrick. *Tentmaking: The Life and Work of Business as Missions*. Colorado Springs: Authentic, 2005.

Manzano, Jojo, and Joy C. Solina, eds. *Worker to Witness: Becoming an OFW Tentmaker*. Makati: Church Strengthening Ministry, 2007.

Smith, Linda Tuhiwai. *Decolonizing Methodologies: Research and Indigenous Peoples.* 2nd ed. London/New York: Zed Books, 2012.

Spindler, George D. *Education and Cultural Process: Anthropological Approaches.* 3rd ed. Long Grove: Waveland, 1997.

Vaka'uta, Nāsili. "Border Crossing/Body Whoring: Rereading Rahab of Jericho with Native Women." In Havea, Neville, and Wainwright, *Bible, Borders, Belonging(s)*, 143–155.

———. *Reading Ezra 9–10 Tu'a-Wise: Rethinking Biblical Interpretation in Oceania.* International Voices in Biblical Studies 3. Atlanta: Society of Biblical Literature, 2011.

———. "Tālanga: Theorizing a Tongan Mode of Interpretation." *Alternative* 5, no. 1 (2009): 127–139.

Van der Meer, Antonia Leonora. *Missionários Feridos: Como Cuidar dos que Servem.* Viçosa: Ultimato, 2009.

Yachnin, Paul. "Instruments of Knowledge: Toward the Reform of the Ph.D. Dissertation." Council of Graduate Schools. Accessed 20 January 2017. http://cgsnet.org/sites/default/files/DissFwd_Print%20All%20Papers.pdf.

16

Boldly Go! Tracking Trends in Comparative Literature

Havilah Dharamraj

When God was about to create the world by his word, the twenty-two letters of the alphabet descended from the terrible and august crown of God whereon they were engraved with a pen of flaming fire. They stood round about God, and one after the other spake and entreated, 'Create the world through me!'" Each request was declined with a fitting reply. The last but one to step up was *beth*, who pleaded that it was the right candidate since all dwellers in the world-to-be would begin their days with the blessing of God: *Baruch atta Adonai* ("Blessed are you, O Lord). God granted the wish of *beth* and began the account of the created world with it: **Bereshith bara Elohim** ("In the beginning God created...").¹

The point of the Jewish fable is the unparalleled privilege of participation in the communication of God. Indeed, more than anything, Israel prided itself on being the recipient of the Torah. Of interest to this essay is that the story reminds us of the wonder of the Christian canon – that divine thoughts were captured by alphabets and words, phrases and syntax, grammar and idiom, sentences and paragraphs. Whether orally delivered by prophets or copied by

---

1. Louis Ginzberg, *Legends of the Jews*, vol. 1, trans. Henrietta Szold (Philadelphia: JPS, 2003), 4. The *aleph* refrained from putting itself forward, and was rewarded at the even more momentous occasion of the giving of the Law to Israel at Sinai. That pronouncement would commence with *aleph*: *Anoki Adonai* ... ("I am the Lord ...." Exod 20:2).

scribal hands, the sacred communication was now incarnated into the human language and would have to find its place among other arrangements of words.

In India, the Christian canon has always had to compete with texts that also claimed to be divine revelation(s). When it first entered through the trading routes, perhaps in the first century, the sacred texts of Hinduism had been around for a couple of millennia – boasting of both the aural and the text-ensconced, and tiered as *shruti* ("that which was heard" by the sages as divine revelation) and as *smriti* ("that which was remembered" and passed on through the teachings of the sages).[2] When the Bible came again, this time through the gateways of colonial rule and more forcefully than before,[3] it was preceded by another scripture. The Qur'an had already been around in India for almost a millennium as the sacred text of the Muslim rulers.[4] There is no environment as competitive for a sacred text as India. The canons of major world religions jostle for space, while acknowledging as demographically lesser rivals the Parsi *Zendavesta* and the sacred writings of the reform movements within Hinduism – Buddhism, Jainism, and Sikhism.

In recognition of this plurality of religions context, most Indian Christian theological institutions offering tertiary level education throw in a course in World Religions. Anything more than that happens in the few institutions that have a department of religions, where master's and doctoral students may have an opportunity to study the Christian sacred text comparatively with others that claim divine revelation. However, the text-based departments (Old Testament and New Testament), especially in evangelical institutions, usually give scant attention to the texts of other religions.

This is strange considering that students in Biblical Studies regularly compare the biblical text with ancient West Asian literature. Who can study the creation narratives in Genesis 1–2 without reference to *Enuma Elish*, or

---

2. The entry of the Aryans onto the Indian sub-continent may be dated between 1500 and 1300 BC. John Keay, *India: A History* (London: Harper, 2010), 27.

3. The first European Protestant missionaries were the Pietists Bartholomew Ziegenbalg and Heinrich Plütschau, dated to 1706. The century following saw a tremendous burst of missionary activity in India as across the rest of the "pagan" world. For a global overview, see Paul E. Pierson, "Why Did the 1800s Explode with Missions?," *Christianity Today*, accessed 3 April 2017, http://www.christianitytoday.com/history/issues/issue-36/why-did-1800s-explode-with-missions.html.

4. Muslim entry into India began c. 663 AD. Keay, *India*, 181.

the flood account in Genesis 6–9 without poring over the *Epic of Gilgamesh* to make comparative tables? Similarly, the Pentateuchal legal literature is examined against contemporaneous Mesopotamian and Hittite law codes; Proverbs is compared with collections from the Egyptian courts; and the Song of Songs is argued to have a secular origin based on its affinities with Egyptian love songs.

However, these exercises may themselves be the obstacle, keeping faculty and their students so ecstatically absorbed in the ancient world that they haven't thought of taking these texts out to converse with contemporary ones; alternatively, these departments might think that such conversations are detrimental to the doctrine of inspiration.[5] "See what happens when the ecumenicals try it," they might say, wagging a cautionary forefinger. Between the insularity and the paranoia, there is the general reluctance to engage with alterity, the "otherness" of other sacred texts.[6]

This chapter makes the secular interdisciplinary method of Comparative Literature its starting point, and attempts to nudge theology – especially Biblical Studies as it is practised in religiously pluralistic environments – towards following where Comparative Literature is going. A definition of this method that has remained relevant across half a century is as follows: "Comparative Literature is the study of literature beyond the confines of one particular country and the study of the relationships between literature on one hand and other areas of knowledge and belief, such as the (fine) arts, philosophy, history, the social sciences, the sciences, religion, etc. on the other.

---

5. The reluctance to engage with other sacred scriptures is often a reflection of the polarizing mindset of the European missionaries from the eighteenth century downwards: "Hindu scriptures were compared to a forest in which one could get lost, to poison, to a disease, and a false light; in contrast, Christian scriptures pointing the way to human salvation, were a life-giving potion, a medicine, and compared to the welcoming light of a home. Such contrasts were not just confined to tracts but were also elaborated in book-length works." Hephzibah Israel, *Religious Transactions in Colonial South India: Language, Translation and the Making of Protestant Identity*, Palgrave Studies in Cultural and Intellectual History (New York: Palgrave Macmillan, 2011), 45.

6. In my experience, students who are first-generation Christians with a Hindu background are particularly resistant to researching Hindu sacred texts and traditions.

In brief, it is the comparison of one literature with another or others, and the comparison of literature with other spheres of human expression."[7]

The Common Reader

In secular Comparative Literature, and certainly in theological investigation using Comparative Literature, it is worth emphasizing that the method "is not . . . an end in itself." It is "as a means of discovery that comparison enables us to discover relations, differences, hidden causes, questions not before asked."[8] The method itself is not rocket science. On the contrary: "Comparative literature scientifically endorses some of the intuitions we have as common readers."[9] "The common reader"[10] has in his or her head a "mental encyclopaedia" within which "connections are made among literary works, most of these connections consisting of comparisons across languages, time, space, cultures, arts, discourses." The cognitive exercise of "literary comparison" is, then, "reading a work through other works."[11]

Traditionally, Comparative Literature has been largely production-centred. That is, the purpose of the comparatist was to establish a vector of influence pointing from an older work to a later one, to show how the production of the latter was shaped. This is what we might do in Islamic Studies when we compare, say, the Quranic account of the "son of the sacrifice" with Genesis 22, the account of Abraham's near-sacrifice of Isaac. The direction of influence (we may even call it "borrowing") being incontestable, the comparatist takes the Hebrew text as the norm against which to examine the continuities and discontinuities of the younger version. Beyond this, the comparatist may wish

---

7. Henry H. H. Remak, "Comparative Literature: Its Definition and Function," in *Comparative Literature: Method and Perspective*, eds. Newton P. Stallknecht and Horst Frenz (Carbondale: Southern Illinois University Press, 1961), 3. The method is young, only about two centuries old. Its history in retrospect begins with the French School, with its Eurocentric bias. With the coming of the concept of "world literature," we have the American School.

8. César Domínguez, Haun Saussy, and Darío Villanueva, "Preface," *Introducing Comparative Literature: New Trends and Applications* (London: Routledge, 2016), xvi.

9. Domínguez et al., "Preface," ix.

10. See the origin of the phrase from Samuel Johnson borrowed by Virginia Woolf, in Domínguez et al., xi.

11. Domínguez et al., xi.

to investigate the historical route of influence; and, being a theologian, (s)he will be intrigued by the theological import of the continuities and discontinuities.

In recent times, however, interest has shifted to reception-centred influence, giving rise to questions that may sound absurd: "How does *Fifty Shades of Grey* influence the Song of Songs?" The "influence" here, of course, is in the mind of the reader who has read (or viewed) the much-hyped *Fifty Shades* and also mused (at some point earlier or later) on the place of the Song of Songs in the biblical canon. This is how the reader creates "some kind of whole" "out of whatever odds and ends he can come by."[12] In such a scenario, the task of the comparatist is even more adventurous than before: the task is to examine how the *reading* of the biblical text is influenced by other literature.

The Common Reader and His or Her Community

A second influence on the Common Reader comes from what is called the *public meaning* of a given piece of literature. To explain, let's take Plato's complaint about the written word (as against the spoken): "[O]nce a thing is put in writing, the composition, whatever it may be, drifts all over the place, getting into the hands not only of those who understand it, but equally of those who have no business with it . . ."[13] This creates a corpus of meaning(s) of the text generated by a collective or a community. Indeed, as a literary work "moves through time and space it accrues meaning, sheds meaning, provokes meaning."[14] In historiography, this is the *longue durée* – the long stretches of time over which imperceptible changes can happen. In Comparative Literature, the *longue durée* of circulation and transmission of a text (perhaps including orality) creates public meaning.[15]

---

12. Virginia Woolf, *The Common Reader*, ed. Andrew McNeilie (San Diego: Harcourt, 1984), 1; cited in Domínguez et al., "Preface," xi.
13. Plato, "Phaedrus," in *The Collected Dialogues of Plato Including the Letters*, ed. Edith Hamilton and Huntington Cairns (Princeton: Princeton University, 1961), 521.
14. Michael Lucey, "A Literary Object's Contextual Life," in *A Companion to Comparative Literature*, ed. Ali Behdad and Dominic Thomas (Chichester: Wiley-Blackwell, 2011), 128. See Kumkum Sangari's treatment of this idea using Mughal art as an illustration: "Aesthetics of Circulation: Thinking Between Regions," *Jadavpur Journal of Comparative Literature* 50 (2013–14): 9–38.
15. Lucey, "A Literary Object's Contextual Life," 121.

As an example, let's take the Hindu mythological story of Sati, the princess who marries against her father's wishes. When, on one occasion, she discovers that her father has calculatingly insulted her husband, her fury takes the form of self-immolation. Derived from Sati's name is the Hindi word *sateetva* ("Satiness") which refers to womanly virtue, as well as the pre-colonial practice of *sati* in which a widow immolates herself on the funeral pyre of her husband. Writing about this in a national newspaper, Arshia Sattar questions the association of the legend with the practice of *sati* and the exaltation of *sateetva*. The very fact that Sattar does so demonstrates the potential of a *longue durée* to alter the meaning of the circulated and transmitted text.[16]

Then there is Sita, the female protagonist of the Hindu epic the *Ramayana*, described thus on a blog: "The popular image of Sita that so powerfully shapes the Indian womanhood is essentially that of a very docile person, someone who gives unbounded love but accepts injustice, cruelty, neglect, humiliation and banishment quietly, uncomplainingly. The ideal wife archetype is perceived as a martyr, willingly sacrificing herself for the purposes of her man, with no purposes of her own."[17] The blogger is a certain Satya Chaitanya, a corporate trainer. Having set out this conception of Sita's characterization, he labours at length over the original Sanskrit text by Valmiki to demonstrate that Sita's "popular image" is flawed. Again, what we see is that public meaning triumphs over the particularities of the text's professed meaning.

Our Indian Christian Common Reader inhabits a world in which (s)he might encounter the Sati or Sita texts (in translation or in comic book form), but the greater likelihood is that (s)he will be familiar with the public meaning of these narratives. The implication is that, beyond the textual "odds and ends" (such as *Fifty Shades* influencing how one reads the Song of Songs), the Common Reader brings to his or her reading "acquisitions that are not simply personal." These are acquisitions "that are related to that person's trajectory through a particular social universe, related to her or his interaction with

---

16. Arshia Sattar, "Sati, Symbol of Empowered Woman," *The Hindu*, 3 March 2017, accessed 24 April 2017, https://www.pressreader.com/india/the-hindu/20170303/282918090244603.
17. Satya Chaitanya, "Reimagining Indian Womanhood: Sita as a Woman of Substance," *Inner Traditions* (blog), 10 July 2009, accessed 24 April 2017, http://innertraditions.blogspot.in/2009/07/reimagining-indian-womanhood-sita-as.html.

that universe."[18] So, when our Indian Christian Common Reader comes to, say, the biblical book of Ruth, (s)he could bring to it – imperceptibly and subliminally – the public meaning accrued by the Sati and Sita texts. (S)he is reading as a reader immersed in half a millennium's worth of transmission of the profile of the ideal Indian woman.

So far, the theologian-comparatist's task has multiplied twice over: in addition to addressing literary influence from within the personal experience of the Common Reader, (s)he addresses the influence of the public meaning of literary works from the "particular social universe" of the Common Reader. But there's more.

What the Common Reader Thinks Is Literature

A third consideration about the Common Reader is that, in an age beyond Gutenberg, our Common Reader has become a "digital native."[19] This demands a catch-up with new forms of literature created by "technologies of the word"[20] – think of the narrative art of augmented reality games like *Pokémon Go*.[21] According to the Bernheimer Report, "Comparative Literature should include comparisons between media, from early manuscripts to television, hypertext, and virtual realities. The material form that has constituted our object of study for centuries, the book, is in the process of being transformed..."[22] Indeed, "digital Humanities" makes necessary "a fundamental rethinking of

---

18. Lucey, "A Literary Object's Contextual Life," 121.
19. For the term, see Marc Prensky, "Digital Natives, Digital Immigrants," in *On the Horizon* 9, no. 5 (October 2001): 1–6. Also available online at https://www.marcprensky.com/writing/Prensky%20-%20Digital%20Natives,%20Digital%20Immigrants%20-%20Part1.pdf, accessed 26 April 2017.
20. J. Walter Ong, *Orality and Literacy: The Technologizing of the Word* (London: Routledge, 1982); cited in Domínguez et al., *Introducing Comparative Literature*, 130.
21. Eric Johnson, in "Full Transcript: Niantic CEO John Hanke Talks Pokémon Go on Recode Decode," thinks that augmented reality (AR), compared with virtual reality that isolates the player, is "far more interesting and promising... for humanity" because "AR is designed to add, enhance the things you do as a human being: Being outside, socializing with other people, shopping, playing, having fun" (4 October 2016, Recode.net, https://www.recode.net/2016/10/4/13166612/john-hanke-niantic-pokemon-go-recode-decode-podcast-transcript).
22. Charles Bernheimer, "The Bernheimer Report, 1993: Comparative Literature at the Turn of the Century," in *Comparative Literature in the Age of Multiculturalism*, ed. Charles Bernheimer (Baltimore: Johns Hopkins University, 1995), 45.

how knowledge gets created, *what* knowledge looks (or sounds, or feels, or tastes) like, *who* gets to create knowledge, *when* it is 'done' or published, *how* it gets authorized and disseminated..."[23] In an exegesis class, I've often found it instructive to study a popular blogged sermon alongside all the traditional course material – but that's only getting our toes wet in the surf as we stand looking out at the ocean of digital "literature" heaving before us.

It's not just that the material form has changed, but that the democratization of reading and writing that Gutenberg ushered in[24] has gathered speed to give rise to a landslide of those who write without having (sufficiently) read – an avalanche of work that might be called "postliterature."[25] It is an age in which "the boundaries between high and low culture, between advertising and art have been erased."[26] Thus, when *The Shack* was doing the rounds in churches about a decade ago, we intuitively brought this piece of Christian pop literature into the classroom to analyse it alongside whatever doctrine of God the students were studying from standard Western or Indian theologians.

In case we're thinking all this well exceeds the remit of theology and theologizing, we should recall here that even Socrates got it wrong. Socrates was of the opinion that "written words were dead letters, mere simulacra of authentic, living discourse which," he claimed, got "written on the soul of the student."[27] Then, in response to the next great turn cranked in by the printing press, came Marshall McLuhan's *The Gutenberg Galaxy: The Typographic Man* (1962). McLuhan submitted that the printed word has led humankind to schizophrenia and alienation.[28] For good or for ill, we have crossed over from the Gutenberg Galaxy of print forms into deeper space. Theology and theologizing have kept pace with each new expression of literature, and, sooner or later, will have to negotiate with the digital revolution. Meanwhile, there

---

23. Todd Presner, "Comparative Literature in the Age of Digital Humanities," in Behdad and Thomas, *Companion to Comparative Literature*, 195.
24. Domínguez et al., *Introducing Comparative Literature*, 136.
25. Domínguez et al., 134.
26. Efraín Kristal, "Art and Literature in the Liquid Modern Age," in Behdad and Thomas, *Companion to Comparative Literature*, 118.
27. Domínguez et al., *Introducing Comparative Literature*, 130.
28. See a review at Wayne J. Urban, "Marshall McLuhan and the Book: A Reconsideration," *Historical Studies in Education*, Spring 2004, accessed 3 April 2017, http://historicalstudiesineducation.ca/index.php/edu_hse-rhe/article/view/438/589.

is another negotiation Comparative Literature has to make on behalf of the Common Reader.

The Common Reader's Other Sources

A fourth dimension of influence on the Common Reader that may need to be factored in is the arts. The question Comparative Literature is asking now is whether the method should confine itself to oral and written textual traditions. Should it embrace the arts also?

Common to literature and the arts is the Aristotelian concept of *mimesis* – the fact that all the arts are imitative, and, what is more, that they all imitate the same subject: human reality.[29] Pantini takes the argument a step further by pointing out that Comparative Literature is the meeting point for the arts. Being the only word-based art, it is the sole verbalizer of the comparative threads running across the plastic (e.g. painting, sculpture, film) and the performance arts (e.g. music, dance, theatre).[30]

For an illustrative example, we could return to the *Ramayana*. Consider its multiple *avatars*: the literary form is Valmiki's Sanskrit textual composition, a hoary text available in many translations; it is performed in various dance traditions; it is sung by local troubadours; it is the subject of the folk art Madhubani style of paintings[31] which has received a GI tag;[32] it was a massively successful television series that ran for seventy-eight episodes in 1987–88 and entered the *Limca Book of Records* as the "world's most viewed mythological serial." Such an "intersemiotic transposition from one sign-system to another"

---

29. Domínguez et al., *Introducing Comparative Literature*, 107.
30. Domínguez et al., 108.
31. Neha Das, "Recounting Ramayan through Madhubani Art," *Deccan Herald*, 15 October 2014, accessed 24 April 2017, http://www.deccanherald.com/content/435958/recounting-ramayana-through-madhubani-art.html.
32. A geographical indication (GI) is an identification given to certain products which correspond to a specific geographical location or origin (e.g. a town, region, or country) in order to protect the product from being duplicated. E.g. Darjeeling tea was the first GI-tagged product in India, in 2004–05.

has been termed "transduction."³³ Which other discipline could analyse and critique and synthesize trans-arts transduction but Comparative Literature? Think of how impoverished a study of the consumption and appropriation of the *Ramayana* would be if we limited it to extant textual traditions. More critically, think of how alarmingly inadequate would be our understanding of the Common Reader, to whom all these various sign-systems are the bits and pieces by which (s)he constructs his or her idea of the whole.

With this, we have described the new ground that lies before the theologian-comparatist.

The task has moved on from text-related enquiry to reader-oriented investigation. The comparatist works from the point of view of the Common Reader addressing four areas of influence on the meaning of a text: (1) other texts within the experience of the Common Reader; (2) the public meaning of these other texts as generated within the social universe of the Common Reader; (3) digital "literature," some of which could be low-brow "postliterature"; (4) the plastic and performance arts into which the text gets transducted.

If this seems a little overwhelming, let us talk briefly about where we could start.

How the Common Reader Joins (or Doesn't Join) the Dots

We said that the Common Reader makes connections so as to construct a whole – so, for example, the whole may be his or her idea of what a married Indian Christian woman should be. What are the "dots" that the reader "joins" to make up this whole? In other words, what does a comparatist look for when (s)he sets about the comparative task?

The current paradigm in Comparative Literature is to pay attention to the empirical evidence available. "If between two distinct literary systems,

---

33. Roman Jakobson, "On Linguistic Aspects of Translation," *Selected Writings II* (The Hague: Mouton, 1971), 260–266; cited in Domínguez et al., *Introducing Comparative Literature*, 111. The term is borrowed from genetics, where it describes the process of the uptake of donor DNA by a recipient organism.

or between a literary work and that of another artistic medium whether it be plastic or musical, there appears a common element . . . then a fundamental theoretical element will appear; that is, an invariant of literature."[34] Sometimes the invariant is a genre itself – the genre of beast-fables, ubiquitous across India (*Panchatantra*), the Persian-Arab world (*A Thousand and One Nights*), and Europe (*Aesop's Fables*), and reaching westwards up to Iceland and south to Borneo.[35]

More often, the invariant is a theme – universal examples are the turn of the seasons, death, love, or war – or images – the adulteress, the miser. However, even where the content of the invariants matches across literatures, the meaning extracted often does not. Reflecting on this, David Palumbo-Liu helpfully refers us to the classical European rhetorical terms *comparatio* and *similitudo*. *Comparatio* "enforces the comparison of apples with apples and oranges with oranges." *Similitudo*, however, "encourages the comparison of apples with objects much further afield than oranges. *Comparatio* enforces preexisting similarities, whereas *similitudo* posits new resemblances, stretching the limits of a code."[36]

Our Common Reader often does a *comparatio* – sometimes consciously, but more often subliminally. An example would be what my MTh student Philip Ewan Yalla found when he examined the possible influence of the public meaning of the ancient Hindu legal treatise *Manusmriti* on the Indian Christian's attitude to widowhood. He began with the working premise that the common Indian Christian's point of view on widows and widowhood was informed by biblical texts (e.g. from the book of Ruth). However, what Philip found through in-depth interviews was that Indian Christians, especially in rural areas, think of widowhood as deeply inauspicious – an idea not present

---

34. Domínguez et al., *Introducing Comparative Literature*, 15. This discovery of "invariants" is what moved comparative literature from its Eurocentric bias to become "world literature," or to use another popular phrase, "literature without borders." René Étiemble is credited with formalizing the idea: "Comparative literature . . . allows the discovery of what I will call literary invariants, without which in all ages, everywhere, there would not be a form of beauty." *Hygiène des lettres: Savoir et goût* (Paris: Gallimard, 1958), 166; cited in David Palumbo-Liu, "Method and Congruity: The Odious Business of Comparative Literature," in Behdad and Thomas, *Companion to Comparative Literature*, 48.

35. Domínguez et al., *Introducing Comparative Literature*, 65.

36. Natalie Melas, "Versions of Incommensurability," *World Literature Today* 69, no. 2 (1995): 276–277; cited in Behdad and Thomas, *Companion to Comparative Literature*, 56–57.

in the Bible, but present in both the *Manusmriti* and in its public meaning, as substantiated by the plastic art of popular film. So deeply entrenched is the inauspiciousness of widowhood that a Christian widow may avoid being present at (or may be required to be absent from) family weddings. Is the Common Reader unconsciously using *comparatio* to arrive at the inference that widows are inauspicious in both the Bible and the *Manusmriti*? If so, (s)he is joining "dots" between the *Manusmriti* on the one hand and selected biblical texts on the other: that is, (s)he infers that Naomi is widowed as a punishment for having left Israel to make her home in ungodly Moab, the enemy of Israel; did she herself not say, "[T]he Almighty has made my life very bitter" (Ruth 1:20)? And thus the link may be made: widowhood is inauspicious.

This is where the theologian-comparatist comes in with the corrective: the *comparatio* made is by no means an exact match and, therefore, is untenable; the case is more *similitudo*, with incongruities – even a whole *structure* of incongruities[37] – waiting to be unearthed.

Besides correcting the faulty Do-It-Yourself comparisons the Common Reader might make, the theologian-comparatist can also help the Common Reader recognize patterns in "dots" that are crying out to be joined. This requires a creative-thinking and theologically reflective comparatist. For an example, we must start with the idea of the *tertium comparationis*.

The *tertium comparationis*, that is, the common denominator between two artefacts being compared, need not always be as obvious as genre (e.g. love songs) or versions of the same narrative (e.g. Abraham and the Son of the Sacrifice in the Bible and the Quran). The *tertium comparationis* can be the comparatist him- or herself. Haun Saussy put this rather cheekily. When a comparatist setting out to compare Mayan hieroglyphics with the fish markets of Gloucester, Massachusetts, is asked to provide the common denominator between them, the answer could well be: "They don't have anything to do with each other – yet. What they have in common is me, or my attention."[38]

So what does the Ancient West Asian goddess Asherah have in common with Mother Mary venerated in Catholic South India? The *tertium*

---

37. Palumbo-Liu, "Method and Congruity," 46–59.
38. Haun Saussy, "Comparisons, World Literature and the Common Denominator," in Behdad and Thomas, *Companion to Comparative Literature*, 62.

comparationis was an MTh student, Madan Kumar. He made his starting point the archaeological finds at Khirbet el-Qom and Kuntillet Ajrud, where inscriptions mention "Yahweh and his Asherah." He considered side by side the religious and economic environments of Canaan. Here was polytheism practised by an agro-economy which required productivity (of field and barn and womb) – a combination that demanded a fertility goddess. He allowed that for this reason, popular Yahwism may have awarded the "bachelor" YHWH a suitable wife in the form of Asherah. Madan made a persuasive transfer of this possibility to Indian Catholicism as exemplified in a famous shrine in a town called Velankanni. Here the worship of Mary is hugely popular, drawing devotees from across the various religious faiths.[39] Hinduism, like the religions of ancient West Asia, has a pantheon sizzling with female deities mediating all forms of prosperity, and also places a high value on progeny – "may you have a thousand sons" is the traditional marriage blessing. Comparing the oral narrative traditions surrounding the Indian Marianic basilica with the idea of "Yahweh and his Asherah," Madan postulated that popular Catholicism meets the demand for a fertility goddess by way of Mother Mary (bearing her Infant Jesus). Her popularity, Madan concluded, was comparable to Asherah's in ancient Israel. The theologian-comparatist was in a position to help a Common Reader join a set of dots that (s)he couldn't have seen on his or her own – the result being a nuanced picture of Indian Christian idolatry.

Thus, *comparatio* and *similitudo*, and the *tertium comparationis*, are promising starting points for comparative studies.

Conclusion

This article argues that the *incarnation* of divine communication into human language, and, therefore, into the category of sacred texts, cries out for the rough and tumble of engagement rather than for the high privilege of golden isolation. For the sake of relevant theology, missional application, and pastoral practice in an increasingly religiously plural world, Biblical Studies should –

---

39. Donna Fernandes, "The Virgin Mary Brings Different Faiths in India and Pakistan Together," *The Indian Economist* (now Qrius.com), 18 April 2017, accessed 24 April 2017, http://theindianeconomist.com/virgin-mary-faiths/.

without undermining the evangelical privileging of Scripture – make (much more!) space for the method of Comparative Literature. More important is that theological education catches the spirit of adventure. If it won't "boldly go where no man has gone before,"[40] it should at least follow where the secular use of the method is going: beyond the text, and into the public meaning of texts, into the arts, and into (cyber) space itself!

Discussion Questions

1. For your particular context, what are two or three pieces of classical literature and at least one contemporary piece of literature that you believe have profoundly impacted people in your context? In particular consider significant religious texts. In what ways has your school interacted with non-Christian literature? To what extent do you believe that this engagement is satisfactory or insufficient, and why?

2. Briefly describe a piece of non-Christian literature or story which has points of connection with a biblical narrative or teaching. How might these points of connection enrich our understanding of the biblical text?

3. What are some of the features of the world inhabited by the "Christian Common Reader" in your context? Describe one or two ways in which there is dissonance between this world and genuine Christian values, and why. Briefly explain how comparative studies might clarify and guide local Christians to a better understanding and embrace of biblical teaching.

4. As you consider emerging generations of young people in your context, what are some of the key forms of "literature" and other sources through which meaning and worldview is formed? Describe at least one way in which there is dissonance between these sources and the way that Christian ministry is currently practised.

5. Try to imagine a creative form of advanced theological studies through which a student might help "Common Readers" to join the dots, and hence hold

---

40. *Star Trek!*

potential for connecting with and impacting society. Describe some possible areas, themes, or ideas for a master's-level thesis relevant to your context.

Bibliography

Behdad, Ali, and Dominic Thomas, eds. *A Companion to Comparative Literature*. Chichester: Wiley-Blackwell, 2011.

Bernheimer, Charles. "The Bernheimer Report, 1993: Comparative Literature at the Turn of the Century." In *Comparative Literature in the Age of Multiculturalism*, edited by Charles Bernheimer, 39–48. Baltimore: Johns Hopkins University, 1995.

Chaitanya, Satya. "Reimagining Indian Womanhood: Sita as a Woman of Substance." *Inner Traditions* (blog), 10 July 2009. Accessed 24 April 2017. http://innertraditions.blogspot.in/2009/07/reimagining-indian-womanhood-sita-as.html.

Das, Neha. "Recounting Ramayan through Madhubani Art." *Deccan Herald*, 15 October 2014. Accessed 24 April 2017. http://www.deccanherald.com/content/435958/recounting-ramayana-through-madhubani-art.html.

Domínguez, César, Haun Saussy, and Darío Villanueva. "Preface." In *Introducing Comparative Literature: New Trends and Applications*, ix–xviii. London: Routledge, 2016.

Étiemble, René. *Hygiène des lettres: Savoir et goût*. Paris: Gallimard, 1958.

Fernandes, Donna. "The Virgin Mary Brings Different Faiths in India and Pakistan Together." *The Indian Economist* (now *Qrius.com*), 18 April 2017. Accessed 24 April 2017. http://theindianeconomist.com/virgin-mary-faiths/.

Ginzberg, Louis. *Legends of the Jews*, vol. 1. Translated by Henrietta Szold. Philadelphia: JPS, 2003.

Israel, Hephzibah. *Religious Transactions in Colonial South India: Language, Translation and the Making of Protestant Identity*. Palgrave Studies in Cultural and Intellectual History. New York: Palgrave Macmillan, 2011.

Jakobson, Roman. "On Linguistic Aspects of Translation." *Selected Writings II*, 260–266. The Hague: Mouton, 1971.

Johnson, Eric. "Full Transcript: Niantic CEO John Hanke Talks Pokémon Go on Recode Decode." Recode.net, 4 October 2016. https://www.recode.net/2016/10/4/13166612/john-hanke-niantic-pokemon-go-recode-decode-podcast-transcript.

Keay, John. *India: A History*. London: Harper, 2010.

Kristal, Efraín. "Art and Literature in the Liquid Modern Age." In Behdad and Thomas, *Companion to Comparative Literature*, 108–119.

Lucey, Michael. "A Literary Object's Contextual Life." In Behdad and Thomas, *Companion to Comparative Literature*, 120–135.

Melas, Natalie. "Versions of Incommensurability." *World Literature Today* 69, no. 2 (1995): 275–280.

Ong, J. Walter. *Orality and Literacy: The Technologizing of the Word*. London: Routledge, 1982.

Palumbo-Liu, David. "Method and Congruity: The Odious Business of Comparative Literature." In Behdad and Thomas, *Companion to Comparative Literature*, 46–59.

Pierson, Paul E. "Why Did the 1800s Explode with Missions?" *Christianity Today*. Accessed 3 April 2017. http://www.christianitytoday.com/history/issues/issue-36/why-did-1800s-explode-with-missions.html.

Plato. "Phaedrus." In *The Collected Dialogues of Plato Including the Letters*, edited by Edith Hamilton and Huntington Cairns, 475–525. Princeton: Princeton University, 1961.

Prensky, Marc. "Digital Natives, Digital Immigrants." In *On the Horizon* 9, no. 5 (October 2001): 1–6.

Presner, Todd. "Comparative Literature in the Age of Digital Humanities." In Behdad and Thomas, *Companion to Comparative Literature*, 193–207.

Remak, Henry H. H. "Comparative Literature: Its Definition and Function." In *Comparative Literature: Method and Perspective*, edited by Newton P. Stallknecht and Horst Frenz, 3–57. Carbondale: Southern Illinois University, 1961.

Sangari, Kumkum. "Aesthetics of Circulation: Thinking Between Regions." *Jadavpur Journal of Comparative Literature* 50 (2013–14): 9–38.

Sattar, Arshia. "Sati, Symbol of Empowered Woman." *The Hindu*, 3 March 2017. Accessed 24 April 2017. https://www.pressreader.com/india/the-hindu/20170303/282918090244603.

Saussy, Haun. "Comparisons, World Literature and the Common Denominator." In Behdad and Thomas, *Companion to Comparative Literature*, 60–64.

Urban, Wayne J. "Marshall McLuhan and the Book: A Reconsideration." *Historical Studies in Education*, Spring 2004. Accessed 3 April 2017. http://historicalstudiesineducation.ca/index.php/edu_hse-rhe/article/view/438/589.

Woolf, Virginia. *The Common Reader*. Edited by Andrew McNeilie. San Diego: Harcourt, 1984.

Section III

Innovative Forms of Advanced Theological Studies

> Finally, when the house catches fire, they decide to dig a well.
> (South Indian proverb)

Contextualized theology has almost become a cliché today. But the "contextualized theology" is generally done in Western writing patterns. Perry has on several occasions challenged Arab and Armenian scholars to consider the primary approaches to meaningful communication in their own local contexts, and to communicate "contextualized ideas" in "contextualized forms." Generally the response has been: "But this would never be accepted or read beyond our own local community!"

In the globalization of distinctly Western patterns of communication and thought, our current approaches to advanced theological study too often teach people to answer questions that nobody is asking. We train emerging leaders to learn and then teach in culturally inappropriate patterns, answering questions using thought processes which people in the local context find unconvincing in their cultural frames of thinking. We haven't realized that the time to dig a well is now – not after we see that irrelevance has caused theological education to auto-combust.

Drawing on many of the issues raised earlier in the collection, in this final section of our collection we investigate alternative forms of scholarship in advanced theological studies to traditional assignments, theses, and dissertations. While at first glance many of these forms may appear "non-academic," our experience is that they require more work, more engagement between text and context, and much more creativity than a traditional thesis. At the same time, when emerging leaders in the Majority World are empowered to use locally significant approaches, both the commitment to the process and the end result are enhanced.

The first suggestion of portfolios is not new to global higher education. Already there is a growing recognition that a single piece of work (though substantial) rarely satisfies the desired outcomes of advanced study. Joanna Feliciano-Soberano (Academic Dean, Asian Theological Seminary, Philippines) guides us through both the philosophy and the process of portfolio development as an often preferable means of demonstrating doctoral competency.

The traditional dissertation is to some extent a relic of an era of non-digital technologies. With the expanding technological capabilities available to us today, innovative possibilities abound. Marvin Oxenham (Program Leader in Theological Education, London School of Theology) has critically engaged with the literature, theoretical commitments, and practices associated with digital scholarship, and introduces us to this rapidly changing world.

In stark contrast to the depersonalizing approach of much advanced theological study, Sam Ewell was enabled in his PhD at the University of Birmingham to use an autoethnographic approach to doing "theology from the middle." The end result is an extraordinarily rich engagement with the work of Ivan Illich. Sam's voice is evident on every page of his thesis. In his chapter he describes his journey and sketches the shape and approach he took.

In much of the Majority World the preferred rhetorical patterns are through story, proverb, and poetry, rather than the linear-rationalist argumentation generally required in advanced study. The final four chapters present samples of what quality scholarship might look like in these contextually significant forms.

Havilah demonstrates how a major theological issue in the book of Judges might be addressed through the classical form of multi-layered narrative. Due to space restrictions in this collection the sample she gives is a smaller piece at the master's level. However, it is clear that comparable work could be completed as a major master's or doctoral project. Dwi Maria Handayani (Bandung Theological Seminary, Indonesia) similarly uses dialogue as a form through which to develop a master's-level thesis proposal.

Xiaoli Yang (University of Divinity, Australia) brings us an insightful reflection on poetry as theology. As is common through much of the Majority World, Xiaoli finds poetry a preferable vehicle for engaging with God, and for reflecting theologically on the world in which we live. More than this, Xiaoli points to the creative act itself as part of God's essential character. Xiaoli provides samples of what this might mean in practice, including the work of advanced theological studies. Our collection closes with a brief anthology of poems, suggesting different ways in which this extraordinarily profound form of communication might enrich our learning and theological expression.

You have probably noticed that most of the chapters in our collection produced by non-Caucasian women have fallen into this final section on innovative forms. This was not intentional. While a limited sample, nonetheless the implications are significant and simply reinforce the central concerns of the collection as a whole. If the church is to benefit from the full richness of its resources – male and female, from every tribe and nation – then it is imperative that innovative forms be embraced and extended.

17

Exploring the Possibilities of Portfolio as an Alternative to the Traditional Dissertation

Joanna Feliciano-Soberano

Introduction

It would be a refreshing learning experience if we who have gone through the phases of a traditional dissertation could sit together (over coffee or tea) and relive those moments. And then to imagine together what could have been done differently, now that we have experienced the bigger realities of our vocations and ministry contexts. For us in the teaching vocation, I am sure one of the threads of discussion would be the challenges of teaching in increasingly multicultural classrooms. Reflecting on my many years of teaching, I can think of many stories.

For example, late last year, I taught a small group of Asian students in Manila on a doctoral-level course. The advantage for me in this two-week intensive course was that I got to know each student quite well. Aside from their families and faith stories, I discovered aspects of their personal journeys in the quest for knowing, the experiences they brought to the table, and the competencies that had been developed. Because the pedagogies applied were highly participative and collaborative, I got to hear each one speak. I found them to be confident as they articulated their ideas even in their not-so-perfect English. My frustration began when the written articulations were submitted. And so the dilemma of the teacher: Is it fair for these equally gifted students to be subjected to the same writing box as are native English speakers?

Another story. I was chosen to be part of the dissertation committee for a pastor completing his DMin program. The more I get to know this pastor, the more I come to admire his gift of leadership within the community of faith. He is a reflective practitioner, and one who has successfully built transformational ministries. But the rigorous academic exercise has taken him away from his family and ministry already. Is there an alternative dissertation process and format for this pastor which will honour what he has accomplished already and which will then encourage him to strengthen and develop his competencies for the sake of the ministry?

Clearly, there is a growing mismatch between the traditionally accepted outcomes of higher learning in theological education and the changing demands of ministry contexts.[1] This paper delineates what a Dissertation by Portfolio is and argues for its usefulness as a legitimate alternative to a traditional dissertation, particularly for students of different cultures and languages, and for those whose goal is to develop as quality reflective practitioners in their chosen fields. This paper argues for the breadth, contextual relevance, creativity, and versatility of a portfolio approach to doctoral research.

The Concept of an Integrated Portfolio

Most of us are already familiar with the idea of portfolios. The *Cambridge English Dictionary* defines "portfolio" simply as "a collection of drawings, documents, etc. that represents a person's, especially an artist's, work." There

---

1. Actually, the call for reassessment of the value of the traditional doctoral dissertation has been made since the early 1990s. See the article by Peter Monaghan, "Some Fields Are Reassessing the Value of the Traditional Doctoral Education," *The Chronicle of Higher Education* 35, no. 29 (1989): A1.

are many of us who use "Portfolio Assessment"[2] as a way to measure the learning of our students. In the early 1990s, electronic portfolios surfaced, in which electronic technologies are used to design and present works.[3] Recently, a faculty-initiated portfolio system called Polaris was created for mechanical engineering students to showcase their best works, to reinforce the link between academy and practice, and as a metacognitive strategy to reflect on learning and monitor achievement.[4]

If one Googles "portfolio images," a host of portfolio collections is revealed in a variety of genres and sizes. By its very nature, a portfolio invites works of all kinds that speak of creativity, practicability, originality, usefulness, teamwork, and being cutting edge, contextual, relevant, meaningful, experiential, exploratory, authentic, and long term – the sort of learning outcomes advocated in the twenty-first century.

This basic definition and imagery of portfolio is the feature of an emerging model of dissertation, Dissertation by Portfolio (DbP), an approach originally developed by Crowther and Hill[5] for technical research projects. The use of portfolio in doctoral education has already become a trend worldwide.[6] Crowther and Hill elaborate the use of portfolio at doctoral level: "In the case of dissertations, the portfolio is seen as a means of supplementing the traditional dissertation format in order to enable a wide range of characteristics to be presented. There are also potential benefits in terms of how the process of building a portfolio can further improve learners' abilities, especially for

---

2. We ask students to collate significant pieces of work at the end of a course so that we can determine the satisfactory achievement of course benchmarks.
3. Helen Barrett and Joanne Carney, "Conflicting Paradigms and Competing Purposes in Electronic Portfolio Development," *Educational Assessment* (July 2005): 1, http://electronicportfolios.com/portfolios/LEAJournal-BarrettCarney.pdf.
4. Marilyn M. Lombardi, "Authentic Learning for the 21st Century: An Overview," *EDUCAUSE Learning Initiative* (2007): 1–12, https://www.educause.edu/ir/library/pdf/ELI3009.pdf.
5. This paper utilizes the term "Dissertation by Portfolio," or DbP, taken from Paul Crowther and Richard Hill, "Dissertation by Portfolio: An Alternative Approach to the Traditional Thesis," *Student Engagement and Experience Journal* 1, no. 2 (2012): 1–12, doi:10.7190/seej.v1i2.28.
6. See T. W. Maxwell and Glenda Kupczyk-Romanczuk, "Producing the Professional Doctorate: The Portfolio as a Legitimate Alternative to the Dissertation," *Innovations in Education and Teaching International* 46, no. 2 (2009): 6; and Nell Duke and Sarah Beck, "Education Should Consider Alternative Formats for the Dissertation," *Educational Researcher* 28, no. 3 (1999): 33.

employment and life-long learning."⁷ A dissertation by portfolio is not just a collection of work or a general portfolio with loosely connected pieces. A DbP is qualified as distinctly integrative because it is conceptualized with a connecting thread that weaves the pieces of work together. It also serves as a demonstration of the fulfilment of expected outcomes.

Purposes of Portfolios

The intention of a portfolio, and particularly the specific audience of readers, is very important because "it impacts form and content significantly."⁸ In education, portfolios are commonly used as assessment tools to measure learning and accountability. Both of these purposes are significant for our discussion of DbP.

In the portfolio for learning, the student authors, owns, and makes decisions on the approach, content, and progress of the portfolio. This kind of portfolio is used as a learning resource and as a formative assessment tool to monitor and coach the learning progress of the student. The emphasis is clearly on the "process of creating" a portfolio and on the "voice" of the learner.⁹

Portfolio for accountability is a summative assessment to "document and assess the achievement of externally defined skills or competencies" or achievement of standards of performance. Portfolio for accountability is often required for certification or graduation.¹⁰

But a word of caution from Barrett and Carney: the two purposes could be conflicting when combined in one portfolio. For example, a portfolio for learning may have gaps that will not be helpful for someone trying to show achievement on performance.¹¹ The key is to be mindful of the purpose and audience of the portfolio, and to "design a balanced system for assessment and learning."¹²

---

7. Crowther and Hill, "Dissertation by Portfolio," 5.
8. Barrett and Carney, "Conflicting Paradigms," 3.
9. Barrett and Carney, 2.
10. Barrett and Carney, 2.
11. For a more detailed comparison of formative assessment and summative assessment, see Barrett and Carney, 6.
12. Barrett and Carney, 8.

Models of Integrated Portfolio

The structure and process of the integrated portfolio may be demonstrated using multiple models. I here present two.

First, there is the Greek Temple Model by Maxwell and Kupczyk-Romanczuk, posited particularly for the professional doctorate.[13] They contend that the traditional dissertation's strength in terms of its focus and in-depth analysis is also its weakness in that it often falls short in relevance for the professional workplace. The workplace is now characterized by "complexity and intensity" with diverse demands, calling for a range of potential research questions, not just one.[14] Consequently, an integrated portfolio may be more relevant for the professional doctorate in that it incorporates a collection of works that are germane to the professional workplace. Like artists honing their skills for various expressions of art, the professional doctoral student is also challenged to explore possibilities in research and presentation, and in acquiring and developing competencies.

Maxwell and Kupczyk-Romanczuk[15] posit two architectural images which can help clarify how the proposed integrated portfolio differs from a traditional dissertation. The form and process of a traditional dissertation is likened to building a skyscraper. This towering architecture is built on a very deep foundation and eventually emerges to be a single edifice that narrows significantly as it gains height. Skyscrapers boast of connectivity and strength that can be explored within. In contrast, the integrated portfolio as a dissertation is likened to building a Greek temple with its complex appearance. The Greek temple starts from a very broad but solid base on which columns are constructed to reach the roof. The roof is overarching. The design of each column may vary, depending on the artist. The Greek temple stands as a work of art that images breadth, beauty, strength, creativity, and novelty.

The specifics of the integrated portfolio using the Greek temple simile are encapsulated in table 17.1.

---

13. Crowther and Hill, "Dissertation by Portfolio"; Maxwell and Kupczyk-Romanczuk, "Producing the Professional Doctorate."
14. Maxwell and Kupczyk-Romanczuk, "Producing the Professional Doctorate," 6.
15. Maxwell and Kupczyk-Romanczuk, 10.

Table 17.1: Parts of the Temple Model of Integrated Portfolio Summarized and Adapted from Maxwell and Kupczyk-Romanczuk[16]

The Roof or Pediment	The integrative thread, the "linking paper" that gives coherence to the whole portfolio. This could be in the form of one paper, or a "combination of development of themes and diagrammatic presentations" holding the pieces of research together.
The Columns or Pillars	Columns are the research pieces. The row of columns, or peristyle, supports the roof. Columns vary in design, size, and appearance and are situated on a solid base.
The Base or Foundation	The solid base is the foundation of the temple, representing the professional experience of the researcher that he/she brings to the topic of research.
The Learner	The researcher is the artist who conceptualizes the portfolio, bringing his/her experiences, standing on the base of the temple symbolizing the "voice" and "validity" of the research.

In the Greek Temple Model, the critical piece of the structure is the overarching pediment. Additionally, the professional experience of the researcher is a distinguishing quality of the integrated portfolio. This is why the researcher is represented in the structure of the portfolio, positioned standing on the base or foundation to symbolize the validity of the researcher's own voice, "especially in terms of the authenticity of the researcher as an experienced professional and hence the credibility that is brought to bear upon the analysis."[17]

Muldoon builds on the Greek Temple Model in her work "What Does a Professional Doctorate Portfolio Look Like?" Figure 17.1 is Muldoon's interpretation of Maxwell and Kupczyk-Romanczuk's temple model as she reflected on her own integrated portfolio for the nursing profession.[18]

What she helpfully adds to the model is the way she imaged the components of the temple: the pediment includes the personal reflection of the researcher; the base is composed of supporting documents aside from the professional experience of the researcher; and the pillars could be three research questions in cluster. To get started, she suggests matrix planning, "a method of conceptualization of the research task by using key elements

---

16. Maxwell and Kupczyk-Romanczuk, 9–10.
17. Maxwell and Kupczyk-Romanczuk, 10.
18. Robyn Muldoon, "What Does a Professional Doctorate Portfolio Look Like?," *Ergo* 1, no. 3 (2010): 38. Used by permission.

of research design as row and column headings," as shown in the in-process matrix in table 17.2.[19]

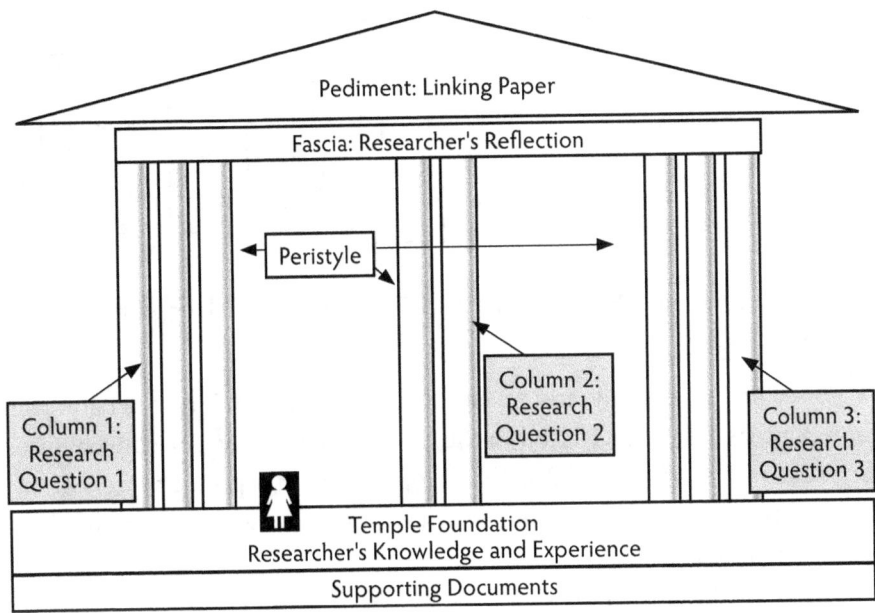

Figure 17.1: Muldoon's Interpretation of Maxwell and Kupczyk-Romanczuk's Temple Model

Muldoon reimages the Greek Temple Model for an integrated portfolio as shown in figure 17.2.[20]

Table 17.2: In-Process Matrix for Research Design

Research Questions	Sub-Questions	Data Source	Data Analysis	Output	Temple Part	Possible Publication

---

19. Muldoon, "What Does a Professional Doctorate Portfolio Look Like?," 37–38.
20. Muldoon, 40. Used by permission.

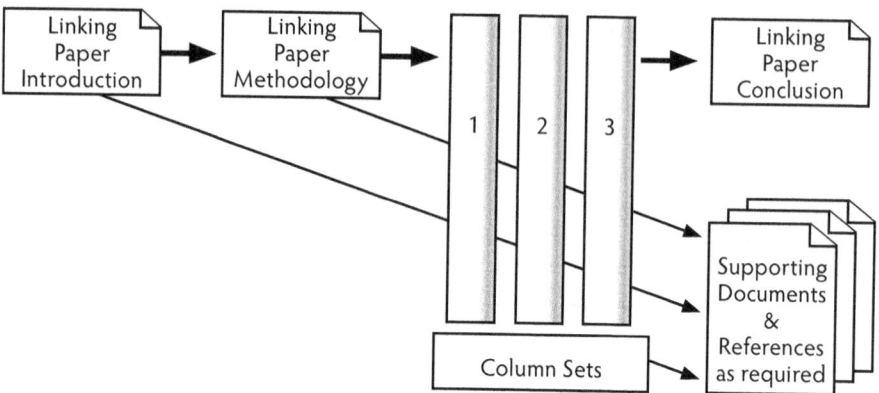

Figure 17.2: Muldoon's Reimaging of the Greek Temple Model for an Integrated Portfolio

A second model, and most recent, is that developed by Crowther and Hill for a master's-level dissertation in the field of technology. For convenience, let us call it the Artefact Model. They proposed the six specific aspects of the DbP[21] with descriptions and their corresponding number of requirements as represented in table 17.3.

Each aspect of the portfolio as presented in table 17.3 is referred to as "evidence," although the term "evidence" refers more particularly to the first three aspects – artefact, annotation, and critical reflection. A piece of evidence may include one or more artefacts. The pieces of evidence are produced by the learner as a result of experiences and should be tied to the learning outcomes or purpose of the portfolio "to make sure it is relevant and part of a cohesive whole."[22] Clusters of artefacts are held together and described by an "overall reflective summary." The DbP roadmap to developing a portfolio begins with a research question, works through a demonstration of the ability to create and produce evidence of the student's work, and ends with an integrative artefact.[23]

---

21. Crowther and Hill, "Dissertation by Portfolio," 6–9.
22. Crowther and Hill, 5.
23. Crowther and Hill, 7.

Table 17.3: Various Aspects of a Dissertation by Portfolio, Abridged and Adapted from Crowther and Hill

Artefact (many per DbP, minimum of three)	A tangible product that documents an activity or experience. This can be an audio file, video file, picture or pictures, written text (report, email, feedback, online discussion, project plan), diagram, table, model, design, or anything that is produced as a result of some relevant activity.
Annotation (many per DbP, minimum of three)	A description that shows what, by whom, when, and why the artefact was produced. It should also explain "what" it shows: some problem solved or learning progression.
Critical Reflection (many per DbP, minimum of three)	An explanation or argument for the inclusion of the artefact and its annotation. Why was it included within the portfolio? What does it illustrate about learning?
Overall Reflective Summary (one per DbP)	A scholarly piece of writing that connects the evidence together to "make sense" of the individual items. Essentially this aspect takes the individual pieces of evidence and tells a story about what has been achieved over the duration of the work.
Index/Contents (one per DbP)	Some form of indexing that enables the reader to navigate the portfolio.
Mapping Matrix of Criteria to Evidence (one per DbP)	A table that relates each piece of evidence to the relevant assessment criteria.

Crowther and Hill apply the same assessment criteria for the traditional dissertation as the marking grid for a DbP:[24]

1. *Knowledge of the domain:* Critically review the relevant literature within the domain of discourse and identify, set, and justify the focus for the investigation.
2. *Justification of the approach:* Select, apply, and evaluate a suitable methodological approach.
3. *Description of the research and discussion of the outcomes:* Conduct the research program and discuss the outcome of the research.
4. *Quality of the report (portfolio in this case) and presentation of the argument:* Draw valid conclusions from the evidence gathered and produce an academic dissertation.

---

24. Crowther and Hill, 8.

The two models of DbP presented above share the following assumptions: (1) the significance of the integrative thread; (2) the importance of the intended outcomes that should shape the portfolio; (3) the varied forms of evidence or artefacts; and (4) the intention to bridge the gap between theory and practice. The Artefact Model of a dissertation by portfolio is aimed to be a coherent, integrated program of research-based work. The strength of the model is that it allows the learner to conceptualize the whole portfolio and make decisions about the kinds of evidence needed. The gap I see in this model of DbP is that it is conceptualized to fit the learning outcomes of a traditional dissertation. In my opinion, the possibilities for a portfolio in terms of creativity and relevance should not be confined within the strict marking grid of the traditional dissertation.

What I find as the strength of the Greek Temple Model, aside from the breadth of possibilities of evidence, is the intentional inclusion of ownership and the voice of the researcher as a critical piece in the portfolio. I see the very active engagement of the researcher – from conceptualization, to actual research, to presentation – as the fundamental shift from the traditional dissertation.

In both models the role of the dissertation adviser is no longer to direct the whole portfolio but is now limited to coaching and assessment. More importantly, because of the nature of DbP as an integrated collection of evidence produced by a student, supervisors, mentors, and coaches are likely to get to know their students far beyond their academic competencies.

Possibilities for DbP in Theological Education

While I would advocate for the DbP to be applied in all doctoral programs,[25] this paper primarily focuses on the professional doctorate, as the DbP is appropriate and significant for advanced professional studies. Maxwell and Kupczyk-Romanczuk describe the purpose of a professional doctorate as follows: "The professional doctorate is a program of research, scholarship and advanced study which enables candidates to make a significant contribution to

---

25. As a critical response to the "mismatch between academically oriented doctoral programs and professionally oriented doctoral students." See Doug Archbald, "'Breaking the Mold' in the Dissertation: Implementing A Problem-Based, Decision-Oriented Thesis Project," *The Journal of Continuing Higher Education* 58 (2010): 10.

knowledge and practice in their professional context. In doing so, the candidate may also contribute more generally to scholarship within the discipline or field of study. Professional doctorate students should be required to apply their research and study to problems, issues or other matters of substance which produce significant benefits in professional practice."[26]

In theological education, several doctoral degrees are clustered within the professional doctorate: for example, PhD in Intercultural Studies or Missions, Pastoral Studies, Christian or Religious Education, Counselling, Homiletics, and Community Development; and also DMin, ThD, EdD, and DMiss programs.

The Greek Temple Model provides the flexibility for us to imagine and reimagine the DbP. The key to the successful building of an integrated portfolio is the defined purposes or learning outcomes. In the professional doctorate, it is important that the outcomes of a dissertation should provide "significant benefits in professional practice."[27]

A. *Proposed Outcomes of a Dissertation by Portfolio*

The twin purpose of the portfolio – namely, portfolio for learning and portfolio for accountability – should be fundamental to the DbP. The portfolio should not only demonstrate the attainment of high levels of thinking skills (according to Bloom's and Fink's taxonomies)[28] and development of competencies (conceptual thinking, problem-solving skills, skill of effective communication, and skill of research and collaboration); the portfolio itself should also serve as a helpful resource for students and teachers, and contribute knowledge to the field.

---

26. Maxwell and Kupczyk-Romanczuk, "Producing the Professional Doctorate," 4.
27. Maxwell and Kupczyk-Romanczuk, 4.
28. B. Bloom et al., *Taxonomy of Educational Objectives, Handbook 1: Cognitive Domain* (London: Longman, 1956); L. Dee Fink, *Creating Significant Learning Experiences: An Integrated Approach to Designing College Courses* (San Francisco: Jossey-Bass, 2003).

I therefore propose two overarching assessment criteria to serve as guidelines for the development of a DbP for the professional doctorate, followed by six outcomes that might serve as a marking grid for the portfolio.[29]

Assessment Criteria

1. The portfolio represents a personal work based on a clearly defined area of inquiry that reflects a research focus and process.
2. The portfolio is composed of an organized series of related works that form a coherent piece of work in the area of expertise or vocation.

Benchmarks

At the culmination of the portfolio, the student should have demonstrated achievement of the following benchmarks (marking grid):

1. Understanding of the key concepts related to the research questions (foundational knowledge).
2. Design of integrated, relevant, and clear research methods to provide needed data for further development of the topic.
3. Identification, selection, analysis, and evaluation of key findings and discussions on the research topic posited in literature and presented through a variety of sources (e.g. PPT's, seminars, interviews, case studies, immersion, team projects, or other forms of personal engagement).
4. Presentation of key findings and personal experiences in creative ways.
5. Creation of a matrix to show the connections and relevance of information or data for each piece of the portfolio.
6. Documentation of personal involvement and awareness of the process of learning (metacognition).

The proposed benchmarks or outcomes are specific enough for students and DbP coaches or supervisors to make decisions as to the number and kinds of artefacts needed.

---

29. Some ideas on guidelines were adapted from Ross McCormick, "Faculty Guidelines to Thesis, Dissertation, Research Portfolio," accessed 15 January 2017, https://www.fmhs.auckland.ac.nz/assets/fmhs/faculty/FOR/future-postgraduates/docs/guidelines_thesis_dsstion_resrchportfolio.pdf.

B. A Proposed DbP for Doctorates in Education (PhD and EdD)

Doctoral candidates in education (PhD and EdD) will most likely be offered a position of educational leadership upon completion, and DbP is particularly relevant for preparing a person for a vocation such as dean. In a PhD or EdD in education, what might a DbP in preparation for work as a dean look like?

The portfolio should follow the learning outcomes suggested above. A possible conceptualization might include the steps, descriptions, and suggestions shown in table 17.4 (using the Greek Temple Model).

Table 17.4: A Proposed DbP for Doctorates in Education (PhD and EdD)

Step 1 and Step 8 *RQ* What are the factors that contribute to the effective role of the dean in my context? What is the value of this knowledge for me and for others?	The main RQ is the integrative thread or the linking paper of the whole portfolio. Although naming the RQ is the first step, the candidate will build an integrative essay which will be completed when each pillar of the portfolio is accomplished.	
Step 2 *Sub-RQs* What information is already out there? What data would be helpful for me?	**Step 3** *Research Methodology* How will I obtain the data needed?	**Step 4** *Evidence or Artefacts and Possible Modes of Presentation* What is the research saying, and what are the implications? How will I present data and analysis that is creative?
RQ1 What does the literature (primary and secondary) say about the critical role of the dean?	Literature research	1. Annotated bibliography of primary and secondary sources on the topic 2. A scholarly essay explaining the role of the dean according to literature 3. A summary of new innovations in instructional leadership

RQ2 Why is the vocation important? What are the expected tasks of a dean of a seminary?	1. Field research (interviews of at least 5 key people in deanship position, current and retired) 2. Shadowing (spend at least a week with a person known to be a high-impact dean) 3. Attend a dean's seminar: observe and document (Propose an alternative research design if this is not possible) Or attend and observe an academic strategic planning retreat or other initiatives led by the dean 4. Collaborate with two or more deans to develop a detailed graduate level course on "Instructional Leadership"	1. Video presentation with permission 2. A documented experience of shadowing and lessons learned in PPT answering the RQ 3. A collage of activities in a dean's seminar with a summary of presentations, highlighting key observations A creative visual presentation of the experience with corresponding explanation on the critical role of the dean 4. A PPT presentation or a document
RQ3 What are the success indicators?	1. Literature research 2. Field research (interviews with or questionnaires from at least 3 of each of students, faculty, and staff) When do they say that the dean has effectively fulfilled his/her role? 3. Field research (interviews with a cluster of current and retired deans with the same questions as in #2 above)	1. PPT or critical reflection essay 2. Video presentation, or rap, or poetry, or presentation of "in vivo" quotes 3. A presentation of quotes from the deans as PPT or video with a synthesis at the end
		Form and Presentation

Step 5 *The Researcher's Experience* 1. What are the experiences I bring to this research? 2. What have I been learning and what has contributed to my learning in this field? (metacognition) 3. Valuing the RQ and the experience	This is the foundation of the research.	Stories of experiences in a collage, or essay that includes the suggested strands in step 5
Step 6 *Documentation in Appendices*		Actual evidence of research (e.g. letters asking for permission to do research, gathered data, other evidence of field experiences)
Step 7 *A Matrix or Index of Contents*		Can be a Table of Contents

Note that the building of columns for the temple is not just a haphazard collection of research materials and presentation. Each piece of research design requires an analysis of data and the identification and summary of key findings with implications for learning and practice. In other words, no matter how the artefact is presented, the data is carefully drawn out of the research design. The media for presentation of the data can also be diverse, particularly in the light of recent developments in technology. The beauty of the whole portfolio is seen in the way the *linking paper* now weaves all the pieces of the portfolio together to provide an answer to the main RQ. Other possible evidence might include:

1. Actual interviews and observations of instructional leaders in various contexts to determine best practices (to be presented as a journal article or a PowerPoint presentation delving into the role of the dean);
2. Work with a consultant trying to assist an institution in implementing academic initiatives;

3. Collaboration with colleagues in designing a curriculum workshop for faculty, and actual delivery with summary statements and assessment;
4. Design and conduct of an impact assessment of curriculum.

A DbP for my Asian students would have been a more meaningful dissertation process. The traditional approach which confines the candidate within the cloisters of the program restricts possibilities and opportunities for sourcing knowledge "out there" and for developing "real-world skills."

C. A Proposed DbP for a DMin Program

What is a possible alternative dissertation for the pastor mentioned at the start? Following the assessment criteria as previously given, a DbP for a DMin program might have the following steps and components:

1. *Intended audience and purpose statement* (e.g. for church leaders and students).
2. *An overarching research question* (e.g. How does one start a ministry platform other than church planting? and a corollary RQ: What are key factors that contribute to the growth of this ministry?).
3. *Evidence*: the artefacts are data from research methodologies connected to the RQs. Suggested research design and evidence are shown in table 17.5.

Table 17.5: Proposed Research Designs and Presentation of Evidence for DbP or a DMin Program

Research Design	Evidence or Artefact	Presentation
Literature Research	An annotated bibliography of primary and secondary sources	Essay form or a paper presentation
	A critical reflection on some popular trends of leadership in new ministries (e.g. movement leader, servant leader, steward leader)	

Field Research	A collection of stories from leaders who started a new ministry and succeeded, with synthesis and analysis	Video presentation
	A collection of stories from leaders who started a new ministry and failed, with synthesis and analysis	Video presentation
	An immersion experience or field observation of a church leader actually doing ministry, and conduct of an impact assessment	A collage of pictures with descriptions
		An article written on the combination of stories in a local Christian magazine, with analysis
Learning from Educators	Partnering with educators and designing a curriculum for church leaders on ways to start and sustain ministry based on literature research, interviews, observations, and immersion experiences	A written form of the detailed curriculum design and materials to be used
	Partnering with educators and other pastors and conducting 2 seminar-workshops for a small group of pastors and church workers (around 20). Planning for the event, promoting and delivering the curriculum, with assessment	Documentation with pictures

4. *The experience as the foundation of the DbP.* A DMin student like the pastor has started a ministry and the ministry has flourished under his leadership. He will submit a document explaining the planning steps or initiatives taken, and the ways these initiatives were achieved, and will include an assessment of his learning (metacognition).
5. *The index of contents of the portfolio*, in a document form.
6. *The linking paper* is the purposeful integrative thread that weaves all the pieces of evidence (including experiences) together into one story that responds to the two stated RQs with personal reflections. The linking paper can be in the form of a journal article or a paper the pastor would present in a seminar.

A DbP for the DMin student/pastor would have been a fitting learning task which valued the richness of his leadership experiences and which would hone other skills, like teaching and training others.

D. Some More Clarification on the Distinctives and Process of DbP

I had the chance to bounce back ideas from this paper with some of my colleagues. There were some expressions of hesitancy regarding the legitimacy of the DbP. As I pondered over our conversations, I gathered that the pushback is actually connected with the versatile nature of the portfolio and concern that this flexibility might compromise the required higher levels of thinking. Given another opportunity, our continuing conversation would explore together the ways critical thinking could be demonstrated and assessed, because assessments of learning and for learning carry numerous indicators. Consequently, DbP coaches and supervisors need to be oriented fully to the format and purposes of a portfolio.[30]

Another hesitancy is based on the gargantuan task of completing a DbP. It is definitely a big task if developed towards the end of a program. However, the distinct advantage of a DbP over the traditional dissertation is that there is the potential for the student to begin to conceptualize and build the "Greek Temple" during the first semester of study.[31] From the beginning of the program, students can also document significant experiences in the past or those which are concurrently happening in the present that have significantly contributed to their shaping as scholars and practitioners. Students can also be on the look-out for seminars, workshops, immersion experiences, and other possibilities of sourcing and acquiring knowledge beyond the classroom. The DbP is not intended to be a culminating activity of the doctoral program, but a formative process. Assessment of learning lies not only in the final product, but also in the actual process of building a portfolio. And so the researcher

---

30. Maxwell and Kupzcyk-Romanczuk raise the issue of the unpreparedness of DbP supervisors and readers for the task. They observe that, because present academics have only the traditional dissertation as their experience, they bring this expertise in evaluating portfolios. Maxwell and Kupczyk-Romanczuk, "Producing the Professional Doctorate," 11–12.

31. With the implication that a doctoral course on Research Methods should be offered during the first semester of coursework.

can strategize, take risks, and make critical decisions in the process (including redefining RQs). The "defence" also invites possibilities in terms of creativity, modality, and audience composition. Can we imagine presenting the defence in rap?[32] Why not?

Can we possibly apply DbP in the more academically inclined doctoral programs? I believe so. If we aim for the strict standards of a traditional dissertation to be imposed on a DbP, then the Artefact Model will be helpful in structure and process. However, if we bring flexibility in our standards, then the Greek Temple Model may be more helpful. Such flexibility may entail the resourcing and presentation of artefacts and research pieces in different forms and media, even in the use of local language and contextually sensitive expressions.

If we continue to insist that the goal of a dissertation is simply "to meet the requirements for receiving a doctoral degree, proving that one has mastered the skills necessary to succeed in one's chosen scholarly field,"[33] then we lose much. In particular, we miss out on bringing the exploratory and cutting-edge approaches to research, and the opportunities offered by emerging technologies, all of which resonate well with DbP. More importantly, we miss out on honouring the experiences and learning goals of students. In contrast, the approach of DbP advances the development of "real-world" skills, life-long and life-wide learning, which are very limited in the traditional dissertation. I believe that DbP redefines what academic and professional excellence means.

Concluding Thoughts: Bridging the Theory and Practice Divide

Authenticity in teaching compels us to ask this question: Should the required means for completion of a doctoral program be the same for everyone? The intended outcomes of twenty-first-century learning for postgraduate work are about more than finishing a rigorous and focused research. The conversation has

---

32. See the recent article by Fernanda Zamudio-Suaréz, "An Activist Defends His Dissertation in Rap," *The Chronicle of Higher Education*, 27 February 2017, http://www.chronicle.com/article/An-Activist-Defends-His/239335.
33. Duke and Beck, "Education Should Consider," 31.

now shifted to the potential for impact that we can imagine in the dissertation process. At this turn of the century, conversations pertaining to the many limitations of the traditional dissertation have been widely addressed, including in other chapters in this collection – not that another mould is perfect, but an alternative model might be more responsive to the changing times, to the multicultural realities, and to the changing demands of ministry contexts. The integrated portfolio as an emerging model bridging theory and practice will continue to be explored and improved. The suggestions given in this chapter are a possible starting point for implementing DbP as we seek missional impact in the service of God's kingdom.

Discussion Questions

1. Describe one or two key ways in which a portfolio might better serve the process of developing missional leadership for the church than would a traditional dissertation.

2. One of the greatest concerns in contemporary higher education is that the traditional dissertation approach to advanced studies produces people who are competent in research, but oftentimes weak or incompetent in communication, teaching, and administration. These latter areas are becoming an increasing concern for accrediting agencies. What elements of your own current role were not adequately addressed in your doctoral studies? How might these elements be brought into a portfolio for doctoral examination? What would you include in such a portfolio?

3. What are two or three of the most significant barriers to the implementation of Dissertation by Portfolio in the advanced studies programs of your school? Suggest one or two specific and tangible actions that you and other leaders at your school might take to address these concerns.

4. Consider a significant leader in the church in your region who might benefit from greater depth of reflection on practice. With one or two others sketch out what a portfolio of theory and practice might look like for such a leader, through which he or she could demonstrate appropriate levels of synthetic, evaluative, creative, and communication competencies.

5. The examples given in this chapter have focused on advanced ministerial studies, but mention has also been made of the relevance of a portfolio for other fields. With one or two others sketch out what a portfolio dissertation might look like in one of the following areas of emphasis: biblical studies; church history; theological studies.

Bibliography

Anderson, Lorin, and David Krathwohl, eds. *A Taxonomy for Learning, Teaching, and Assessing: A Revision of Bloom's Taxonomy of Educational Objectives*. 1st ed. New York: Longman, 2001.

Archbald, Doug. "'Breaking the Mold' in the Dissertation: Implementing a Problem-Based, Decision-Oriented Thesis Project." *The Journal of Continuing Higher Education* 58 (2010): 99–107.

Barrett, Helen. "Electronic Teaching Portfolios: Multimedia Skills + Portfolio Development = Powerful Professional Development." In *Society for Information Technology and Teacher Education International Conference 2000*, edited by Dee Anna Willis, Jerry Price, and Jerry Willis, 1111–1116. Waynesville: Association for the Advancement of Computing in Education, 2000. http://electronicportfolios.com/portfolios/3107Barrett.pdf.

Barrett, Helen, and Joanne Carney. "Conflicting Paradigms and Competing Purposes in Electronic Portfolio Development." *Educational Assessment* (July 2005): 1–14. http://electronicportfolios.com/portfolios/LEAJournal-BarrettCarney.pdf.

Bloom, B., M. Engelhurt, E. Furst, W. Hill, and D. Krathwohl. *Taxonomy of Educational Objectives. Handbook 1: Cognitive Domain*. London: Longman, 1956.

Brandenburg, Robyn, and Jacqueline Wilson. *Pedagogies of the Future: Leading Quality Teaching and Learning in Higher Education*. 1st ed. Rotterdam: Sense, 2013.

Crowther, Paul, and Richard Hill. "Dissertation by Portfolio: An Alternative Approach to the Traditional Thesis." *Student Engagement and Experience Journal* 1, no. 2 (2012): 1–12.

Dewey, John. *Experience and Education*. 1st ed. New York: Collier Books, 1938.

Duke, Nell, and Sarah Beck. "Education Should Consider Alternative Formats for the Dissertation." *Educational Researcher* 28, no. 3 (1999): 31–36.

Fink, L. Dee. *Creating Significant Learning Experiences: An Integrated Approach to Designing College Courses*. 1st ed. San Francisco: Wiley & Sons, 2003.

Kilbourn, Brent. "Defense." *Teachers College Record*, 15 June 2016. https://www.tcrecord.org/content.asp?contentid=12543.

Lombardi, Marilyn. "Authentic Learning for the 21st Century: An Overview." *EDUCAUSE Learning Initiative* (2007). https://www.educause.edu/ir/library/pdf/ELI3009.pdf.

Maxwell, T. W., and Glenda Kupczyk-Romanczuk. "Producing the Professional Doctorate: The Portfolio as a Legitimate Alternative to the Dissertation." *Innovations in Education and Teaching International* 46, no. 2 (2009): 1–17.

McCormick, Ross. "Faculty Guidelines to Thesis, Dissertation, Research Portfolio." Accessed 15 January 2017. https://www.fmhs.auckland.ac.nz/assets/fmhs/faculty/FOR/future-postgraduates/docs/guidelines_thesis_dsstion_resrchportfolio.pdf.

Monaghan, Peter. "Some Fields Are Reassessing the Value of the Traditional Doctoral Dissertation." *The Chronicle of Higher Education* 35, no. 29 (1989): A1.

Muldoon, Robyn. "What Does a Professional Doctorate Portfolio Look Like?" *Ergo* 1, no. 3 (2010): 35–43.

Patton, Stacey. "The Dissertation Can No Longer Be Defended." *The Chronicle of Higher Education*, 11 February 2013. http://www.chronicle.com/article/The-Dissertation-Can-No-Longer/137215.

Thomas, Rebecca Arlene. "The Effectiveness of Alternative Dissertation Models in Graduate Education." Master's thesis, Brigham Young University, 2015.

Vella, Jane. *Taking Learning to Task: Creative Strategies for Teaching Adults*. 1st ed. San Francisco: Jossey-Bass, 2001.

Yung, Hwa. "Critical Issues Facing Theological Education in Asia." *Transformation* 12, no. 4 (1995): 1–6.

Zamudio-Suaréz, Fernanda. "An Activist Defends His Dissertation in Rap." *The Chronicle of Higher Education*, 27 February 2017. http://www.chronicle.com/article/An-Activist-Defends-His/239335.

18

Digital Scholarship

Marvin Oxenham

I write as a scholar who has been awarded his PhD through a theoretical dissertation, obtained in a Russell Group British university and successively published through an academic editor. I examine and supervise students and work with colleagues committed to the provision of conventional British PhDs. All this is to say that my personal experience with advanced studies is traditional, conservative, and paper-shuffling.

What I will argue for in this chapter is not concerned with the search for a *better* way, but for possible *different* ways of doing advanced studies in theological education. The PhD remains a specific product with a venerable history, a vast body of literature on methodology, and a distinct sharpened focus, producing graduates who will normally be scholars, writers, and academics with a mastery of a discipline, and providing an original contribution to one area of knowledge. The thesis this chapter shares with the friends and colleagues writing this book is that there might be different ways of doing advanced theological studies and that some of these different ways might be explored through the changes that are brought by digital technology and in particular by the Internet.

With such a vast remit and quickly changing landscape, the scope of the chapter cannot but be illustrative, in the hope of sparking imagination and igniting new paradigms and discussions around higher research in theology. This chapter may be alien and difficult for some readers, mostly due to the fact that we are exploring what might be unfamiliar ground. The first part of the chapter, where we deal with the laws of technology and connectivism, is also quite dense and theoretical, although I have tried to build bridges into an audience that may not necessarily be specialized in such matters. If you make it through these pages you will probably find greater enjoyment in the more practical sections on digital scholarship, where you will hopefully also find some concrete ideas to spark your imagination. This chapter might anticipate the times in some contexts but I would like to think, however, that in a few years some may come back and have an "Aha!" moment, as the digital revolution becomes commonplace even in our ivory towers of theological education.

Laws of Technology

The choice of words in giving the title to this chapter is an interesting initial exercise as terms like *online* or *digital* are both complex and narrow at the same time. Also, to simply use *technology* is too broad as it encompasses all practical uses of scientific discoveries. Focusing in particular on *information technology* as that branch of technology concerned with the use of "computers and other electronic equipment to store and send information"[1] is another option, but the term IT is not immediately associated with education and much less with scholarship. The choice has therefore fallen on the title "Digital Scholarship" as a compromise, but one that immediately clarifies the key question this chapter investigates, which is: In what ways can/does the use of digital technology that is found in computers, the Internet, and other electronic equipment, and is capable of finding, storing, organizing, and developing information and knowledge, impact advanced research and scholarship in theology? Some initial considerations concerning the so-called laws of technology (here applied to information technology) will set us out on our exploration.

---

1. "Information Technology," *Cambridge Dictionary* online, http://dictionary.cambridge.org/dictionary/english/information-technology.

Underestimating Long-Term Effects

The First Law of Technology[2] claims that we tend to overestimate the short-term impact of new technologies while underestimating their longer-term effects. In a pungent short article for *The Observer*, John Naughton, the Open University's emeritus Professor of the Public Understating of Technology, draws an analogy of the Web with the printing press. When Gutenberg invented the printing press, the short-term impact was greatly acclaimed, as within forty years over 30,000 titles had been printed and published. But no one could have envisioned the longer-term effect of the printing press and its impact, for example, in fuelling the Reformation, enabling the rise of modern science, or in creating new social classes of clerks, teachers, and intellectuals.[3]

The First Law of Technology clearly applies to the work of Sir Tim Berners-Lee, who in 1989 invented the Web. Already today we can see that the changes are momentous and deeply impact the world of education and research: "Our new information landscape is digital bits in the ether instead of ink dots on paper. There is no foreseeable future in which we go back to analog."[4] Everyone in my generation recalls that, before the Internet, information was characterized by ink on paper, and as such it tended to be expensive, scarce, isolated, static, and slow to change. The mechanisms of publication were reserved for experts, the dissemination of results was relatively limited, and careful filtering always occurred before publication. After the Internet, this landscape becomes "bits in the ether," and these are now free or low-cost, abundant, hyper-connected, interactive, and in real time. The mechanisms of publication are also revolutionized as they become participatory, exponential (in dissemination and reach), and generally published first and filtered later. When it comes to research institutions, however, they tend to continue to

---

2. The label "First Law of Technology" is disputed, as other laws might claim the status "first," "second," etc., and there is no authoritative list. This law is also known as Amara's Law, as it was created by Roy Amara, scientist at Stanford Research Institute and president of the Institute for the Future.

3. J. Naughton, "Thanks, Gutenberg – But We're Too Pressed for Time to Read," *The Observer*, 27 January 2008, accessed 27 October 2016, https://www.theguardian.com/media/2008/jan/27/internet.pressandpublishing.

4. Scott McLeod, "Schools Are Supposed to Help Students Master the Dominant Information Landscape of Their Time," *dangerously ! irrelevant* (blog), 28 November 2016, http://dangerouslyirrelevant.org/2016/11/schools-are-supposed-to-help-students-master-the-dominant-information-landscape-of-their-time.html.

consolidate their abilities in ink dots, and do not excel in digital bits. While it is true that there are many who likely overestimate the current "digital revolution," the short-term impact before our eyes is already phenomenal and we must confess our difficulties in foreseeing the even greater long-term effects. What will it mean for scholars in forty years' time to have had constant, increasingly agile access to billions of pages of information, and immediate publication combined with global, instant, media-rich networking abilities with the rest of society? If we are, in fact, faced with a momentous cultural revolution that is driven and supported by digital technology, how do we respond as theologians and theological educators?

The responses to culture that Niebuhr presents in *Christ and Culture*[5] provide a scaffold for our options. Do we go *against* advances in digital technology as they impact higher research, and adopt a stance of resistance and traditionalism? Do we see *the work of God in* these advances and embrace them together with the epistemological challenges they bring? Or, as this chapter assumes, do we see that *Christ is above the cultural revolution*, and hence seek out the best elements of what digital technology brings and allow these changes to transform us, while at the same time engaging as active agents of transformation within the discipline of education that will align digital technology with kingdom truths and values?

Ageing Quickly

There are a number of other so-called laws of technology[6] that we will simply mention as we see how they also relate to the future of advanced studies in theology. Probably the most famous is Moore's Law (named after Gordon Moore, co-founder of Intel©), which states that the performance of hardware doubles about every two years. We have all seen our computing devices become smaller and more powerful, and what was inconceivable ten years ago is now indispensable. The examples that are featured in this chapter itself will likely be dated by the time the book is printed, and in five years' time readers will

---

5. H. Richard Niebuhr, *Christ and Culture* (New York: Harper & Row, 1975).
6. Steve Arndt, "4 Laws of Technology and How They Impact Your Business," 13 November 2014, accessed 27 October 2016, http://smarndt.com/2014/11/4-laws-of-technology-and-how-they-impact-your-business/.

smile at them as archaeological artefacts. This trend is destined to continue, so getting comfortable with old technology is probably not an option and we would do well to include critical consideration of and engagement with these growing developments as a standard feature in the methodological sections of all advanced studies.

Too Much Information

Segal's Law[7] provides another perspective, as it claims that a man with a watch knows what time it is, but a man with two watches is never sure. What this is saying is that too much information can become a curse as it impacts our ability to process information, make connections, be analytic and synthetic, and propose theses and decisions as a result. In a way, this is not new to advanced academic studies, and part of the process that leads to "doctoralness" is exactly the ability to process and stay on top and in control of vast amounts of data without losing the plot. But digital technology is exponentially enhancing the production of and the accessibility to even more information, and in one generation we have moved from a context of scarcity of available information, where one had to struggle to find valid and pertinent sources, to a context of an overabundance of information, where the key competences deal with filtering out and being selective.

The incredible power of search engines on the Internet poses both opportunities and challenges, especially as key words yield hundreds of thousands of results and we must be taught new search tactics. New issues will arise about the "appropriateness" of information found on the Web as the explosion in quantity will inevitably generate an issue of quality, and we can anticipate an avalanche of material in the network that will not qualify as scholarly or advanced (or even true and decent). Filtering and selectivity have become crucial competences for today's advanced research scholar, and we need to develop training programs that are fit for purpose.

---

7. Arndt, "4 Laws of Technology."

The Vehicle Is Designed for the Journey

Another law of technology is called Conway's Law,[8] and observes that all software, technological systems, and operations reflect the organizational structures that produce them. In other words, the vehicle is designed for the territory and the journey. If you are being given a freight train, it is designed to travel in specific circumstances, with set destinations and determined cargo capacities and speed. You cannot therefore enter the train and uncritically try to use it should your purposes be different, such as having an agile transportation vehicle to deliver pizza. The system will determine the journey. This law may seem to relate mostly to business and not to advanced studies, but as scholars we need to be aware that most of the technology we are engaging with is not value-free nor purpose-free. It is usually designed with some purpose in mind, which may not align perfectly with our purposes.

Sociologist Thorstein Veblen labelled the term "technological determinism," which is the fear that technology will shape human behaviour.[9] This fear is not new, and has accompanied the promises of emerging educational technologies over at least the last twenty years, from computers, to CD-ROMs and virtual reality, and today through the Internet, smartphones, social media, and gamification. While on the one hand, as theologians, we hold to the place of human agency and to the evaluative capacities of created beings to critically use new technologies, on the other hand, we would be naïve to claim that technologies have no impact on our pedagogy or educational philosophies, even as theological educators. Understanding these technologies deeply is a first step in the right direction of critical, transformative engagement.

Sometimes the technologies are also reflecting philosophical commitments and these are even more important to discern as theological thinkers who are using them. For example, many virtual learning environments and online educational tools are geared to build educational experiences on presuppositions of a connectivist pedagogy (see below), which is not value-free and with which we need to critically engage even as we use these tools. Software design lends itself to selected uses and predictable abuses, such as "trolling" generated by the ability to post anonymous comments on YouTube,

---

8. Arndt.
9. Cited in M. Weller, *The Digital Scholar* (London: Bloomsbury, 2011), 10.

or oversimplistic classifications in social media that lead to a dumbing-down of content as "people lower their behavior to meet that of the software."[10]

What does this entail for advanced scholars? First, they will not uncritically embrace any and all technology, but will first determine what that technology is meant to reflect, do, and express, and then critically relate it (in part, in full, or not at all) to the studies at hand. But it also challenges scholars to take ownership within the digital revolution, not simply as passive recipients, but becoming active participants in the design, in the shaping, and in the commissioning of digital technologies that are fit for purpose.

Constructivism, Connectivism, and Advanced Research in Theological Education

We turn now to consider briefly an example of the deeper underlying issues that are at play in digital scholarship, by looking at the constructivist and connectivist presuppositions that are behind some of the trends we are about to examine. It is important to realize that, as we discuss the implications of technology-enhanced research in theology, we are not just considering surface issues pertaining to research habits, publication strategies, or the convenience of technological gizmos, but we are actually facing some important epistemological shifts. In this brief section we will glance at constructivism and connectivism as among the most significant of these shifts on the horizon.

Understanding Constructivism

First, a brief overview of constructivism as the broader theory within which connectivism sits. Constructivism is a learning theory that says that individuals construct their own understanding of the world through their experiences of the world and their reflective work on those experiences. Compared with an idealist, Platonic vision of reality that presents a vision of truth and knowledge "out there" that has to be accessed somehow, the constructivist vision configures the individual as the creator of her/his own knowledge. There are important pedagogical implications in constructivism which we will not consider here, but in relation to research, a constructivist view critically places

---

10. Weller, *Digital Scholar*, 183.

the researcher as an epistemological locus of what is being researched and not an investigator of what can be known. Simply put, the researcher is an inside *part of the research* and not simply an external *agent of research*. Compared with idealist notions of research that were about discovery and interpretation of reality, constructivist research has to do with problem-solving, and with the interpretation of subjective and contextual experiences. So whereas a piece of advanced research in an idealist vision might have been titled "The Place of Women in Ministry as Prescribed in Romans 15," a constructivist title would likely read "Exploring Meanings of Women's Ministry in 21st Century Bangkok."

Understanding Connectivism

Connectivism is a little more difficult to define, but it can be seen as a sub-category of constructivism with which it shares basic assumptions.[11] What connectivism adds is a more nuanced definition of what knowledge is and how it is constructed, focusing in particular on *how* individuals generate knowledge in connection with one another. Concerning the nature of knowledge, AlDahdouh et al. observe that "Connectivists claim that the background or the general climate has recently changed: a new generation of researchers, connectivists, propose a new way of conceiving knowledge. According to them, knowledge is a network and learning is a process of exploring this network."[12] Instead of standing on the shoulders of giants and applying modernist methodologies of reason and logic, connectivism implies that it is impossible to build on previous theories and that new conceptual frameworks need to be constructed around phenomena and experiences. This knowledge is not static but fluid. What is right today might be outdated and wrong tomorrow. Whereas "All previous theories recognize knowledge as an object or state to be acquired or built in the learner's mind . . . [c]onnectivism, in contrast, conceives it as a process, which is alive and moving, a shifting reality."[13]

---

11. S. Downes, *Connectivism and Connective Knowledge: Essays on Meaning and Learning Networks* (2012), http://www.downes.ca/files/books/Connective_Knowledge-19May2012.pdf.
12. Alaa A. AlDahdouh, António J. Osório, and Susana Caires Portugal, "Understanding Knowledge Network, Learning and Connectivism," *International Journal of Instructional Technology and Distance Learning* 12, no. 10 (October 2015): 3–21 (3).
13. AlDahdouh et al., "Understanding Knowledge Network," 12.

The digital information age is a foundational player in connectivism that claims that knowledge is *in the network*, and individual participation in that network is the road to research and discovery. It is, in a way, a democratization of knowledge, where the boundary between content-consumers and content-generators becomes blurred, as do the lines between the researcher, the object of research, and the community within which that research takes place. To state it plainly, the researcher does not access the digital network to *find and retrieve* information, but is a dynamic part of the network that *is the information* itself. If, as connectivism claims, knowledge does not have one source but is distributed among learners and things, and the connections of the latter are the route to knowledge, the technologies developed in the digital era are responsible for inaugurating a quantum leap forward.

Web 2.0

On a less philosophical and more popular level, what has come to be known as Web 2.0 is a good example of this shift. Web 2.0 has had profound implications for many fields, including education, as it marks a distinct break from the so-called Web 1.0 Internet applications of the 1990s and early 2000s. This break witnessed the facilitation of "interactive" approaches in which information is shared "many-to-many," over and against "broadcast" forms of exchange that were being transmitted from one-to-many.

Examples of broadcast forms of exchange in the so-called Web 1.0 are typically one-way, authoritative, in the hands of the few, static, and non-interactive, such as the *Encyclopedia Britannica,* Amazon, and websites. Web 2.0 instead is the place where communication and information uploading comes from all participants, authority and initiative is spread to individuals, and content changes from being static to being dynamic. Web 2.0 is about shared creation, collaboration, and communication, examples being Wikipedia, eBay, and blogs.

When it comes to advanced research, we can use this vocabulary as a diagnostic tool. We see, for example, that when scholars publish in digital journals rather than print journals, there is not deep change happening. For although the publication is using digital means, an online journal is still very safely within the Web 1.0 category and far from connectivist commitments. The same can be said about using an online library rather than a physical one.

As scholars, however, engage with each other in blogs, shared data sites, or wikispaces in shaping their research, deeper change is on the horizon.

Critiques of Connectivism

Connectivism is a relatively recent theory and not without critics, and there is ample ground for critical theologizing on both constructivism and connectivism. We will not engage with these critiques in this chapter, but suggest that this is a field of very important higher research in the future. As you read the pages that follow on digital scholarship and we deal with concepts of openness and the functions of the increasingly populated space of digital tools for research, keep connectivism in mind. For some, technology is simply another way to conduct research within the framework of previous learning theories, while for others, technology itself has paved the way for a new learning theory to emerge; for it is true that education can change the Web, but it is also true that the Web can change education.

The Digital Scholar

Martin Weller, Professor of Educational Technology at the Open University, has written *The Digital Scholar*,[14] a discerning and forward-looking text on which I have built this section (effectively this is a sort of extended book review). *The Digital Scholar* is written broadly to discuss how technology is transforming scholarly practice, and its findings provide a good structure for the discussion that follows as we explore digital scholarship in theological education. At the heart of Weller's work is the conceptualization of "digital scholarship," which is most useful as we think of technology-enhanced research in theological education. Admittedly, for some this might come across as an oxymoron, but that is probably part of the prejudice that Weller helps to tame. The brief definition of a digital scholar is one who employs "digital, networked and open approaches to demonstrate specialism in a field,"[15] and we will now turn to each of these to investigate how they mark key shifts in the practice of scholarly writing.

---

14. Weller, *Digital Scholar*.
15. Weller, *Digital Scholar*, 4

Digital

First, advanced *digital* writing means that content is digitized in terms of having different media, different possibilities of sharing, no limits on length in order to be published, and economic accessibility. Hence a piece of digital scholarship will not be limited to the support of the written page but might use combinations of text, images, interactive tools, surveys or tests, video, audio, and hyperlinks. Particular attention falls on hyperlinks that provide a powerful tool to connect one digital piece of information to another and allow new opportunities of navigation and multidimensional writing. Search functions are also enhanced by digital writing, as content can easily be searched and collated. Among other things, digital writing means that authoring tools and approaches to production will vary from simple word processors to more elaborate software and online tools.

Networked

Second, digital scholarship is defined by Weller as *networked* writing, which entails an ease of distribution and communication of ideas over the global network. As large peer networks have become inexpensive and uncumbersome, and face-to-face environments are no longer essential, unprecedented levels of knowledge globalization have quickly come within reach. Networked writing opens the doors to the massification and greater democratization of scholarship as the costs and obstacles that scholars had to face in a non-digital age are being removed, allowing a new wave of production by specialists in many fields that may never fit into the canonical mould of academics.

Digitally networked research also means joint authorship and a *culture of sharing* unfinished products and even stages of development. The notion of a WikiThesis is an example of this, where a number of authors share in writing a thesis through the technological tool of a wiki.[16] A WikiThesis can be articulated as a sophisticated piece of writing that might appeal to scholars with key criteria of defensibility, accuracy, originality of interpretation, and formal wording.[17] This is a slight variation of the popular Wikipedia, which

---

16. Interestingly, "wiki" comes from a Hawaiian term meaning "fast."
17. "WikiThesis," accessed 28 October 2016, Wikimedia, https://meta.wikimedia.org/wiki/WikiThesis.

effectively is a piece of advanced research with encyclopaedic objectives that, rather than assemble the experts of the world and publish volume upon volume (as we would see in *Encyclopedia Britannica*), remains an open platform where continual edits can be brought about as knowledge and understanding develop.

Open

Third, advanced writing for digital scholars is *open*, which means that there is free sharing that coincides with the advent of Web 2.0 tools, cloud computing, and a more democratic and generous mentality. In 2013 alone over 500,000 pieces of scholarly research were made available through open access across the disciplines.[18] There is a growing architecture of participation where content sharing becomes the default posture outside of institutional control, which usually means more ideas, more experimentation, and more innovation, but, as mentioned above, less refinement and quality control. In short, it has never been more risky to operate in the open and yet it has never been more vital to operate in the open.[19]

The openness of digital scholarship has significant implications for the shelf life of research, for the speed, volume, and global distribution of production that is featured on the Internet makes knowledge obsolete more quickly. Advanced research that is "closed" and "static" ages quickly and by the time a book or article is completely written, peer reviewed, edited, printed, and distributed, it may be time to rewrite it again. "Open" research, on the other hand, can be constructed to be continually expanding and quickly updated.

Forms of open scholarship in theology might, for example, follow the approach taken by MoodleDocs,[20] the site where documentation and downloads are provided for the well-known virtual learning environment Moodle©. Moodle is continually releasing new versions of its platform and new fixes to new problems as they emerge, which makes writing manuals complex. So, rather than writing a book on "How to Use Moodle 3.0," which would probably become obsolete by the time it was published, MoodleDocs

---

18. "Open Scholarship," Wikimania 2014, accessed 27 October 2016, https://wikimania2014.wikimedia.org/wiki/Open_Scholarship#cite_note-1.
19. M. Weller, "The Paradoxes of Open Scholarship," *The Ed Techie* (blog), 13 December 2016, http://blog.edtechie.net/openness/the-paradoxes-of-open-scholarship/.
20. https://docs.moodle.org/.

takes the approach of an open and growing database with information that is regularly updated and where the user can select the software version which is most appropriate. This, combined with discussion forums that are open to questions from users, serviced by competent developers, and easily searchable, makes MoodleDocs a very versatile and continually updated piece of "advanced research." Of course, there is also a core of information on MoodleDocs that does not change and does not need to continually be rewritten.

In advanced research in theology, we might imagine a similar research project called "#SocialJusticeInAthensDocs" where there would be a core of basic information that would not change, but with a growing selection of "versions" that would be updated continually by a group of scholars and covering social justice in urban Athens in 2000, then during the economic crisis, then before Turkey closed its borders, then after Turkey strikes a deal with the EU, and so on.

Boyer's Aspects of Scholarship and Their Relation to Information Technologies

Boyer's definition of scholarship,[21] based on researching what over 5,000 scholars actually do, remains among the most influential definitions. He has identified four aspects of scholarship: discovery, integration, application, and teaching, and we will now consider them in turn to explore how changing technologies might impact them.[22]

Discovery

Discovery is the first dimension of scholarship, focusing on the creation of new knowledge. The growing accessibility and power of computing tools allows scholars to generate unprecedented amounts of data, provides them with new possibilities of sharing this data in scholarly communication, and allows new ways of combining data. This can take the form, for example, of group research with distinct phases of shared planning, data collection, data analysis, and

---

21. E. Boyer, *Scholarship Reconsidered: Priorities of the Professorate* (San Francisco: Jossey-Bass, 1990).
22. Weller, *Digital Scholar*, 42.

reflection through the use of social networks, blogs, feeds, Google Scholar and Alerts, online surveys, and interviews.[23] In this context, advanced research in theology might, for example, be dealing with the production, sharing, and accessibility of datasets in biblical languages or missiological trends, forming clusters of networks and communities that build and share datasets. Discovery and production of datasets can also happen through other means than text, as through sharing Excel data in Google Drive or through video and audio. Some of the discoveries that have had great impact and popularity in recent years have, for example, taken the form of video, as in the widely viewed TED Talks.[24]

When we speak of discovery, "granularity" is an interesting theme, by which we simply mean that valid discovery may have to do with very small "grains" rather than a massive harvest. The act of sharing these "research buds" (perhaps through a blog) as they are developing offers a chance to get feedback, pushback, and further idea-generating dialogue. Advanced technologies set no limits to the length of a discovery before it can be brought out: it can be as short as a Tweet or an initial intuition, or as long as an extended Facebook conversation with peers.

Discovery also has to do with finding and retrieving information, and here probably most of the readers of this chapter will already have engaged with the advantages of the search functions of emerging technologies. In the age of the digital resource, some wonder about the future of a physical library. The piece of research illustrated in figure 18.1[25] represents the results that CIBER discovered in collecting data about how people actually use the British Library and JISC websites. A couple of elements can be noted. The first is that, overall, there is more searching happening in digital environments (electronic tables of content and journal websites) than in physical libraries. The second is that there is a clear difference when the ages of researchers are compared, with younger researchers clearly preferring tools like Google Scholar and older researchers holding to traditional patterns of visiting libraries. Interestingly, both age groups rely significantly on personal recommendations, but it is likely

---

23. Weller, *Digital Scholar*, 56–57.
24. http://www.ted.com.
25. UCL, "Information Behaviour of the Researcher of the Future: A Ciber Briefing Paper," 11 January 2008, p. 13, https://www2.warwick.ac.uk/study/cll/courses/professionaldevelopment/wmcett/researchprojects/dialogue/the_google_generation.pdf.

that many of these are also occurring in digital network environments. Hence, discovery trends into the future would seem to confirm a digital preference.

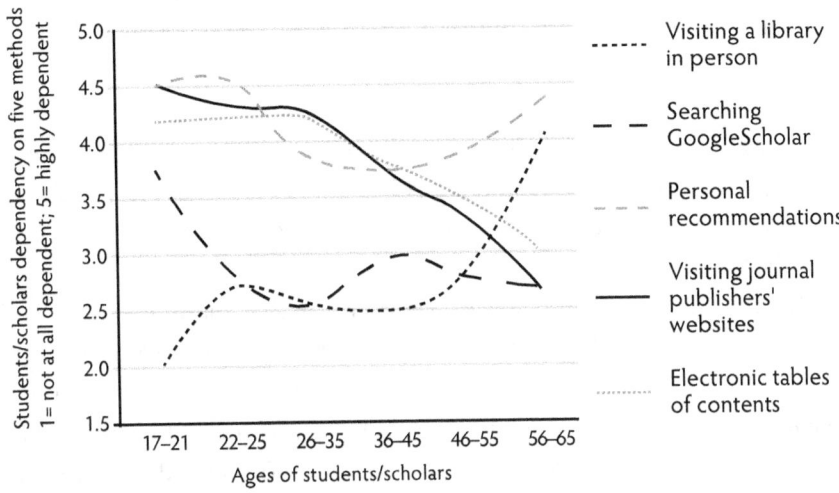

Figure 18.1 A Comparison of Students/Scholars of Different Ages[26]

Integration

Integration is a second dimension of scholarship that focuses on making connections, on interdisciplinary work, on placing specialties in a larger context, on illuminating data, and on educating non-specialists.

Advanced research that expresses integration through information technologies can take many shapes, from very simple hyperlinking to very complex schema. For example, a PhD student, as he was working on his literature review in a growing body of interdisciplinary research, used Google Scholar and built a Web app called Bibnet. Through this he produced a diagram that visually shows connections between citations of authors in various fields.

---

26. A comparison of students/scholars of different ages in terms of how dependent they said they were on five methods of finding articles that might interest them. Adapted from CIBER/UCL, 2008, 13.

This work enabled him to make a series of remarkable discoveries about his topic that would otherwise have remained obscure or difficult to identify.[27]

When we discuss integration in research, journals play an important role and can be "seen as the battleground between new forms of scholarly activity and traditional systems."[28] Publication in journals can be plagued by long publication times and high subscription costs, and can also be seen as restrictive as it does not allow dynamic content and has rigid parameters around word limits. Access is also an issue, especially in less developed countries that cannot afford expensive journal subscriptions, which in turn feeds into the discussions around the democratization of knowledge which should resonate loudly with global theologians.

The main point as we discuss integration is that many journals tend to be "disciplinary" and do not encourage interdisciplinary connections or communication aimed at non-specialist audiences.[29] Journals are about a specialism and are for specialists, and they can foster fragmentation rather than the pursuit of unified knowledge. The "open nature" and culture that comes with advanced technologies combined with more flexible and versatile classification techniques (where the same work can "occupy many shelves simultaneously"[30]) can help open new doors to integration and interdisciplinary research.

Academic blogging communities are very good examples of integration, as a phenomenon characterized by willingness to share thoughts and ideas at an early stage. Blogs enhance integration through having loose boundaries and making an effort to address a wider range of audiences; operating "at the intersection of personal and professional life, unlike a journal, their content is not bounded by discipline."[31] Blogs are also constructed to highlight the importance of input from others by providing platforms within which to launch collaborative projects, daily gather information from many sources, and enable instant ongoing conversation. Sadly, research in theology is typically done in

---

27. Jon Dron, "Scraping Google Scholar to Write Your PhD Literature Chapter," 13 October 2016. https://landing.athabascau.ca/bookmarks/view/2002574/scraping-google-scholar-to-write-your-phd-literature-chapter.
28. Weller, *Digital Scholar*, 47.
29. Weller, 65.
30. Weller, 65.
31. Weller, 67.

isolation and there might be lessons to be learnt from other disciplines (e.g. science) where teamwork is more the established norm.

Application

Application is a third dimension of scholarship that looks to engagement with the wider world outside academia, public engagement, citizenship, input into policy, and media discussion. By application, we do not mean activity done by the researcher to transform the knowledge gained into praxis, but the extent to which research is engaged with and applied to the broader public. In terms of communicating with non-specialist audiences Weller points out that distribution over the Internet rules over other media (e.g. television) and in particular that user-generated content that is Web 2.0 dwarfs institutional, directive contributions.[32]

Although the type of outlet will depend on the type of output, in general we see advanced research increasingly reaching the public through data and open source repositories, open access journals, individual websites and blogs, OER (open educational research) projects, conference sites, video channels, community forums, social media groups, and public engagement sites.[33] Wikipedia receives much bad press among academics, and many critiques are fair, but since it is a place where anyone can become an editor, why not consider it as a platform for engagement and global dissemination? Not many people in the world will read our latest publication on the role of Christianity in feminism, but an appropriate edit on our part in the Wikipedia article on "feminism" will instantly access a global readership.

Unfortunately this is an uphill journey as the "establishment" is still looking to the printed page as the "proper" academic venue of publication and as the means to measure the career of an academic and the ranking of a university. In the future, however, academics may be asked about their blog subscribers, LinkedIn networks, YouTube channel hits, and Twitter followers.

---

32. Weller, 79.
33. Weller, 79.

Teaching

Teaching is the final dimension of scholarship listed by Boyer, as research is considered consequential as it is understood by others. The area of teaching and delivery is one where digital advances have made the deepest impact, but this is not the place to discuss online education. Sadly, online education can get a bad press because it is so easy to do badly, but there is no denying that it is currently the most fertile arena in which traditional and culturally weighted theories and practices of teaching and learning are being reassessed. Advanced theological research must not only find ways of expressing itself in response to digital technologies that are quickly moving from marginality to dominance, but also do higher research itself into the theological and educational dimensions of online education.

Drawbacks and Conclusions

As scholars do, one must keep a critical eye both on the evangelists in the pro-technology camp and on the doomsday prophets in the ban-technology camp. Both sides can easily fall into extreme views which are inaccurate and unhelpful. As Weller reminds us, "the pro-camp will make . . . outlandish claims . . . about the imminent revolution, the irrelevancy of higher education and the radically different net generation. The anti-technology camp will decry that it destroys social values, undermines proper scholarly practice, is always superficial and is even damaging our brains."[34] As most of this chapter has been generally positive towards the place of technology in advanced theological education, in conclusion it is fair to consider a few of the counterbalancing drawbacks and dangers.

A popular argument critiquing digital scholarship relates to the danger of breadth prevailing over depth. Quick blogging and tweeting research communities can, in fact, produce volume at the expense of rigour. Similarly, the bounds of interdisciplinary research can become so vaporous that there is no backbone to pull it all together into something meaningful, leaving no more than assorted thoughts in a sort of postmodern "pastiche."[35]

---

34. Weller, 155.
35. A technical word that I would advise you to "Google."

In 2008 Nicholas Carr wrote an article entitled "Is Google Making Us Stupid?"[36] that stirred up a debate and helped focus the attention on something that many users of the Internet were beginning to sense. That is, that our attention span is getting shorter, that we tend to skim rather than read deeply, and that our memories are less exercised, for we know that we can retrieve data easily rather than needing to memorize it. All this amounts to superficiality, which goes against the grain of scholarship. In *The Shallows: What the Internet Is Doing to Our Brains*,[37] Carr further argues that advanced research will have increased challenges as the "raw materials" of students' minds coming to do the research will be "less exercised." Our human brain has abilities to set high-level goals that are complex and need to exercise cognitive control that comprises a triad of attention, working management, and goal management. The task of continually switching from one quick activity to another, such as what we see in the typical "skimming and scrolling" activities for which much online content is designed, can degrade performance and impact cognition, decision-making, and the learning process. The huge amount of information through digital sources and the vast parade of technological resources at our fingertips can distract, giving the impression of progress, but impede attention and achievement of high-level goals typical of advanced studies.[38]

There are also some possible pitfalls in researching in open communities. Weller, for example, advises of the dangers of creating "echo chambers" where "as the amount of information available increases, there is an argument that it becomes more difficult to hear distinct and different voices."[39] This is due to the sheer volume of information but also because one can easily form like-minded communities around oneself that will hinder critical thinking rather than promote it. One's research community can also become a source of power, where critiques or opinions voiced by lone scholars can be drowned out and

---

36. Nicholas Carr, "Is Google Making Us Stupid? What the Internet Is Doing to Our Brains," *The Atlantic*, July/August 2008, http://www.theatlantic.com/magazine/archive/2008/07/is-google-making-us-stupid/306868/.
37. Nicholas Carr, *The Shallows: What the Internet Is Doing to Our Brains* (New York: Norton, 2010).
38. John Naughton, "The Internet: Is It Changing the Way We Think?," *The Observer*, 15 August 2010, https://www.theguardian.com/technology/2010/aug/15/internet-brain-neuroscience-debate.
39. Weller, *Digital Scholar*, 73.

lost. Furthermore, research done in "the open" will probably not have names tagged to conclusions or "authorities" who will have the courage to plant flags and set landmarks, thus potentially defusing some of the pugnacious nature of some of the best and most original research.

A concern for quality is also connected to publication approaches that are typical of the Web 2.0. This is because these approaches are simple and accessible to all and the temptation is only one click away to publish something quickly that is not really thought through at all. Weller suggests that we are seeing a shift in filtering of quality "from pre- to post-dissemination."[40] In other words, whereas a peer-assessed journal will evaluate the quality of an article *before* it is published, an unfiltered blog post will demonstrate whether it is a reputable and worthy contribution to research only *after* its reception and much interaction. Andrew Keen argues that the abundance in quantity is creating "an endless digital forest of mediocrity."[41]

As open access journals become an expression of an open digital culture, a warning should be sounded against predatory and scam journals[42] that fester in the world of digital scholarship. These journals are often of mediocre quality, with many shoddy articles and unrigorous or non-existent review procedures (often, however, overstating their rigour, peer process, and long list of reviewers). These journals are, however, appealing both to academics, who see them as a quick route to increase their publication lists for career advancement, but also to universities who might "close one eye" as long as they are meeting the publications quota.

Open publication also presents other drawbacks, most notably those of intellectual property rights and sustainability. Concerning intellectual property rights, this remains a complex issue, as many open cloud services are privately owned and legal borders can become fuzzy. Concerning sustainability, there is a simple question of who is going to pay scholars for their time in producing research if it is then put into the open freely. This may not be the case for contracted faculty members who often are paid by their universities to do

---

40. Weller, 157.
41. Cited in Weller, 157.
42. See Alex Gillis, "Beware! Academics Are Getting Reeled in By Scam Journals," *University Affairs*, 12 January 2017, http://www.universityaffairs.ca/features/feature-article/beware-academics-getting-reeled-scam-journals/.

research, but it can become an issue for freelance scholars who try to make a living through their publication. The conundrum of publishing one's work on sites like Academia.edu is keenly felt by many scholars who also need to pay their bills.

Conclusion

Alas, it is no secret that many academics are not enthusiasts of digital technologies. As a matter of fact, probably most of those reading this chapter have done so with scepticism. And you may remain largely unconvinced, for the things that may be lost in digital scholarship may be very clear to you and alarming, whereas the gains are still unfocused.

And as we have seen, the world of advanced research may be better in some respects because of digital technology, but it may also be much worse. Where the difference lies is still unclear. What is clear and certain is that there *is and will be* a difference, and while we should not uncritically dance around the straw-fires of trends, neither should we passively sit by as the Bastille is stormed, disappearing into irrelevance with our archaeological artefacts. There is a revolution coming and the changes it brings will be central to much that will happen in the future of education and theological education. As Weller reminds us,[43] in all revolutions some things will disappear, other things will remain, and other things yet will be new.

As theological educators we should not be passive spectators. Rather, we should engage thoughtfully as those who are privileged to have time, capacity, and a distinctive transformative theological perspective. Together with attentive engagement, we should also invest incisively to become proficient, unbarbaric digital immigrants who, where necessary, will act disruptively in accreditation policy, institutional strategy, and individual efforts. "For scholars it should *not* be a case of you see what goes, you see what stays, you see what comes, but rather you *determine* what goes, what stays and what comes."[44]

---

43. Weller, *Digital Scholar*, 169.
44. Weller, 184.

Discussion Questions

1. Briefly discuss some ways in which you personally have seen the "laws of technology" at work both in your personal life and in your experience of theological education. To what extent is technology available in your context, and how is it influencing the way people think and act?

2. From your own experience, what are two or three of the greatest benefits for theological education that you have seen from technological developments over the past twenty years or more? What is your greatest fear, and why?

3. Briefly consider the material on constructivism and connectivism. How have you seen each of these theories at work in your own pilgrimage of learning? Even more importantly, how would you critically engage with these theories from a theological point of view?

4. Consider in turn each of the three elements of digital scholarship suggested in the chapter: digital, networked, and open. Describe one or two ways in which your school has already embraced these elements. Suggest at least one specific and significant step that your school might take to better embrace the move towards digital scholarship.

5. The chapter describes Boyer's four aspects of scholarship: discovery, integration, application, and teaching. In your own school, how do you see technology impacting each of these areas? In the light of the discussion of Boyer's model given in this chapter, suggest at least one way in which technology might better enhance the work of scholarship at your school.

Bibliography

AlDahdouh, Alaa A., António J. Osório, and Susana Caires Portugal. "Understanding Knowledge Network, Learning and Connectivism," *International Journal of Instructional Technology and Distance Learning* 12, no. 10 (October 2015): 3–21.

Arndt, Steve. "4 Laws of Technology and How They Impact Your Business." 13 November 2014. Accessed 27 October 2016. http://smarndt.com/2014/11/4-laws-of-technology-and-how-they-impact-your-business/.

Boyer, E. *Scholarship Reconsidered: Priorities of the Professorate*. San Francisco: Jossey-Bass, 1990.

Carr, Nicholas. "Is Google Making Us Stupid? What the Internet Is Doing to Our Brains." *The Atlantic*, July/August 2008. http://www.theatlantic.com/magazine/archive/2008/07/is-google-making-us-stupid/306868/.

———. *The Shallows: What the Internet Is Doing to Our Brains*. New York: Norton, 2010.

Downes, S. *Connectivism and Connective Knowledge: Essays on Meaning and Learning Networks*. 2012. http://www.downes.ca/files/books/Connective_Knowledge-19May2012.pdf.

———. "Scraping Google Scholar to Write Your PhD Literature Chapter," 14 October 2016. http://www.downes.ca/post/65932.

Gillis, Alex. "Beware! Academics Are Getting Reeled in By Scam Journals." *University Affairs*, 12 January 2017. http://www.universityaffairs.ca/features/feature-article/beware-academics-getting-reeled-scam-journals/.

McLeod, Scott. "Schools Are Supposed to Help Students Master the Dominant Information Landscape of Their Time." *dangerously ! irrelevant* (blog), 28 November 2016. http://dangerouslyirrelevant.org/2016/11/schools-are-supposed-to-help-students-master-the-dominant-information-landscape-of-their-time.html.

Naughton, John. "The Internet: Is It Changing the Way We Think?" *The Observer*, 15 August 2010. https://www.theguardian.com/technology/2010/aug/15/internet-brain-neuroscience-debate.

———. "Thanks, Gutenberg – But We're Too Pressed for Time to Read." *The Observer*, 27 January 2008. Accessed 27 October 2016. https://www.theguardian.com/media/2008/jan/27/internet.pressandpublishing.

Niebuhr, H. Richard. *Christ and Culture*. New York: Harper & Row, 1975.

UCL. "Information Behaviour of the Researcher of the Future: A Ciber Briefing Paper." 11 January 2008. https://www2.warwick.ac.uk/study/cll/courses/professionaldevelopment/wmcett/researchprojects/dialogue/the_google_generation.pdf.

Weller, M. *The Digital Scholar*. London: Bloomsbury, 2011.

———. "The Paradoxes of Open Scholarship." *The EdTechie* (blog), 13 December 2016. http://blog.edtechie.net/openness/the-paradoxes-of-open-scholarship/.

19

Doing Theology from the "Land of Samba":
Integrating Personal Experience in the Task of Advanced Theological Research

Samuel Ewell

In so much of advanced research, the person of the researcher may appear at the beginning and the end, but otherwise disappears off the page. This so-called "objective" approach which isolates the "object" being researched from the researcher is, however, problematic for both practical and theological reasons. This is because every researcher is always already bringing personal experience into the research process. Therefore, while the voice of researcher *qua* person can be *muted*, it cannot be simply "turned off" – nor should it be.

As a doctoral researcher, I was fortunate to be able to keep my own voice and experience at the centre of my research. In what follows I want to show that this personal "baggage" is not necessarily a burden to "get rid of," but actually can be a kind of hidden treasure worthy to be researched and shared with others. This chapter is a description of how this happened in my case.

My own introduction to academic theology and research began when I was a seminary student at Duke Divinity School in the late 1990s. As a seminarian, I was fortunate to become friends with and learn from a number of doctoral students whose reading knowledge and academic rigour seemed to leave us "seminarians" behind. Unfortunately, my impression of doctoral research at that time was less about learning to reflect deeply and theologically about one's lived experience and social location, but that it was more like a club for specialists who wrote texts on each others' texts (i.e. research on each other's research). Therefore, I did not go straight into a doctoral program after seminary, precisely because I thought it meant spending four to six years researching something that only eight other people in the world might read! So I left seminary highly motivated to live out the theology that I learned in seminary, but totally unmotivated to do academic research on it.

My understanding of theology (in general) and academic research (in particular) would soon change as a result of my journey into "the land of samba." That is, my doctoral research emerged directly out of a deep desire to make sense of my intercultural experience as a US national married to a Brazilian, living as a missionary in Brazil from 2003 to 2010. At a formal level, my doctoral research[1] explores the cultural, political, and ethical questions related to Christian mission by reappropriating the life and thought of the Roman Catholic priest and intellectual Ivan Illich. *Yet, at the most fundamental level, my experience as a missionary serves as the narrative matrix and lens for the entire research agenda.*

As a researcher, I was fascinated not so much with answering questions about Illich (i.e. establishing myself as an aspiring scholar in "Illich studies"), but rather with the way that Illich responded to my personal questions. Therefore, I was drawn neither towards writing a "theology of Ivan Illich"-type thesis, nor towards writing a spiritual memoir. I was drawn towards doing theology in the space emerging between Illich's life and thought and my own, and yet it was not at all clear to me how to move from gathering research to "writing up."

Full disclosure: for the first four years of my doctoral program, I struggled to find a form for my thesis that fit the function that I needed. I knew that I had to meet the formal requirements for a doctoral thesis, yet I also intuited that the energy for the research came from attending and responding to my personal questions. The breakthrough came when I submitted a draft chapter using personal narrative as a way to frame the question: Why Illich? My supervisor

---

1. Samuel Earl Ewell III, "Prolonging the Incarnation: Towards a Reappropriation of Ivan Illich for Christian Mission and Life Together" (PhD diss., University of Birmingham, 2014).

responded enthusiastically, in effect saying: "You have just written the first chapter of your thesis. The shape of personal narrative and journey in Brazil gives you a form for presenting your scholarship on Illich in a compelling way."

Looking back on my experience as a doctoral student at a major research university, I realize now how fortunate I was to work with a supervisor who did not just tolerate, but actively encouraged me to locate myself in – that is, to bring my voice and experience into – the production of my research.

I say that I am fortunate because I was enabled to swim against the current of a dominant, yet debilitating tendency in advanced theological research: namely, the tendency to objectify knowledge as something to be found and studied in isolation from lived experience. This tendency, common to theology as well as to the social sciences, prefers to isolate a researching "subject" from a researched "object" based on the assumption "that a person's background identity, personality, experience and world-view needed to be subjugated to the need for a scientific kind of method."[2] This assumption, while still dominant, has been called into question on the grounds that the subject/object dichotomy is a false one.[3]

A growing number of researchers recognize that locating oneself in the activity of research is not a liability at all; rather it is a more reflexive, authentic way of "showing one's work" and where one takes a stand.[4] Indeed, if "knowledge is formed through the encounter, that is . . . in the space between the self and the other,"[5] then the questions is: Wouldn't advanced theological researchers want to locate those encounters and give voice to lived experiences out of which theological imagination emerges? Perhaps the time has come for us to say collectively: there is every reason to do so!

In what follows I will reflect on how I found a way to voice my lived experience in my doctoral thesis. In doing so, I assume that the researcher

---

2. Michael Pears and Paul Cloke, "Introduction," *Mission in Marginal Places: The Praxis* (Milton Keynes: Authentic, 2016), 3.

3. Geoffrey C. Ward and Ken Burns, *The War: An Intimate History, 1941–1945* (New York: Knopf, 2007), 52.

4. For a broad range of contributors who advocate for the integration of lived experience into advanced research, see the essays in Pears and Cloke, *Mission in Marginal Places*, as well as those in Christian Scharen and Aana Marie Vigen, eds., *Ethnography as Christian Theology and Ethics* (London: Continuum, 2011).

5. Pears and Cloke, "Introduction," 18.

accesses knowledge through encounter – by facing and responding to a lived experience with other people, places, and even written texts. Therefore, I will explore how my research is framed as a theological response to encounters that have become generative "turning points," or *viradas*,[6] on my own journey in and beyond Brazil. What follows is not the back-story but a summary of the content of the thesis itself, for these *viradas* frame each chapter by generating the questions to which Illich responds. You will see throughout that my own story in dialogue with Ivan Illich's life and thought is front and centre. Through what follows you will get a taste of how personal identity and struggle can be, perhaps even should be, prominent and unambiguous in advanced theological studies.

Virada One – Being Turned Towards Brazil: An Exercise in Being Immersed and "In Between"

In the first section of my dissertation I traced my personal journey into Brazil, as a way of situating the background for my research. I focused on how the experience of doing theology from more than one place might entail a movement from rupture to the renewal of one's theological imagination. What follows is a summary of how I explore the questions that arose from my missionary experience as the narrative context for my research.

The story of my being turned towards Brazil began definitively on 29 May 1999 when I married Rosalee Velloso da Silva, a Brazilian born and raised in São Paulo, Brazil. We took our wedding vows from the book of Ruth, recognizing and celebrating that, through our life together, somehow our peoples' lives

---

6. In my doctoral thesis as well as in this chapter, I use the Portuguese word for "turning point" – *virada*. *Virada* is not an explicitly religious term, for in *futebol*, you might speak of how an important play or goal *virou o jogo* [changed the game] or *deu uma virada* [turned the game around], but you can also speak of a *virada na sua vida* [turning point in one's life], and it is in this more general, but stronger sense that I am using the term. In using it I refer to an encounter or event that leads to enduring change in one's perceptions, attitudes, and way of life. In the light of the Christian tradition, conversion is a way of talking of the ongoing movement of being changed and being turned towards life in and with God. *Viradas*, then, are a way of talking about significant episodes of encounter within that continual movement of "being turned."

would be joined as well. In the light of those vows, there is a real sense in which our journey together to Brazil was a Ruth narrative-in-reverse. In our case, *her* people would become *his* people.

In July 2003, we arrived in Brazil. For Rosalee, it was a return trip to her home country; my arrival in Brazil, however, was an immersion into a whole new world. Suddenly, I was no longer just an English-speaking American, but also a *gringo* who could hardly speak a complete sentence in Portuguese. As an immersed language-learner of Brazilian Portuguese, I was learning what anyone who has become fluent in a second language through immersion will tell you: learning to speak another language goes far beyond learning to say foreign words. *Futebol* may translate into English as the sport that Americans call "soccer," but Brazilians will tell you that *futebol* is not just a sport primarily played with your feet, but rather a quasi-religious phenomenon whose own "liturgical season" comes to a climax every four years with the World Cup. On another, deeper level, as a language learner I became acutely aware of how becoming fluent in another language involves becoming immersed in another way of life.

In fact, one of the key "turning points" of my first two years in Brazil was this insight regarding the Christian life (in general) and missionary existence (in particular) as disruptive yet transformative realities of immersion. I was married to a Brazilian, the father (by 2006) of three Brazilian citizens, a permanent resident of Brazil, a fluent and comfortable speaker of Portuguese (accent included), and a convert to *futebol* and Brazilian percussion. How could I be just a foreign outsider or another *gringo*? Surely I was becoming more than just a *gringo*. And yet I knew I would never speak Portuguese like my children, nor "get Brazil" like a Brazilian. I knew somehow that I would never become Brazilian. Perhaps even more unsettling than recognizing that I would never become Brazilian was accepting that I could never just "reset" my previous identity and sense of belonging as an American. By 2007, I had internalized a range of Brazilian cultural cues, gestures, and perceptions in the midst of being estranged from certain features of my "United States of American-ness." I was traversing two distinct, yet overlapping, linguistic and cultural fields, and I found myself in a space of "in-between-ness," that of an outsider-insider. From that space, I began to ask: Is this "in-between-ness" simply about being fated to a kind of "no man's land," a cultural black hole whose gravity holds me suspended between "never-going-back-to-being-just-American" and "never-fully-arriving-as-Brazilian?" In fact, I was entering a sense of liminality that missiologist Paul Hiebert describes as an "outsider-insider."[7]

Interestingly, however, the more subtle and challenging struggle that I encountered as a missionary was not negotiating a transcultural identity and a new cultural-linguistic framework. Rather, the real struggle came from trying to navigate the institutional matrix operating between the seminary, sanctuary, and street.[8] As a missionary navigating "in between" institutions in Brazil and the US, I came to recognize that theological production and formation (seminary), visions for "gathered church" (sanctuary), as well as the strategies and financial basis for social transformation (street) were, in large part, contained within a disorientating dialectic – either institutional reproduction of or resistance to what came from the North. Even more disorientating, however, than the challenge of traversing the North–South barriers was the sense that much of what I was seeing, and was even involved in, between these three Ss was counterproductive – that is, much of the institutional activity seemed to work against and even undermine the original intent. Thus, in the seminary, the work of facilitating theological learning and formation became locked into the production, dissemination, and defence of theological *certainties*; in the sanctuary, the ecclesial vocation to worship God and make disciples mutated into an emphasis on attracting and serving members as primarily passive religious *consumers*; and on the streets of places like João Turquino, neighbour-love towards the marginalized ended up objectifying the poor, effectively "othering" them as *clients*.

In my experience as a missionary, then, a deeper challenge than becoming a *brasicano* was the disintegration through becoming aware of the subtle forms of alienation. Learning to speak Portuguese, to eat *feijoada*, to play *futebol*, to enjoy *MPB* – these were not my obstacles. My biggest obstacle came from the challenge of learning to live "in" and "out" of institutional realities without

---

7. Paul Gordon Hiebert, "The Missionary as Mediator of Global Theologizing," in *Globalizing Theology: Belief and Practice in an Era of World Christianity*, ed. Craig Ott and Harold A. Netland (Grand Rapids: Baker Academic, 2006), 300.

8. I borrow this triad from theological educator Ched Myers, which he develops in "Between the Seminary, the Sanctuary, and the Streets: Reflections on Alternative Theological Education," *Ministerial Formation* 94 (July 2001): 94.

being "of" them. The tension for me was not between Christian identity and some other cultural identity (American or Brazilian), but rather discerning between the freedom of the Christian life *vis-à-vis* being conformed within the horizon of institutionalized expectations linked to the "good intentions" of missionary presence. Indeed, I only discovered a way forward on my journey by undergoing a second *virada* – namely, making friends (and through them) encountering a Christian intellectual named Ivan Illich.

Virada Two – Being Turned Towards Ivan Illich: An Exercise in Doing Theology With and After Illich

In the second *virada* of my thesis, I documented my encounter with Ivan Illich. What follows is a summary of that encounter, and specifically how that encounter happened in the most "Illichian" way – that is, in the context of friendship.

In November 2007, I was introduced through a mutual friend to a Brazilian named Claudio Oliver. Claudio would become not only my closest friend in Brazil, but also a kind of *irmão mais velho* (an older brother). During my first visit to his home city of Curitiba, what I recall most was Claudio's enthusiastic description of his master's research in education on Paulo Freire, Leo Tolstoy, and Ivan Illich. I had read a lot of Freire and some Tolstoy, but I had never heard of Ivan Illich. That initial visit ended with two parting shots from Claudio: meditate on Matthew 10:16, and read Illich's 1968 address to North American short-term missionaries in Latin American, entitled "To Hell With Good Intentions."[9] Simply from the title, I immediately recognized that Illich was going to be an important thinker for me. By the time I arrived at home and looked through the text, I knew I had found a guide, someone clearing a path and pointing beyond the counterproductive fallout of "good intentions."

Illich's 1968 address no doubt intended to challenge the adequacy of "good intentions," but it went beyond merely pointing out how good intentions can

---

9. Ivan Illich, "To Hell with Good Intentions," 1968, accessed 22 July 2010, http://www.davidtinapple.com/illich/1968_cuernavaca.html.

lead to harmful outcomes. Rather, his more fundamental insight had to do with the recovery of a deeper sense of missionary awareness, that is, both (1) the recognition of the arena in which our actions of service and mission take place; and (2) the capacity to renounce "good intentions" in order truly to act for the sake of what is good, what is right, or what is fitting.

As a US national serving as a missionary in Brazil, I was deeply affected by Illich's talk. Although written in 1968, nearly forty years before I first read it, his message for "do-gooders" pricked the insular, missionary bubble that had slowly formed around me. Over the next few days, I mulled over "To Hell With Good Intentions" many times, always hovering over the last lines: "Come . . . to enjoy our flowers. Come . . . But do not come to help."

I knew that I had not gone to Brazil out of a sense of duty to help needy Brazilians; I knew that I didn't even need to leave Durham, North Carolina, for that. I went because I was married to a Brazilian, and I believed in the promises of our marriage vows that "her people had become my people." I went because I sensed a growing desire to become part of this people, to become immersed in their way of life. We moved to Brazil, then, as a response to a growing desire and a call to *be there*, not primarily to go as helpers. But somewhere along the way, "being there" had been hijacked by "good intentions." Somewhere along the way, planning projects had gone astray from the path of personal presence. Suddenly, Illich's proposal, "Come, but not cast in the role of helper," led me to reflect back upon what being in Brazil *could* mean.

Fundamentally, the insight of Illich's message challenged my burdensome temptation to "fix" all that was wrong about Brazil by playing the role of "do-gooder." At the same time, the more I read Illich, the more I realized he was not letting "do-gooders" like me off the hook. He was not advocating disengagement, but a different kind of presence, a more aware, more subversive presence. I realized that if I were going to take Illich as my guide, I was going to have to question not only my intentions and actions, but also the arena in which Christian witness has unfolded in Brazil. More generally, I realized that by taking Illich as my guide, I would have to question the certainties and assumptions that shape the way Christians imagine their place and role in relation to God's "good intentions" for the whole world.

As I continued to turn my understanding of Illich and my own experience towards one another, I was able to frame the answers I found through my scholarship on Illich as a response to the two basic questions that gripped my imagination as a missionary:

- First, given the history of Christian missionary expansion in its colonial and neo-colonial forms, and the fallout of such expansion as what Eduardo Galeano poignantly termed "the open veins of Latin America,"[10] on what *basis* do we go on fulfilling the "Great Commission" (Matt 28:16–20) as Christ's disciples?
- A second question, intimately related to the first, is: What makes it possible to embody a distinctively Christian presence that is *missionary* without being *manipulative*?

Driven by those questions, I focused my research on Illich around finding answers to those questions. By bringing together his explicitly theological commentary, focused on the incarnation, with his earlier social criticism and his focus on conviviality, I showed how they operate in tandem as complementary expressions of his "Incarnational Christianity."[11] In doing so, I demonstrated that Illich offers a threefold contribution to contemporary accounts of Christian mission, related to:

- his understanding of the incarnational logic of mission;
- his diagnosis of the social conditions which undermine and corrupt the incarnational movement;
- his insights (i.e. the recovery of conviviality) for regenerating incarnational mission and the cultivation of "life together" as responses to wider social concerns, such as economic and ecological crises.

In sum, I found answers through Illich that satisfied not only my questions as a researcher, but also my questions as an intercultural missionary. Along the way, I discovered that the very form of my thesis needed to envelop my research on the life and thought of Ivan Illich (as theological guide) inside my own personal narrative (as the generative context of the research questions).

---

10. Eduardo Galeano, *Open Veins of Latin America: Five Centuries of the Pillage of a Continent*, trans. C. Belfrage, 1973, 25th anniversary ed. (New York: Monthly Review Press, 1997).

11. David Cayley, *The Rivers North of the Future: The Testament of Ivan Illich as Told to David Cayley* (Toronto: House of Anansi, 2005), 41.

As an exercise in doing theology with and after Illich, then, there is a distinct logic to the form of my thesis. It is worth noticing that the form fits the function of integrating personal narrative, experience, voice, and academic scholarship. That is, the very form of my thesis allows me *to follow Illich's lead as a theological guide for navigating my experiences of "turning points" on a journey.*

One could say the thesis bears a musical (rather than linear) logic that moves from beginning to end by introducing a theme (journey), a set of dissonant variations on that theme (detours), and a sense of resolution of those variations in relation to the original theme (re-turn). To describe the thesis in terms of a musical form also sets up a third and final *virada* that informs my research: how my experience with the cultural form of Brazilian samba itself became a tool for reflection and research.

Virada Three – Being Included in the Samba Circle: An Exercise in "Overhearing the Gospel According to Samba"

Another aspect of my writing brought the *roda de samba* (samba circle) into dialogue with my experience and Illich's thought. Interestingly, one of the most decisive "turning points" of my missionary experience in Brazil did not happen in a church but rather in a *roda de samba* (samba circle). Through my participation in the *bloco* (samba ensemble), I came to a new awareness of how formation and participation were at the core of both musicianship and discipleship. The more I struggled and grew as a percussionist, the more I came to recognize how the experience of joining the *bloco* serves as a parable for Christian discipleship, the interpersonal process of formation and participation in Christ.

The more I was drawn into this Brazilian cultural form, the more I began to imagine my experience of togetherness inside the *roda* as a parable for the incarnational logic of Christian discipleship and mission. While the *roda* offered an array of insights which could be developed theologically, I was caught not only by the energy of the music, but also by the relational dynamics of embodiment and interdependence.

First, the emphasis on the movement and presence of the body in samba echoes Illich's emphasis on *embodiment* as a precondition for the Christian life. In both samba and discipleship, the body is indispensable: we neither "samba" nor "follow" without our bodies' actions as well as their interactions with other bodies.

Second, in the *roda* I glimpsed a parable of inclusion into conditions of interdependence that is intrinsic to life together in the body of Christ. Just imagine the simple phrase of an *agogô*, a kind of cowbell that usually produces only two pitches or notes. Voiced, the phrase might sound like this: Ding . . . ding-dong . . . dong-ding . . . ding-ding-ding . . . dong-ding. This kind of phrase is not complicated, and by itself is musically uninteresting. But put the *agogô* part with the pulsating bass lines of the *surdos*, and you have bass and treble calling and responding. Add the *caixas*, or snares, and you can begin to feel the samba's groove, or swing. If you add the *repiques*, the *tambourins*, and the *rocars*, you then have all the *naipes*, or sections, working together, all playing different parts but as one group. Thus, different members are all playing simple parts that sound complex and incredibly beautiful – *together*. As experienced samba players often point out, the most difficult challenge in playing samba in a *bloco* is not executing the notes of the phrases in isolation (i.e. playing "right"); it is executing the notes in full synchronization with the group (i.e. playing together). In Illich's terms, the relationships in the *roda* embody not only complementarity, but also conviviality, a term which for Illich refers to a sense of "individualized freedom in personal interdependence."[12]

As I play the *agogô*, I am aware that the *agogô*-ness of the *agogô* is most fully expressed in the *roda*. For it is in the *roda* that its distinctiveness – its unique voice – and its relatedness – its capacity to build up other voices – establish harmony and a sense of proportion. As I play the *agogô*, I am also aware that I am a *gringo*, a foreigner surrounded and included by Brazilians within their *roda de samba*. Yet, through being included in the *roda*, I no longer see myself as a *gringo*, nor am I magically transformed into a Brazilian. Like the *agogô*, I have a distinct voice, yet a voice that belongs in the *roda*. I am "in between," but I know that I am *in*, a *brasicano* who is a co-participant in the *roda*. My experience of being included in the musical space of the *roda*, as a foreigner, is parabolic of another inclusion: inclusion in the body of Christ. Thus, the *roda* is

---

12. Ivan Illich, *Tools for Conviviality* (London: Marion Boyars, 1973), 11.

parabolic of being included in the space of the incarnation, the personal space that, Illich insists, Christians are called to inhabit and to "prolong."[13]

All of which is to say: through the experience of being included in the *bloco* (samba ensemble), I discovered a way of integrating the musical imagination of the *bloco* with a theological imagination which was being increasingly shaped by my continuing encounter with Illich. Being immersed in the *roda de samba* took me deeper into the intercultural immersion, beyond the grammar, rhythm, and inflection of Brazilian Portuguese, directly and more deeply into "the poetic, the historical, and the social aspects"[14] of Brazilian reality, which Illich saw as essential elements of the preparation for the study of missiology. Therefore, a virtuous circle began between Illich and the "samba circle": Illich guided me to take the "samba circle" seriously as part and parcel of my intercultural formation, and the "samba circle" became a primary context in which Illich's insight came alive.

Conclusion: Research as an Exercise in "Beginning in the Middle"

Like all doctoral researchers, as a doctoral candidate I knew that the defining function of doctoral research, so the standard definition goes, is to make "an original contribution to knowledge." I knew I had to tick that "original contribution" box, and I did that by reappropriating Ivan Illich for contemporary theology to fill a research gap – that is, by demonstrating that he offers a compelling contribution to contemporary accounts of Christian mission.

But I also knew that the basic function of research (in general) was not "to fill research gaps in an academic field" but to answer questions by gathering information. As discussed earlier, my questions were not determined by a research gap in an academic field, but rather by a gap between my lived experience as a missionary in Brazil and my theological imagination struggling to catch up with that experience.

---

13. Ivan Illich in Cayley, *Rivers North of the Future*, 207.
14. Ivan Illich, *The Church, Change and Development* (Chicago: Urban Training Center, 1970), 87.

Therefore, filling a "research gap" in relation to Illich in the field of theology was not the driving factor for my research into Illich. The deeper reason for turning to Illich was that, since 2007, Illich had become the most challenging and reliable guide that I had encountered while navigating Christian/missionary existence in Brazil and beyond. More than anyone else, Illich had influenced me by naming the air I breathed as a missionary, by navigating a similar path in the Americas, and by inspiring me to embrace both the truth that comes to us in Jesus (Eph 4:21) and "the world that has come upon us."[15]

The methodological assumption that eventually informed my entire doctoral thesis is taken from Rowan Williams: "I assume that the theologian *is* always beginning in the middle of things."[16] Williams argues here that the theologian neither begins at the beginning, in the sense of "starting from scratch," nor begins at the end by securing a standpoint that provides a complete and totalizing overview. Rather, the theologian is always already "placed" within history, and, therefore, works from "a practice of common life and language already there, a practice that defines a specific shared way of interpreting human life as lived in relation to God."[17] For my purposes here, "beginning in the middle" is a shorthand for the methodological approach by which I (1) reflected theologically upon my own social location (involving "movement" and "placement") and (2) challenged the objectification of theological knowledge by making that reflection-upon-location visible in the thesis itself.

In putting the matter in this way, I am suggesting that my approach of "beginning in the middle" allows the notes of theological reflection to resound in an *ethnographic* key. In pointing to the ethnographic character of my research, I am not pointing to the use of particular ethnographic techniques.

---

15. W. J. Jennings, *The Christian Imagination: Theology and the Origins of Race* (New Haven: Yale University, 2010), 290.

16. Rowan Williams, *On Christian Theology*, Challenges in Contemporary Theology (Oxford: Blackwell, 2000), xii. Williams makes this reference to "beginning in the middle" in the prologue to his collection of essays in *On Christian Theology*. Although he makes no direct reference to Dietrich Bonhoeffer here, this trope of "beginning in the middle" can be found in Dietrich Bonhoeffer, *Dietrich Bonhoeffer Works*, vol. 3, *Creation and Fall: A Theological Exposition of Genesis 1–3*, ed. G. L. Müller and A. Schönherr, trans. D. W. Bloesch and J. H. Burtness (Minneapolis: Fortress, 1997), 30.

17. Williams, *On Christian Theology*, xii.

After all, I did not move to Brazil to do "fieldwork." I did not live in Brazil for seven years as a "participant observer," but rather as a permanent resident – a spouse/father of Brazilian citizens. Therefore, I am referring to ethnographic research not as a set of techniques, but as a research process: "in contrast to quantitative research, ethnography primarily uses an inductive method, which means that rather than apply a broad principle to a concrete situation, it seeks to discover what truth or valuable insight is found within specific locations – discovered in communal and individual stories, cultures, practices, and experiences. Ethnographic methods provide a path *by which* truth emerges, rather than a way to apply truth."[18]

Clearly, my research on Illich is also quantitative and bibliographical, yet my journey as an "outsider-insider" in Brazil required the same dispositions and habits of a good ethnographer. My basic point here is not to argue that my thesis has to be read as ethnographic research. Rather I am suggesting that situating it within the nascent ethnographic turn in theology and ethics is illuminative. Recent edited volumes such as *Ethnography as Christian Theology and Ethics*[19] as well as *Mission in Marginal Places: The Praxis*[20] make a compelling case for placing the voice and located experience of the researcher in the activity of advanced research. This is because it is precisely those ethnographic dimensions, such as (1) embodied knowing, (2) the integration of human experience and (theological) tradition, and (3) critical self-reflection, that allow theological truth to emerge.[21]

Indeed, what the scriptural letters of the apostle Paul, Augustine's *Confessions*, Julian of Norwich's *Revelations of Divine Love*, Vincent Donovan's *Christianity Rediscovered*,[22] Howard Thurman's *Jesus and the Disinherited*,[23] and Gustavo Gutiérrez's *We Drink from Our Own Wells*[24] all have in common

---

18. Christian Scharen and Aana Marie Vigen, eds., *Ethnography as Christian Theology and Ethics* (London: Continuum, 2011), 17.
19. Scharen and Vigen, *Ethnography*.
20. Pears and Cloke, "Introduction," *Mission in Marginal Places*.
21. Scharen and Vigen, *Ethnography*, 61–62.
22. Vincent J. Donovan, *Christianity Rediscovered*, 25th anniversary ed. (Maryknoll: Orbis, 2003).
23. Howard Thurman, *Jesus and the Disinherited*, reprint ed. (Boston: Beacon, 2012).
24. Gustavo Gutiérrez, *We Drink from Our Own Wells: The Spiritual Journey of a People*, trans. M. J. O'Connell (Maryknoll: Orbis, 1984).

is a form of doing theology that does not mute, but rather "voices" personal experience. And when we closely observe the wells of Christian tradition from which we all drink, we recognize that before these sources became Christian "classics" to be canonized and researched, they were produced by Christians doing advanced theological research in the deepest sense – that is, making sense of their experience and contexts as a response to the Word that is "living and active" (Heb 4:12). Moreover, recent theological monographs, such as Mary McClintock Fulkerson's *Places of Redemption: Theology for a Worldly Church*[25] and Angel Méndez-Montoya's *The Theology of Food: Eating and the Eucharist*,[26] offer examples of how advanced researchers are making their own location and experience explicit in doing theology. Therefore, to recognize that we are always already "beginning in the middle" is to recognize that we researchers do not first get our theology sorted and then figure out how to apply it. Rather we discover by "beginning in the middle" that lived experience and advanced research can and should be a movement from the rupture to the renewal of our theological imagination (Rom 12:1–2).

Discussion Questions

1. In what ways have you seen the push for "objectivity" pressed upon you in your own theological studies? To what extent have you been enabled to be a "real" person?

2. List three or four major theological and/or philosophical weaknesses in the classic emphasis on "objective" knowledge. What are some of the dangers or challenges in bringing a greater emphasis on personal subjective experience into advanced studies? How might these challenges be addressed so that we can remain "real" people in our pursuit of meaningful knowledge and understanding?

---

25. Mary McClintock Fulkerson, *Places of Redemption: Theology for a Worldly Church* (Oxford: OUP, 2010).
26. Angel F. Méndez-Montoya, *The Theology of Food: Eating and the Eucharist* (Hoboken: Wiley-Blackwell, 2012).

3. "I assume that the theologian is always beginning in the middle of things" (Rowan Williams). Reflect back on your own life. What have been the major *viradas* ("turning points") in the intersection between your life experiences and your development of theological understanding? How have you seen "beginning in the middle" as a key element in your own pilgrimage?

4. How do you see the dissonance within the 3 Ss – "theological production and formation (seminary), visions for 'gathered church' (sanctuary), as well as the strategies and financial basis for social transformation (street)" – in your context? Suggest one or two possible ways in which you personally and your school as a whole might bring better integration within these three elements.

5. The chapter focuses on "doing theology with and after Illich." Who are the key people in your own experience with whom and after whom your theological thinking has been shaped? How has this taken place?

Bibliography

Bonhoeffer, Dietrich. *Creation and Fall: A Theological Exposition of Genesis 1–3*. Vol. 3 of *Dietrich Bonhoeffer Works*, edited by G. L. Müller and A. Schönherr, translated by D. W. Bloesch and J. H. Burtness (Minneapolis: Fortress, 1997).

Cayley, David. *The Rivers North of the Future: The Testament of Ivan Illich as Told to David Cayley*. Toronto: House of Anansi, 2005.

Donovan, Vincent J. *Christianity Rediscovered*. 25th anniversary ed. Maryknoll: Orbis, 2003.

Ewell, Samuel Earl III. "Prolonging the Incarnation: Towards a Reappropriation of Ivan Illich for Christian Mission and Life Together." PhD diss., University of Birmingham, 2014.

Fulkerson, Mary McClintock. *Places of Redemption: Theology for a Worldly Church*. Oxford: OUP, 2010.

Galeano, Eduardo. *Open Veins of Latin America: Five Centuries of the Pillage of a Continent*. Translated by C. Belfrage, 1973. 25th anniversary ed. New York: Monthly Review, 1997.

Gutiérrez, Gustavo. *We Drink from Our Own Wells: The Spiritual Journey of a People*. Translated by M. J. O'Connell. Maryknoll: Orbis, 1984.

Hiebert, Paul Gordon. "The Missionary as Mediator of Global Theologizing." In *Globalizing Theology: Belief and Practice in an Era of World Christianity*, edited by Craig Ott and Harold A. Netland, 288–308. Grand Rapids: Baker Academic, 2006.

Illich, Ivan. *Celebration of Awareness: A Call for Institutional Revolution.* London: Marion Boyars, 2000.

———. *The Church, Change and Development.* Chicago: Urban Training Center, 1970.

———. "To Hell with Good Intentions." 1968. Accessed 22 July 2010. http://www.davidtinapple.com/illich/1968_cuernavaca.html.

———. *Tools for Conviviality.* London: Marion Boyars, 1973.

Jennings, W. J. *The Christian Imagination: Theology and the Origins of Race.* New Haven: Yale University, 2010.

Méndez-Montoya, Angel F. *The Theology of Food: Eating and the Eucharist.* Hoboken: Wiley-Blackwell, 2012.

Myers, Ched. "Between the Seminary, the Sanctuary, and the Streets: Reflections on Alternative Theological Education." *Ministerial Formation* 94 (July 2001): 49–52.

Pears, Michael, and Paul Cloke, eds. *Mission in Marginal Places: The Praxis.* Milton Keynes: Authentic, 2016.

Scharen, Christian, and Aana Marie Vigen, eds. *Ethnography as Christian Theology and Ethics.* London: Continuum, 2011.

Thurman, Howard. *Jesus and the Disinherited.* Reprint ed. Boston: Beacon, 2012.

Ward, Geoffrey C., and Ken Burns. *The War: An Intimate History, 1941–1945.* New York: Knopf, 2007.

Williams, Rowan. *On Christian Theology.* Challenges in Contemporary Theology. Oxford: Blackwell, 2000.

20

Telling Tales:
Stories That Embox Theology

Havilah Dharamraj

"Spending time with stories" (*katha kaalakshepa*) is a term used to describe the Indian tradition of oral storytelling. It has myriad forms, each specific to the region, to the language, and to the community. The literary form of the stories is most often poetry, and, as such, can be readily rendered into song. Thus, in Tamil Nadu, there is a self-explanatory tradition called *kathaiyum paattum* ("story and song").[1]

Another layer is sometimes added on beyond the aural, as in the example of *kaawad bachana* ("story using a *kaawad*"), practised by troupes of itinerant storytellers in Rajasthan over four centuries. The *kaawad* is a storytelling aid – a small wooden structure with multiple doors that fold in upon each other. Each door opens to reveal paintings of stories, with as many as twenty doors available. As the audience's eye dwells on the pictures, the stories are sung out, making the narration an aesthetic stimulus to both ear and eye.[2] Even more imaginatively layered is the *harikatha* ("stories about [the deity] Hari") which is an astoundingly composite art form. Strung into the main storyline

---

1. Pia Chandavarkar, "Indian Storytellers Struggle to Keep Tradition Alive," *DW Made for Minds*, 2 May 2013, accessed 11 April 2017, http://www.dw.com/en/indian--struggle-to-keep-tradition-alive/a-16765198.
2. Ranee Kumar, "An Ancient Art of Storytelling," *The Hindu*, updated 28 November 2013, accessed 11 April 2017, http://www.thehindu.com/features/friday-review/history-and-culture/an-ancient-art-of-storytelling/article5371732.ece.

are sub-plots and anecdotes, while the presentation itself incorporates music and song, drama and dance, jokes and ready wit.[3]

In these storytelling traditions, the themes are usually religious in nature, rehearsing the myths and legends of Hindu epics. Some traditions, though, like the *kathaiyum paattum*, incorporate fables populated by talking animals to whom are attributed "human characteristics, behaviour patterns, and even ethical propensities."[4] Thus, "the lion is strong but dull of wit, the jackal crafty, the heron stupid, the cat a hypocrite."[5]

Among the collections of fables, the best known is the ancient anthology titled the *Panchatantra*, the "five discourses," a reference to the five sections or books in the collection. Dating back to a timeless oral tradition, the written composition is arguably dated third century BC.[6] Given the extent of its influence (including on the *Arabian Nights* and *Aesop's Fables*), it has been claimed that "No other work of Hindu literature has played so important a part in the literature of the world as the Sanskrit story collection called *Pañcatantra*."[7] The stories use both poetry and prose, the former largely proverbial. What makes the fables intriguing is that each book has a frame narrative into which stories are interrelatedly embedded by "emboxment."[8] Like a set of Russian dolls, the stories are nested into each other, going down to three or even four levels of story-within-a-story.

The purpose of the *Panchatantra* was probably the dissemination of political philosophy and practice, epigrammatically summed up at the end of each fable as a precept to follow. This classifies it as *nītishastra*, "wise conduct,"

---

3. G. S. Amar, "Harikatha," in *Encylopaedia of Indian Literature*, ed. Amaresh Datta (New Delhi: Sahitya Akademi, 1988), 2:1551–1552.

4. Patrick Olivelle, "Introduction," in *The Five Discourses on Worldly Wisdom by Visnusarman*, trans. Patrick Olivelle (New York: New York University, 2006), 25.

5. Arthur W. Ryder, "Translator's Introduction," in *The Panchatantra of Vishnu Sharma*, trans. Arthur W. Ryder (Chicago: University of Chicago, 1925), 12.

6. Olivelle, "Introduction," 20–21.

7. Franklin Edgerton, *The Panchatantra Reconstructed*, vol. 2, *Text and Critical Apparatus*, American Oriental Series 3 (New Haven: American Oriental Society, 1924), 3; cited in Olivelle, "Introduction," 17. For its migration out of India and its influence on literature in Asia and Europe, see Vijay Bedekar, "History of Migration of *Panchatantra* and What It Can Teach Us," Institute for Oriental Study, Thane, 27 December 2008, accessed 11 April 2017, http://www.orientalthane.com/speeches/speech2008.htm.

8. Olivelle, "Introduction," 23.

offered to the royal court, to kings, ministers, and courtiers (much like one possible function of the biblical book of Proverbs). Ryder describes this "wise conduct" (*nīti*) as "the harmonious development of the powers of man, a life in which security, prosperity, resolute action, friendship, and good learning are so combined to produce joy."[9] In other words, the *Panchatantra*, like Proverbs, offers advice on how to maximize life.

However, a fundamental difference between the *Panchatantra* and biblical literature that uses the narrative and proverbial genres is that the *Panchatantra* is unashamedly pragmatic, setting a desirable end over the means to that end. Thus, in the context of court intrigues, deception and counter-deception are endorsed as strategies that a winner uses before these get practised on him or her.[10] *Nīti* is therefore ethically ambiguous – it endorses both values and counter-values towards what is considered a desired end. This is in sharp contrast with the use of the word *nīti* in vernacular translations of the Bible, where *nīti* is the equivalent of the English term "righteousness." Thus, in Proverbs, the "righteous" person follows ethical means in living out life, expecting a God-ordained good end as a result of his or her right choices and actions.

With this historical background, and considering the current movements in India to revive our heritage of storytelling for use in education, in therapy, and in coaching,[11] we provide a sample "essay" at master's level submitted for the course "Exegetical Study of an Old Testament Book: Judges." The form of the essay mimics the *Panchatantra*: that is, it consists of fables set in a frame narrative with emboxment down to three levels. The third level uses a *Panchatantra* story, familiar to most Indian children. The footnotes demonstrate the basic expectation for scholarly engagement and for analysis of an issue, and could be more substantial.

It is possible that this or other forms of storytelling, ancient or modern, can be used for master's- and even doctoral-level dissertations, either as a single

---

9. Ryder, "Translator's Introduction," 10.
10. Olivelle, "Introduction," 40–41. Contra, for example, Ryder, who sees only positive ethics in the *Panchatantra*. "Translator's Introduction," 5–10.
11. See Indian Storytelling Network, founded in 2011 by Geeta Ramanujam, with chapters in major Indian cities: http://www.indianstorytellingnetwork.org/. See also the Kahani Project: http://thekahaniproject.org/.

continuous story or as a portfolio of stories.[12] Such a piece of work would use very substantial footnotes to show the theological reflection and critical engagement with scholars.

The primary question driving this master's-level course assignment is a *Panchatantra*-oriented theological issue: *Does the book of Judges present a devious God who strategically changes sides in order to win?*

The Watering Hole

"I am puzzled," the pupil said. (He had been studying the book of Judges all week.) "I am puzzled that God empowers all these sorts of leaders."

"All these sorts . . . ?"

"A coward of a man . . ."

"Barak?"

"And a power-hungry gangster . . ."

"Jephthah?"

"And a muscle-man who can't think beyond gratifying his body . . ."

"Samson."[13]

"Does God not care about who he backs?[14] *I mean to ask, whose side is God on?"*

---

12. Steps on this journey have already taken place. See, for example, Aminta Arrington, "Hymns of the Everlasting Hills: The Written Word in an Oral Culture in Southwest China" (PhD diss., Biola University, 2014); and W. Jay Moon, *African Proverbs Reveal Christianity in Culture: A Narrative Portrayal of Builsa Proverbs Contextualizing Christianity in Culture*, American Society of Missiology Monograph Series 5 (Eugene: Pickwick, 2009).

13. The book of Judges contains seven cycles of stories arranged in a downward moral spiral in which the successive judges are increasingly flawed. Robert G. Boling makes this summary statement: After Othniel, "[t]he remainder of the period was filled . . . with major and minor malfunctions, deviations from the Othniel standard." *Judges: Introduction, Translation and Commentary*, Anchor Bible 6A (London: Doubleday, 1975), 83. A full development of this schema may be found in Dennis T. Olson, "The Book of Judges: Introduction, Commentary and Reflections," in *The New Interpreter's Bible* (Nashville: Abingdon, 1998), 2:762–765. (Of course, this raises the question of the place of judges in Heb 11 alongside the heroes of faith. For explanations, see Barry G. Webb, *The Book of Judges*, New International Commentary on the Old Testament [Grand Rapids: Eerdmans, 2012], 55–57, 418; Daniel I. Block, *Judges, Ruth*, New American Commentary 6 [Nashville: Broadman & Holman, 1999], 70.)

14. See Olson, "Judges," 850–851, which reviews the Samson story to infer that "the Lord works in mysterious and seemingly contradictory ways," and finally reaches the ethically problematic conclusion that "God seems constrained to work through such devious and sinful means in the disordered context of a splintered and rebellious Israelite nation" because "God is free to

"Let me tell you a story."

Once upon a time, the great forest to the north was ruled by a lion.[15] He was as strong and fearsome as he was wise. But most important was that he cared for his subjects and for the forest they lived in. He watched over the shoals of little fish in the ponds with as much attention as he gave to the herds of trumpeting elephants. He was a good king.

The forest, as we said, was a great one. It ran up over the Aravalli hills, and swished down into deep gorges. Streams hurried through it. Springs broke through the forest floor, swirling into pools. Some of these pools were deep. Even if the streams dried up in the heat of summer, the pools remained. They shrank, but were still there – watering holes that kept animals alive till the monsoon rains came again. It was important to attend to these watering holes, so at each the lion king appointed a regent. He himself spent his days patrolling the far reaches of the forest.

Our story is about one such watering hole, whose regent was a wild rabbit,[16] a clever one. The pool, long and narrow in shape, was always busy. Fish darted. Tadpoles swarmed. Frogs wetly plopped about from water to lotus pads to land. Herons alighted on the rim, and waded in hopefully. Kingfishers flashed in the trees that bent down into the water. A peacock would come by now and then. What you couldn't always see was a great long beast that slithered about between the reeds at the pool's edge – a crocodile. At the near end of the pool was a broad green ring of short grass, tunnelled through into a maze of wild rabbit warrens. At the far end, the long pool slapped against a wide semi-circle of rock that

---

contravene the very laws God has given to Israel."

15. In the *Panchatantra*, the lion "is the king of the wild, the king of all animals, his only rival being the elephant. He is noble and brave . . ." Olivelle, "Introduction," 29.

16. The hare in the *Panchatantra* "is small but crafty and smart, and can outwit his larger and stronger rivals." Olivelle, "Introduction," 29. In my story, the traditional hare had to morph into a wild rabbit for the sake of the plot: rabbits burrow, while hares live on the surface of the ground.

rose up and up into a rather spectacular cliff-face. It was a pool to which you would want to take your cellphone and selfie stick.

When the monsoon came each year, the pool would swell with the rain. Often, the water got into the low-lying warrens. The rabbits would evacuate and move further up the slope till the monsoon quietened down and the water level fell to normal. During one such monsoon, as the watering hole began to creep outward, greedily lapping up the land at its edges, the rabbits found they had a far more serious problem than simply being temporarily homeless.

An ugly black snake[17] had arrived in an anthill halfway up the slope, and found that rabbits were an easy catch, especially if they were being flushed out of their warrens. So it decided to stay a while. It had a cosy hole in the ground, waterproofed by the hard mud of the anthill. And there was the guarantee of a daily meal.

With each week, the rabbits lost relatives and lost courage. The regent thought a while and remembered the story of the thirsty crow.

> *One hot summer day, a thirsty crow finally found a pot with some water in it. Perched on the rim, the crow bent down to get himself a drink. He couldn't reach the water. What was he to do? He looked around and saw pebbles on the ground around. He picked up the pebbles and dropped them into the pot one by one. With each pebble, the water rose. The crow got his drink and flew off satisfied.*[18]

Think hard and work hard, and you can find a solution to any problem, said the wisdom of the ancients. Inspired, the rabbit-

---

17. In the *Panchatantra*, "the snake (especially the cobra) is much feared; there can be no friendship with a snake ... [It is a] common image of danger lurking in the most unexpected of places ..." Olivelle, "Introduction," 30–31.

18. See a version in "Tales of Panchatantra: The Thirsty Crow," accessed 14 April 2017, http://www.lehren.com/kids/fairy-tales-kahaniya/tales-panchatantra-thirsty-crow-kids-animated-story-20160712.

regent came up with a plan. "Why should only our homes be flooded?" he asked. "Let's make our problem the snake's problem as well. We'll burrow a tunnel from the pool to the anthill."

It didn't take too long to dig the tunnel. The rabbits all gladly took turns at it. Soon, the tunnel was within inches of the pool-water at one end and the anthill at the other end. What was needed now was a distraction. Someone had to get the snake out while the rabbits linked up the pool and anthill. The regent said he would create the distraction. He was brave and cunning, but he wasn't the swiftest. There were nimble young ones that could readily outrun him, but the regent said this task was his to do.

So off he went to the anthill just as it was the snake's usual mealtime. The snake, now grown plumper and rounder on her regular rabbit-diet, was just then sliding out of her hole. To her surprise, here was a meal hopping right up to her. Just as she prepared to strike, the rabbit changed direction and leaped up the slope. The snake could see that this wasn't a particularly fast rabbit, and followed eagerly. The other rabbits quickly set to work on flooding the anthill.

The regent was going as fast as he could, but the snake was zig-zagging in upon him. Just when it seemed that the victory would be won – but at the cost of the regent's life – something unexpected happened. Out from the grey monsoon sky, an eagle swooped down. He could have taken either the rabbit or the snake – either would have made him a good lunch. But at that moment, the rabbit slid under a lantana bush and the snake, only seconds behind the rabbit, was surprised by the eagle. Hearing the rush of wings, the rabbit threw a frantic look behind. There was the snake being carried away into the sky. She was writhing mightily, but there was no hope of escape.

The monsoon clouds rolled on, moving noisily north. The sun came out again, and scolded the swollen pool back to its place. The warrens become habitable. The snake faded into a cautionary tale for young rabbits. There was peace again.

"Hmm," said the pupil, thoughtfully. "God is on the side of those who get on with the job?"

"Ehud put to use all that he could – left hand, 18-inch dagger, a mind that could work out a daring assassination..."

"And work out a brilliant war plan. Where does God come in?"

"He supplies the coincidences.[19] The careless guards, a corpulent tyrant who makes himself even more vulnerable by dismissing his guard, the defecation which wins Ehud time to muster his troops."

"Same with Jael, I suppose?"

"With a few changes. A strong right hand, a hammer, and a tent peg..."

"Warm words, warm milk, and a warm rug..."

"And the ability to pull off a daring assassination."

"And God provides the rest. A freak thunderstorm over Tabor..."

"Which brings Sisera to Jael's door."

"Just when her pro-Sisera husband is away. I get it. Even cowardly Gideon. He figures the war plan – the three hundred trumpets would have signalled as many regiments. He cleverly tricked the enemy."

"And God, for his part, provided the panic."

"So, yes. God works for those who work for his people.[20] But, what about the others in the book – the self-gratifying ones who get divine empowerment anyway?"

"Let me continue the story."

---

19. Olson, for example, tables "the high number of fortuitous coincidences" in the Ehud story. "Judges," 773.

20. The first phase of Judges covers three cycles of deliverance featuring in succession Othniel, Ehud, and the trio of Deborah–Barak–Jael. The pattern, largely, is that of a judge who uses his/her resourcefulness and courage, sometimes in covert ways. Does this warrant the kind of conclusion Webb reaches on Ehud? "[Ehud's] deceptions have been providentially directed and guaranteed by Yahweh... We can't explain his choice of Ehud... Why a devious assassin?... [Yahweh's] activity assumes a new character here. It is secretive, deceptive, and less accessible to human perception and explanation than it was in the Othniel episode." *Judges*, 169. Similarly, Olson comments on the moral ambiguity of Jael's actions. "Judges," 783. Block attempts an answer with: "[I]n the dark days of the governors the tools available to God are crude." *Judges*, 171. A much more helpful and biblically consistent reading is to appreciate the underlying moral emphasis in these stories. As Susan Niditch explains at length in her chapter "The Ideology of Tricksterism" in *War in the Hebrew Bible: A Study in the Ethics of Violence* (Oxford: OUP, 1993), 106-122: The Ehud and Jael stories "are dominated by the contest between those occupying a marginal place in society and the powerful, those at the centre of society with the capacity to oppress." Similarly, Olson, "Judges," 782. Thus, God does not trespass the boundaries of biblical *nīti* ("righteousness") any more than does the regent rabbit.

The years passed, and the rabbit died of ripe old age. Not waiting for the lion, the creatures of the pool elected their next regent – a smooth-talking mongoose. The creatures wanted someone who ensured that they wouldn't ever be terrorized by a snake again. With that in mind, a mongoose seemed the best option.[21]

When our story resumes, it is springtime. Birds began to poke around for twigs that held the promise of a nest. The *ber* trees around the pool were clustering over with glistening fruit, bloodshot-green. And suddenly, one day, the pool had a horde of unexpected visitors – monkeys.[22] On their way through the forest, they came upon the ripening fruit, and decided to stay over the *ber* season. Monkeys are not known for behaving themselves. And these monkeys were rowdier than usual. They set up an ear-deafening chatter all day long as they leaped from branch to branch stuffing themselves with *ber*. They scared the squirrels and birds away from their fair share of fruit. What was worse, they began to raid the bird nests, both on the trees and in the bushes by the water. The young ones, especially, took a great liking to bird eggs, sucking them with noisy delight.

The birds gathered together – bulbuls, koels, parrots, wild pigeons, mynahs, and even a peacock – and marched off to the regent. They complained bitterly. The mongoose was sitting at the entrance to his hole in the rocks, his brown coat shining and his bushy tail curled neatly around his forelegs. He listened attentively, and assured the birds he would talk to the monkeys and ask them to leave.

What passed between the mongoose and the monkeys no one knew, but things became much worse. The monkeys now began to catch the birds. A bird could barely alight on a branch and it would fall into the nimble paws of a lurking monkey. Watching

---

21. In the *Panchatantra*, the "mongoose's claim to fame is its eternal and innate enmity with snakes. In a country infested with snakes one can understand the popularity of the mongoose." Olivelle, "Introduction," 30.
22. The ubiquitous monkey, in the *Panchatantra*, "is playful, but fickle and foolish." Olivelle, "Introduction," 30.

closely, the inhabitants of the pond figured that the monkeys and the mongoose had made a deal. The monkeys were allowed to stay and do as they pleased as long as they supplied the mongoose with a plump bird or two every mealtime.[23]

The monkeys grew increasingly uncontrollable, and as the weeks passed they began to take the mongoose for granted. Rather than give him his bird-meals, they began to eat the birds themselves. The mongoose was outraged at this open disrespect. He slunk off to report the situation to the lion. And this is the story the lion told him:

> *There was once a monkey who lived on a jamun tree by the river. When the tree fruited, he would spend all day enjoying the sweet purple fruit. A crocodile came by, and the monkey generously threw him down some fruit. And with that, a friendship began. The monkey and the crocodile would talk and eat all day until it was time for the crocodile to return to his home on an island in the river.*
>
> *One day, the monkey gave him some extra jamuns to take back to his wife. The crocodile's wife had never tasted anything so good. "If this fruit is so sweet," she remarked, "how much sweeter the monkey should be, since he eats nothing but jamun all day. Dear husband, bring me that monkey's heart as a special treat."*
>
> *Of course, the crocodile was horrified at the thought. The monkey was a dear friend. But his wife would not relent. Unable to bear her nagging, he consented. The next day, he invited the monkey home to meet his wife. The unsuspecting monkey readily agreed. He clambered down onto the crocodile's back, and they began the journey across the water. Halfway*

---

23. In the deteriorating cycles of the judges, this is the situation in the second phase. Gideon turns upon his own people at Succoth and Peniel. Abimelek, the self-appointed judge, inflicts a massacre on his subjects at Shechem.

through, the crocodile couldn't help telling the monkey the reason why he was taking the monkey home. The monkey thought fast.

"Your wife is welcome to eat my heart!" exclaimed the monkey. "Why didn't you tell me before, though? I keep my heart safe in a hole in the jamun tree. We must go back and get it. I'd be delighted to offer it to your dear wife."

The foolish crocodile turned around and swam back to the shore. The monkey nimbly leaped off the crocodile's back into the safety of the jamun tree. "Of course I don't keep my heart anywhere but in my body!" said the monkey. "Be off, you treacherous creature! And never come back!"[24]

On hearing the lion's story, the mongoose began to see how the monkeys could be dealt with. He returned to the pool and went straight to the crocodile.[25] It didn't take long for them to work out a scheme. The next morning, the crocodile offered the younger monkeys his back if they wanted to get their greedy paws on the eggs that lay beyond their reach – in the tall bushes that grew further into the pool. A whole community of herons had nested there and were so far safe from the monkey menace. The monkeys were eager to go. A ride on the back of a crocodile was exciting in itself. With the promise of heron eggs added on, the proposal was irresistible.

Slowly the monkey population began to diminish. Those that took the joyride in search of heron eggs never returned. The crocodile was growing fatter by the day. He smiled more. But we know by now that crocodiles aren't very clever. They tell things

---

24. See a fuller version in Ryder, "The Monkey and the Crocodile," in *Panchatantra*, 381–388.
25. In the *Panchatantra*, the crocodile "represents hidden danger lurking beneath the inviting waters of a lotus pond . . . It is vicious, with a face and body to match its character . . . when the monkey became friends with the crocodile the Indian listener would immediately think: 'Oh Oh! He's in trouble!'" Olivelle, "Introduction," 27.

to monkeys that they shouldn't. And so, one day, as he ferried a loadful of chattering monkeys to their death, the crocodile told them not to expect to live long. In their alarm, the monkeys leaped into the water. Nearly all of them drowned, but one made it back. When the monkeys heard the story the bedraggled youngster told, they hopped up and down in fury. Lately, they had been planning to move on. The *ber* season had ended and the nests had long been emptied. But before they left, they now had one last thing to do. And that was to teach the mongoose a lesson: Don't mess with monkeys. The mongoose got the mauling of his life.

The monkeys departed satisfied, but much depleted in number. As for the mongoose, he dimly figured that the lion – in telling him the story – had subtly worked against both him and the monkeys.[26] But there was nothing he could do about that. Bruised and shame-faced, he dragged himself off. No one saw him again.

"Ah," said the pupil, eyes narrowed. *"God may sometimes intentionally stir up disharmony?"*

"That's a disturbing thought, isn't it? Think of how he handles the civil war."

"Twice he advises Israel to go up against Benjamin . . ."

"But notice that he does not promise victory."

"And in both battles Israel is routed. He sets them up for defeat."

"A defeat which Israel well deserved."

"Is this how it works, then: God can play off one party against another, because both parties are in the wrong and need equally to be disciplined?"[27]

---

26. The lion does not directly provide advice, but instead tells a story that brings to a head the animosity between the erstwhile partners in crime. This is the parallel to how the Jotham–God pair bring about the destruction of Shechem and Abimelek, the two parties deserving judgement. Jotham tells a fable (Judg 9:7–15) and God stirs up animosity between Shechem and Abimelek (Judg 9:23). That this is *nīti* in the sense of biblical righteousness is well explained in Olson, "Judges," 818, with reference to the tower of Babel as an example. There, God stirs up internal conflict to bring to an end the rebellion of powerful communities. Further, Webb explains how Israel should have seen this as a chilling warning that their evil could similarly turn YHWH against them. *Judges*, 296; also, 281.

27. God punishes "Benjamin for its disobedience, just as the two previous battles had been God's judgment on the other tribes of Israel." Olson, "Judges," 885.

"Which means that even if one party wins this battle and the other wins that battle, God is on the side of neither party."

"Whose side is God on, then?"

"Let me finish the story."

> With the exit of the mongoose, the creatures unanimously agreed that the crocodile should be their leader. After all, it had been the crocodile who had eaten up (literally!) their enemy, the monkeys. So the crocodile became regent.
>
> Meanwhile, I should tell you that there was a reason why the lion patrolled the edges of his realm. Humans had begun to live quite close to the forest. They often came in to hunt beasts. Their traps killed some and maimed some. Some creatures they ate. Others they took away to sell. Some others they killed for what goods they could extract out of them. As time went by, they grew bolder and bolder.
>
> In our story, spring passed into summer. In many a pool, the sun licked up the water to the last drop, leaving the bottom dry to the point of cracking. The beasts of the forest began to suffer thirst. The pool in our story had shrunk, but not quite as much as some others had, for the spring was a deep one. Animals that usually drank from other watering holes began to come to this one. The humans turned this to their advantage, and began to lay traps in a wide circle around the pool. There were three of them that had ventured this deep into the forest. They had set up camp not far from the watering hole. Their traps caught little animals and big ones, from rabbits to deer. Occasionally, a pit trap caught an elephant. There was much distress around the pool.
>
> The deer[28] decided to appeal to the crocodile. He lay in the water, half-submerged, his beady eyes watching. He heard out the deer's request for protection against the hunters. Then he

---

28. The deer, in the *Panchatantra*, "is associated with the peace and tranquillity of forest hermitages. The deer is also the typical object of the hunt; indeed, the Sanskrit word for deer (*mṛga*) is related to the verb to hunt (*mṛgayate*) . . . [so] the deer always appears with a hunter close behind." Olivelle, "Introduction," 27–28.

explained that it was really too hot for him to bother himself. But he was very willing, he said, to eat a human if it came within striking distance. In fact, he had been waiting for a chance to try human meat for a long time now. It was up to the deer to make the arrangement.

The deer were disappointed. Their regent was not only lazy but greedy. There were stories to say that nothing good came of that combination.[29]

> On a hill lived a lazy jackal. Rather than hunt for his food, he lived off what he could find. One day, a huntsman came by the hill and, sighting a boar, shot an arrow at him. The boar was fatally wounded but charged at the huntsman. In the fight that ensued, both human and boar died. The jackal came by and was delighted at the compounded meal that lay before him. Greedy fellow that he was, he decided that he wouldn't spare anything, not even the bowstring – in fact, he was going to start with the bowstring (an appetiser!) before going on to the main meal. He snapped the high-tension bowstring with one greedy bite. The string recoiled and struck him, killing him instantly.[30]

The deer agreed that such a poor regent as this crocodile must be got rid of. After some thinking they came up with a strategy that would eliminate both problems – greedy humans, and lazy crocodile. They would lure the hunter to the pool's marshy edge (in which the crocodile wallowed), and then plunge into the water. (Deer are strong swimmers when they need to be.) That would put the human within the reach of the self-serving crocodile.

---

29. The phase three judges are Jephthah and Samson. Neither cares for the interests of the people. Indeed, "Jephthah [was motivated] by ambition and pagan values, Samson was driven by lust." Block, *Judges*, 471.

30. See a version in "Panchatantra Story: The Greedy Jackal," *explore2enjoy* (blog), 22 October 2010, accessed 14 April 2017, http://explore2enjoy.blogspot.in/2010/10/panchatantra-story-greedy-jackal.html.

Much like the lazy and greedy jackal, these two parties would meet their end.

It happened just so. The crocodile tasted his first human, and he liked what he ate. It was far better than monkey. He grinned a toothy grin, congratulating himself on his cunning. One way or another, he was now at the top end of the hunting sequence he had created: deer hunted by humans, and humans hunted by crocodile. But humans are clever too. After one of the hunters got fooled by the deer (and ended up inside the crocodile), the remaining two humans carefully surveyed the situation and made their plans.

Meanwhile, the deer had swum across to the far end of the pool and found a haven against the cliff-face. With the diminishing of the pool this summer, a narrow arc of land had emerged, enough for the herd. They now had the length of the pond, and the crocodile, between them and the hunters. The hunters had no way to reach the herd of deer unless they eliminated the crocodile. To the hunters, the prospect of getting their hands on a full herd of deer, trapped in a rocky cul-de-sac, was eminently inviting. They proceeded to act.

Armed with a net and an arsenal of rods, the hunters came for the crocodile. The crocodile wasn't in a mood to give in easily. Mud splashed in all directions as the net fell over the great beast. He thrashed this way and that, and even managed to get a few bites of his assailants. Just when the rods had done their deadly work and victory was presumed, an unexpected sound set the air vibrating.

It was the roar of the lion. Even as the hunters tried to gauge the direction from which the beast was coming, another roar shook the air, this time from a different side. (Did you know that lions are good ventriloquists? The confused prey sometimes actually ends up moving towards the lion!) Roar followed roar, and the humans, thoroughly muddled about both the direction and distance of the peril, backed towards the pond in panic, almost falling over the dead crocodile. To their dismay, the crocodile wasn't quite dead. The creature reared up to play his final act. In one fluid movement he took both the hunters. One, he tore asunder in his jaws. The other, he slashed to death with a sweep of his lethal tail. Then he subsided into the black ooze, and his beady eyes glazed over.[31]

Now you could see the lion. He was standing on the cliff at the far end, a ripple of yellow incandescence. One minute he was there, and the next he was gone.

"So whose side is God on in the book of Judges?"

"Let's think ... At different times, he's on different sides. Sometimes he lets the Moabites and Midianites get the upper hand, but that's because he's against sinning Israel. When Israel repents, he empowers this judge or that, and Israel is the winning side."

"But we mustn't read his empowerment of the judge as endorsement of that judge. He's not necessarily on the side of the judge."

"Not necessarily."

"So a self-gratifying judge can be empowered without being endorsed."

"Because the empowerment serves God's larger purpose – the deliverance of Israel."[32]

"But, as we said, God can also be against Israel when Israel sins."

"Of course. He doesn't overlook Israel's flaws either."[33]

"So God is on God's side alone?"

"He is. That's because he is always on the side of the right ... and who is more completely and consistently right than God himself?"

---

31. This is Samson's relationship with the Philistines: he loves them, he hates them. He loves their women and slaughters their men, just as the crocodile loves human flesh but sees humans as its enemy. God permits Samson to make his choices, but ensures that he gets his returns for the investment made in this judge in terms of Israel's deliverance from the Philistines. To this end, God sends the Spirit "in power" whenever Samson encounters the Philistines (Judg 14:19; 15:14). Like the crocodile, Samson is interested only in his self-gratification, but pays with his life, while God's plan for Israel's liberation continues unaffected. There is biblical *nīti* in this in that the righteousness of God is displayed in the justice meted out to a wilful judge.

32. Olson well observes the decreasing effect of Spirit-empowerment on the successive judges. "Judges," 802, 831. When it comes to the last judge, Samson, Block sums up his divine empowering thus: "[I]ronically, by the free exercise of his own immoral will, Samson serves as an agent of the Lord's ethical will." *Judges*, 472.

33. Besides the multiple times God works against Israel by handing Israel over to oppressors, a good verbal example of God "going up" or turning against Israel is in Judg 1:22–36: "[P]reviously God had gone up and fought *for* Israel, but now God goes up and fights *against* Israel." Olson, "Judges," 733, 747–748.

"I get it. The question we should be asking, then, is not 'Whose side is God on?' but—"

"Who is on the LORD's side?"

Discussion Questions

1. What are some of your favourite stories? See if you can match them genre-wise to those found in the Bible (e.g. fable, parable, riddle, hero-story, quest story, tragedy, humour). Pick a matching pair and tease out the similarities and differences (theme, purpose, theological or ethical content, etc.).

2. Why do you think the story has established itself as a didactic form across cultures and across time? What might we have lost in largely excluding this form from advanced theological studies?

3. Discuss at least one Christian story you know that communicates significant theological substance through a narrative form. How did the writer present the theological themes in story form?

4. What are one or two significant ways in which stories have shaped the worldview of people in your local context? Compare this with how your local church ministry uses or does not use stories; and uses stories effectively or ineffectively.

Bibliography

Amar, G. S. "Harikatha." In *Encylopaedia of Indian Literature*, Vol. 2, edited by Amaresh Datta, 1551–1552. New Delhi: Sahitya Akademi, 1988.

Arrington, Aminta. "Hymns of the Everlasting Hills: The Written Word in an Oral Culture in Southwest China." PhD diss., Biola University, 2014.

Bedekar, Vijay. "History of Migration of *Panchatantra* and What It Can Teach Us." Institute for Oriental Study, Thane, 27 December 2008. Accessed 11 April 2017. http://www.orientalthane.com/speeches/speech2008.htm.

Block, Daniel I. *Judges, Ruth*. New American Commentary 6. Nashville: Broadman & Holman, 1999.

Boling, Robert G. *Judges: Introduction, Translation and Commentary*. Anchor Bible 6A. London: Doubleday, 1975.

Chandavarkar, Pia. "Indian Storytellers Struggle to Keep Tradition Alive." *DW Made for Minds*, 2 May 2013. Accessed 11 April 2017. http://www.dw.com/en/indian-storytellers-struggle-to-keep-tradition-alive/a-16765198.

Edgerton, Franklin. *Text and Critical Apparatus*. Vol. 2 of *The Panchatantra Reconstructed*. American Oriental Series 3. New Haven: American Oriental Society, 1924.

Kumar, Ranee. "An Ancient Art of Storytelling." *The Hindu*, updated 28 November 2013. Accessed 11 April 2017. http://www.thehindu.com/features/friday-review/history-and-culture/an-ancient-art-of-storytelling/article5371732.ece.

Moon, W. Jay. *African Proverbs Reveal Christianity in Culture: A Narrative Portrayal of Builsa Proverbs Contextualizing Christianity in Culture*. American Society of Missiology Monograph Series 5. Eugene: Pickwick, 2009.

Niditch, Susan. *War in the Hebrew Bible: A Study in the Ethics of Violence*. Oxford: OUP, 1993.

Olivelle, Patrick. "Introduction." In *The Five Discourses on Worldly Wisdom by Visnusarman*, translated by Patrick Olivelle. New York: New York University, 2006.

Olson, Dennis T. "The Book of Judges: Introduction, Commentary and Reflections." In *The New Interpreter's Bible*, 2:762–765. Nashville: Abingdon, 1998.

Ryder, Arthur W., trans. *The Panchatantra of Vishnu Sharma*. Chicago: University of Chicago, 1925.

Webb, Barry G. *The Book of Judges*. New International Commentary on the Old Testament. Grand Rapids: Eerdmans, 2012.

21

Proverbs as Theology

Dwi Maria Handayani

Introduction

When I studied in the US, my American friend Joo used to take me to her house. I remember the first time I visited her: I was so fascinated by the different kinds of written information on the board and on the door of her fridge. As an Indonesian, I discovered how much I am an oral person. I was brought up in an oral culture where knowledge is passed from one generation to the next orally.[1] My parents never wrote me any sort of information. They just talked to me and asked me to remember everything.[2]

As is common in oral cultures, Indonesians love to socialize.[3] In that social interaction "historical events, moral values, religious values, custom,

---

1. A. Tella and A. O. Issa, *Library and Information Science in Developing Countries: Contemporary Issues* (Hershey: IGI Global, 2011), 98.
2. Douglas E. Ramage confirms this: "Indonesia is still in an oral culture. Decisions by the president, for example, are not always written down – they are relayed personally." Douglas E. Ramage, *Politics in Indonesia: Democracy, Islam, and the Ideology of Tolerance* (Abingdon: Psychology Press, 1997), x. "A recent study conducted by John Miller, president of Central Connecticut State University in New Britain, puts Indonesia in the second-lowest rank of 61 measurable countries for its 'literate behavior characteristics,' everything from numbers of libraries and newspapers to years of schooling and computer availability." Stefani Ribka, "As Illiteracy Rate Lowers, RI Struggles with Reading Habits," *The Jakarta Post*, 24 March 2016, http://www.thejakartapost.com/news/2016/03/24/as-illiteracy-rate-lowers-ri-struggles-with-reading-habits.html.
3. Carol Johnson, Vera Mackie, and Tessa Morris-Suzuki, *The Social Sciences in the Asian Century* (Canberra: ANU, 2015), 185.

fantasy stories, songs, spells, proverb, and ancestor's advice"[4] will be discussed. I find this same kind of learning process happens in me. I definitely love to talk more than to write. I am not used to writing down all information. I like to memorize material by talking about it with somebody. Therefore, this article is a reflection of my style of learning. This is a conversation about a Critical Discourse Analysis approach and how it might be used in a piece of doctoral research.

"Do you think they have a good service?" I asked Iljo, my best friend, who lives in Manila.

It was a hot day in Manila. I disliked the heat. The humid weather could spoil my mood. We were off class and planned to have a foot massage at Palengke.

"I have never gone to this salon before. But I heard they provide a good massage, and you can order coffee too," Iljo said. Getting a foot massage with manicure and pedicure is one of our favourite activities in Manila. For only 360 pesos, we can go home with beautiful feet and nails.

We got a *jeepney*[5] in front of the church and headed towards a beauty salon in Palengke. Soon after that the three of us, Iljo, Jane, and I, were sitting comfortably in pedicure chairs next to each other, with our feet soaking in hot water.

I was busy picking the colour for my nails when the lady spoke to me in Tagalog. "I am sorry, I don't speak Tagalog, I am an Indonesian," I said.

"She asked if you would like an extra massage on your shoulder," Iljo translated to me.

"Oh, no thank you."

I had almost fallen asleep on my chair when I heard Jane say, "I just submitted my proposal. I hope I will get good feedback."

"What is your topic of research?" asked Iljo.

---

4. Karin Czermak, Philippe Delanghe, and Wei Weng, "Preserving of Information Value in Oral Tradition of Minangkabau Society, West Sumatera, Indonesia" (paper delivered at UNESCO Conference on Language Development, Language Revitalization and Multilingual Education in Minority Communities in Asia, 6–8 November 2003, Bangkok, Thailand), 1.
5. Public transportation in Manila.

"I am going to do an exegetical study on some problematical passages in Acts," Jane answered with hesitation in her voice.

Iljo, Jane, and I are classmates. We are doing our doctoral studies. As a social worker, Jane had hoped that she could relate her dissertation to the work that she is doing, but unfortunately our program director insists that she needs to write a pure Biblical Studies dissertation.

"Ouch! Not too hard, please," I said to the lady as she put strong pressure on my calf.

"How about you, Ria? What is your topic of research?" Jane asked me.

"I am going to write about proverbs. Proverbs are very popular in my culture. Politicians, artists, teachers, parents, religious leaders, they all use proverbs," I answered.

"Oh, you mean traditional proverbs? Not the book of Proverbs?" Iljo responded quickly.

"I plan to do research on the role proverbs play in everyday life."

"Friend, remember you are a biblical scholar, not a sociologist." Every time Iljo wants to emphasize something she always calls me "friend."

"Won't you learn from my experience?" asked Jane.

"I don't like this. You two are looking for trouble," Iljo said. "If you want to graduate, you'd better limit yourself to exegetical writing or biblical theology."

"How would you design your research, Ria?" Jane interrupted.

"First, I need to collect traditional proverbs in society. Then I will analyse their role in everyday life. After that, I will analyse their theological meaning and compare them with biblical concepts on the same topic, especially from the book of Proverbs."

"Can you imagine how our program director will react to your proposal?" asked Iljo, rolling her eyes.

"I know, but I'll still try."

"Why are you so interested in proverbs?" Iljo asked, with curiosity in her tone.

"Because I like culture, and proverbs are very closely associated with cultures, I would like to understand how proverbs are defined by the cultural context."[6]

---

6. The *New Dictionary of Cultural Literacy* defines "proverbs" as "short, pithy sayings that reflect the accumulated wisdom, prejudices, and superstitions of the human race." Eric Donald Hirsch, Joseph F. Kett, and James S. Trefil, *The New Dictionary of Cultural Literacy* (New York: Houghton Mifflin Harcourt, 2002), 47. The words "prejudices" and "superstitions" suggest that proverbs

"Can you give me an example of your traditional proverbs?" asked Jane.

"For example, in my culture there is a proverb about women that says, '*Swarga nunut, neraka katut*' ('If the husband goes to heaven, the wife will go with him; if the husband goes to hell, he will also take his wife with him'). It means that women do not have rights to their own salvation."

"Oh, wow, that is such a dangerous concept!" Iljo responded.

"We in the Philippines also have proverbs," my masseuse suddenly said, jumping into the conversation.

"Really *ate*[7]? Can you give me an example?" I said.

"*Aanhin pa ang damo, kung patay na ang kabayo*," she answered quickly.

"It means, 'What good is the grass if the horse is already dead?'" Jane translated. "This proverb is usually used to express useless effort. Nothing can be changed."

"What methodology are you using?" asked Iljo.

"Hmm, I want to do Critical Discourse Analysis," I answered.

"What is that?" asked Jane.

"It is a methodology that analyses the role of language in society. It focuses on how social relations are constructed through written and spoken texts in communities."[8]

"I've never heard about that before," said Jane.

---

are closely related to the formation of society. They reflect the real situation of the people.

7. "Big sister" in Tagalog.

8. According to van Dijk, critical discourse analysis is a special approach to the study of text and talk. It is a method used to analyse the relations between discourse structure and power structure. Critical discourse analysis studies how the structure, strategies, and style of language and verbal interaction play a role in society. Teun A. van Dijk, "Principle of Critical Discourse Analysis," *Discourse and Society* 4, no. 2 (1993): 250–252. Wodak and Meyer consider critical discourse analysis as a paradigm characterized by principles such as problem-oriented "interests in de-mystifying ideologies and power" through the investigation of language – written, spoken, or visual. Critical discourse analysis aims to gain an accurate comprehension of how language functions in social institutions. Ruth Wodak and Michael Meyer, *Methods for Critical Discourse Analysis* (Thousand Oaks: SAGE, 2009), 3. McGregor argues that critical discourse analysis forces the researcher to see language not as an abstract entity but as words that have meaning in a historical, social, and political context. S. L. T. McGregor, *Critical Discourse Analysis: A Primer* (Halifax: Mount Saint Vincent University, 2010), 2. Fulcher asserts that critical discourse analysis can be seen as a way of understanding social interactions. R. Fulcher, *Critical Discourse Analysis* (New York: Longman, 2010), 7.

"Yes, it is an approach that is used in sociolinguistic study."[9]

"So basically you are comparing the Javanese proverbs and the Old Testament proverbs, right? What makes this Critical Discourse Analysis approach different from other methods of comparison?" asked Iljo.

"I think that with Critical Discourse Analysis you are not just comparing the texts but also the worlds behind the texts," Jane explained as she tried to understand.

"You mean that behind every proverb there is a deeper meaning that forms the structure of society?" Iljo asked.

"Exactly! I believe that by unmasking the written word or proverb we can have a deeper understanding of the values and beliefs of a society."[10]

"Is it possible that in ancient times, those who created proverbs did so to establish their power?" Jane interrupted. "You know sometimes people used language as a means of power."

"That is very possible. I see your point, Jane," said Iljo. "How can Critical Discourse Analysis help you to discover what is behind the text of proverbs?"

"Well, the issue of power has been at the core of the CDA project. The aim of Critical Discourse Analysis is to reveal what kinds of social relations of power are present in the text."[11]

"How?" Jane and Iljo responded in unison.

"Wow, I've got you both interested, huh? Well, there are three levels of discourse. First, we need to investigate the social factors which contributed to

---

9. This approach was introduced in the 1970s when some linguistics scholars started to recognize the role of language in structuring power relations in society. In the early 1990s, some scholars created critical discourse analysis as a network, following a small symposium held in Amsterdam in January 1991. Wodak and Meyer, *Methods for Critical Discourse Analysis*, 5.

10. Barajas says, "Values and beliefs are codified and manifested in all aspects of linguistic communication, such as popular expressions, shared vocabulary, oral traditions, conversational rules and modes of interaction, and even linguistic modes of creativity." Elías Domínguez Barajas, *The Function of Proverbs in Discourse: The Case of a Mexican Transnational Social Network* (Berlin: Walter de Gruyter, 2010), 50. Mieder asserts, "Proverbs, like riddles, jokes or fairy tales, do not fall out of the sky and neither are they products of a mythical soul of the folk. Instead they are always coined by an individual either intentionally or unintentionally." Wolfgang Mieder, *"Proverbs Speak Louder Than Words": Folk Wisdom in Art, Culture, Folklore, History, Literature and Mass Media* (Bern: Peter Lang, 2008), 14.

11. David Machin and Andrea Mayr, *How to Do Critical Discourse Analysis: A Multimodal Introduction* (Thousand Oaks: SAGE, 2012), 24.

the text; second, the way in which the text was produced and how this affects interpretation; and third, the text itself as the product of the first two stages."

"Any examples?" asked Iljo.

"Sure, I will give you another proverb about women."

"I think in proverbs women are mostly associated with beauty, and men with intelligence,"[12] said Jane.

"Actually it depends on the culture. *Ate*, do you have a Tagalog proverb about women?" I asked my masseuse.

"Yes, hmm . . . *magkapangit-pangit ng babae ay may sariling buti*."

"The ugliest woman has her own goodness," Jane translated for me.[13]

"Wow, that is a positive view on women. It is very different from the proverbs about women in my culture," I said.

"Really?"

"Yes; here's another example: *tiga ikang abener lakunya ring loka, iwirnya, ikang iwah, ikang udwad, ikang janmasri, yen katelu, wilut gatinya, yadin pweka nang istri hana satya budhinya dadi ikang tunjung tumuwuh ring cila*."

"Oh wow, what is that?" Jane said, as she let out a big yawn between her words.

"Very long, isn't it? It means: There are three things that cannot walk straight on earth: a river, a vine, and women. Three of them are intricate. If there is any upright woman, a flower will grow out of stone."

"A very negative view on women!" said Iljo.

"Absolutely! Critical Discourse Analysis will help me analyse why the views on women are so low and negative in Javanese culture."

"So what are possible social factors which contributed to the proverbs?" Iljo asked.

"They could be varied, such as social structure: class, status, age, ethnic identity, and gender. Or the social culture surrounding the text, such as politics, the economy, religion, education, and so on."[14]

---

12. Mineke Schipper, *Never Marry a Woman with Big Feet: Women in Proverbs from Around the World* (New Haven: Yale University, 2003), 41.
13. Leonardo N. Mercado, *The Filipino Mind* (Washington, DC: CRVP, 1994), 113.
14. Norman Fairclough, *Language and Power* (Abingdon: Routledge, 2013), 28–33.

"How do you investigate the production process of the texts? That would be very difficult!" Iljo said, as she looked down at her red painted toes.

"Many of the proverbs actually came from the old books of Javanese philosophy, which were written at the royal palace."[15]

"I see; so actually you can analyse why the royal family were producing these kinds of proverbs," said Jane while she tried to hold back another big yawn.

"Yes, and Critical Discourse Analysis will help us to reveal unseen connections within texts. It will also help us to identify areas of 'social wrong,' such as injustice, inequality, racism, danger, suffering, prejudice, and other similar issues."[16]

"How will you relate that to the biblical proverbs?" asked Iljo.

"There are several steps I need to do. First, I need to choose a proverb topic in both texts. If I choose a proverb on women in Javanese culture, I need to find a similar topic in Old Testament proverbs."

"That is very obvious."

"After that, I need to ask some questions relating to power, such as: 'Who is depicted as in power and over whom? Who is depicted as powerless and passive? Who is exerting power and why?'"[17]

"Can you do that with biblical proverbs?"

"Why not? Old Testament proverbs are also a reflection of culture."

"Absolutely! For example, 'proverbs concerning the *good wife* and the *quarrelsome wife* take on different meanings in a context where a married couple were rarely in close daily contact.'"[18]

"Maybe you should also analyse the texts themselves with the exegetical method that biblical scholars usually use."

"Of course I will do that as well."

---

15. The earliest Javanese literature about women is *Kakawin* poetry. "*Kakawin* were produced at the royal courts that flourished in Java from the eighth to the fifteenth centuries, and in Bali from the ninth until the early twentieth century." Helen Creese, "Images of Women and Embodiment in *Kakawin* Literature," *Intersections* 5 (May 2001), accessed 17 April 2017, http://intersections.anu.edu.au/issue5/creese.html#n11.

16. Norman Fairclough, *Critical Discourse Analysis: The Critical Study of Language* (Abingdon: Routledge, 2013), 231.

17. McGregor, *Critical Discourse Analysis*.

18. John J. Pilch, *The Cultural Life Setting of the Proverbs* (Minneapolis: Augsburg Fortress, 2016), back cover.

"How do you do that with the Javanese proverbs?"

"I still have no idea about that."

"Zzzzz." Suddenly we heard a gentle snore from Jane's chair.

"I need a coffee; can I have a black coffee, please? Jane! Wake up! Do you want a coffee?" Iljo said with her loud voice.

The waiter came to take her order. He stood in front us, holding his pad and waiting, a good-looking young man with a tattoo of an eagle on his left arm. "You guys are so boring," he said with a smile.

"Hey, you were listening to our discussion! You are right. That's why I fell asleep," Jane said.

"I am a theological student too. I'm doing my master's in theology. Now can I take your order?" He was looking at Iljo.

"Black coffee, please," Iljo said.

"How about you, *ate*?"

"What is your name?" I asked.

"Fernando. And I like your topic of research. I am currently researching the theological concept behind Tagalog folk songs."

"Hey, I want my coffee!" Iljo yelled at us.

"OK, I want a latte, please."

"Me, too," Jane said.

Fernando left and we looked at each other, smiling.

"Are you sure you can find sets of Javanese traditional proverbs that you can compare with the biblical proverbs?" Jane said with a grin as she tried to bear the pressure in her shoulder from the therapist.

"Absolutely! Last month I sat with my grandma – she could recall nearly fifty proverbs in one night," I said.

"Ouch!" Jane cried out. "Stop! Please stop."

"I am sorry," the masseuse said. "Your shoulders are so stiff."

"Yeah, I'm stressed out."

"Try to relax, Jane. Stop thinking about your proposal . . . Our program director is just too hard on you. Don't let him define your life. *If you let someone put the calf on your shoulders, it will not be long before he claps on the cow*," I said.

"I know. I am trying to relax here. Anyway, I like your topic, Ria."

The smell of coffee entered the room. Fernando walked towards us with a tray in his hands: "Here are your coffees, *ate*. My supervisor is here in the coffee shop. Please stop by after you are all done with your nail spas. I will introduce you to him."

"Thank you, Fernando. Very kind of you. We will be there in a minute," I said.

After we had finished our nail spas we moved to the coffee shop area. The top half of the walls was painted black, while the lower part was boarded, with the panels painted white. One big quote was written on the wall: "Coffee should be black as hell, strong as death, and as sweet as love."

Fernando greeted us and escorted us to a table. A man with a book in his hands was sitting at the table.

"Dr Raymond, this is *ate* Jane, *ate* Ria, and *ate* Iljo," Fernando introduced us properly to his supervisor.

"Please, come and take a seat," Raymond said as he pulled out three chairs for us.

"Thank you," I said.

"So, tell me about yourselves. You are theological students?"

"Yes, sir, we are doing our doctorate program at Shalom Seminary," Jane answered politely.

"Please don't call me 'sir.' You can call me *kuya*."[19]

"They are doing their research on traditional proverbs. It's very interesting," Fernando interrupted.

"Really? I love that," Raymond responded.

"Well, Ria is doing proverbs. I am just doing a plain exegetical research," said Jane.

"Tell me about your research, Ria," Raymond said as he reached for the last piece of his sandwich.

"I am interested in traditional proverbs, to see if there are any similarities or differences with the Old Testament proverbs."

"Any particular theme?"

"Yes, proverbs about women."

"Interesting! Do you know that there are many different expressions about a good wife in different proverbs?"

---

19. "Big brother" in Tagalog.

"Yes; for example, in the book of proverbs a good wife is described as a treasure and crown for her husband. In Java, a good wife is pictured as a beautiful sunset or a broken pepper."

"Ha ha! I know another one: *A wife is like a blanket: cover yourself, it irritates you; cast it aside, you feel cold*," said Raymond.

"What about this: *Darkness covers everything except a bad wife.*"

"Wow, you two are really enjoying this, huh?"

"Ha ha! I'm sorry! Anyway, what kind of approach are you using?" asked Raymond.

"Critical Discourse Analysis."

"Interesting! I am sure Critical Discourse Analysis will help you to dig into the cultural setting of the proverbs."

"Exactly, but I still have no idea how to do a textual analysis for the Javanese proverbs."

"Well, the principle is similar to biblical textual analysis. The first thing you need to do is to examine the structure of the text. What you need to do here is find the basic structural frame of the proverb. There are many books about this; one is written by Neal R. Norrick. You can check in the library."[20]

"OK, I can do that; and then what?"

"Then you need to analyse the function of the sentences – whether they are declarative or indicative, interrogative, imperative, or exclamatory."[21]

"That's it? Easy," said Iljo.

"You may also try to identify linguistic and rhetorical mechanisms. Such as 'word group,' grammar, figures, and so on."

"Word group?" asked Jane.

"Yes, you need to see the text use of words that have a common contextual background. For example, the vocabulary may be drawn directly from military, agriculture, shepherding, or just romance language."

"OK."

---

20. Neal R. Norrick, *How Proverbs Mean: Semantic Studies in English Proverbs* (Berlin: Walter de Gruyter, 1985), 51.

21. M. Mac Coinnigh, "Structural Aspects of Proverbs," in *Introduction to Paremiology: A Comprehensive Guide to Proverb Studies*, ed. Hrisztalina Hrisztova-Gotthardt and Melita Aleksa Varga (Berlin: Walter de Gruyter, 2015), 115.

"Next, you need to check the grammatical features. In many proverbs you will not find the subject, but you need to identify that because in Critical Discourse Analysis you need to assume who is in power as it usually does not appear explicitly in the text."

"Hmm."

"After you do all the investigations, then you can interpret your data."

"It could be theological interpretation, right?"

"Of course, and compare that with what you find in the Old Testament proverbs."

"Last, you can present your findings and suggestions for the benefit of Javanese women," Jane added.

"Absolutely!" Raymond said as he wiped his mouth. "Excuse me, I need to go to my class now, but it was great to see you all. See you in my office, Fernando."

"Yes, sir. I will be there at 4 p.m."

"Thank you, *kuya*," Jane, Iljo, and I responded almost at the same time.

"Wow, it is like we are *killing two birds with one stone*," Iljo said.

"Yes, thank you, Fernando, we got a great lesson from your supervisor," said Jane.

"You are welcome, *ate*."

Discussion Questions

1. To what extent is interdisciplinary reflection on Scripture allowed/welcomed/encouraged in your programs of study? Are your classes in Biblical Studies strictly according to traditional historical-critical exegetical analysis, or do you also have students work with other critical approaches so as to dialogue between the text and the context? Explain.

2. In its advocacy for alternative approaches to methodology, this chapter has intentionally been shaped as a narrative rather than in a linear-empiricist form. If you were on a thesis-approval board and received this chapter as the methodology component of the proposal, what would be your reaction? Why?

3. In what ways does the narrative approach to proposal-writing resonate with normal communication patterns in your local context? One of the key elements

of contemporary accreditation is the ability to communicate to "ordinary" people. How might a narrative approach such as this be a possible bridge to better communication between your students and their context?

4. Critical Discourse Analysis (CDA) seeks to bridge the gap between text and context. In what ways might this approach be helpful in biblical research, particularly in advanced theological studies? What concerns do you have?

5. With one or two others, try to sketch out the contours of a contextually significant doctoral project using CDA as the primary research methodology.

Bibliography

Barajas, Elías Domínguez. *The Function of Proverbs in Discourse: The Case of a Mexican Transnational Social Network*. Berlin: Walter de Gruyter, 2010.

Creese, Helen. "Images of Women and Embodiment in *Kakawin* Literature." *Intersections* 5 (May 2001). Accessed 17 April 2017. http://intersections.anu.edu.au/issue5/creese.html#n 11.

Czermak, Karin, Philippe Delanghe, and Wei Weng. "Preserving of Information Value in Oral Tradition of Minangkabau Society, West Sumatera, Indonesia." Paper delivered at UNESCO Conference on Language Development, Language Revitalization and Multilingual Education in Minority Communities in Asia, 6–8 November 2003, Bangkok, Thailand.

van Dijk, Teun A. "Principle of Critical Discourse Analysis." *Discourse and Society* 4, no. 2 (1993): 249–283.

Fairclough, Norman. *Critical Discourse Analysis: The Critical Study of Language*. Abingdon: Routledge, 2013.

———. *Language and Power*. Abingdon: Routledge, 2013.

Fulcher, R. *Critical Discourse Analysis*. New York: Longman, 2010.

Hirsch, Eric Donald, Joseph F. Kett, and James S. Trefil. *The New Dictionary of Cultural Literacy*. New York: Houghton Mifflin Harcourt, 2002.

Johnson, Carol, Vera Mackie, and Tessa Morris-Suzuki. *The Social Sciences in the Asian Century*. Canberra: ANU, 2015.

Mac Coinnigh, M. "Structural Aspects of Proverbs." In *Introduction to Paremiology: A Comprehensive Guide to Proverb Studies*, edited by Hrisztalina Hrisztova-Gotthardt and Melita Aleksa Varga, 112–132. Berlin: Walter de Gruyter, 2015.

Machin, David, and Andrea Mayr. *How to Do Critical Discourse Analysis: A Multimodal Introduction*. Thousand Oaks: SAGE, 2012.

McGregor, S. L. T. *Critical Discourse Analysis: A Primer*. Halifax: Mount Saint Vincent University, 2010.

Mercado, Leonardo N. *The Filipino Mind*. Washington, DC: CRVP, 1994.

Mieder, Wolfgang. *"Proverbs Speak Louder Than Words": Folk Wisdom in Art, Culture, Folklore, History, Literature and Mass Media*. Bern: Peter Lang, 2008.

Norrick, Neal R. *How Proverbs Mean: Semantic Studies in English Proverbs*. Berlin: Walter de Gruyter, 1985.

Pilch, John J. *The Cultural Life Setting of the Proverbs*. Minneapolis: Augsburg Fortress, 2016.

Ramage, Douglas E. *Politics in Indonesia: Democracy, Islam, and the Ideology of Tolerance*. Abingdon: Psychology Press, 1997.

Ribka, Stefani. "As Illiteracy Rate Lowers, RI Struggles with Reading Habits." *The Jakarta Post*. 24 March 2016. http://www.thejakartapost.com/news/2016/03/24/as-illiteracy-rate-lowers-ri-struggles-with-reading-habits.html.

Schipper, Mineke. *Never Marry a Woman with Big Feet: Women in Proverbs from Around the World*. New Haven: Yale University, 2003.

Tella, A., and A. O. Issa. *Library and Information Science in Developing Countries: Contemporary Issues*. Hershey: IGI Global, 2011.

Wodak, Ruth, and Michael Meyer. *Methods for Critical Discourse Analysis*. Thousand Oaks: SAGE, 2009.

22

Poetry as Theology:
A Creative Path

Xiaoli Yang

Personal Encounter

Poetry has played a significant part in my life. I was born and grew up in Mainland China at the end of the Cultural Revolution. Like millions of Chinese in my generation, I not only learned to recite many classical Chinese poems at school, but I was also quickly swirled into the "poetry fever" of the 1980s. Just waking up from the tormented national trauma, Chinese people began to engage in critical self-reflection and re-position themselves in a newly articulated social reality. Many of them expressed their most significant life issues such as identity, community, and freedom through poetry. During the so-called "Second Chinese Enlightenment,"[1] poetry reading and writing became a way of life in modern China amongst both the social elite and the common people.

As a teenage girl who was eager to explore the world ahead of me, I bought and read many poetry books by both native and foreign writers, wrote some poems, and even won a few prizes. I fell in love with this "inner music" behind the chaotic world. One day, I strolled down the street and bought a poetry book in a street booth. I went home and read it as I would any other poetry book. What

---

1. Edmond Tang, "The Second Chinese Enlightenment: Intellectuals and Christianity Today," in *Identity and Marginality: Rethinking Christianity in North East Asia*, Studies in the Intercultural History of Christianity 121, ed. W. Usdorf and T. Murayama (Frankfurt: Peter Lang, 2000), 55–70.

fascinated me was the line: "One thing I ask from the Lord . . . that I may dwell in the house of the Lord all the days of my life, to gaze on the beauty of the Lord and to seek him in his temple." "Who wrote such beautiful lines? Who is this 'beautiful Lord' the poet is writing about?" I wondered. Years later, I discovered that it was from the book of Psalms – the songs of poetry in the Hebrew Bible.

After migrating to Australia and soon becoming a Christian, I went to a Bible college for several years and was quickly drawn to the poetics in the Bible including the Wisdom literature, the visions of the prophets, and the parables of Jesus. I read them in many of my devotional hours and decided to enrol on a course to study the book of Psalms "properly." My encounter in the first class was, however, with the rational, scientific, compartmentalized, and linear analysis of grammar and structure, which was called "exegesis." I was acquainted with this historical-critical exegetical methodology. What surprised me was the loss of awe and appreciation of the richness in the poems in the way that I knew them as a child. I was puzzled, and somewhat disappointed by this sort of rational, clinical way of reading and the presuppositions behind it in the academy.

I have been through tertiary education in both Eastern and Western worlds, and know that there are certainly places for this sort of analysis for one to enter into the texts. However, I was still surprised by the extent of scientific deconstruction or "mind-control" of the texts, and the fact that the beauty and aroma that naturally arise from the poetry were lost, ignored, or pushed down. It seemed that anything that had to do with aesthetics, emotion, heart, and vulnerability needed to become secondary to a rational and logical mind in the academic pursuit. This sidetracks theological thought into academic and logical assumptions rather than grasping the biblical author's attempt to declare the wonder of a relationship with a saving and righteous God. The disorientation and struggle continued as I waded through the strongly rationalist theological study. Meanwhile, poetry that connected with my heart and spirit became an important resource for personal spiritual formation and growth. While much of the understanding of faith is rational and systematic in this set mould of training, poetry continues to call me towards home – a place where I am at ease to create metaphors and tell stories in relation to God, the world, others, and myself. It is in this space that I find personal joy in grasping a covenantal relationship with an eternal God.

The tension I sensed was not only the cultural disparity between the East and the West, but also the supposed different standpoints of two vocations: the creative poet and the systematic theologian. As Paul Fiddes comments on the interchanges between artists and theologians, "literature tends to openness and doctrine to closure."[2] This is the "messy middle" or "broken middle"[3] that I have been living in. The triple alienation as a migrant, poet, and Christian gave birth to the following poem.[4]

LOST

You live
between
lines

Being pushed
in and out
as a stranger

Squeezing
between
Even tears have
no weight

You are deaf
though grasping voices
You are mute
though knowing words

Communication
seems necessary
but never
ever
works

---

2. Paul S. Fiddes, *The Promised End: Eschatology in Theology and Literature*, Challenges in Contemporary Theology (Oxford: Blackwell, 2000), 6–7.
3. Gillian Rose, *The Broken Middle: Out of Our Ancient Society* (Oxford: Blackwell, 1992).
4. Xiaoli Yang, "Lost," *Southerly* 57, no. 4 (1997–98): 59.

This sense of "otherness" or "dislocation" finally merged in my PhD dissertation that brought poetry and faith together in dialogue. Initially my proposal was an auto-ethnographic study of my own poetry that expressed a search for identity and home as a Chinese migrant, in conversation with the changing cultures around me. Unfortunately, the embodying nature of the project was turned down because it was "too self-focused and emotive," there were "no secondary resources to back up your claim," and it was not "philosophical and objective enough" for a PhD. Instead, another proposal that created a dialogue between a well-known Chinese poet and Jesus in the Gospel of Luke was accepted. Although poetry occupies 10 percent of the whole dissertation, I still largely conformed to the Western approach of a dissertation. While many positive comments were made, one person said to me: "you write like a poet, lacking precision." He did not realize that the poetic language is precisely incarnated words that embody the voice of the East – a "poetic epistemology" that I attempt to introduce to Western readers.

The Western scientific "intellectual elitism" or "mind tower," deeply influenced by the Enlightenment, dominates Western academia. As Perry Shaw describes, "the classic approach to higher level research is linear, specific, analytic, hypothesis-driven, and individualistic-competitive . . . far more likely to suit the thinking processes of white Western males than women in general, or than students from collectivist societies."[5] This classic approach is certainly one way of thinking, but not *the* only way, especially in the field of humanities and the arts. It limits the scope for theological reflection and poetic imagination. Increasingly it loses its capacity to engage with a multicultural, pluralistic, and visual-based postmodern world. Christian theology with universal context-free presuppositions is not only presumptuous, but also it does not bring home meaning to cultures that honour poetry, music, and narratives as the primary vehicles of communication. If the task of theological training is to equip leaders holistically, then the task to engage with them creatively through their heart language and the language of the heart is critical. This is especially urgent as the global church has now largely shifted from the West to the South and the East.

---

5. Perry Shaw, "'New Treasures with the Old': Addressing Culture and Gender Imperialism in High Level Theological Education," in *Tending the Seedbeds: Educational Perspectives on Theological Education in Asia*, ed. Allan Harkness (Quezon City: Asia Theological Association, 2010), 54–55.

My personal journey in this global context prompted me to ask whether poetry can contribute to theology as a way of knowing and therefore shape theological education. This chapter examines the crucial role of poetry in Chinese culture. It then explores "poetic epistemology," drawing resources from neuroscience, mystics, and classical Chinese understanding. Using my own dissertation as an example, it demonstrates a way of poetry–theology dialogue that is mutually enriching. It argues that poetry writing is a theological act and therefore poetry should be taken seriously, not only as a tool for communication, but also as the creative movement of God within the human heart. It concludes that poetry should be considered as a theological discourse for future theological education.

The Crucial Role of Poetry in Chinese Culture

As with many regions of the Majority World, poetry has a long historical, cultural, and religious tradition in China, and therefore has been deeply rooted in the Chinese soil. The *Book of Poetry* (or *Poetry*, *Shijing*, 诗经) is the earliest poetry collection in China, dating from the tenth to the seventh century BC. It includes a total of 305 poems of the Zhou dynasty (1046 BC–256 BC). The most distinguished early poet is Qu Yuan 屈原 (340 BC–278 BC), known for his work called *Questions to Heaven* (*Tianwen*, 天问). His deepest yearning is expressed with great intensity in the 373 lines of poetry. This poem has been regarded by the Chinese as the most magnificent work of its kind throughout the ages.

The Confucian tradition affirms the important role of poetry. In the *Analects* (*Lunyu*, 论语), Confucius (551 BC–479 BC) refers to the fact that he reads the classic Chinese book *Poetry*. In the chapter "Shuer" (述而) he writes, "What the Master used the standard pronunciation for were the *Poetry*, the *Documents*, and the performance of the rites. For all these he used the standard pronunciation" (子所雅言，诗、书、执礼，皆雅言也).[6] In the following chapter, "Tai Bo" (泰伯): "One is roused by the *Poetry*, established by ritual, and

---

6. Confucius, *The Analects*, trans. Raymond Stanley Dawson (Oxford: Oxford University, 2000), 25.

perfected by music" (兴于诗，立于礼。成于乐).⁷ In the chapter "Jishi" (季氏): "Without learning *Poetry*, one cannot speak" (不学诗，无以言).⁸ *Poetry* also records the idea of a personified Heaven (*Tian*, 天), who is described as the creator of the universe and has a distinct personality.

Though the languages and forms of poetry have changed dramatically over the years, poetry has long been used and regarded highly by the Chinese. In Confucian tradition, for example, one had to pass a poetry-reciting exam in the Imperial Examination System (*Kejuzhi*, 科举制) before one could become a respected government official called "Zhuangyuan" (状元). Poetry reached its climax in the Tang dynasty (618–907 AD) through the famous "Three Saints of Poetry" – Libai (李白), Dufu (杜甫), and Bai Juyi (白居易). During the development of literary or political movements, when ideologies and thoughts have interacted intensely, poetry has been the common way of communication.

The famous modern Chinese poet Bingxin 冰心 (1900–1999) wrote, "Only a star, in this endless darkness, has fully expressed the loneliness of the universe" (只是一颗孤星罢了！在无边的黑暗里/已写尽了宇宙的寂寞).⁹ The heart speaks and the emotions are stirred and released through the "star" in the darkness, namely poetry. Here is the beautiful portrayal of poetry shining in "the dark night of an utter alienation from the 'available' world."¹⁰ Clearly, within Chinese culture and history, poetry occupies a special space as the heart language of Chinese culture, for it is that form which speaks about the richest cosmic themes.

Poetry in the Human Heart

Poetry is not only the heart language of Chinese culture, but also the language of the human heart. Blaise Pascal said that "the heart has its reasons which reason knows nothing of." Such reasons, however, can be articulated, if not proven, through poetry. This is because poetic language has the capacity to

---

7. Confucius, *Analects*, 29.
8. Confucius, 68.
9. Bingxin 冰心, Zhenglin Xu, 许正林, and Guangming Fu, 傅光明, *Bingxin Shi Quanbian* (Bingxin's Complete Poems) (Hangzhou: Zhejiang wenyi chubanshe, 1994), 65.
10. Rowan Williams, "Poetic and Religious Imagination," *Theology* 80, no. 675 (1977): 180.

activate pictures, metaphors, and images that the brain uses to explain the world. "Metaphor is pervasive in everyday life, not just in language but in thought and action."[11] With pervasive metaphors, the poetic voice can trigger imagination, creativity, and emotions.

Western philosophers have developed metaphysics and ontology to help them to define the world around and beyond them. However, unlike Chinese people, who adopt holistic thinking and seek their place in harmonious relationship with the external world, Western philosophers tend to start their inquiries by standing "outside" the world of reality and seeking to understand it through logic and rationality.[12] Influenced by the dominance of Plato and his followers, Western intellectual history has proceeded with the fundamental assumption that the rational universe is intelligible and that reason is the primary tool to unveil the hidden principles. As Colin Brown describes this approach, "Behind all the complex machinery of nature there was a rational mind, and this could be known by the right use of reason. Given the right data, it was possible to draw up a map of reality, provided that one made the correct logical deduction."[13] Western culture consequently tends to divide reality into parts by logic and reason. Adolf Reichwein points out that "we see this world as a separated whole, whose unity is in no way impaired by the fact that other worlds with other actualities maintain a parallel existence . . . All these worlds had their separate existences, because each had its own separate laws."[14] In contrast to the Western norm of compartmentalized and linear thinking, philosophers in the East, since Laozi and Zhuangzi, have advocated the use of one's whole being to approach the universe. The diagram shown

---

11. George Lakoff and Mark Johnson, *Metaphors We Live By* (Chicago: University of Chicago, 1980; 2nd ed., 2003), 3.
12. Xiaoli Yang, *A Dialogue between Haizi's Poetry and the Gospel of Luke: Chinese Homecoming and the Relationship with Jesus Christ*, Theology and Mission in World Christianity (Leiden: Brill, 2018), 173–174.
13. Colin Brown, *Philosophy and the Christian Faith: A Historical Sketch from the Middle Ages to the Present Day* (Downers Grove: InterVarsity, 1968), 48.
14. Adolf Reichwein, *China and Europe: Intellectual and Artistic Contacts in the Eighteenth Century*, trans. J. C. Powell, History of Civilization, 1st ed. (London: Routledge & K. Paul, 1968), 75.

in figure 22.1 illustrates the different ways of thinking in the two cultures.[15] The linear logical stairs in the West contrast to the circular evolving stairs or double helix in the East.

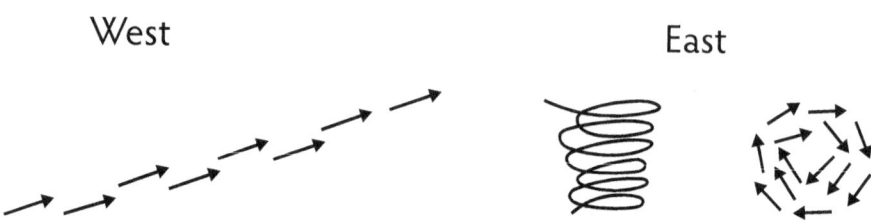

Figure 22.1: The Different Ways of Thinking in the West and the East

Different cultures have different ways of thinking and different worldviews. One of the most influential series of experiments conducted by Richard Nisbett and his team found that people in the East tend towards thinking that is relational, holistic, circular, and communal in its relation to the world; in contrast, people in the West tend towards thinking that is rational, logical, linear, and individualist in problem-solving.[16] The recognition of the diversity of our cultures and different mindsets is a catalyst for innovative approaches to learning and training. The proposal is to provide different methodologies in a Western-dominated academic world. The work of Nisbett and others affirms the validity of poetic epistemology as an appropriate method of knowing and training for the Sino-mind. Beyond the recognition of the diversity of approaches, here is also an invitation for the East and the West to learn from each other and cultivate the whole person in order to reach their full potential.

Neuroscientists of the twenty-first century have developed a more comprehensive understanding of the human brain. They discovered the connectedness within our human system and how the heart is intimately

---

15. The diagram is partly taken from Denis Lane, *One Mind Two Worlds* (Littleton: OMF International, 1995), 16; the paragraph is partly taken from Xiaoli Yang, *A Dialogue between Haizi's Poetry and the Gospel of Luke*, 173–174.

16. Richard E. Nisbett, *The Geography of Thought: How Asians and Westerners Think Differently . . . And Why* (New York: Free Press, 2003); and R. E. Nisbett, I. Choi, K. Peng, and A. Norenzayan, "Culture and Systems of Thought: Holistic versus Analytic Cognition," *Psychological Review* 108, no. 2 (2001); see also Shaw, "New Treasures with the Old," 50–52.

connected with the way we use our brain and body to respond to the world around us. According to Doc Childre and his colleagues' research, "heart intelligence" can shift perception and direct the flow of emotions.[17] The heart can be like a fully functioning brain that provides an intellectual gateway to other brains. Luiz Pessoa's research goes beyond the traditional understanding of cognition/emotion interaction, suggesting the complex *integration* of cognition and emotion in the brain.[18] Drawing from the discovery of the scientists, Richard Rohr argues for the importance of poetry as a contemplative stance: "All of the poetry and songs about the heart 'knowing' were not just idle chatter; we now have scientific validation that the heart shares brain-like functions. The connection of the prefrontal lobes to the heart has been demonstrated electromagnetically and at the neural and hormonal levels too."[19] This is very similar to the Chinese path of gaining knowledge. The Chinese etymology of "thinking" (*si*, 思) is made up of mind (*xin*, 囟, meaning fontanel) on the top and heart (*xin*, 心) at the bottom, as shown in figure 22.2.[20]

Figure 22.2: The Chinese Etymology of "Thinking"

For the ancient Chinese, understanding derives from the heart and is grasped through the fontanel. The fontanel sits between the cranial bones of

---

17. Doc Childre, Howard Martin, and Donna Beech, *The HeartMath Solution: The Institute of HeartMath's Revolutionary Program for Engaging the Power of the Heart's Intelligence*, 1st ed. (San Francisco: HarperCollins, 1999), 28–34.
18. Luiz Pessoa, "Cognition and Emotion," *Scholarpedia* 4, no. 1 (2009): 4567. http://www.scholarpedia.org/article/Cognition_and_emotion.
19. Richard Rohr, "The Evolving Brain," Center for Action and Contemplation, 8 December 2015, accessed 15 March 2017, https://cac.org/the-evolving-brain-2015-12-08/.
20. *The Dictionary of Han Language*, "s.v. 思 (si)," accessed 18 March 2017, http://www.zdic.net/z/19/zy/601D.htm.

an infant, as a tunnel for *Qi* ('因为之通气')[21] while the baby is in the womb. Its pulsation echoes with the heartbeat. The character "heart" (*xin*, 心), in the shape of a heart, refers to the organ of a heart, but also the "thinking of the heart" (*xinsi*, 心思) or the "will of the heart" (*xinyi*, 心意). Ancient Chinese understood that the heart is a thinking organ and that thoughts are products of the human heart. When considering something, one is using one's heart to think.

In classical Chinese hermeneutics, the epistemological issue of heart (*yixin weizhi*, 以心为知) finds unity with the ontological source of the world through a poetic path. The shared ontological-epistemological goal is to achieve harmony with "Dao" (道), in the language of ethics – "perpetual unity of the Self with Heaven" (*tianren heyi*, 天人合一). This understanding of the connection between the heart language of poetry and the ontological Dao offers some wisdom for today's theological training that is heavily based on linear and cognitive thinking.

The discovery of neuroscience is not totally alien to the spiritual practice of the Western world especially amongst mystics. Many of their writings are love poems expressing their deepest heartfelt longing for God. One of the most prominent mystics, St John of the Cross (1542–1591), writes poetry drawing on a wide range of imagery from his experience, the Scriptures, contemporary poetry of his day, the Greek classics, and his observations of nature and life around him. His mystical experience of journeying to be in union with God cannot be adequately explained by rational dialogue or other forms of logic. He parallels his experience with the utterances of the Spirit (Rom 8:26–27), when words are not adequate to express what is in our hearts, and the Spirit of God steps in and evokes a poetic language in imagery that gives voice towards knowledge of God.[22] The mystics in Western spiritual tradition learned a long time ago that poetry has a special role in contemplation. The sudden "peak experiences" shared by poets and mystics allow them to transcend ordinary daily life.[23]

---

21. "Kangxi Zidiang, 康熙字典" (The Dictionary of Kangxi), accessed 17 March 2017, http://ctext.org/kangxi-zidian/31/3/zh. Koubu (口部), Three (三), 4. 三.
22. St John of the Cross, "A Spiritual Canticle of the Soul and the Bridegroom Christ," Christian Classics Ethereal Library, http://www.ccel.org/ccel/john_cross/canticle.html, 7.
23. Colin Wilson, *Poetry and Mysticism* (San Francisco: City Lights, 1986).

It is from René Descartes' famous statement "I think, therefore I am" (*Cogito ergo sum*) that Western culture from the Enlightenment onwards has taken rationalism to its extreme in a belief that reason is inwardly connected with the truth of the world. Romanticism reacted and promoted "I feel, therefore I am." Many mystics, however, have taken the intellect in a total negation – "I think, therefore I don't exist." In Chinese tradition, it becomes "I think (*si*, 思) from the knowledge of the heart, therefore I am." Confucius understands this and says: "Learning without thought is labour lost; thought without learning is perilous" ('学而不思则罔, 思而不学则殆').[24] Holistic spiritual formation within a theological framework requires not just cognitive information, but revelation that is connected with the heart that can function like a brain. The deepest convictions of our heart are often formed by narratives and the attached images, symbols, sounds, and music that are embodied in poetic imagination. Expressed in the form of metaphors and emotion, poetry can be used as a creative epistemological path towards God, for it speaks of the deepest human longing to know and be known. In this sense, everyone is a poet.

Poetry in Theological Reflection and Theology in Poetic Imagination

How can dogma and doctrine move to the level of experience that engages with our heart? Conversely, how can the poetic voice of the heart be described by dogma and doctrine? The heart cannot live on facts, principles, and propositions alone. It needs to be awakened to respond, to touch, and to feel. Especially since Hans Urs von Balthasar's attempt to address the dissociation between cognitive-based theology and creativity-based arts in his vision of a "theological aesthetics," Western theologians realize more and more the importance of developing cognitive thinking that connects with the heart. Richard Viladesau develops a "transcendental" theology of aesthetics – a theology of revelation in relation to three dimensions: feeling and imagination, beauty, and the

---

24. Confucius, "Lunyu, Weizheng" (The Analects), Chinese Text Project, http://ctext.org/analects/wei-zheng, 15.

arts.[25] Elaine Graham and her colleagues offer useful theological reflection methods including "theology by heart" (the living human document), seeking to transform the heartfelt inner life into a theological resource.[26] However, they neither mention poetry specifically, nor indicate how theology might inform creative writing.

The interplay between theology and poetry can be both creative and dialogical. While theology needs to be "constantly broken open" by images and cultures in changing contexts, poetry needs theology to reflect, critique, and interpret. The mutually enriching relationship enables the two to both "heighten and deepen" their sensitivity to certain human experience that they would otherwise not notice.[27] Amos Yong emphasizes that the orthopathic sphere concerns the affective dimension of the human constitution: the beautiful for which human beings deeply yearn.[28] "This aesthetic vision, however, can be reduced neither to cognitively construed propositions (orthodoxy) nor pragmatically resolved constructions (orthopraxis); rather, it operates at the interior level of the human will, imagination, and heart."[29] This dialogue uses poetry as the basic resource for theological reflection and theology as the discerning party for poetic imagination.

Attentive listening as an act of love and respect becomes a primary task in the theology–poetry conversation. If poetry bubbles from heart knowledge, it requires attentive listening by sitting together and paying attention to the other. Through "holy listening," we come to appreciate the poetic heart language and discern where God is and what God is doing in the other and in our world; we become a place of welcome and "hospitality," an empowering "teacher" or a

---

25. Richard Viladesau, *Theological Aesthetics: God in Imagination, Beauty, and Art* (New York: Oxford University, 1999).

26. Elaine L. Graham, Heather Walton, and Frances Ward, *Theological Reflection: Methods* (London: SCM, 2007), 18–45.

27. Jason Goroncy, *"Tikkun Olam" – To Mend the World: A Confluence of Theology and the Arts* (Eugene: Wipf and Stock, 2013), 5; also Fiddes, *Promised End*, 6–7.

28. "Orthopathic" refers to right aesthetics, in contrast to "orthodoxy" (right belief) and "orthopraxis" (right action).

29. Amos Yong, "Missiology and Mission Theology in an Interfaith World: A (Humble) Manifesto," *Evangelical Interfaith Dialogue* 5, no. 2 (Fall 2014): 4–6.

facilitating "midwife" who provides the life-giving God-spaces.[30] Theological education needs to consider this *micro* aspect seriously as we hold the *macro* vision of empowering the future leaders in this globalized and pluralistic world.

Here I will use my dissertation as an illustration. My research is a face-to-face encounter between the Christian story and the poetic voice of contemporary China through active listening to each other. It is an example that combines Western philosophical articulation and Eastern poetic imagination by attentively listening to both parties in mutual respect and humility. It creates a dialogue between the Chinese soul-search found in Haizi's (1964–1989) poetry and the gospel of Jesus Christ through Luke's testimony. The proposal of this dialogue is that the common language of the poet Haizi and the Lukan Jesus provides a crucial and rich source of data for an ongoing table conversation between culture and faith. It creates a contextual poetic lens to appreciate a generation of the Chinese homecoming journey through Haizi's poetry, and to explore its relationship with Jesus Christ. The study examines Haizi's existential quest, and the resonance in Jesus's life and his answer in communion with God.

I sought to build bridges between theological articulation and poetic imagination, between the cultural division of the East and the West, and between the sacred and the secular through the voices of Haizi and the Lukan Jesus. From a deep conviction, I advocated that the topic of homecoming bears universal significance, as well as particularity for this generation of Chinese in Post-Mao China. If I had not known Jesus as revealed in the Scripture, I probably would walk a similar path as the poet Haizi, and would not be able to introduce the Christian path of homecoming to contemporary China. If I had not introduced Haizi, the post-Christendom Western theological academy where I have been trained and nurtured as my "natural home" would not have understood contemporary Chinese culture through this poetic lens. Rowan Williams is right: "the theologian *is* always beginning in the middle of things."[31] Standing in this existential "middle," I ask the question: "Where is God? What

---

30. Margaret Guenther, *Holy Listening: The Art of Spiritual Direction* (London: Darton, Longman & Todd, 1992). The three images of hospitality, teaching, and midwifery are used to illustrate the role of a spiritual director.
31. Rowan Williams, *On Christian Theology*, Challenges in Contemporary Theology (Oxford: Blackwell, 1999), xii; emphasis added.

is he doing? What are we going to do about it?" I seek to locate the "hidden driveshaft" that helps to shape the creative tension. In *The Holy Trinity and the Law of Three* by Cynthia Bourgeault, the two polarities (such as theory and practice, heart and mind, good and evil) call forth a third reconciling or harmonizing principle, forming a ternary system that facilitates creativity.[32] My "messy middle" is in fact a gift that enables me to hold the tension with discernment and creativity.

As a midway player of the two-way traffic, it is my hope to communicate an authentic "Chinese Jesus" to Chinese readers, and make a contribution to the Western theological academy, in a way that ensures that not only are the voices from contemporary Chinese culture through Haizi heard, but also that two centuries of scientific historical-critical analysis of the contents of the Bible are examined and placed within the continuum of human culture, especially the poetic tradition. Hans-Georg Gadamer's hermeneutics that opens "horizons" of meaning fits well with the purpose of the dialogue. In his "dialogue-play" model, the truth that emerges belongs to neither of the parties and hence transcends both, leading transformation into a communion in which neither party remains what it was.[33] The shared language therefore becomes the communion between the two where truth and understanding arise. Gadamer retained Heidegger's emphasis on the "linguisticality" or poetic understanding of human ontology, but saw the dynamic "fusion of horizons," which is available through a transformative understanding of others as the most important enrichment of being.[34] This indeed frees one up for imagination, authentically expressing whichever "middles" the dialoguing partners are from.

The dissertation came out of a personal journey of integration and dialogue between theology and poetry, concerns for the Post-Mao generation who are struggling to find their identity and life purpose, and the lack of appreciation of poetry in the theological environment. I am one of the Post-Mao generation who has gone through the struggles in that context and is still in the current

---

32. Cynthia Bourgeault, *The Holy Trinity and the Law of Three: Discovering the Radical Truth at the Heart of Christianity*, 1st ed. (Boston: Shambhala, 2013), 3, 16.
33. Hans-Georg Gadamer, *Truth and Method*, 2nd revised ed. (New York: Continuum, 2000), 368, 379.
34. David Vessey, "Gadamer's Critique of Heidegger's Account of Authentic Relations to Others," accessed 2 April 2015, http://www.davevessey.com/Vessey_Gadamer_Heidegger.htm.

Western context as a migrant, poet, pastor, and lecturer. I am also one trained in the Western theological academy, a product of the collapsing Western post-Enlightenment culture that needs to be self-critiqued. By locating my own historical, cultural, and economic context, I acknowledge the limitations of my interpretation, and that constant discernment is required to establish that which is of lasting significance.

Like a gateway, poetry opens up fertile ground for spiritual inspiration and imagination in and beyond the engagement between contemporary Chinese culture and the Christian gospel. In this way, a creative Christology is formed, opening potential multiple views of Jesus as Dao, Host of *Huijia* (homecoming), Harmonizer of yin and yang, and the Great Poetry.[35]

This is an example of using poetry as a resource for theological reflection, and theological truth being expanded by poetic imagination. While it opens the doors for both disciplines with cultural sensitivity, the discourse and presuppositions still largely fit within the current Western academic model. More than a dialogue between two separate entities, I propose the possibility of poetry as theology with a lucid boundary between the two.

Conclusion: Poetry As Theology

If poetry derives from the utterances of the human heart, then the child-like "innocent" writing process is an authentic expression of being human, whether the poet realizes the presence of the divine or not. For Confucius, one thing that embraces all three hundred pieces in *Poetry* is "having no depraved thoughts" (思无邪).[36] In the inter-rationality of life and the cosmos, the "pure writing" not only expresses one's own interior self, but also bears witness to one's encounter with others, the world, and God. Poets instinctively sense the call that, alongside the rest of creation, they are invited not just to watch, but to participate in the divine dance or the great poetry writing of the triune God. By embracing the language and breathing with human struggles and pain,

---

35. Xiaoli Yang, "China—Christianity—Jesus," in *Encyclopedia of the Bible and Its Reception* (*EBR*), ed. Steven L. McKenzie et al. (Berlin: De Gruyter, 2017), 14:30–32.
36. Confucius, "Lunyu, Weizheng," 2.

poetry opens up a new horizon of an un-manifested world and in doing so brings eschatological hope that endures.

The poetic writing process becomes an incarnational act, for poets use nothing but the languages and images of the cultural context they are living in. This "impossibility of absolute innovation" is described by Rowan Williams: "the artist has no option but to take his material from the world as it is."[37] It is in the poetics of everyday that theology is formed. According to William A. Dyrness, poetic theology was part of God's intention throughout biblical history. The Protestant church needs to recover aspects of contemplative spirituality through poetic theology in which the embodiment of story takes place in the settings of our daily lives.[38] Before words and images are recreated, poets need to be deeply immersed in the world, listening in silence to the music behind the elements of the world. As a contemplative stance, poetry opens the gate to "the world hidden within the world,"[39] the un-manifested within the manifested natural world, the deeper reality beyond what we can see. Ontologically speaking, it is a creative gateway that opens up a world that connects with the treasures of the human heart and the reality of God. Like a priest who has eyes to perceive the depths of the unknown where God dwells, the creative process of a poet is revelatory just as in theology. This creative path, whether in lament over suffering or hope in God, becomes participation and co-labouring in God's continuing creative movement in the world. Together with the creation, the poetic incarnational act participates in the "groaning in one great act of giving birth" (Rom 8:22). The poetic voice echoes with the sound of the agony of birth pain and of joy in receiving new life.

Can theology turn to this aspect of embodiment, as the poets embody their insights, pain, love, and dreams in poetic form? Can the poetic rhythm carry us along in theological discourse, so that beauty and the truth become one? Going beyond intercultural, interdisciplinary, and interfaith approaches, poetry communicates directly at the heart level and evokes things like love,

---

37. Williams, "Poetic and Religious Imagination," 180; Goroncy, "*Tikkun Olam*," 15.
38. William A. Dyrness, *Poetic Theology: God and the Poetics of Everyday Life* (Grand Rapids: Eerdmans, 2011).
39. Freya Mathews, "An Invitation to Ontopoetics: The Poetic Structure of Being," *Australian Humanities Review* 43 (Dec. 2007), http://www.australianhumanitiesreview.org/archive/Issue-December-2007/EcoHumanities/EcoMathews.html.

healing, freedom, and forgiveness that doctrines or creeds alone cannot. Jesus from the Trinity, the Word become flesh, invites us to sing and write in sacred poetry, joining him in the divine dance. Aren't those poems I wrote earlier from authentic human experience also theological? Why must theological reflection be cognitive and scientific, rather than poetic and imaginative, which can also reflect the all-encompassing reality of God? Theological educators need to consider poetry seriously as a theological discourse and the writing process as a theological act.

Putting aside my personal struggle with language, individualist culture, and a linear way of thinking in Western academia mentioned at the beginning of this chapter, I am not promoting the dichotomy of rational thinking and creative imagination. My recommendation is that we take off the lens that we are so acquainted with to perceive what academic study is, and try to put on a poetic lens that may give us another view and see where that will take us. Holistic theological training needs to involve not just a cognitive plane, but also hands and hearts; not just spoken words, but also feelings and experiences. May we never lose our wonder and awe at the world around us, and never forget the poetic treasure in the human heart. It is time for the poetic epistemological lens to be used as a way forward towards the openness to truth, beauty, and goodness in which academic research should fundamentally abide.

Let me finish with a poem:[40]

Theology

> systemizes our thoughts
> of the eternal mass
> into categories
>
> creates words of
> paradox and abstraction
> and labels them
> in the safe box of our doctrines

---

40. Xiaoli Yang, "Theology," in *Imagine*, eds. Janette Fernando and Maree Silver (Montrose: Poetica Christi, 2016), 16.

we think

the epistemology of God

and God winks

Discussion Questions

1. What are one or two of your favourite poems? Why do you particularly value these poems? Describe some ways in which poetry has shaped the hearts and minds of people in your own local context.

2. In her opening reflection Xiaoli talks about how the Psalms shaped her early journey to knowing God, and her subsequent frustration with the "loss of awe and appreciation of the richness in the poems" when she undertook a "clinical" study of the Psalms at Bible college. To what extent does Xiaoli's experience resonate with you, or do you know of others who have felt similar joys and/or frustrations? Explain.

3. Briefly discuss the theological value of "aesthetics, emotion, heart, and vulnerability" in knowing God, and hence their significance for theological education. How might the encouragement of poetic expression be a significant way of embracing affective learning in theological studies?

4. To what extent might poetry and other innovative approaches show greater respect to the interconnectivity between the cognitive and affective in the brain than do empirical-rationalist approaches?

5. As we look at an increasingly global Christian community, what are one or two of the rich benefits that might be gleaned through poetry? How might poetry and other innovative approaches be pathways to incorporating Majority World holism as a counterpoint to the precision of Minority World empirical-rationalist approaches to knowing? Why might this be particularly significant for theological studies?

6. Try to imagine what a poetic project for a master's or doctoral submission might look like. You may like to consider both the material given in this chapter

and Sam Ewell's description of his "autoethnographic" PhD.[41] How might the creative and dialogical interplay of theology and poetry be encouraged and embraced? What might be some of the key elements that would affirm both cognitive and affective competencies of the candidate?

Bibliography

Bingxin 冰心, Zhenglin Xu, 许正林, and Guangming Fu, 傅光明. *Bingxin Shi Quanbian* (Bingxin's Complete Poems). Hangzhou: Zhejiang wenyi chubanshe, 1994.

Bourgeault, Cynthia. *The Holy Trinity and the Law of Three: Discovering the Radical Truth at the Heart of Christianity*. 1st ed. Boston: Shambhala, 2013.

Brown, Colin. *Philosophy and the Christian Faith: A Historical Sketch from the Middle Ages to the Present Day*. Downers Grove: InterVarsity, 1968.

Childre, Doc, Howard Martin, and Donna Beech. *The HeartMath Solution: The Institute of HeartMath's Revolutionary Program for Engaging the Power of the Heart's Intelligence*. 1st ed. San Francisco: HarperCollins, 1999.

Confucius. *The Analects*. Translated by Raymond Stanley Dawson. Oxford: Oxford University, 2000.

———. "Lunyu, Weizheng" (The Analects). Chinese Text Project. http://ctext.org/analects/wei-zheng.

The Dictionary of Han Language. "s.v. 思 (si)." http://www.zdic.net/z/19/zy/601D.htm.

Dyrness, William A. *Poetic Theology: God and the Poetics of Everyday Life*. Grand Rapids: Eerdmans, 2011.

Fiddes, Paul S. *The Promised End: Eschatology in Theology and Literature*. Challenges in Contemporary Theology. Oxford: Blackwell, 2000.

Gadamer, Hans-Georg. *Truth and Method*. 2nd revised ed. New York: Continuum, 2000.

Goroncy, Jason. *"Tikkun Olam" – To Mend the World: A Confluence of Theology and the Arts*. Eugene: Wipf and Stock, 2013.

Graham, Elaine L., Heather Walton, and Frances Ward. *Theological Reflection: Methods*. London: SCM, 2007.

Guenther, Margaret. *Holy Listening: The Art of Spiritual Direction*. London: Darton, Longman & Todd, 1992.

"Kangxi Zidiang, 康熙字典" (The Dictionary of Kangxi). http://ctext.org/kangxi-zidian/31/3/zh.

---

41. Sam Ewell, "Doing Theology from the 'Land of Samba,'" in this collection.

Lakoff, George, and Mark Johnson. *Metaphors We Live By*. Chicago: University of Chicago, 1980; 2nd ed., 2003.

Lane, Denis. *One Mind Two Worlds*. Littleton: OMF International, 1995.

Mathews, Freya. "An Invitation to Ontopoetics: The Poetic Structure of Being." *Australian Humanities Review* 43 (Dec. 2007). http://www.australianhumanitiesreview.org/archive/Issue-December-2007/EcoHumanities/EcoMathews.html.

Nisbett, Richard E. *The Geography of Thought: How Asians and Westerners Think Differently . . . And Why*. New York: Free Press, 2003.

Nisbett, R. E., I. Choi, K. Peng, and A. Norenzayan. "Culture and Systems of Thought: Holistic versus Analytic Cognition." *Psychological Review* 108, no. 2 (2001): 291–310.

Pessoa, Luiz. "Cognition and Emotion." *Scholarpedia* 4, no. 1 (2009). http://www.scholarpedia.org/article/Cognition_and_emotion.

Reichwein, Adolf. *China and Europe: Intellectual and Artistic Contacts in the Eighteenth Century*. Translated by J. C. Powell. History of Civilization. 1st ed. London: Routledge & K. Paul, 1968.

Rohr, Richard. "The Evolving Brain." Center for Action and Contemplation, 8 December 2015. https://cac.org/the-evolving-brain-2015-12-08/.

Rose, Gillian. *The Broken Middle: Out of Our Ancient Society*. Oxford: Blackwell, 1992.

Shaw, Perry. "'New Treasures with the Old': Addressing Culture and Gender Imperialism in High Level Theological Education." In *Tending the Seedbeds: Educational Perspectives on Theological Education in Asia*, edited by Allan Harkness, 47–74. Quezon City: Asia Theological Association, 2010.

St John of the Cross. "A Spiritual Canticle of the Soul and the Bridegroom Christ." Christian Classics Ethereal Library. http://www.ccel.org/ccel/john_cross/canticle.html.

Tang, Edmond. "The Second Chinese Enlightenment: Intellectuals and Christianity Today." In *Identity and Marginality: Rethinking Christianity in North East Asia*, Studies in the Intercultural History of Christianity 121, edited by W. Usdorf and T. Murayama, 55–70. Frankfurt: Peter Lang, 2000.

Vessey, David. "Gadamer's Critique of Heidegger's Account of Authentic Relations to Others." http://www.davevessey.com/Vessey_Gadamer_Heidegger.htm.

Viladesau, Richard. *Theological Aesthetics: God in Imagination, Beauty, and Art*. New York: Oxford University, 1999.

Williams, Rowan. *On Christian Theology*. Challenges in Contemporary Theology. Oxford: Blackwell, 1999.

———. "Poetic and Religious Imagination." *Theology* 80, no. 675 (1977): 178–187.

Wilson, Colin. *Poetry and Mysticism*. San Francisco: City Lights, 1986.

Yang, Xiaoli. "China – Christianity – Jesus." In *Encyclopedia of the Bible and Its Reception (EBR)*, edited by Steven L. McKenzie et al., 14:30–32. Berlin: De Gruyter, 2017.

———. *A Dialogue between Haizi's Poetry and the Gospel of Luke: Chinese Homecoming and the Relationship with Jesus Christ*, Theology and Mission in World Christianity. Leiden: Brill, 2018.

———. "Lost." *Southerly* 57, no. 4 (1997–1998): 59.

———. "Theology." In *Imagine*, edited by Janette Fernando and Maree Silver. Montrose: Poetica Christi, 2016, 16.

Yong, Amos. "Missiology and Mission Theology in an Interfaith World." *Evangelical Interfaith Dialogue* 5, no. 2 (Fall 2014): 4–6.

23

Verse by Verse:
The Use of Poetry in Advanced Theological Education

Havilah Dharamraj, Xiaoli Yang,
Grace al-Zoughbi Arteen, and Karen Shaw

"Class, when you write your essay, don't tell me what you *feel*, tell me what you *think*!" This instruction from a tutor is rather familiar, perhaps? If so, it gives us a good idea of the place advanced theological education makes (or does not make) for poetry. If traditional Western theological education can be imagined as a basketball player, the "basket" it has in mind is the cognitive domain. Imagine it squinting up its eyes with concentration as it takes aim at the rational-analytical faculties of the student. Only if its spatial skills are really wretched might it unintentionally hit the emotional or the behavioural. Small wonder, then, that our students know more *about* God but are moved less *for* God.

Among the discernible losses of theologians abandoning poetry is that we have left behind us the age of the great hymn writers. Indeed, the decline of hymn writing appears to correlate directly with the rise of empiricist-rational approaches to theological education. Theology that arose from the subjective, affective domain has been largely elbowed out into "popular Christian literature" by an approach to theology that has focused on the objective, and firmly foregrounded it in advanced education.

Following on from Xiaoli Yang's chapter "Poetry As Theology: A Creative Path," which persuasively argues for poetry from the theoretical perspective, this chapter provides four samples of poetry, annotated to show how poems can engage the various domains of learning.

Xiaoli Yang makes suggestions for using a poem as the bridge between the biblical text and the practice of it.

Grace al-Zoughbi uses poetry in theological education, such as the sample provided here, to catalyse an intermeshing of head, heart, and hands.

Karen Shaw's poem shows how a poem could be used in the classroom to investigate a whole range of ways we can think about God, feel about God, and serve God better.

Havilah Dharamraj submits a poem as a substitute for a standard essay, with the poem providing evidence of the affective learning and the footnotes showing cognitive learning.

It happens that all four samples are by women. That is by coincidence, but it may reinforce a central tenet of this collection: that the current paradigms of advanced theological education are more likely to suit men than women, and these limitations impoverish the church.[1]

The regional spread is exhilaratingly global: Chinese, Palestinian, American, and Indian. The first two pieces are composed in regional languages; the second two are in a language that originated in Britain, but is now thoroughly appropriated by the populations that have inherited it.

Havilah Dharamraj

Sample 1: Xiaoli Yang

多和少的人 **(Duo he Shao de Ren)**

很多人都喜欢来筵席
Henduoren dou xihuan lai yanxi
享用美味佳肴
Xiangyong meiwei jiayao

---

[1]. The topic of culture and gender is addressed in greater depth in Perry Shaw's chapter in this collection, "Culture, Gender, and Diversity in Advanced Theological Studies."

却很少人愿意留下
Que henshaoren yuanyi liuxia
独饮苦杯
Duyin kubei

很多人都喜欢说一说
Henduoren dou xihuan shuoyishuo
唱一唱，想一想
changyichang, xiangyixiang
却很少人甘心走一回
Que henshaoren ganxin zouyihui
让心和头的距离缩小
Rangxin he tou de juli suoxiao

很多人都喜欢指点一下
Henduoren dou xihuan zhidian yixia
评个理还个公道
Pinggeli huangegongdao
却很少人乐意回转
Que henshaoren leyi huizhuan
把头埋在双臂下
Ba tou maizai shuangbi xia

很多人都喜欢被重视
Henduoren dou xihuan bei zhongshi
被抬举前呼后拥
Beitaiju qianhuhouyong
却很少人真心跪下
Que henshaoren zhenxin guixia
为人端水洗脚
Weiren duanshui xijiao

很多人都喜欢走大路
Henduoren dou xihuan zoudalu

却很少人找到窄门
Que henshaoren zhaodao zhaimen
很多人都被召
Henduoren dou beizhao
却很少人被选上
Que henshaoren beixuanshang

Many and Few

Many like to come to the banquet
To enjoy the exquisite food
Few are willing to stay behind
Drink the bitter cup alone

Many like to say a bit
Sing a bit, and think a bit
Few are willing to walk
Shorten the distance of mind and heart

Many like to point the finger
To judge what is right or wrong
Few are willing to return
And hide the head in the arms

Many like to be valued
Favoured with many attendants crowding round
Few are willing to kneel down
Carry water to wash others' feet

Many like to walk on the broad road
Few find the narrow gate
Many invited
Few chosen

Poetry writing is a response to a divine invitation to engage with the world in images and metaphors in a way that creeds and doctrines alone cannot.

The images in this poem came to me naturally as I watched many leaders in emerging churches I trained choosing to carry their cross and walk on the narrow road as disciples of Jesus. The intermingling of the biblical stories and daily lives is formed in poetic rhythm such that one cannot tell where the inspiration is initially from. As such, theological reflection and poetic imagination become one. While mystery, beauty, and metaphors remain in affective learning, scriptural articulation stays in the cognitive domain. As one contemplates the poem, the learning can be both cognitive and affective.

Students can be asked to read and appreciate the poem as it is, and to share any feelings and resonance in their imagination. After this affective learning, they can be invited to write down the correlated stories or images in the Bible (see examples below). The next step is to exercise two-way reflections in order to gain dual understanding and enrichment – that is, to reflect on how the way of the cross reflected in the poem helps them to have deeper understanding of the related verses, and vice versa. In the to-and-fro dialogue, it is hoped that students will understand both the Scripture and the reality of following Jesus at a deeper level.

- *The first paragraph:* Many wanted to be fed and healed by Jesus, but Jesus was left alone in Gethsemane, even by his disciples. No one shared his bitter cup (Matt 26:36–46; Mark 14:32–42).
- *The second paragraph:* Many encounters Jesus had with the Pharisees show how the Pharisees knew the law of God but refused to make any heartfelt changes (Matt 15:8; 19:8; Mark 3:5; 6:52; 7:6).
- *The third paragraph:* Job's friends thought they were right, and Job also wanted to get justice from God (book of Job); those who brought before Jesus the woman caught in adultery left with shame after Jesus asked them which of them did not commit sin (John 8:3–4).
- *The fourth paragraph:* The Pharisees loved to sit in important places (Matt 6:2; 23:6; Mark 12:38–39; Luke 11:43; 14:7–10; 20:46). Even Jesus's disciples competed for a place of honour (Mark 9:34–35). Jesus, however, washed his disciples' feet, including the feet of the one who was to betray him (John 13:1–14).
- *The fifth paragraph* is from Matthew 7:13–14; 22:14.

Sample 2: Grace al-Zoughbi Arteen[2]

In Jesus Our Destiny Is Sure

Born and raised in Bethlehem, I am inspired every day to think and write about the Word who became flesh in a manger a couple of minutes from where I live. I desire to share Jesus with my people and encourage them to set their eyes on him, the Bread of Life, through my simple lines of poetry. Of course, there is no better place to start doing so than the House of Bread[3] (Beit il Khobz بيت الخبز)!

Living in a war-torn land and in the midst of intense conflict, I hope this poem will be a great reminder for my Palestinian students and whoever reads it that tomorrow, no matter what happens, is secure in the hands of the Almighty. Not only in Palestine, but in other places of the world, there is constant turmoil; the forces of darkness, it seems, are in almost every walk of life! However, even as the individual lights of love dwindle, we are reminded by the apostle John that it takes only one single light to dispel the darkness, for the darkness cannot comprehend it (John 1:5)! My prayer is that people will be encouraged to see the Light of Jesus that overcomes all darkness as they meditate on these words.

In Jesus Our Destiny Is Sure	fī yasū' ḍamān almaṣīr	في يسوع ضمان المصير
In a mean manger he became poor	fī midhwad ḥaqīr ṣār faqīr	في مذود حقير صار فقير
Lord of glory, humbly leaving much	rabb almajd tawāḍū' tārikan alkathīr	رب المجد تواضعَ تاركاً الكثير
Perfection of beauty shone like a bright planet	kāmil aljamāl 'ashraq kalkawkab almunīr	كامل الجمال أشرق كالكوكب المنير
He came a Saviour to give liberation	jā' mukhalliṣan kay yu'ṭī attaḥrīr	جاء مخلّصاً كي يعطي التحرير
For my sake and your sake he endured the blame	min 'ajlī wa'ajlak aḥtamal atta'yīr	من أجلي وأجلك احتمل التعيير

---

2. Grace teaches Biblical Studies at Bethlehem Bible College. She particularly likes to encourage students to read and write meditations and poetry inspired by the Scriptures. By doing so, she hopes to motivate her students in their walk with the Lord and rise above the challenges of living in an occupied nation.

3. Bethlehem means literally "House of Bread."

Forgave the sinner and the tormented and the wicked	ghafar lilkhāṭī walmuʿadhdhab washarīr	غفر للخاطي والمُعذَّب والشرير
And satisfied with good things the great multitude	waʾashbaʿ bilkhayrāt aljamʿ alghafīr	وأشبع بالخيرات الجمع الغفير
He gave them the bread of life and every measure	aʿṭāhum khubiz alḥayāt wakull tadbīr	أعطاهم خبز الحياة وكل تدبير
All passes and disappears, so come to the Almighty	alkull yumḍī wayazūl, fataʿāl lilqadīr	الكل يَمضي ويزول، فتعال للقدير
I, the daughter of Bethlehem, call like the evangelist	ʾana ibnit bayt laḥm ʾunādī kalbashīr	أنا ابنة بيت لحم أنادي كالبشير
I bear witness to him, for I am no longer a prisoner of Satan	ʾashhadd ʿanhu falam taʿudd lishshayṭān ʾasīr	اشهد عنه فلم تَعُد للشيطان أسير
Jesus alone ensures justification	yasūʿ waḥdahu yaḍmin attabrīr	يسوع وحده يضمن التبرير
He renews your life and heals your broken heart	yujaddid ḥayātak wayushfī qalbak alkasīr	يجدد حياتك ويشفي قلبك الكسير
He dispels darkness and orders change	yubaddid aẓẓalām wayaʾmur bittaghyīr	يبدد الظلام ويأمر بالتغيير
Let us follow his footsteps and complete the path	linaḥtadhi khuṭāh wanakmil almasīr	لنحتذي خطاه ونكمل المسير
Jesus remains the strongest support and greatest companion	yasūʿ yabqā ʾawfā sand wakhayr samīr	يسوع يبقى أوفى سند وخير سمير
Hang on to him and he will save you from bitter darkness	tuʿalliq bih yunnajīk min ẓalām marīr	تعلّق به ينجّيك من ظلام مرير
His mercy has strengthened us and his love every day is abundant	raḥmatuhu quwiyat ʿalaynā waḥubbahu kull yawm wafīr	رحمته قويت علينا وحبّه كل يوم وفير
For you and for me from his own he grants much grace and honour	lī walak min ladunihi niʿma waʾikrām kathīr	لي ولك من لدنه نعمة وإكرام كثير

Sample 3: Karen Shaw[4]

God Is the Great Salvage Man

God is the great salvage man,
rummaging intently through
the mounds of human refuse and
collecting, as if treasures,
> soiled consciences
> shattered dreams
> empty wrappings
> rotting legacies
> depleted hopes
> dented destinies
> tangled thoughts
> mangled morals
> broken hearts
> chipped shoulders
> excess libido
> rusted relationships
> holey excuses
> scraps of faith

God smiling all the while,
and saying to Himself,
"What I could make of this!"

7 October 2015

Study Questions

1. Make observations, using quotations from the poem, about the author's understanding of the following theological themes:

   a. The nature and character of God

---

[4]. Karen has been reading and writing poetry as a means of both theological reflection and personal spiritual nourishment since childhood. She finds strong biblical and historical support for this practice. She particularly appreciates the works of John Donne, George Herbert, and Luci Shaw.

b. Hamartiology
   c. Soteriology
   d. Another field of theology of your choice, such as biblical anthropology, incarnation, or eschatology.

2. Find at least three parallels between this poem and the parables of Luke 15.

3. What is the nature of the "treasures" collected by the "Great Salvage Man"? What do you think the writer was trying to accomplish through the lengthy list that makes up the centre of the poem? If you had written the list, what items would you have left out and what new ones would you have added, and why?

4. No single human word or metaphor is adequate to describe God fully. Find at least six biblical metaphors for God and fill in the chart below:

Metaphor	Reference	What is true in this metaphor	Limitations of the metaphor
Bird parent	Ps. 91:4	E.g. God is protective of his children	E.g. in contrast to God's protection of his children, a hen's protection ceases when the chicks grow up

Now address these questions related to the poem: Is it insulting to God to describe him as a "salvage man" rummaging through garbage? Defend your answer. What is true in this metaphor? What is one way in which it might be misused? To what degree are the biblical metaphors a definitive collection of verbal pictures of God, and to what degree are they an invitation to believers to find new, contextual metaphors for God?

5. The author writes, "Once, while stopped at a traffic light, I watched a Syrian man rummage with his son through a dumpster in downtown Beirut. The father looked humiliated, but he smiled hopefully when his boy excitedly

showed him a broken chair that might be fixed and sold for a bit of cash. This recollection provided the metaphor I needed as I meditated on God's delight in saving damaged humanity." Describe a poignant memory and write a theologically rich poem or parable which captures, both cognitively and affectively, the central metaphor of your memory.

6. How might you use the poem "God Is the Great Salvage Man" in a current practical ministry situation? This could be preaching, counselling, evangelism, teaching, catechism, or discipleship. Describe the people you are serving, how the poem would be used, and the result you hope to achieve.

Sample 4: Havilah Dharamraj[5]

This poem could well be submitted by a master's-level student as an assignment in a New Testament, Theology, or Religions course at SAIACS. The question the assignment might treat could be: *What are aspects of salvation that you, as an Indian, consider significant?*

The poem has a storyline, imitating the story-telling traditions in India. Thus, there is a plot which moves from crisis to resolution of crisis; characters with some degree of characterization; and dialogue. The creative element is the redistribution of the traditional "seven sayings from the cross" to the three characters so as to emphasize and demonstrate the *affective learning* from the assignment. (Of course, this redistribution will need to be read as poetic licence, and the reader will need to "suspend" theological hair-splitting.)

The *cognitive learning* is from the theological ideas embedded. These are the aspects of salvation that the student explains are significant especially within the Indian context. The four ideas are marked by footnotes. In the actual assignment they would be explanatory and amply show the level of engagement with both the biblical text and secondary literature.

---

5. Havilah wrote (rather ridiculous) rhyming verse in her schooldays and hoped to study English Literature. She ended up with Biochemistry. Shifting to Old Testament later on brought her back to literature, even if not in English. She is grateful for the opportunity to help students appreciate the beauty of Hebrew poetry.

The Bridge

Once upon a time long ago
Between Earth and Paradise there ran a fiery gulf

The ancient stories said that it had not always been so
And that the divide was the deed of humankind
And for that deed, Paradise was ever lost to us

On the other side of the chasm
In Paradise
The Mediator said to God
Father, forgive them for they know not what they do

And God, on the Paradise side
Nodded and said
Let us make a bridge then
For too long the cry of humankind has come up to me –
My God, my God, why have you forsaken me?[6]

I watched as he laid across that great rift
a beam of Judean timber
    spindly
        roughly hewn
            and, frankly speaking, cheap
                with not a grain of good in it
And I thought
Will that suffice!\[7]

God must have read my mind
For he turned from his labour and said, smiling
Truly I say to you, Today you will be with me in Paradise

---

6. This stanza and the one preceding treat Idea 1: Salvation has its origin in God rather than in humans (contra other religions on the Indian sub-continent, such as Hinduism and Islam, in which salvation is by works).

7. Idea 2: Incarnation. A human on a material cross effects salvation for all people across all time. This contrasts at multiple levels with the Hindu concept of *avatar*, wherein deity assumes material form also for salvific purposes.

He set across the shaft a crossbeam
And looked up at the Mediator standing beside him
And the Mediator said
Into your hands I commend my spirit[8]

Then God laid that Perfect One upon the tree
In the burning heat of that bottomless abyss
(*I thirst*)
And he hammered the willing flesh into the wood with Roman nails

We stood on either side of that gulf, God and I
For three long hours
The anguished sky around us mutely dissolving into darkness
And at last I heard a voice say
(I thought it trembled just a bit)
It is finished[9]

So I stepped softly across the bridge to Paradise
And said to God
(How else could I introduce myself?)
Behold, your son!

Ash Wednesday, 2010

Discussion Questions

1. Consider some of the dominant types of poetry in your own local context, including contemporary forms (e.g. rap). What roles do these types and forms play in society?

---

8. Idea 3: The voluntary nature of Christ's sacrifice, which stands out in a culture in which any sacrifice is on the part of the devotee rather than deity; an example is the self-mutilation practised at certain religious festivals of both Hinduism and Islam.

9. Idea 4: The complete and unique nature of salvation whereby Christ is the only way back to God, an exclusive claim contrary to the pluralistic approach of popular Hinduism.

2. Consider different elements of classroom instruction in your advanced programs of study. How might poetry play a role in each of these? For example, how might poetry be used:

    a. As an opening point of discussion in a class?
    b. As a dialogue partner with a text of Scripture or a central theological theme?
    c. As a means for addressing a key personal or social issue in (say) an ethics class?
    d. As an option as an assignment for students who are so inclined?
    e. Other suggestions?

3. What are some of the main barriers you see to the use of poetry that result in its rare use in theological education? For example, to what extent are your faculty familiar/comfortable with poetry as a medium? What concerns would you have about grading? Suggest one or two practical steps by which these barriers might be reduced.

4. How might the church benefit from theologically informed poetry?

Epilogue

Little by little, the cotton thread becomes a turban. (Urdu Proverb)

Change needs patience, but change in our approach to advanced studies particularly needs patience. Sometimes it can seem a little like a Russian novel – "long, tedious, and everyone dies in the end"[1] – as there are a variety of external and internal tangles that confront those who long to weave together innovation that better serves the development of theological leadership.

Externally, we have to negotiate the secular education structure, and we have to answer to accrediting agencies. In much of the world the Western hegemony of global higher education is seen in the uncritical absorption of Western standards that have questionable validity in Majority World contexts. In some places theological schools are bound by government standards that are based on models now rejected in the West, but which have locally become inflexible and virtually sacrosanct. It will take courage for theological schools to challenge the powers that be for the sake of an education that better serves the local context.

Worth noting is that in much of the Minority World the secular academy is (sadly) ahead of the church, and in many places the accrediting agencies are pushing for more innovation and effectiveness than are the colleges. Awareness of these trends can further support the advocacy for change.

Internally, there are also problems. Most faculty members have done little if any serious study in educational theory. Frequently, the dominant voices are faculty who are more comfortable as traditional scholars than as theological leaders. In addition, theological faculty are generally those who have succeeded in the system and are consequently very reluctant to question the system to which they have devoted so much of their lives. It is therefore difficult for

---

1. Mark G. Yudof, "School Finance Reform in Texas: The Edgewood Saga," *Harvard Journal on Legislation* 28 (1991): 499–505, http://scholarship.law.berkeley.edu/facpubs/2207, quoted in Linda Cannell, *Theological Education Matters: Leadership Education for the Church* (Newburgh: EDCOT, 2006), 45.

established faculty to initiate much-needed reform. As Parker Palmer points out, "Changing a university is like trying to move a cemetery. You get no help from the inhabitants."[2]

We trust that you have found the suggestions in this book both challenging and helpful. However, you may feel overwhelmed, unsure of where to begin. If so, be assured that you are not alone! We are all on a journey as we seek increasingly more effective means of accomplishing God's great missional purposes in this world, in our regions, and in our schools. That journey begins with one step.

From our own experience the pathway to innovation is often best completed incrementally. We would encourage you to consider beginning with experimental pieces within master's-level courses, then perhaps attempts at interdisciplinary integrative courses, then opening wider possibilities for final master's projects, culminating in substantial innovation at the doctoral level. However, as Evan Hunter puts it in his early chapter of this collection, the context "is conducive to innovation."[3]

Take a moment to imagine how it would be if:

- Our master's and doctoral candidates were genuinely excited about what they were doing, rather than seeing much of the work as a series of mindless hoops they needed to jump through.
- Examiners looked forward to reading what was produced, knowing that it would be gripping and significant.
- Church leaders were in eager anticipation of the results, knowing how much their churches and communities would benefit.
- Local church members read the end product and said, "This is exactly what we need!"
- Jesus himself was excited about the difference the work of his people's best minds was having as the church sought to impact the world in his name.

---

2. Parker Palmer in Parker J. Palmer and Arthur Zajonc, *The Heart of Higher Education: A Call to Renewal; Transforming the Academy through Collegial Conversations* (San Francisco: Jossey-Bass, 2010), 127.
3. Evan Hunter, in this collection.

Only as we dream and then take steps that move us towards those dreams can we hope to be faithful to our calling as leaders of God's kingdom people. The cotton thread can eventually become a turban! May God grant us his grace, strength, and wisdom in our joint endeavour.

Bibliography

Cannell, Linda. *Theological Education Matters: Leadership Education for the Church.* Newburgh: EDCOT, 2006.

Palmer, Parker J., and Arthur Zajonc. *The Heart of Higher Education: A Call to Renewal; Transforming the Academy through Collegial Conversations.* San Francisco: Jossey-Bass, 2010.

Yudof, Mark G. "School Finance Reform in Texas: The Edgewood Saga." *Harvard Journal on Legislation* 28 (1991): 499–505. http://scholarship.law.berkeley.edu/facpubs/2207.

About the Contributors

Stephanie Black, PhD, currently based in Dublin, Ireland, serves as an international theological education specialist with Serge in partnership with World Outreach of the Evangelical Presbyterian Church. She is also Affiliate Associate Professor of New Testament at Fuller Theological Seminary. Her doctoral work was in biblical Greek and linguistic theory. She describes her many years teaching in theological higher education in Ethiopia, Kenya, and India as an ongoing journey of discovery – about God, about herself, about culture, and about the gospel: "It's theology on safari!" She is grateful to the students and colleagues from around the world who have joined and guided her in this journey.

Larry W. Caldwell, PhD, is Academic Dean and Professor of Intercultural Studies at Sioux Falls Seminary in Sioux Falls, SD. In addition, he is Director of Training and Strategy for Converge Worldwide. Prior to this, he and his family were missionaries with Converge for twenty-one years in Manila, Philippines, where he was Academic Dean and Professor of Missions and Bible Interpretation at Asian Theological Seminary, as well as Director of the Doctor of Missiology program of the Asia Graduate School of Theology, Philippines. Larry teaches regularly on contextualization and cross-cultural Bible interpretation (ethnohermeneutics) at missionary training institutions throughout the world. He has authored dozens of books and articles, and for several years edited the *Journal of Asian Mission*. His latest book is *Doing Bible Interpretation: Making the Bible Come Alive for Yourself and Your People*.

Ashish Chrispal, PhD, is a pastor, grassroots missionaries' trainer, and theological education facilitator. Ashish has served with Overseas Council for the last ten years equipping seminaries in Asia to rethink theological education through being missional and ministry-oriented with a scholarly focus for the Lord's glory.

Paul Allan Clark is the Director of Education and Engagement with Overseas Council, where he oversees the Institute for Excellence. Pastoral and missionary experiences combine into a life as teacher, discipler, and facilitator of transforming theological education and Christian leaders. During twenty-five years in Brazil, Paul discovered his joy in transforming leaders for ministry. He completed his PhD in Theology through the Programa Doutoral Latino-Americano and Facultad Internacional de Educación Teologica in 2017. Paul is married to Karen, and they have five married children and nine grandchildren, spread across the Americas.

Havilah Dharamraj is Academic Dean and Head of the Department of Old Testament at the South Asia Institute of Advanced Christian Studies, Bangalore, India. She has a doctoral degree from the University of Durham, UK, in narrative theology. For long years she laboured under the misconception that creative writing was for "popular" publications, while academic work had not much use for the imagination. In her writing thus far, she has been trying to sneak in her mind-boggling Indian heritage of poetic, epic, and narrative literature. This book assures her that she can now do this without apology.

Samuel Ewell served in Brazil as a missionary from 2003 to 2010 with his wife Rosalee and their three children James, Isabella, and Katharine. Since 2010 the Ewells have resided in Birmingham, UK, where Sam has recently completed his PhD on Ivan Illich and Christian witness (*Faith Seeking Conviviality*, publication forthcoming with Wipf and Stock). As an ordained minister and member of Companions for Hope, a Christian collective based in Summerfield-Winson Green, Sam combines prison and community engagement, urban agriculture, and theological facilitation as a way of cultivating abundant community at the edges of inner-city Birmingham, especially among the "discarded." Sam's research interests include the intersection of Christian spirituality and practical theology, exploring personal, social, and ecological transformation in the midst of the "throwaway culture."

Joanna Feliciano-Soberano is Academic Dean and Chair of the Christian Education Department at Asian Theological Seminary (ATS) in Manila, Philippines. She earned her ThM degree in Spirituality from Regent College in Vancouver, BC, and a PhD in Educational Studies from Trinity International University in Deerfield, IL. She is married to Fernando and they have a grown-up son. Joanna has worked as a full-time faculty member at ATS since 1998.

She has been a GATE Associate (Global Associates for Transformational Education) since 2012. Her ministry involvement with ATS and with GATE has provided her with opportunities for growth in leadership and in teaching. These learning experiences have also strengthened her resolve to be a high-impact teacher.

Dwi Maria Handayani, PhD, is a Langham Scholar graduated from Asia Graduate School of Theology, Manila. She serves at Bandung Theological Seminary as program director for the MTh program. As a faculty member she teaches Biblical Studies and Sociology. She is also a trainer at Langham Preaching Indonesia and actively speaks in seminars in relation to Muslim and Christian studies.

Allan Harkness, PhD (Murdoch, W. Australia), is working with Asian seminaries in leadership, curriculum development, and faculty enrichment. Now living in New Zealand, he has twenty-six years of experience in Asian theological education, including as the founding dean of AGST Alliance (2004–15), a role which included supervising and overseeing students completing research programs up to doctoral level. He has been disquieted when his students have struggled to move successfully through the standard thesis/dissertation hoops, so he is pleased to be part of the critically reflective discourse represented by this book. To continue to dialogue, Allan may be contacted at allan.harkness@gmail.com.

Evan Hunter, PhD (Trinity Evangelical Divinity School), has served as Vice President (Scholar Network) of ScholarLeaders International since 2004, drawn by the commitment to developing leaders for the Majority World church. He brings a passion for both the church and the seminary to his work with ScholarLeaders and as editor of the *InSights Journal for Global Theological Education*. In his role, he has had the privilege to work with hundreds of gifted women and men who serve in theological education across Africa, Asia, Latin America, the Middle East, and Eastern Europe. From his vantage point, he sees significant opportunities for schools to develop new, contextually engaged training models that will both meet the demand for equipping for kingdom service and creatively address some of the mounting pressures on theological education. Evan and his wife Becky live in Minnesota, where they keep up with their three very active sons.

Caleb Hutcherson serves as Faculty Development Lead and Lecturer in Historical Theology at the Arab Baptist Theological Seminary, Beirut, Lebanon. After completing his ThM at Dallas Theological Seminary, Caleb and his wife, Nicolette, replanted themselves in Beirut, Lebanon, to partner with the Lebanese Baptist Church in theological education and compassion ministries. Creative experimentation is somewhat of a tradition for Caleb, having grown up in a family that often did things a little differently. His theological mentors all had extensive backgrounds of ministry outside of "Western" frameworks; they encouraged creativity in their classrooms and inspired Caleb to embrace innovation as he came to theological studies. Caleb is currently a PhD candidate at the International Baptist Theological Study Centre at Vrije Universiteit Amsterdam. His research explores the dynamics of practising theological reflection in Arab-Muslim contexts.

John Jusu earned his PhD in Educational Studies from Trinity International University in Deerfield. He currently serves as Regional Director for Overseas Council in Africa and is also on the faculty of Africa International University in Kenya. His doctoral work was in understanding the epistemological frameworks of Africans preparing for pastoral and teaching ministries of the church in Africa and how that understanding might influence the production of learning materials and the pedagogy of such learners. In the light of this expertise, John serves as curriculum consultant for More Than a Mile Deep-Global, Supervising Editor for the *Africa Study Bible*, Senior Researcher for the Africa Leadership Study, and Associate of GATE (Global Associates for Transformational Education). He is also involved in faculty development for many educational initiatives in Africa. John is married to Tity. They have three children.

César Lopes has been working in theological education in Brazil since 2000. He was among the first students of South American Theological Seminary (SATS, Brazil), joining the faculty after graduation, and in 2013 completed the PhD in Education Studies program at Trinity Evangelical Divinity School, where he received support from both Langham Partnership and ScholarLeaders

International. César is married to Amanda and they have two daughters, Giovana and Luiza. He currently serves as Academic Dean for an online program of pastor formation for the Independent Presbyterian Church in Brazil and on the Board of Directors of CETI (Center for Interdisciplinary Theological Studies), an organization based in Costa Rica offering certificate and master's programs that cater to Latin America in general.

Bassem Melki is Dean of Students at the Arab Baptist Theological Seminary. He also serves as a consultant to the Peacemaking Initiative Team of ABTS's Institute for Middle East Studies. Bassem's deep concern is to have Christ's message of reconciliation lived out in practice in contexts of conflict. To deepen his understanding of possible pathways to culturally relevant and biblically faithful approaches to peacemaking, Bassem is pursuing a PhD in Biblical Peacemaking through the International Graduate School of Leadership, Philippines. He would never have entered this program if it were not for the non-traditional approach to advanced studies promoted, including the option to use action research as the methodology for his final project. Bassem is married to Roula and they have two children, Samantha and Brandon.

W. Jay Moon, PhD, is a Professor of Evangelism and Church Planting at Asbury Theological Seminary in Wilmore, KY. In addition, he directs the Office of Faith, Work, and Economics at Asbury Theological Seminary. Prior to this, he and his family were missionaries with SIM for thirteen years, including nine years serving in Ghana, West Africa, doing church planting and water development among the Builsa people. It was in Ghana that he first learned about oral cultures as he learned and collected local African proverbs. He has authored three books, the latest being *Intercultural Discipleship: Learning from Global Approaches to Spiritual Formation*, published by Baker Academic. In his spare time, he has developed digital hybrid books for the new digit-oral generation of learners.

Marvin Oxenham is an interdisciplinary scholar, holding completed degrees in theology, philosophy, and education, having done his doctoral work at King's College London in educational philosophy and later specializing in online and distance education. He is also a practitioner in theological education, having served as Academic Dean at the London School of Theology, where he currently holds the post of Director of Online Education and Program Leader for the MA in Theological Education, an innovative postgraduate and doctoral program aimed at providing professional and scholarly educational training for global theological educators. He also serves as Coordinator for the European Evangelical Accrediting Association (ICETE member) and has been Regional Consultant for Europe for Overseas Council. Marvin was born and lives in Rome, Italy.

Ian Payne is Principal and Lecturer in Theology at South Asia Institute of Advanced Christian Studies, Bangalore, India. He has his PhD in Theology from the University of Aberdeen, UK, focused on epistemology and pedagogy and Karl Barth. He is author of *Wouldn't You Love to Know? Trinitarian Epistemology and Pedagogy*. The son of New Zealand missionaries, he grew up in India. After being an architect in New Zealand, he studied MTh at SAIACS in the mid-1990s, accompanied by his wife and three daughters. He returned as faculty and has been Principal at SAIACS from 2008. From building church buildings, he has been drawn into the excitement of building the church. He hopes this present collection will enhance the educational adventure for many.

Lal Senanayake is the President of Lanka Bible College and Seminary. He is a graduate of Lanka Bible College, University of Nottingham, and Trinity International University (TIU). He earned his PhD in Educational Studies at TIU as a scholar of ScholarLeaders International. He has served at Lanka Bible College and Seminary for over twenty-five years in several capacities – from being a student to being the current president. Lal has many years of experience in pastoral care and counselling ministry. In addition to teaching at LBCS Lal has a passion for writing for the Majority World. This book has provided a great platform to speak to the context of theological education in the Majority World.

Karen Shaw, DMin, is Assistant Professor of Cross-Cultural Ministry at the Arab Baptist Theological Seminary in Beirut, Lebanon. Karen has a particular interest in the significant role that affect plays in personal and corporate faith. She regrets that poetry and photography have been almost completely absent from her theological studies. Karen has been living in the Middle East since 1990, engaging in a variety of ministries. She currently shepherds the

International Community Church in Riyadh as-Sulh. Karen is married to Perry and they have two adult children in Australia.

Perry Shaw, EdD, is Professor of Education at the Arab Baptist Theological Seminary in Beirut, Lebanon, and the author of *Transforming Theological Education*. Perry and his family have been serving in the Middle East since 1990. Over the years Perry has enjoyed a highly eclectic education that includes such diverse studies as mathematics, pastoral training, education, sociology and psychology, Greek exegesis, intercultural leadership, and Arabic language and history. This with his years living in the Arab world has given him an appreciation for the rich untapped resources of the global church, resources that he believes have been stifled in traditional approaches to theological studies. His commitment to this collection emerges out of a desire to see the whole global church benefit from the depth of wisdom and understanding that is found in its rich diversity of peoples and cultures.

Xiaoli Yang, PhD, has been serving in Australia and Asia as a lecturer, pastor, and mentor over the last twenty years. In her teaching at the University of Divinity in Australia and theological seminaries in Asia she adopts creative methodologies to build bridges between the secular and the sacred, the East and the West, theology and poetry. The embracing of the diverse approaches to theological studies in this volume affirms not only her unique voice as a Chinese migrant, poet, and theologian, but also the imaginative poetic epistemology in theological research.

Rafael Zaracho (PhD in Theology, University of St Andrews) is a professor at Instituto Bíblico Asunción in Paraguay. He is part of the Anabaptist tradition in which knowing and following Jesus are crucial elements of the everyday life of being a disciple. His contribution to this book is part of his desire to create and promote discerning communal spaces. His invitation is to promote and create spaces for diverse and multiple models of teaching, learning, and final works. He is married to Rut and they have two children Sofía (nine) and Sebastian (four).

Grace al-Zoughbi is a Christian Palestinian from Bethlehem who serves as a lecturer in Biblical Studies at Bethlehem Bible College. She was an undergraduate student at the college and finished her MA at the London

School of Theology in 2010. Her thesis sought to explore the ways in which women can seek to defend and promote personal dignity, particularly within strongly patriarchal contexts. Grace is currently working on her PhD through the South African Theological Seminary. In her day-to-day life, she participates in leading a variety of programs through her local church in Bethlehem and is also involved in various translation projects. Grace joined the staff of BBC in 2011, and she is currently the head of the Biblical Studies department.

Author Index

A

Adams, T. 163
Aikenhead, G. 149
Aitchison, C. 24
AlDahdouh, A. 358
Alfaro, C. 149
al-Ghazali 240
Allen, D. 210
Alves, R. 259
Amar, G. 394
Amstutz, D. 150
Anderson, David 131
Anderson, L. 46, 80
Anderson, R. 194, 257
Ango, S. 103
Apfelthaler, G. 151
Apple, M. 157
Archbald, D. 338
Arndt, S. 354, 372
Arrington, A. 278, 396
Arroyo, M. 153
Arteen, G. 447, 452
Asselin, M. 112

B

Bali, M. 57
Banks, C. 146, 156, 157
Banks, J. 146, 156, 157
Barajas, E. 415
Baron-Cohen, S. 101
Barrett, H. 331, 332
Barrows, H. 210
Barth, K. 168, 169, 257, 470
Bauman, C. 98

Bauman, Z. 172
Baumgartner, L. 98, 120
Becker, R. 25
Beck, S. 331, 347
Bedekar, V. 394
Beech, D. 433
Behera, M. 90
Belenky, M. 102
Beltechi, A. 25
Bennett, M. 80
Berhane, M. 128, 130
Bernheimer, C. 315
Beyer, B. 122
Bhatti, D. 234, 235, 237, 239, 241, 244, 246
Bingxin 430
Bjuremeark, A. 23
Black, S. 11, 30, 92, 99, 104, 127, 149, 202, 465
Blake, N. 152
Bleier, H. 24
Bliss, A. 135, 136
Block, D. 396, 400, 406, 408
Bloom, B. 45, 50, 57, 150, 276, 339
Bonhoeffer, D. 387
Boomershine, T. 279
Borkowski, N. 25
Bosch, D. 159
Boud, D. 23, 25, 28, 31, 36, 210, 217
Bourgeault, C. 438
Boyer, E. 34, 363, 368, 372
Braga, R. 198
Brandenburg, R. 349
Brennan, S. 147

Brookfield, S. 122, 160
Brown, C. 431
Brynjolfson, R. 190
Bull, B. 70, 84
Burns, K. 377

C
Caffarella, R. 98, 120
Caine, G. 192
Caine, N. 192
Caldwell, L. 33, 203, 287, 288, 291, 293, 465
Cameron, H. 234, 235, 237, 239, 241, 243, 244, 246
Canagarajah, A. S. 2, 128, 130, 133, 137, 141
Cannell, L. 461
Carney, J. 331, 332
Carr, N. 369
Cayley, D. 383, 386
Chaitanya, S. 314
Chandavarkar, P. 393
Chang, P. 30
Checkland, P. 238
Childre, D. L. 433
Choi, I. 30, 98, 432
Chow, W. 27
Chrispal, A. 9, 13, 15, 192, 465
Clark, P. 28, 34, 36, 99–101, 151, 156, 187, 198, 279, 465
Cloke, P. 377, 388
Colwill, D. 31
Conde-Frazier, E. 236
Confucius 429, 435, 439
Connor, U. 128, 135
Costas, O. 158
Cranton, P. 151
Cronshaw, D. 192
Crowther, P. 331–333, 336, 337
Cunningham, S. 45, 53, 54

Cushner, K. 147
Czermak, K. 412

D
Dahlgren, M. 23
Danby, S. 23–25, 27, 31
Das, N. 317
Das, R. 260
Dearborn, T. 190
Dei, G. 147
Deininger, F. 260
de Klerk, B. 190
DeLanghe, P. 412
Demarest, B. 111
Dewey, J. 211
Dharamraj, H. 3, 99, 151, 156, 276, 278, 309, 393, 447, 448, 456, 466
Dick, B. 235, 237, 240–244, 247
Dietz, G. 146
Dimen-Schein, M. 281
Doch, B. 210
Doiron, R. 112
Dokecki, P. 236
Domínguez, C. 312, 313, 315–319
Donovan, V. 388
Dorfman, P. 29
Dowes, S. 358
Duce, C. 234, 235, 237, 239, 241, 244, 246
Duke, N. 331, 347
Durkheim, E. 113
Dyrness, W. 440

E
Edgerton, F. 394
Eguizabal, O. 260
Ehrenberg, R. 25
Elashmawi, F. 98
English, M. 122

Enns, M. 31, 99
Epstein, D. 145
Escobar, S. 158, 255
Étiemble, R. 319
Ewell, S. 55, 56, 152, 198, 211, 326, 375, 376, 443, 466

F

Fairclough, N. 416, 417
Feletti, G. 210, 217
Feliciano-Soberano, J. 326, 329, 466
Ferenczi, J. 260
Fernandes, D. 321
Ferris, R. 190
Fiddes, P. 427, 436
Fink, L. D. 46, 339
Fischer, R. 99
Fisher, M. 11
Ford, P. 68
Foucault, M. 154
Francesco, A. 115
Freire, P. 122, 161, 198, 200, 211, 216, 235, 237, 241, 381
Frings, T. 102
Fu, G. 430
Fulcher, R. 414
Fulkerson, M. 389

G

Gabrys, B. 25
Gadamer, H-G. 438
Galeano, E. 383
Gardner, H. 222
Geertz, C. 281
Gettier, E. 176
Gilbert, R. 31
Ginzberg, L. 309
Gold, B. 115
Golde, C. 23, 25
González, J. 253, 259

Goroncy, J. 436, 440
Gorski, P. 152
Govindarian, V. 37
Graen, G. 29
Graham, E. 234, 247, 436
Green, B. 31
Greene, M. 2
Greenwood, D. 235
Griffiths, M. 186
Groh, S. 210
Guenther, M. 437
Gunton, C. 174
Gushee, D. 241
Gutiérrez, G. 388

H

Hall, E. 114, 115, 117
Handayani, D. 99, 278, 327, 411, 467
Harder, C. 236, 237
Harkness, A. 3, 10, 30, 32, 33, 61, 74, 89, 169, 291, 428, 467
Harper, A. 299
Harris, P. 98
Havea, J. 300
Hawk, L. D. 154, 155
Healey, J. 277
Heggelund, M. 25, 32
Hibbert, E. 203, 205
Hibbert, R. 203, 205
Hiebert, P. 277, 380
Higgs, P. 33
Higuera-Smith, K. 154, 155
Hiha, A. 72, 73
Hill, B. 77
Hill, G. 52
Hill, R. 331–333, 336, 337
Hirsch, E. 413
Hmelo-Silver, C. 218
Hofstede, G. 28, 29, 149
Holst, J. 122

hooks, b. 260
Horton, M. 235, 241
House, R. 29, 30
Hung, W. 212
Hunter, E. 3, 10, 21, 22, 26, 34, 95, 145, 195, 235, 289, 462, 467
Hutcherson, C. 102, 187, 200, 233, 239, 468

I
Illich, I. 152, 326, 376, 378, 381–388, 390, 466
Ingalhaliker, M. 101
Ingram, D. 147
Inhelder, B. 47
Israel, H. 311
Issa, A. 411

J
Jakobson, R. 318
Janik, A. 138
Jegede, O. 149
Jenkins, P. 52
Jennings, W. 387
Jeyaraj, J. 190
Johnson, C. 411
Johnson, E. 315
Johnson, M. 431
Johnson, T. 1
Jonassen, D. 212
Jordan, B. 291
Jost, L. 262, 263
Jusu, J. 102, 187, 209, 220, 235, 468

K
Kahn, P. 212
Kamande, P. 128, 131–133, 136–138, 140, 141
Kang, N. 5, 44

Kaplan, R. 128, 129, 133–135, 139, 149
Keay, J. 310
Kegan, R. 194, 200
Kelsey, D. 33, 34
Kendall, J. 46
Kett, J. 413
Kilpatrick, W. 211
Kincheloe, J. 145
Kinsler, R. 255
Kirk, J. A. 10
Kitsantas, A. 122
Kivunzi, P. 128, 130, 131, 136, 137, 140, 141, 143
Kjesbo, J. 303, 304
Knowles, M. 74
Kolb, D. 150
Koyama, K. 256
Krathwohl, D. 46, 80, 150
Kraybill, D. 253, 257, 258
Kristal, E. 316
Kuh, C. 25
Kumar, M. 77
Kumar, R. 393
Kupczyk-Romanczuk, G. 331, 333, 334, 338, 339, 346

L
Lai, P. 299
Lakoff, G. 431
Lalitha, J. 154, 155
Lan, L. 138
Lawson, K. 33, 54
Lee, A. 23–25, 27, 28, 31, 36, 37
Leonard, D. 25
Leonard, R. 141
Leshner, A. 200, 201
Levin, M. 235
Lewin, K. 237, 239, 240
Lewis, G. 111

Lewis, J. 190
Lingenfelter, J. 120
Lingenfelter, S. 120
Little, A. 113
Liu, R. 212
Lombardi, M. 331
Long, T. 199
Lonu, V. 128, 131–133, 136–138, 140, 141
Lopes, C. 11, 145, 193, 468
Lucey, M. 313, 315
Lun, V. 99
Luszcz, M. 221

M
Mac Coinnigh, M. 420
Machin, D. 415
MacIntyre, A. 176
Macionis, J. 113
Mackie, V. 411
Major, C. 222
Maki, P. 25
Malsen, G. 24
Manathunga, C. 27
Mansour, J. 29
Manzano, J. 299, 300
Margetson, D. 217
Marincovich, M. 217
Martin, H. 433
Martin, J. 84
Marzano, R. 46
Masschelein, J. 152
Mathews, F. 440
Maxwell, T. 331, 333, 334, 338, 339, 346
Mayr, A. 415
McArthur, J. 152
McDonough, G. 281
McGregor, S. 414, 417
McLaren, P. 153

McPeck, J. 122
Meek, E. 171
Melas, N. 319
Melki, B. 102, 187, 200, 233, 239–242, 469
Méndez-Montoya, A. 389
Mendieta, E. 145
Mennin, S. 222
Mercado, L. 416
Merriam, S. 98, 120, 123, 151, 162
Meyer, M. 414, 415
Mezirow, J. 102, 150
Mieder, W. 415
Miller, C. 202, 411
Mishra, R. 112
Monaghan, P. 330
Moon, J. 242, 396
Moon, W. J. 99, 129, 269, 270, 278, 279, 282, 469
Morin, E. 191
Morris-Suzuki, T. 411
Morrow, R. 147
Moust, J. 219, 222
Mowat, H. 234, 242, 244, 247
Muldoon, R. 334, 335
Mutuku, G. 128, 130, 131, 136, 137, 140, 141
Mwangi, J. 190
Myers, C. 380

N
Na, J. 98
Nakane, I. 149
Nakosteen, M. 240
Nashon, S. 131
Naughton, J. 353
Ndyamiyemenshi, N. 128, 130–133, 137, 138, 140, 141
Nerad, M. 25, 32
Neufeld, A. 258

Neville, D. 300
Newbigin, L. 17, 171, 172, 177
Newbrough, J. 236
Niditch, S. 400
Niebuhr, H. R. 354
Nieto, S. 153
Nisbett, R. 30, 96–100, 105, 106, 139, 432
Norenzayan, A. 432
Norrick, N. 420
Ntseane, P. 151

O

Ogalo, G. 128, 131–133, 136–138, 140, 141
O'Gorman, R. 236
Olivelle, P. 394, 395, 397, 398, 401, 403, 405
Olson, D. 396, 400, 404, 408
Ong, J. W. 315
O'Rourke, K. 212
Osmer, R. 197
Osório, A. 358
Ott, B. 45, 53, 54, 190, 192, 259
Oxenham, M. 202, 211, 282, 326, 351, 469

P

Padilla, R. 158, 255
Palmer, P. 462
Palumbo-Liu, D. 319, 320
Panetta, C. 129, 134
Pare, A. 24
Parker, D. 101
Patton, S. 105, 186
Payne, I. 11, 84, 167, 171, 191, 470
Pears, M. 377, 388
Peng, K. 30, 432
Pessoa, L. 433
Philbin, M. 102

Phillips, D. 211, 212
Phillips, E. 73, 78
Piaget, J. 47, 212
Pierson, P. 310
Pilch, J. 417
Plato 176, 313, 431
Polanyi, M. 178, 180
Popper, K. 209
Portugal, S. 358
Preiswerk, M. 255, 258–260
Prensky, M. 315
Presner, T. 316
Priest, R. 95
Pugh, D. 73, 78

Q

Quezada, R. 149

R

Raj, P. 190
Ramage, D. 411
Ramsden, P. 71
Reagan, T. 120, 145
Reichwein, A. 431
Reike, R. 138
Reynolds, F. 223
Ribka, S. 411
Riebe-Estrella, G. 43, 94, 95
Rockwell, E. 148
Rogers, K. 73, 78
Rohr, R. 433
Rose, G. 427
Roth, J. 256, 257, 260
Ryder, A. 394, 395, 403

S

Sabra, G. 242
Sachs, J. 282
Sande, B. 128, 130–133, 137, 138, 140, 141

Sangari, K. 313
Sattar, A. 314
Saussy, H. 312, 320
Savin-Baden, M. 213, 222
Scharen, C. 377, 388
Schiff, L. 78
Schipper, M. 416
Schmidt, H. 219, 222
Scholes, J. 238
Schön, D. 237, 242
Schwartz, P. 222
Schwartz, S. 98
Schwarz, E. 80
Semali, L. 145
Senanayake, L. 11, 30, 109, 158, 193, 470
Shaw, I. 33, 45, 53, 54, 64
Shaw, K. 447, 448, 454, 470
Shaw, P. 3, 11, 30, 43, 63, 72, 73, 89, 91, 121, 139, 154, 191, 242, 259, 260, 264, 265, 279, 289, 428, 432, 448, 471
Shulman, L. 47
Skirka, L. 98
Sleeter, C. 153
Small, S. 75
Smith, A. 101
Smith, K. 196, 197
Smith, L. 292
Solina, J. 299
Somekh, B. 235, 242
Sousa, D. 192
Sowell, R. 33
Spindler, G. 119, 120, 292
Spiro, R. 221
Spradley, J. 281
Stanton, A. 102
Starcher, R. 27
Stassen, G. 241
Stevens, R. P. 105

Stick, S. 27
St John of the Cross 434
Sugimoto, C. 2, 74, 105
Sul, S. 98
Swinton, J. 234, 242, 244, 247
Sybertz, D. 277

T
Tamblyn, R. 210
Tang, E. 425
Tella, A. 411
Teme, D. 128, 130–133, 137, 138, 140, 141
Tennent, T. 5
Thurman, H. 388
Ting-Toomey, S. 116
Tippins, D. 212
Tobin, K. 212
Todhunter, C. 238
Torres, C. 147
Toulmin, S. 138
Townsend, B. 62
Tracy, D. 157
Trefil, J. 413
Triandis, H. 98
Trimble, C. 37
Turner, E. 281
Turner, V. 280, 281

U
Urban, W. 316

V
Vaka'uta, N. 300
Vaka'uta, N. 300, 301
Van der Meer, A. 299
van Dijk, T. 414
Vessey, D. 438
Vigen, A. 377, 388
Viladesau, R. 436

Villanueva, D. 312
Vygotsky, L. 212

W
Wainwright, E. 300
Walker, G. 23, 25
Walton, H. 436
Wanak, L. 260
Ward, C. 99
Ward, F. 436
Ward, G. 377
Watson, R. 102
Webb, B. 396, 400, 404
Webb, G. 222
Weller, M. 356, 360, 363, 366, 369, 371
Weller, R. 361, 367–371
Weng, W. 412
Wheeler, B. 24
Willetts, J. 27
Williamson, M. 102
Williams, R. 387, 390, 430, 437, 440
Wilson, C. 434
Wink, W. 186
Wodak, R. 414, 415
Wolterstorff, N. 171
Wood, P. 221
Woolf, V. 312, 313
Wright, H. 131
Wright, N. T. 171, 177

X
Xu, Z. 430

Y
Yachnin, P. 296
Yang, X. 100, 151, 156, 278, 327, 425, 427, 431, 439, 441, 447, 448, 471
Yong, A. 436

Yudof, M. 461

Z
Zachariah, R. 122
Zacharias, R. 122
Zajonc, A. 462
Zamudio-Suaréz, F. 2, 347
Zaracho, R. 28, 35, 73, 102, 133, 235, 253, 255, 278, 471
Zhongshe, L. 138
Ziolkowski, T. 103, 185
Zull, J. 192

Subject Index

A

accents of the Spirit 255, 256
accreditation 57, 58, 103, 217, 249, 371, 422
action research 102, 187, 233–249, 469
Aesop's Fables 319, 394
aesthetics 196, 426, 436, 442
affective, affectivity 94, 102, 106, 204, 265, 436, 442, 443, 447, 448, 451, 456
Africa 1, 6, 11, 22, 23, 27, 58, 92, 99, 100, 105, 127, 129, 131, 141, 172, 187, 202, 213, 239, 248, 269, 270, 467, 468, 469
Africa International University (AIU) 27, 128, 468
Akrofi Christaller Institute 27, 280
Analects 429
anthropology, cultural 96, 146, 148–152, 155, 156, 161, 162, 193
anthropology, theological 198, 455
Arab Baptist Theological Seminary (ABTS) 187, 234, 239, 243–245, 468, 469, 470, 471
architecture 56, 260, 333, 362
Aristotle 317
Asia 6, 9, 19, 22, 27, 29, 30, 33, 58, 68, 98, 99, 105, 115, 172, 321, 394, 465, 467, 471
Asia Graduate School of Theology (AGST) 10, 27, 299, 467
Asian Theological Seminary 326, 465, 466
Association for the Study of Higher Education (ASHE) 62
Association of Theological Schools (ATS) 26
A Thousand and One Nights, Arabian Nights 319, 394
Australia 22, 49, 80, 327, 426, 467, 471
autoethnography, autoethnographic 55, 326, 428, 443

B

Bandung Theological Seminary 327, 467
Bangalore Adaptations 52, 54
Beirut Benchmarks 33, 45, 52, 54, 57, 175, 182
Bethlehem Bible College 452, 471
Biola University 278, 409
Bloom's taxonomy of educational objectives 45, 46, 48, 50, 51, 57, 80, 121, 150, 269, 273, 274, 276, 277
Bologna Declaration, Bologna Process 25, 33, 52
Book of Poetry 429
Borneo 319
Boyer's Aspects of Scholarship 363
Brazil 22, 160, 198, 376–382, 384, 386–388, 466, 468
Buddhism 180, 310

C

Cameroon 299, 302

Cape Town Commitment (CTC) 64, 66, 67
Carnegie Initiative on the Doctorate (CID) 25
Chicago Manual of Style 297
China 1, 24, 78, 97, 115, 425, 429, 437
China Graduate School of Theology (CGST) 27
Church of North India 15
collaborative, collaboration 27, 28, 34, 35, 73, 74, 94, 133, 195, 204, 209, 216, 220, 222, 253, 259, 261, 262, 266, 267, 302, 330, 339, 359, 366
collectivism, collectivist, communitarian 29, 35, 63, 73, 74, 151, 162, 428
colonialism, colonial 57, 90, 100, 145, 226, 297, 304, 310, 383
Columbia University 198
Common Reader 181, 312–315, 317–322
Community development 339
comparative literature. *See* literature, comparative
competencies 49, 50, 53–55, 59, 69, 149, 162, 224, 330, 332, 333, 338, 339, 348, 443
comprehensive examinations 62
confessionalism 179
Confucius 429, 435, 439
connectivism, connectivist 352, 356–360, 372
conscientization 211
constructivism, constructivist 211, 212, 357, 358, 360, 372
contextualization, contextuality 27, 95, 105, 151, 241, 302, 465
contextual theology 278
conviviality 383, 385

Council for Higher Education Accreditation (CHEA) 49
credentialism, credentials 66, 69, 111, 118, 186
critical contextualization 277
criticality, critical thinking 57, 79, 111, 121, 122, 133, 138, 181, 346, 369
critical reflection 112, 119, 153, 180, 225, 238, 242, 243, 336, 337, 342, 344
critical self-reflection 159, 388, 425
cultural differences 28, 31, 81, 114, 148, 295
cultural hegemony 2, 45

D

dance 198, 277, 279, 317, 371, 394, 439, 441
Dao 434, 439
Descartes 171, 435
deterritorialization 153
dialectics, dialecticism 97
dialogue 45, 48, 99, 117, 119, 121, 123, 152, 154, 156, 159, 187, 204, 211, 258, 327, 364, 378, 384, 421, 428, 429, 434, 436–439, 451, 456, 459, 467
digital humanities 315
digital hybrid books. *See* digital literature; *See* digital literature; *See* digital literature; *See* digital literature
digital literature 316, 318
digital revolution 316, 352, 354, 357
digital scholarship 326, 351, 352, 357, 360–362, 368, 370–372
discipleship 67, 70, 71, 82, 85, 272, 277, 384, 385, 456

discourse, discourse analysis 16, 37, 134, 141, 242, 312, 316, 337, 412, 414–417, 420–422, 429, 439–441, 467
dissertation 4, 16, 17, 23, 25, 31, 32, 34, 35, 37, 45, 52, 54, 56, 58, 61, 67, 72–78, 93, 94, 104, 133, 138, 151, 177, 184–186, 198, 201, 224, 242, 255, 278–281, 289, 295–300, 305, 326, 329–331, 333, 336–339, 344, 346–349, 351, 378, 395, 413, 428, 429, 437, 438, 467
doctorate by publication 55
drama 56, 277, 279, 280, 394
dualism, dualistic 151
Dublin Descriptors 45, 49, 51
Duke Divinity School 375

E

empirical, empiricist, empiricism 3, 10, 37, 43, 44, 89–91, 94, 102–104, 186, 197, 245, 318, 447
English (language) 5, 14, 16, 17, 78, 79, 127–130, 136, 137, 297, 300, 330, 379, 395
enlightenment 43, 59, 90, 94, 98, 103, 425, 428, 435, 439
epistemology 30, 168–170, 175, 177, 183, 244, 428, 429, 432, 442, 470, 471
ethnocentrism 176
ethnography, ethnographic 199, 274, 291, 387, 388
ethnohermeneutics 287–290, 300–303, 305, 465
Europe 1, 2, 22, 25, 49, 97, 151, 185, 319, 394, 467, 470
European Evangelical Accrediting Association (EEAA) 470

F

faculty training 69, 100
faithful intentions 253, 256, 257, 259, 266
field education 265
fog index (language) 69
fragmentation 5, 37, 156, 172, 204, 255, 366
Fresno Pacific Biblical Seminary 262

G

gamification 356
Germany 185
Ghana 269, 270, 280, 469
Gilgamesh, Epic of 311
Google 168, 331, 364, 365
Great Commission 383
guru-gola 112, 125
Gutenberg 315, 316, 353

H

hidden curriculum 10, 61–66, 69–72, 76, 78, 80, 82, 84
high-context culture/communication 114–117, 121, 125
Hindu 14, 173, 310, 311, 314, 319, 394, 457
holism, holistic 5, 25, 30, 31, 34, 52, 82, 90, 97–99, 104, 105, 110, 118, 123, 151, 158, 162, 170, 197, 201, 203, 205, 223, 273, 278, 280, 284, 431, 432, 435, 441, 442
homiletics 56, 339
hospitality 436, 437
humanities 43, 75–77, 178, 180, 196, 205, 245, 246

I

Iceland 319

identity 95, 97, 119, 139, 140, 177, 238, 377–381, 416, 425, 428, 438
Imperial Examination System 430
incarnational mission 383, 384
indigenous 90, 130, 145, 147, 154, 273, 276, 277, 292, 301
individualism, individualist 30, 73, 151, 172, 176, 432, 441
Indonesia 327, 411, 467
inferiorization 153
Instituto Bíblico Asunción 261, 265, 471
integration 27, 28, 34, 35, 37, 48, 51, 109, 116, 119, 120, 125, 141, 151, 156, 157, 163, 187, 196, 197, 199–205, 210, 227, 236, 238, 243, 248, 264, 363, 365, 366, 372, 388, 390, 433, 438
Intercultural Studies 339, 465
interfaith dialogue 123
International Council for Evangelical Theological Education (ICETE) 3, 19, 26, 33, 45, 53, 54, 57, 64, 65, 67, 77, 82, 175, 241
Islam 173, 240, 457, 458

J

Jainism 310
Japan 97, 115
John of the Cross 434
joint or multi-author doctoral projects 73, 133, 253

K

Kenya 3, 80, 127, 283, 465, 468
kingdom of God 1, 10, 67, 71, 182, 257
knowing, embodied 388
knowledge, experiential 96
knowledge(s), emancipatory 145, 147, 148, 152, 155, 158–163
knowledge(s), local 11, 145, 147, 148, 152, 153, 155, 156, 158–163
Korea 1, 97, 115

L

Langham Partnership, Langham Ministries 16, 296, 468
Lanka Bible College and Seminary (LBCS) 11, 109, 470
Latin America 22, 29, 58, 99, 105, 254, 255, 383, 467, 469
Lausanne Congress on World Evangelization 64, 194
learning, collaborative 28, 38, 74, 215, 220, 228, 237, 264, 267
learning community 217, 253, 258, 266
learning, experiential 212, 213, 247
learning, local 269, 270, 273, 277
learning, problem-based (PBL) 74, 187, 209–211, 222, 223
learning, social 117–119, 121
learning styles 43, 53, 71, 75, 76, 123, 150, 155, 159, 294
learning, transformative/transformational 150, 169, 279
Lebanon 52, 64, 234, 243, 259, 468, 470, 471
liberation theology 16, 241
life-long learners/learning 218, 220, 332, 347
linear-empiricist, linear-rationalist 2, 4, 56, 91, 93, 326, 421
literature, comparative 181, 182, 311–313, 315, 317, 318, 322
liturgy 56, 257
London School of Theology 326, 469, 472

low-context culture/communication 114–116, 121, 125

M
Mandarin 296
Manusmriti 319
Māori 72
matrix planning 334
Maya, Mayan 320
mentoring 228, 265
metacognitive, metacognition 112, 122, 211, 218, 228, 331, 340, 343, 345
metalearning 72
Middle East 1, 22, 75, 99, 115, 239, 248, 467, 469, 470, 471
midrash 288
missiology 238, 299, 386, 465
missional 13, 15, 18, 19, 33, 52, 53, 56, 64, 65, 67–70, 74, 79, 81, 84, 85, 156, 175, 180–184, 192, 249, 321, 348, 462, 465
modernism, modernist 52, 58, 171, 172, 179, 183, 358
multiple intelligences 72, 222
music 55, 56, 120, 156, 198, 281, 317, 384, 394, 425, 428, 430, 435, 440
Myers Briggs Type Indicator (MBTI) 74

N
Nairobi Evangelical Graduate School of Theology (NEGST) 27, 128, 135
narrative 9, 99, 151, 156, 162, 177, 179, 182, 245, 278, 281, 310, 314, 315, 320–322, 327, 376, 378, 383, 384, 394, 395, 409, 421, 428, 435, 466
Native American 75, 135

neo-colonial 383
Nepal 167
neuroscience 196, 429, 434
New Zealand 72, 169, 300, 467, 470
null curriculum 62

O
occultism 302
Open University 353, 360
oral learners 273, 278, 280, 281
oral literature 273, 274, 277, 283
oral, orality 94, 124, 129–131, 136–138, 142, 151, 159, 160, 162, 263, 269, 272, 276, 277, 280, 283, 296–298, 303, 313, 317, 321, 393, 394, 411, 415, 469
orthopathy, orthopathic 436
orthopraxis 436
Overseas Council 9, 19, 187, 465, 468, 470

P
Panchatantra 319, 394–398, 401, 403, 405
Paraguay 254, 261, 471
Paremiology 420
Parsi 310
Pathways College 169
peacemaking 233, 240, 469
Peace Studies 34, 187
phenomenology 169
Philippines 80, 299, 300, 326, 414, 465, 466, 469
political science 152
polygamy 302
portfolio 55, 326, 329, 330, 332–341, 343, 345, 346, 348, 349, 396
positivism 185
postcolonialism 146, 154

postliterature 316, 318
postmodernism, postmodern 52, 172, 177, 179, 183, 200, 303, 368, 428
power distance 29
praxis 154, 211, 216, 234, 235, 238, 249, 367
pre-colonial 314
problem-based learning (PBL) 102, 210–224, 227–229
proposal (dissertation) 62, 239, 240, 243, 327, 412, 413, 418, 421, 428
proverb(s) 1, 9, 129, 130, 136, 138–140, 185, 269–273, 276–280, 282, 283, 292, 311, 325, 326, 395, 411–421, 461, 469

Q
QS World University Rankings 44
qualitative research 136, 244
quantitative research 388
Questions to Heaven 429
Qur'an 310, 320

R
Ramayana 314, 317, 318
rationalism, rationality 44, 53, 65, 99, 146, 172, 176, 179, 216, 431, 435
reconciliation 227, 234, 236–239, 469
reflective practice 242, 243
reflectivity 199
relationality 199
reverse innovation 36
rhetoric, contrastive 128
rhetoric, intercultural 11, 127–129, 131, 134
rhetoric, persuasive expert 129
Russian 134, 394, 461

S
samba 198, 375, 376, 384–386
Sanskrit 14, 17, 314, 317, 394, 405
Sati 314, 315
scientific method 43, 44, 103, 123, 186
Senior Seminar 262–264, 267
Sikhism 310
Singapore 16
Sioux Falls Seminary 302, 465
Sita 314, 315
smart phones 356
social construction of reality 114
social media 356, 357, 367
social transformation 380, 390
sociology 16, 152, 199, 221, 467, 471
Socrates 316
South Asia Institute of Advanced Christian Studies (SAIACS) 3, 11, 18, 170, 182, 295, 456, 466, 470
spiritism 302
spiritual disciplines 53
Sri Lanka 11, 109, 112, 113, 117, 118, 120, 121
stakeholders 65, 66, 70, 71, 77, 80–85, 132, 139, 140, 159, 235, 249
story, stories, storytelling 5, 9, 13, 14, 91, 105, 129, 135, 151, 159, 169, 176, 198, 202, 245, 269–273, 277, 279, 280, 283, 292, 309, 314, 322, 326, 329, 330, 337, 343, 345, 378, 388, 393–398, 400–406, 409, 412, 426, 437, 440, 451, 456, 457
subalternization 5, 153
supervised practice 73, 265, 267
supervisor(s), supervision 28, 36, 59, 65, 70, 73, 79, 93, 139, 186, 200, 204, 246, 247, 262, 265,

Subject Index   487

295, 338, 340, 346, 376, 418, 421
Swahili 140, 296

T
Tagalog 412, 414, 416, 418, 419
teach, teaching 11, 15, 16, 18, 22, 24, 25, 32, 53, 64, 66–69, 78, 83, 91, 92, 94, 109, 110, 112, 119, 120, 122, 127, 134, 146–148, 150, 155, 157, 160, 171, 182, 183, 185, 198, 204, 217, 219, 220, 224, 226, 243, 254, 260, 266, 269, 272, 273, 291, 303, 310, 322, 325, 329, 346–348, 363, 368, 372, 404, 437, 456, 465, 467, 468, 470, 471
technological determinism 356
technology, laws of 352, 354, 372
TED Talks 364
Tertiary Education Quality and Standards Agency (TEQSA) 49
theological aesthetics 435
theological circumcision 186
theological leaders, theological leadership 1, 3–6, 10, 11, 19, 21, 24, 27, 31–33, 36, 37, 53, 91, 94, 95, 105, 187, 235, 249, 461
theological reflection 77, 91, 104, 197, 234, 242, 244, 265, 387, 396, 428, 435, 436, 439, 441, 451, 454, 468
Theology and Development 34
theology, practical 16, 139, 178, 197, 199, 245–248, 263, 302, 466
thesis statement 136
Tonga 299, 300
Torah 309
Torch Trinity Graduate University (TTGU) 19

transduction 318
Trinity, Trinitarian 169, 174, 175, 183, 441
Turkey 3, 363

U
Union Biblical Seminary 16, 17
United Kingdom 97, 254
United Kingdom Quality Assurance Agency for Higher Education (QAA) 49, 55
United States 49, 97, 185, 379
University of Aberdeen 470
University of Auckland 300
University of Birmingham 55, 326
University of Divinity, Australia 327, 471
University of Glasgow 56
University of Michigan 96

V
VARK (Visual, Audio, Read/write and Kinaesthetic) 75
vernacular 14, 15, 256, 266, 395

W
Web 2.0 359, 362, 367, 370
Wikipedia 359, 361, 367
wikispaces 360
WikiThesis 361
witchcraft 221, 302

Y
YouTube 356, 367

Z
Zendavesta 310

Global Hub for Evangelical Theological Education

Mission

ICETE advances quality and collaboration in global theological education to strengthen and accompany the church in its mission.

Objectives

As a global hub for evangelical theological education, ICETE is recognized for its reliable capacity to:

1. Develop, disseminate, mutually validate, harmonize, and inspire quality in theological education, aimed at fostering reciprocal trust among stakeholders, including the church;
2. Cultivate worldwide relationships, stimulated through gatherings, communications for reflection, interactive dialogue, collaboration, and practice in support of the church's mission; and
3. Train, consult, and provide resources for those involved in theological education, marked by relevance, accessibility, and collaborative effectiveness.

ICETE's mission emphasizes its dual focus on quality *and* collaboration through its constituency to strengthen and accompany the church in its mission. The quality aspect of our work addresses the church-academy gap by requiring theological institutions to build strategic partnerships with churches and ministry organizations. ICETE quality assurance seeks to be an agent for change in theological institutions, and consequently in the lives of the next generation of global leaders.

Through collaborative opportunities, our impact begins with theological educators and extends exponentially to training programs, students, church leaders, and the broader community for the sake of the church. Our work targets theological educators across all sectors who prepare thousands of learners serving in hundreds of ministries.

www.icete.info

Langham Literature and its imprints are a ministry of Langham Partnership.

Langham Partnership is a global fellowship working in pursuit of the vision God entrusted to its founder John Stott –

> *to facilitate the growth of the church in maturity and Christ-likeness through raising the standards of biblical preaching and teaching.*

Our vision is to see churches in the majority world equipped for mission and growing to maturity in Christ through the ministry of pastors and leaders who believe, teach and live by the Word of God.

Our mission is to strengthen the ministry of the Word of God through:
- nurturing national movements for biblical preaching
- fostering the creation and distribution of evangelical literature
- enhancing evangelical theological education

especially in countries where churches are under-resourced.

Our ministry

Langham Preaching partners with national leaders to nurture indigenous biblical preaching movements for pastors and lay preachers all around the world. With the support of a team of trainers from many countries, a multi-level programme of seminars provides practical training, and is followed by a programme for training local facilitators. Local preachers' groups and national and regional networks ensure continuity and ongoing development, seeking to build vigorous movements committed to Bible exposition.

Langham Literature provides majority world preachers, scholars and seminary libraries with evangelical books and electronic resources through publishing and distribution, grants and discounts. The programme also fosters the creation of indigenous evangelical books in many languages, through writer's grants, strengthening local evangelical publishing houses, and investment in major regional literature projects, such as one volume Bible commentaries like *The Africa Bible Commentary* and *The South Asia Bible Commentary*.

Langham Scholars provides financial support for evangelical doctoral students from the majority world so that, when they return home, they may train pastors and other Christian leaders with sound, biblical and theological teaching. This programme equips those who equip others. Langham Scholars also works in partnership with majority world seminaries in strengthening evangelical theological education. A growing number of Langham Scholars study in high quality doctoral programmes in the majority world itself. As well as teaching the next generation of pastors, graduated Langham Scholars exercise significant influence through their writing and leadership.

To learn more about Langham Partnership and the work we do visit **langham.org**

www.ingramcontent.com/pod-product-compliance
Lightning Source LLC
Chambersburg PA
CBHW060910300426
44112CB00011B/1405